ORACLE® Oracle Press™

OCP Oracle9*i* Database: Performance Tuning Exam Guide

Charles A. Pack

Osborne/**McGraw-Hill**

New York Chicago San Francisco
Lisbon London Madrid Mexico City Milan
New Delhi San Juan Seoul Singapore Sydney Toronto

Osborne/**McGraw-Hill**
2600 Tenth Street
Berkeley, California 94710
U.S.A.

To arrange bulk purchase discounts for sales promotions, premiums, or fund-raisers, please contact Osborne/**McGraw-Hill** at the above address. For information on translations or book distributors outside the U.S.A., please see the International Contact Information page immediately following the index of this book.

OCP Oracle9*i* Database: Performance Tuning Exam Guide

      67890 FGR FGR 0198765
Book p/n 0-07-219528-2 and CD p/n 0-07-219529-0
parts of
ISBN 0-07-219527-4

Publisher
   Brandon A. Nordin

Vice President & Associate Publisher
   Scott Rogers

Acquisitions Editor
   Jeremy Judson

Project Manager
   Jenn Tust

Acquisitions Coordinator
   Athena Honore

Technical Editor
   Janet Stern

Cover Design
   Damore Johann Design, Inc.

Composition and Indexing
   MacAllister Publishing Services, LLC

This book was composed with QuarkXPress™.

This book is dedicated to my wife Donna and our daughter Jenny.

About the Author

Charles A. Pack is an Oracle Certified Professional DBA with over 15 years of IT experience. His range of experiences includes COBOL, C/C++, Basic, Visual Basic, Clipper, FoxPro, dBase, Prolog, Java, and PL/SQL programming; HP 3000 operations and database administration; network design and construction; Unix and Windows NT administration; and MS-SQL Server and Sybase administration. He earned a bachelor of science degree from Oklahoma State University, an MBA from the University of Oklahoma, and a master of science in computer science from Texas A&M University, Corpus Christi. He teaches Oracle DBA classes at Florida Community College, Jacksonville, and is a regular contributor to the North Florida Oracle User Group. He works for CSX Technology as a DBA project manager responsible for data warehouse, Oracle financials, and PeopleSoft Oracle databases. And he likes to barbecue . . . .

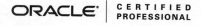ORACLE® | C E R T I F I E D
PROFESSIONAL

About the Oracle Certification Exams

The expertise of Oracle database administrators (DBAs) is integral to the success of today's increasingly complex system environments. The best DBAs operate primarily behind the scenes, looking for ways to fine-tune day-to-day performance to prevent unscheduled crises and hours of expensive downtime. They know they stand between optimal performance and a crisis that could bring a company to a standstill. The Oracle Certified Database Administrator Track provides DBAs with tangible evidence of their skills with the Oracle database.

The Oracle Certified Professional (OCP) Program was developed by Oracle to recognize technical professionals who can demonstrate the depth of knowledge and hands-on skills required to maximize Oracle's core products according to a rigorous standard established by Oracle. By earning professional certification, you can translate the impressive knowledge and skill you have worked so hard to accumulate into a tangible credential that can lead to greater job security or more challenging, better-paying opportunities.

Oracle Certified Professionals are eligible to receive use of the Oracle Certified Professional logo and a certificate for framing.

Requirements for Certification

To become an Oracle Certified Professional Database Administrator for the Oracle9i track, you must pass four tests. These exams cover knowledge of the essential aspects of the SQL language, Oracle administration, backup and recovery, and performance tuning of systems. The certification process requires that you pass the following four exams:

    Exam 1: Introduction to Oracle9i: SQL (1Z0-007)

    Exam 2: Oracle9i Database: Fundamentals I (1Z0-031)

    Exam 3: Oracle9i Database Fundamentals II (1Z0-032)

    Exam 4: Oracle9i Database: Performance Tuning (1Z0-033)

Recertification

Oracle announces the requirements for upgrading your certification based on the release of new products and upgrades. Oracle will give six months' notice announcing when an exam version is expiring.

Exam Format

The computer-based exam is a multiple-choice test, consisting of 56 questions that must be completed in 90–120 minutes.

Contents

PART II

Practice Exams

Acknowledgments

hanks to my Oracle DBA coworkers Nirupam Majumdar, Gunjan Nath, Don Mongeon, Maritza Gonzalez, Yang Jiang, John King, Bill Sullivan, Bill Barker, Tim Stippler, Rich McClain, and Ron Grinam; my boss Nancy Von Dolteren for excusing my occasional outbursts; Bob Just, for your continuous support (no pun intended); and Robert Freeman for perpetually challenging me and making me a better DBA.

A great big special thanks to Janet Stern for her technical editing on this book: her contribution was tremendous!

Thanks to my friends at Osborne/McGraw-Hill, Athena Honore and Jeremy Judson, and Beth Brown, Jeanne Henning, and Barbra Guerra from MacAllister Publishing Services.

Without question, I must thank my parents Charlene and Gus, who didn't seem to mind too much that I brought my laptop computer to their 50th wedding anniversary, and to Christmas dinner, and so on, and so on. Most of all, thanks to my beautiful, wonderful, awesome wife Donna—the love of my life—who continues to encourage and support me, and to our daughter Jenny, who thinks Daddy lives in his office. Now we can go play in the Florida sun . . .

Introduction

his book was specifically written to help you prepare for the Oracle
Certified Professional (OCP) DBA Exam #1Z0-033: Oracle9*i*
Performance Tuning. The book is designed to follow the published test
content checklist for the Performance Tuning exam. Each chapter is
dedicated to a section on the test content checklist, and each bullet
item on the test content checklist is discussed in detail.

The caveat, of course, is that Oracle has the right to change the test content
anytime they choose. This book was written with the test content checklist that was
available to the public at the time. Please keep that in mind before you send me an
e-mail detailing everything that was missed in the content of this book.

Each content chapter begins with a list of subjects that will be covered and ends
with a chapter summary, a two-minute drill, test questions for the chapter, and
answers to the test questions.

I have also included two separate practice exams that are approximately the
same length as the actual OCP exam. You'll find a third practice exam on the CD.
Answers with explanations are provided immediately following each practice exam.
I have attempted to make the exam questions similar in format and difficulty to
the OCP exam questions; some questions will seem trivial, while others may seem
impossible. Any occurrence of one of my questions on the actual exam or vice versa
is purely coincidental.

If you need additional resources to help you prepare for the exam, I suggest you start with the Oracle documentation set, freely available at http://technet. oracle.com. Click on the Documentation link, then click on the Oracle9i Database link. You can drill down to the "Oracle9i Database Performance Methods," "Application Developer's Guide—Fundamentals," "Database Concepts," and "Database Reference." These documents provide the foundation material that you should use when you exercise performance tuning and will give you an edge when preparing for the exam.

Also, Oracle University provides excellent instructor-led training; the Oracle9i Database Performance Tuning class is a great place to gain detailed performance tuning information and practice database performance tuning in a laboratory environment.

If you have any questions, please feel free to e-mail me at charlesapack@yahoo.com.

Enjoy, and good luck!

PART I

OCP Tuning Exam Guide

CHAPTER
1

Database
Tuning Overview

n this chapter, I will discuss

- How this book is organized.
- A brief introduction to each of the chapters in this book.
- A brief tuning overview.
- Resources for advancing your tuning knowledge.

The purpose of this chapter is to describe the basic form and function of this book, to provide you with a brief overview of the contents of the book, to help you understand the basic premise for Oracle Relational Database Management System (RDBMS) performance tuning, and to list some important resources for further study.

How This Book Is Organized

The purpose of this book is to help you pass the Oracle Certified Professional (OCP) Oracle9*i* Performance Tuning Exam #1Z1-033. Therefore, the book is written to cover the subjects listed in the "Test Content Checklist" published by Oracle Corporation that are also available on their web site. Each subject area in the checklist has a chapter in this book, and each bullet item within a subject area will have a section in the chapter. This book is not intended to be an all-encompassing tuning guide. The references section at the end of this chapter lists several excellent resources that will meet your more advanced tuning guide needs.

Each chapter will begin with a brief introduction to the subject and a list of topics covered in the subject area. Each chapter will end with a chapter summary, a line-item recap of important information, and sample test questions that are representative of the chapter content. You will discover that greater emphasis will be given in the text to the topics that are most likely to appear on the exam, and that there will be more end-of-chapter questions related to the more important topics.

Following the subject area chapters, I have included two full-length sample tests and answer keys. This gives you the opportunity to test your knowledge, and it also helps you manage the time available to you during the actual OCP exam. Each sample test is approximately the same length as the actual OCP Performance Tuning Exam, and I have endeavored to make it as difficult as the actual OCP exam.

The sample tests are followed by a glossary of terms. If you're reading one of the subject chapters and you get stuck on a term that you're not familiar with, look in the glossary first. If you don't find the term there, refer to your Oracle documentation set.

Topics Covered in the OCP DBA Tuning Exam

In this section, I will briefly discuss each of the subject areas in the test content checklist and, in doing so, introduce each of the remaining content chapters in this book.

The Oracle Performance Tuning Methodology

Before you begin performance tuning a database, you should take some time to read about and understand the philosophy and methodology that Oracle has developed to performance tune databases. This methodology has evolved over the years through countless performance tuning sessions conducted by numerous tuning experts. The processes that they describe in the methodology, when followed correctly, will result in high-performing databases. These are the tuning methodology topics covered on the exam:

- The roles associated with the database-tuning process

- The dependency between tuning in different development phases

- Service level agreements (SLAs)

- Tuning goals

- The most common tuning problems

- Tuning goals associated with different types of applications

Diagnostics and Tuning Tools

This subject area and chapter focus on the tools that you will use to gather data essential to performance tuning. The most fundamental topic covers data dictionary views and dynamic performance views. The dynamic performance views contain information about events occurring in the Oracle instance, such as information that you will use to answer questions about performance problems. Consider the dynamic performance views of your *instrument panel* into the Oracle instance. Statspack is used to collect and store performance data and generate performance reports. These are the diagnostics and tuning tools topics covered:

- The data dictionary and dynamic performance views related to tuning

- The statistics in the dynamic performance views

- How Statspack collects statistics

■ Using Statspack to collect statistics

■ Using other tools for tuning

■ Using the ANALYZE command

■ The alert log and trace files

Sizing the Shared Pool

This subject is the first to discuss modification to the Oracle instance parameters to improve performance. As you know, an Oracle instance consists of background processes and memory structures. The shared pool is one of the major Shared Global Area (SGA) memory structures, which resides in memory while an Oracle instance is alive. The primary components of the shared pool are the library cache and the dictionary cache. Properly sizing the shared pool is a critical element of performance tuning. We will also discuss hit ratios, one of the most important pieces of data that you will gather. In this chapter, we will

■ Measure and tune the library cache hit ratio.

■ Measure and tune the dictionary cache hit ratio.

■ Size and pin objects in the shared pool.

■ Tune the shared pool reserve space.

■ Describe UGA and session memory considerations.

■ Describe other tuning issues related to the shared pool.

Sizing the Buffer Cache

The second major memory structure is the *buffer cache*. This is where data blocks reside in memory when they are needed by Oracle processes. In general, a bigger buffer cache is better than a smaller one, but as with all things, there is a trade-off. You will learn about the optional buffer pools that you can configure in the buffer cache and how each can be used to improve performance. In this chapter we will discuss the following:

■ How the buffer cache is used by different Oracle processes

■ Tuning issues related to the buffer cache

- Monitoring the buffer cache
- The different pools within the buffer cache
- Creating and sizing multiple buffer pools
- Table caching
- Diagnosing LRU latch contention

Sizing Other SGA Structures

The shared pool and the buffer cache are generally the two largest chunks of memory allocated in the SGA, and their proper configuration has the greatest impact on performance. However, proper analysis and configuration of the remaining SGA structures are also very important. The redo log buffer size can have a great impact on performance if it isn't sized properly. Depending on which features of the database you utilize (Java stored procedures, for example), you may also need to configure the additional SGA structures. This topics in this chapter are as follows:

- Monitoring and sizing the redo log buffer
- Monitoring and sizing the Java pool
- Limiting the amount of Java session memory used by a session
- Monitoring and sizing the large pool
- Configuring multiple DBW processes and I/O slaves

Database Configuration and I/O Issues

Because the disk subsystem is usually the slowest component of the three fundamental pieces of a typical computer (central processing unit [CPU], memory, and disk), it is extremely important that you balance disk input/output (I/O) properly. Slow reads from disk will contribute to slow query responses, while slow writes to disk can cause bottlenecks in the database if the disks can't keep up with write demands. In this chapter, we will

- Describe the reasons for distributing different Oracle file types.
- Describe the reasons for partitioning data in tablespaces.

- Diagnose the inappropriate use of tablespaces.

- Describe the trade-offs between large and smaller block sizes.

- Describe how checkpoints work.

- Monitor and tune checkpoints.

- Monitor and tune redo logs.

Optimizing Sort Operations

Sorting occurs when a Structured Query Language (SQL) select query includes an ORDER BY clause or a UNION operator, when you build an index on data that isn't already sorted, and during various other operations. Ideally, sorting occurs in memory and is very fast. However, it is sometimes necessary to sort to disk, which is slower, and can sometimes lead to performance problems. In this chapter, we will

- Describe how sorts are performed in Oracle.

- Describe the operations that cause sorting.

- Differentiate between disk and memory sorts.

- Describe ways to reduce total sorts and disk sorts.

- Determine the number of sorts performed in memory.

- Set old and new sort parameters.

- Create and monitor TEMPORARY tablespaces.

Diagnosing Contention for Latches

A *latch* is a mechanism that enables one process to modify an SGA data structure while protecting the structure from other processes. A latch can only be held by one process at a time, and a request by a process to get a latch either succeeds or fails; there is no queuing. In the chapter on latches, you will be able to

- Describe the purpose of latches.

- Describe the different types of latches.

- Describe how to diagnose contention for latches.

- Tune parameters to minimize latch contention.

Tuning Rollback or UNDO Segments

Oracle uses rollback segments to maintain read consistency during a transaction and to enable transaction changes to be returned to a before state if it is determined that the transaction should not be committed. Automatic undo management, which uses UNDO segments, is the preferred way of handling undo needs. Rollback segments are available for backward compatibility. The following topics will be covered:

- Using the dynamic performance views to check rollback segment performance
- Defining the number and sizes of rollback segments
- Appropriately allocating rollback segments to transactions
- Understanding the concept of automatic undo management
- Creating and maintaining system managed undo tablespace

Monitoring and Detecting Lock Contention

Locks are used to protect structures such as database tables from conflicting processes. Locks enable session requests to queue up and wait for a resource that another process is modifying. For a simple example, if I am in the process of modifying a row of data in table A, Oracle will place a lock on the row so that you don't change it also, at least not until my transaction is complete. In this chapter, we will

- Define levels of locking.
- Describe possible causes of contention.
- Use Oracle utilities to detect lock contention.
- Resolve contention in an emergency.
- Prevent locking problems.
- Recognize Oracle errors arising from deadlocks.

Tuning Oracle Shared Server

In a dedicated server environment, each user session has a one-to-one relationship with a server process, which is responsible for retrieving data blocks from disk into the buffer cache. In the shared server environment, there is a smaller pool of server processes, and a many-to-one relationship between user sessions and server processes. Oracle shared server went by the name Oracle Multithreaded Server (MTS) in previous versions. We will focus on the following shared server topics:

- Identifying issues associated with managing users in a shared server environment

- Diagnosing and resolving performance issues with shared server processes

- Configuring the shared server environment to optimize performance

Application Tuning

Once we have tuned our memory structures, the database layout, rollback, UNDO, and various other tuning opportunities, we must turn our focus to the actual objects that user sessions manipulate: tables, indexes, clusters, and views. In this chapter, we will

- Describe the role of the database administrator (DBA) in tuning schema objects.

- Explain different storage structures.

- Explain why one storage structure may be preferred over another.

- Explain and describe clustering options.

- Explain the different types of indexes.

- Explain index-organized tables.

- Describe the use of histograms.

- Describe materialized views.

- Explain the use of query rewrites.

Using Oracle Blocks Efficiently

Using blocks of data wisely improves efficiency and can significantly improve performance. On the other hand, the implementation of a bad block usage strategy will cause performance problems, such as row chaining and migration. Sparsely populated data blocks can also lead to increased I/O. In this chapter, you will learn how to

- Describe the correct usage of extents and Oracle blocks.

- Explain space usage and the high watermark.

- Determine the high watermark.

- Explain the use of Oracle blocks.

- Recover space from sparsely populated segments.

- Describe row chaining and row migration.

- Detect chaining and migration.

- Resolve chaining and migration.

- Perform index reorganization.

- Monitor indexes to determine usage.

SQL Statement Tuning

As you gain experience as an Oracle performance tuner, you will discover that your most noticeable performance issues are directly related to SQL statements. However, all the subject areas leading up to this point must be addressed before you begin tuning SQL. In this chapter, you will learn how to

- Describe how the optimizer is used.

- Use SQL Trace and TKPROF.

- Describe how hints are used.

- Explain the concept of plan stability.

- Used stored outlines.

- Collect statistics on indexes and tables.

- Describe the use of histograms.

- Copy statistics between databases.

- OLTP and DSS considerations.

OS Considerations

Regardless of the platform you choose to implement your Oracle database on, certain commonalities exist. This chapter describes some of the basic steps you will need to take to ensure that the operating system (OS) is tuned properly for Oracle databases and is not causing unnecessary problems. Specifically, we will

- Describe different system architectures.

- Describe the primary steps of OS tuning.

- Identify similarities between OS and database tuning.

- Explain the difference between a process and a thread.

- Understand Virtual Memory and paging.

- Configure the Resource Manager.

- Administer Resource Manager.

Tuning Overview

In this section, I'll describe the following topics:

- Why, what, where, when, and how do we performance tune an Oracle database?

- How will I know that my efforts are actually improving performance?

Why Do We Performance Tune?

Oracle designed its RDBMS for performance, flexibility, and stability. As the DBA, you can create and manage a database that performs extremely well or very poorly; the choice is yours. This is mentioned because a well-designed database and a properly configured instance built on an adequately-sized server with quality-performance hardware and a properly tuned OS have the potential to perform extremely well. They also have the potential to perform well below expectations. As the DBA, you have control or influence over these factors. If you work for an organization that paid a lot of money for the hardware, software, and DBA time, then performance expectations will probably be very high. Effective performance tuning will lead to lower hardware costs since you will be able to add more users without affecting performance and without adding more hardware.

Your success as a DBA will be measured primarily on two criteria: Is the database available when needed, and does the database performance meet customer expectations? Availability is usually more dependent on the stability of the OS and hardware than the RDBMS. Rarely does an Oracle database crash on its own; it generally takes an OS panic, a hardware failure, or human error (the DBA) to unintentionally bring a database down.

So, if the instance is up and the database is available, your focus should turn to performance tuning. If availability is not an issue, your customers will expect good performance from the database. They will expect the DBA to understand how to performance tune and deliver a high-performing database.

What Is Performance Tuning?

Performance tuning is part-design and part-troubleshooting. If the database is designed properly, performance issues may never become a significant problem. So, the most successful DBAs are active participants in the database and application design process. By eliminating major design flaws before implementation, you reduce the amount of explaining and redesign after implementation. Design issues include the proper application of relational theory to the logical database design, appropriate indexing strategies based on common access paths, and load balancing data files on disk drives.

The general approach to day-to-day performance tuning is to gather data, identify problems, and continuously remove bottlenecks. You may create new bottlenecks, but they are generally less painful to the end users and you can work on the new problems as they become apparent. Oracle performance tuning is not deterministic; it is iterative and ongoing.

The types of problems include, but are not limited to, poorly designed and/or badly performing SQL statements, long-running transactions, long disk I/O times, memory paging and swapping, and CPU starvation. Each of these problems can be identified with readily available tools, analysis, and a possible solution applied.

Where Do I Tune?

During the design phase, tuning is done at the chalkboard or within a design tool, such as Oracle Designer. Once the database is created, the majority of your tuning exercises will occur within the Oracle database, looking at V$ dynamic performance views and Statspack reports. You will also use OS tools, so some of the tuning will occur at a telnet prompt if your database is on Linux or Unix, or in a MS-Windows utility if your database runs on Windows NT. Oracle Enterprise Manager has a suite of tuning tools, and there are also several third-party tuning aids. It's also a good idea to document your performance tuning findings, so a word processor and a spreadsheet program should be added to your toolset.

How Do I Performance Tune?

As mentioned previously, you should gather baseline data on a regular schedule; this may be daily on a low-volume system or hourly on a high-volume Online Transaction Processing (OLTP) system. This will help you identify historic problems and set expectations for tuning goals. Identifying problems is sometimes very easy, and at other times subtle performance problems can be difficult to trap. Have conversations with your OS and network administrators, application developers, and customers. Learn from them where the perceived bottlenecks are or where they see potential areas for improvement. Use your ears and your eyes. If you overhear someone in the elevator talking about "waiting on the database," you might have a lead that needs investigation. As your experience grows, so will your acumen at detecting, analyzing, and resolving.

When determining what to tune, you should target measurable performance improvements, such as improved query response time, higher hit ratios, reduced CPU consumption (load balancing), reduced I/O, wait times, fewer rollback segment errors, and so on. Query response time can often be improved by adding hints to the query, creating an index on the columns used in the WHERE clauses, or gathering current statistics for the cost-based optimizer. Hit ratios are generally improved by proper sizing of the associated SGA structure. Disk I/O issues are usually resolved by moving database files or moving objects from one tablespace to another. You can significantly reduce CPU utilization if you tune bad SQL. These are just a few of the "how's" to improve performance.

When Do I Tune?

Continuously. As mentioned, in an active database there will always be opportunities for improvement. You should establish a regular schedule to gather data using Statspack or another tool of your choice. You should also continuously monitor your databases for noticeable performance problems, such as response time statistics, for example. When you notice an anomaly or an event that crosses a threshold value, investigate, analyze, and resolve it. Then celebrate.

It's important to stay ahead of your customers when it comes to database performance. If you are diligent, hopefully you won't overhear someone in the elevator talking badly about one of your databases.

How Do I Know If My Performance Tuning Efforts Are Actually Working?

If you have collected baseline statistics, you will be able to compare before and after values for response time, I/O, and hit ratios, and demonstrate empirically that an improvement has been made. If you follow the iterative and continuous approach, you'll see the numbers improve over time. The effect is cumulative.

One of the best performance indicators, and the one that usually gets you the most feedback from your customers, is query response time. Hit ratios and I/O stats are fine measurements to discuss between us DBAs, and we should always strive to improve those numbers, but what the customers really want is improved query response time. Focus on improving query response time as a tuning goal, measure the effects of your efforts, and provide the information to your boss and your customers. Then maybe you'll hear positive comments from the people in the elevator.

To Advance Your Tuning Knowledge

There are several Oracle tuning books on the market, and I expect new titles as Oracle9*i* becomes more pervasive. Here are a few titles that you can use to really expand your knowledge:

Adams, Steve. *Oracle8i Internal Services for Waits, Latches, Locks, and Memory*. O'Reilly and Associates, 1999. ISBN: 1-56592-598-X.

Burleson, Donald. *Oracle High-Performance SQL Tuning*. Oracle Press, 2001. ISBN: 0072190582.

————. *Oracle High-Performance Tuning with STATSPACK*. Oracle Press, 2001. ISBN: 0072133783.

Niemiec, Richard J. et al. *Oracle Performance Tuning Tips and Techniques*. Oracle Press, 1999. ISBN: 007-882434-6.

Vaidyanatha, Gaja, Kirtikumar Deshpande, and John Kostelac. *Oracle Performance Tuning 101*. Oracle Press, 2001. ISBN: 0072131454.

Web sites:

Revealnet Oracle DBA Pipeline: www.revealnet.com/Pipelines/DBA/index.htm

CHAPTER
2

Oracle Performance Tuning Methodology

n this chapter, you will learn the Oracle Performance Tuning Methodology and be taught specifically to

- Describe the Oracle Performance Improvement Method.
- Describe the roles associated with the database tuning process.
- Describe the dependency between tuning in different development phases.
- Describe service level agreements (SLAs).
- Describe tuning goals.
- Describe the most common tuning problems.
- Describe tuning goals associated with different types of applications.

This chapter focuses on the Oracle Performance Tuning Methodology, which has been derived from the experiences of Oracle performance tuning masters over the years. The Performance Improvement Method is defined in the first topic because it lays the foundation for all subsequent topics, which describe specific goals, agreements, roles, and processes that support and help with implementation of the methodology.

Oracle Performance Tuning Method

The Oracle Performance Tuning Method has evolved as the Relational Database Management System (RDBMS), server hardware, networking, and business environment have changed. The biggest influences on the current evolution of the methodology are the Internet and the continuous uptime and high-performance requirement of many self-service online database systems. The primary goal of the method is to produce robust scalable systems. There are eight general steps in the Oracle Performance Tuning Model:

1. Get user feedback.
2. Gather statistics.
3. Look for fully utilized systems.
4. Check for common mistakes made by Oracle users.
5. Build a conceptual model.
6. Propose an action plan and implement it.

7. Validate the performance impact.

8. Repeat steps 5, 6, and 7.

Get User Feedback   Interview the database users, application developers, managers, and business partners. Determine what the current problems are and establish near- and long-term performance expectations. It is very important that you understand what the users perceive as the most significant performance problems. Their observations are often very good clues as to where the tuning opportunities exist. For example, they may not be able to identify the problematic Structured Query Language (SQL) statement, but they will know when a specific report, form, or process performs poorly. Document your findings.

Gather Statistics   Establish a systematic way to gather and store statistics about the database, network, operating system (OS), hardware, and applications that use the database. Gather statistics during peak load times as well as during low usage times. This is especially important if the tuning opportunities are related to network or OS overhead. It is important that you involve your network engineer and system administrator in this process. If you are fortunate enough to have a performance monitoring team, get them involved. It is also very important that you involve the application support or development team; they will be essential in determining and analyzing bottlenecks from the application user's perspective. Store the statistics that you have gathered in a form that can be easily manipulated, such as a database table or spreadsheet. Documenting your observations is the most important part of this phase.

Look for Fully Utilized Systems   If you know that one of the components of the application architecture is overloaded, verify and note it in your initial analysis. For example, if the web application server is servicing twice the recommended number of concurrent users, note it. If users that attach via dialup modems are complaining about application performance, investigate the possibility that the modems are slower or older technology. Also, run hardware and OS diagnostics and determine if there are errors. Again, document your findings.

Check for Common Mistakes Made by Oracle Users   Oracle performance tuning experts have compiled a list of the most prevalent mistakes made by Oracle users, developers, designers, and database administrators (DBAs). As part of your continuous information gathering, you should look for these mistakes. If you see one of these mistakes, put it at or near the top of your list of things to fix. The top ten list of common mistakes made by Oracle users is included in the "Describe the Most Common Tuning Problems" section later in this chapter.

Build a Conceptual Model   Look at the data you have gathered thus far, and try to wrap your mind around what may be causing the problems. Categorize the problems, and rank them according to severity or impact. If some queries perform quite well, and other queries perform very poorly, then you should investigate the application code that submits the poorly performing queries. If the baseline central processing unit (CPU) utilization is very high, then investigate which server OS or database processes are consuming CPU. If all queries are responding poorly at all times and disk input/output (I/O) is extremely high, then investigate swapping, paging, and real memory consumption. If CPU utilization is high, no particular query performs poorly, and you see a significant number of connects and disconnects to the database, then you should investigate your connection management. The information assembled from this stage will help you design an action plan.

Propose an Action Plan and Implement It   For each of the high-severity problems, detail a treatment plan. Note the amount of effort required to make each change, who will make the change, and potential side effects of the change. Note if the change will require a server reboot or instance restart, and the potential service impact to end users. Also create a backout plan to reverse the changes should performance degrade. It is important at this stage that you present your plan to the people who must endorse it, or at least those who are interested in it. Outline the individual changes and the expected cumulative effect. Be prepared to discuss the cost and benefits of each change. Generally, you'll find that some of your team members will oppose changes, while others will embrace the changes. Don't be surprised if you find yourself negotiating which changes should be implemented.

Gather performance data before and after you implement any change. It is preferred that you make one change and measure the impact; however, this isn't always possible. Measure the individual and cumulative impact, and share the information with your team.

Validate the Performance Impact   Nothing impresses end users and managers like improved response time, so be prepared to show actual numbers. Reduced I/O, higher hit ratios, and greater transaction throughput are very important performance indicators. This is also a good time to utilize your spreadsheet and graphing abilities. Compare the actual performance improvement to the expectations. Sometimes you will make a mistake and performance will degrade, so you may need to implement the backout plan. Sometimes you will make an improvement that moves the bottleneck somewhere else, so the effect of the change isn't fully appreciated. Get feedback in the form of soft data (general improvements, user comments, and the feel of the change) and hard data (response times, performance numbers, and statistics) from the end users, systems administrators, and others on the performance tuning team.

Repeat Steps 5, 6, and 7   As noted, the methodology is iterative and continuous. Freeing up one bottleneck might make other bottlenecks apparent. Continuously remove bottlenecks until no one notices that a bottleneck exists. If you follow this methodology, you will notice significant performance improvements. There is, of course, a point of diminishing returns; continuously applying the performance tuning method will result in less obvious or less costly performance problems, some of which the end users will probably not even notice. Performance tuning also takes valuable personnel away from other productive work. So, as the DBA, you must constantly evaluate the trade-off between performance tuning and other DBA activities.

Describe the Roles Associated with the Database Tuning Process

A successful performance tuning implementation requires that several roles be filled. These roles may all be filled by one individual, but it's more likely that a small team of knowledgeable professionals will assemble for the task. You may find that in your organization you need fewer or more roles than those listed here.

Users

The application users will tell you when and where the application performs poorly. They have a feel for the system performance, even if they can't quantify exact performance issues. They know which screens paint slowly and which lookups are less than optimal. In a high-volume online transaction processing (OLTP) environment, such as an order-processing system, the application users can often detect subtle changes in the system performance.

Management

Management will help the performance tuning team understand the gap between actual and expected system performance. They are instrumental at setting performance goals and priorities. More complex tuning environments will require greater participation from the management team. We must not forget that management needs to understand the impact that the performance tuning efforts have on the business, both positive and negative. Management participation is essential for sustained performance tuning efforts.

Application Architect/Designer

The application architect or designer is usually the person most knowledgeable about the assumptions that went into the design of the system and where potential design problems exist. They will have knowledge about how changes to one part of the application will affect other parts, and they will usually have some ideas about potential bottlenecks.

Application Developer

This is the person who is responsible for implementing changes to application code. They probably wrote the SQL, or at least are familiar with the SQL that the application generates. Because the majority of our performance tuning opportunities will be related to poorly performing SQL, the role of the application developer is extremely important.

DBA

The DBA is usually the focal point of the tuning efforts. In most organizations, the DBA is expected to understand how to performance tune and will be held responsible for the results of the tuning efforts. The DBA must have the desire and the skills to performance tune. The DBA will not only be accountable for initialization parameters and database file distribution, but will be expected to know how to find and resolve most of the performance tuning problems.

System Administrator

Regardless of the OS, you will need a knowledgeable system administrator to help identify and document system-related performance issues. They will help identify I/O, CPU, and memory problems. They will also be responsible for working with the OS and hardware vendors to identify and analyze potential problems.

Network Engineer

Most applications have a network component, so you'll need to collect and analyze statistics about the performance of the application over the network. The network engineer will look at throughput and bandwidth issues as well as unnecessary packet overhead.

Performance Engineer

In some organizations, there is a group or individual dedicated to gathering and analyzing performance data. They can help gather and categorize data, and look at the performance picture for the entire application. They may have performance-modeling software, and they are often involved in capacity planning as well.

Describe the Dependency Between Tuning in Different Development Phases

Each of the different phases in the life of an application will require a different focus of your tuning efforts. Also, the process that you follow should be more detailed and rigorous in the design, development, and testing phases than in the production phase. Your goal should be to prevent tuning problems before they reach the production environment.

Application Design and Programming

During the design phase, the database architect or designer is usually responsible for creating an optimal and workable relational database design; however, a conscientious DBA will be closely involved from the beginning. When the coding starts, the developer and code review team should be responsible for creating optimal code. Again, the DBA should be involved in both of these phases.

Design   The focus here is on creating a relational database design that is technically correct and will perform well. There are sometimes trade-offs between normalization and pure performance. The database designer and DBA should focus on the design of schema objects, transactions, and connection management. Pay special attention to expected access paths to tables (search conditions), join conditions between tables, and potential full table scans (FTSs). These designs will lead to your indexing strategy. During this phase, you should also evaluate the use of clusters, index-organized tables, materialized views, and the Oracle Partitioning option for tables and indexes.

Application Coding   Focus on reusable code, that is, SQL statements that will use the same cursor in the shared pool. You can tune this with the use of bind variables or by using the CURSOR_SHARING parameter for nearly identical SQL code. This is also a good time to review the use of indexes for common access paths.

Database Configuration

The DBA is the primary tuner when it is time to configure the database. Although application design and coding will account for the majority of tuning opportunities, it is important for the DBA to get the physical database configuration correct. Your goals should be to reduce I/O and negative effects by or to the OS.

Memory Tuning   When we refer to tuning memory, we're usually referring to the instance's Shared Global Area (SGA). The primary tunable memory components are the shared pool, large pool, Java pool, buffer cache, redo buffer, and the sort area. The sort area is outside the SGA and is allocated for each user when they need to sort; therefore, it has an impact on total system memory usage. The DBA should gather hit ratio statistics for each of the SGA memory structures and tune as necessary. For sorts, compare the number of in-memory sorts and to-disk sorts.

Generally speaking, when we tune memory structures we make them larger; however, be very careful when increasing the size of memory structures. Make sure that modifications are based on statistics that you have gathered and thoroughly analyzed. The important thing to remember when tuning memory structures is not to size your SGA or the sum of all the instance's SGAs on a server to a size larger than the available real memory. Configuring Oracle memory structures to a size larger than real memory will lead to memory paging and process swapping. Even if the combined SGA size for all instances is smaller than real memory, too many users performing sorts can lead to memory paging or process swapping. Paging and swapping will destroy system performance.

I/O Tuning   Once you're satisfied that the memory structures are sized appropriately, turn your focus to analyzing disk I/O. You should have already considered I/O balance when you designed the database, so this is a good time to evaluate your assumptions. Look for long read or write times. You may notice that one or two database files have a significantly larger amount of I/O than the rest of the database files. You may also notice that files on a particular disk drive, controller card, or array have significantly longer read and/or write times than the overall database average. When you see these trends, investigate them. If necessary, redistribute your files to improve load balance and performance.

If you determine that one table generates a tremendous amount of I/O, and you are using the Oracle Partitioning option, investigate spreading I/O across partitions. Also look for excessive or slow redo log file switches. Another area to investigate is excessive reads in tablespaces that contain only tables, which is generally a good indicator of FTS. Long write times may indicate the need for additional DB writer processes. Also investigate rollback segment I/O, which is usually a good indicator of application design issues.

Contention Tuning   When we refer to contention tuning, the goal is to reduce or eliminate the time a process waits for a resource: rollback segment, latch, lock, or free list. Multiple transactions in the same rollback segment can lead to contention. Increasing the number of rollback segments is one way to reduce the contention. Latches are usually held by a process for only a brief instant, but contention can occur when a process holds onto a latch that other processes need. One example of lock contention is when a process locks a table in exclusive mode, and other processes need to update rows in the table. Lock contention is usually resolved by writing the application such that it uses the least restrictive locking level needed and by committing changes as soon as possible. Freelist contention occurs during inserts into a data segment when multiple server processes are competing for access to a limited number of free lists for the segment.

OS Tuning   Depending on the OS, you may or may not have many OS parameters to tune. Also, OS tuning will usually have less impact on the database and application performance than tuning the application or database. Key things to look for are CPU, I/O, swap space, and network bandwidth. Evaluate direct I/O or raw devices. Examine the process scheduler, and ensure that all Oracle processes have the same process priority.

Repeat as Necessary   As you have learned thus far, this is an iterative process. You may find that tuning the I/O leads to better system throughput, which then leads to greater processing demands that initiate a memory bottleneck. Keep tuning until performance is not an issue.

One thing to keep in mind: Adding hardware to alleviate the performance bottleneck is the last option to a tuning exercise. Adding hardware means that you either miscalculated the requirements of your well-tuned application and database, which would be considered a design/architecture issue, or that you've failed to discover, analyze, and resolve some major application or database tuning problem. Again, the goal is scalability. If you haven't tuned the application and database, the problems will get worse as you add more users.

Adding a New Application to an Existing System

When you add enhancements or implement bug fixes to an application, it is extremely important to monitor the changes and watch the effect they have on existing processes. Always monitor the performance impact in the development and user acceptance testing environment before you migrate the changes to the production environment.

Production Troubleshooting and Tuning

This is an abbreviated version of the performance improvement method described previously. Generally, these measures are to resolve unexpected problems that occur after a system moves from development and testing into production. The problems may occur because of an unexpected increase in application or database use. Some refer to this as *emergency tuning* because of the unplanned nature of the exercise. You should follow the same methods used in development and testing, just with a more focused effort:

- Locate the bottleneck and try to understand why it exists.

- Resolve the problem and validate the results.

- Repeat as necessary.

Describe SLAs

An SLA, in this context, is a document that clearly states end-user or management expectations about application performance. In some organizations, the application performance SLA is negotiated between the business partner, customer or end user, and the application development team. For performance tuning, we usually refer to the expectations outlined in the SLA as a set of goals or targets for our efforts. It is important that the DBA or performance engineer contribute to the SLA. Without sound technical guidance, the framers of the SLA may inadvertently create unrealistic expectations. Wording such as all queries will return all required rows in less than one second may be appropriate for a small OLTP system or some queries in a larger system, but definitely not for a large data warehouse. More appropriate wording would be something like all zip-code table lookups will return the city and state columns within five seconds. That's a realistic target that the performance team can work towards.

Before you begin a large-scale tuning effort, make sure that you have an established SLA. Otherwise, the tuning effort will be continuous, but without direction.

Describe the Tuning Goals

Your tuning efforts will vary based on end-user requirements, the type of database application, and priorities. With each type of system, however, you should focus on specific, measurable tuning goals.

Reduce or Eliminate Waits   Application processes shouldn't have to wait for locked or fully utilized resources. Waits for locked tables should be addressed in the application design. Waits for physical resources like disk space should be eliminated through load balancing.

Access the Least Number of Blocks   If you can rewrite a query that will get the same results with fewer block reads, performance will improve. Properly used indexes often reduce the total number of blocks read, leading to improved performance.

Cache Blocks in Memory   Often-used data should be retrieved from memory instead of disk. Measure the buffer cache hit ratio.

Improve the Performance of Specific SQL Statements   If a batch process runs for several hours, it is a good candidate for performance tuning. Long-running queries also affect other user processes by using CPU and causing unnecessary disk reads.

Response Time   End-user query response time is usually the most visible performance issue, and many times poor response time drives the performance tuning effort.

Throughput   One highly visible measure is the amount of work accomplished, or throughput, in the database application. An example would be increasing batch order processing from 100 to 1,000 orders per minute.

Backup and Recovery Time Long backup times can prevent database access or reduce performance. Long recovery times will impact availability. Efforts to improve the backup and recovery process may not be noticed until you're in a crisis recovery mode.

Data Availability For Internet or self-service applications, 24×7 data availability is often part of the SLA. Tuning for availability means that database maintenance occurs with the database online, and with little or no impact to the end users.

Hit Ratios Library cache, dictionary cache, and buffer cache hit ratios are often good indicators of overall instance performance. Hit ratios should be one of the measures you attempt to improve; however, acceptable ratios don't always indicate good performance.

System Memory Utilization Using too much server memory could indicate that you have oversized your SGA or allocated too much memory to user sort areas. Using memory isn't bad, however. Ideally, most of our operations occur in memory, which is usually orders of magnitude faster than operations to disk.

Paging and Swapping If you notice paging or swapping, work diligently to eliminate it. Reduce SGA or sort area allocation until paging or swapping is eliminated.

Scalability Near-linear scalability should be one of your primary goals, and one that is easily measurable.

Share Application Code One of your goals should be to write code that is parsed once and executed many times. This cuts down on overhead in the library cache.

Read and Write Data as Fast as Possible Reduced average I/O times can be achieved by load balancing and redistributing data files to eliminate hot spots. End users may not notice I/O problems, so sometimes this tuning goal takes a lower priority. However, you should not overlook it.

Describe the Most Common Tuning Problems

The most common performance problems are due to application design and implementation, not instance parameters or database configuration. Oracle has identified the ten most common user mistakes; we will translate these into performance problems. We will also identify some additional common performance problems.

Top Ten Performance Problems

In this section, we list the most common mistakes found in Oracle systems. If you find these performance problems on your system, diagnose the impact and fix what you can. If you follow the performance tuning methodology, you should not encounter these problems.

- **Bad connection management**   We see this with applications that do not maintain a persistent connection to the database; instead, they make a connection for an SQL statement and then disconnect. This is not optimal. A good analogy is mass transit versus single-passenger vehicles. Mass transit is more efficient at transporting large numbers of people from one point to another. Databases are the same way; they prefer a small number of persistent connections instead of a large number of transient connections.

- **Poor cursor usage**   The key to good cursor usage is to use bind variables in the application. If you see SQL statements that use literals in the WHERE clause instead of bind variables, investigate.

- **Database I/O not managed properly**   Significant performance problems can occur if database I/O isn't spread across disks and controllers. Monitor for long read and write times.

- **Redo logs too few or too small**   If the redo logs are too small, you can expect a greater buffer cache load and an increased frequency of log switching, which causes more work for the I/O system.

- **Buffer cache issues, not related to size**   Too few rollback segments, freelists, or freelist groups, or an INITRANS value that is too low, can lead to the serialization of data blocks in the buffer cache, which can cause contention.

- **Long-running FTSs**   Long FTSs usually indicate a missing index, missing statistics, or a suboptimal optimizer selection. OLTP systems will suffer the most from long FTSs, but we expect long FTSs in decision support systems. To your users, long FTSs are usually the most noticeable performance problem.

- **Sorts to disk instead of in memory**   At least 95 percent of your sorts should occur in memory. If you see a larger percentage of sorts to disk, investigate.

- **Recursive SQL**   Extent allocation and other SYS chores generate recursive SQL.

- **Schema errors and optimizer problems**   Look for missing indexes or missing statistics.

■ **Incorrectly set init.ora parameters** Be wary of undocumented initialization parameters or setting parameters based on myth and folklore. Verify that the reason an initialization parameter was set is not outdated or incorrect.

Additional Performance Tuning Problems

The top ten list does not cover all potential performance issues. Some of the more common additional problems to look for are listed here. In practice, you will probably encounter several additional types of performance tuning problems.

Relational Design Issues Sometimes the database architect chooses the wrong type of object for an application component or fails to recognize the need for an index. Some of the relational design and implementation issues are as follows:

■ Table and index design, and foreign keys

■ Aggregates, clusters, index-organized tables, partitioning, and views

■ Unnecessary joins that could be resolved by denormalization

Incorrect Hardware Configuration Many factors go into determining the correct hardware configuration for a database server. The architect, DBA, and performance engineer should base the hardware configuration on the number of concurrent users, the amount of interaction, the location of the users, the amount of data read and written, response time requirements, availability, real-time versus batch issues, and database size. Based on this information, the team should establish requirements for CPU, memory, I/O subsystem throughput and capacity, and network capacity.

Limitations of Software and Hardware Components Some components work well with 5, 10, or even 100 users, but fail to perform well at some usage level. These limitations should be determined before a system goes into production. The development and testing teams can use benchmarking, workload testing, extrapolation, and modeling to determine system limitations.

Describe Tuning Goals Associated with Different Types of Applications

Users expect different types of applications to perform a certain way. Your tuning problems and goals will vary based on the type of system that you're tuning. The tuning methods should vary little between the different types of systems.

OLTP System Tuning Goals

Users of OLTP systems expect high performance on inserts, updates, and deletes, sometimes subsecond responses. They also expect common lookup functions to return instantly. Contention is often an issue. Your primary goals should be to improve query response times, improve throughput, ensure that no process waits for resources, and ensure that data is always available when needed.

Decision Support System Tuning Goals

Users of decision support systems expect their reports to take a longer amount of time, but usually not days or weeks. You should focus your efforts on tuning long-running queries and reading as few blocks of data as possible.

Hybrid Systems

With hybrid systems, we have to tune for OLTP as well as for decision support queries. End users will expect excellent response times, and long-running queries should not interfere with online performance. You have to manage the diverse needs of the different users, and prioritize batch versus interactive processes.

Internet/Intranet System Tuning Goals

With web-based systems, we have to tune for wild variability in the number of user connections and requests. Scalability and availability are your primary goals. Fast response time is an essential component of scalability.

Performance and Safety Trade-Offs

The DBA is ultimately responsible for the availability, recoverability, and performance of the database. There are several features of the Oracle9*i* database that help the DBA with the availability and recoverability of the database, but can cause an impact on performance. Please remember, availability and recoverability should not be sacrificed to achieve minimal performance gains.

Archiving   Running the database in archivelog mode enables you to recover a database up to the point of failure. Archiving uses CPU cycles and causes disk writes, so archiving can impact system performance. As the DBA, don't run a production database in noarchivelog mode without full disclosure of the consequences to your application support team and end-user management.

Backups   A cold backup denies user access to the data while the database is backed up. A hot backup can cause user waits and generally slower response times. However, backups are an essential part of database administration. Don't run a database without backups simply to improve performance, unless your end-user management is willing to accept the consequences of a database failure.

Checkpointing, Multiple Control Files, and Multiple Redo Log Members   Each of these features can improve your recoverability, but can also lead to performance issues. Infrequent checkpointing means greater potential for loss of data in case of a failure, while too-frequent complete checkpoints can cause I/O problems. Multiple control files safeguard against the corruption or deletion of a single file, but updating multiple control files takes time. The same goes for multiple redo log members in a group. Several additional members means more I/O, and consequently, a performance hit. To keep the performance impact at a minimum and still keep your recoverability options available, write the control files to different disks. Also, make sure that no two members of the same redo log group are on the same disk. There is almost never a good reason to run a database without multiple control files and multiple redo log members in each redo log group.

Chapter Summary

This chapter introduced you to the Oracle Performance Tuning Methodology. We described the basic steps that Oracle recommends you follow to achieve performance improvements. We described the different roles associated with performance tuning. Although you may not find an individual in your organization for each role, you may find one or more people who are willing to take on more than one of the suggested roles. If you can't fill one of the roles, don't let it prevent you from performance tuning. You learned that it is most important to create a good application and database design; that is your first performance tuning exercise. You also learned that different phases of application development require different performance tuning processes. We also discussed SLAs and why they're important to the performance tuning process. We described several performance tuning goals; some of them will be more important to you depending on the type of application you support or the types of performance problems you see. We then described some of the most common performance problems you will face. If you look for the types of problems described and follow the steps outlined in this chapter, you will see performance improvements.

Two-Minute Drill

- There are eight steps to the Oracle Performance Tuning Method.
- The model is designed to promote iterative and continuous performance improvement.

- The steps are 1) get user feedback, 2) gather statistics, 3) look for fully utilized systems, 4) check for common mistakes made by users, 5) build a conceptual model of your findings, 6) propose and implement an action plan, 7) validate the modifications, and 8) repeat steps 5, 6, and 7.

- Continuous application of this model will reduce and eliminate bottlenecks.

- The roles associated with performance tuning are users, management, a designer, a developer, a DBA, a system administrator, a network engineer, and a performance engineer.

- Each phase of the application development process requires different tuning efforts.

- The designer should be responsible for designing the application for performance.

- The developer should focus on writing reusable and efficient code.

- The DBA should focus on tuning the database configuration: memory, I/O, contention, and possibly the OS. Repeat as necessary.

- Production performance tuning should follow the same general method, only accelerated.

- A service level agreement (SLA) should exist between the parties responsible for the development, maintenance, and use of the system. It should specify performance expectations.

- Specific tuning goals include, but are not limited to, improved throughput, reduced waits, faster response times, higher hit ratios, faster backup and recovery, more in-memory sorts, and reduced I/O.

- The most common tuning problems are related to application design and SQL coding.

- Bad connection management, not reusing cursors, and bad relational design are the most common performance problems.

- Different types of applications will have different tuning goals.

- One of the goals for OLTP systems should be query response time.

- One of the goals for a decision support system should be reducing the total blocks read.

Chapter Questions

1. **Which one of the following is not a role associated with the Oracle Performance Tuning Methodology?**

   A. Oracle DBA

   B. Application developer

   C. Project manager

   D. Network engineer

   E. System (OS) administrator

   F. Pizza delivery person

2. **Which of these statements describe the Oracle Performance Tuning Methodology? (Choose three.)**

   A. Performance tuning is deterministic.

   B. Performance tuning is iterative and continuous.

   C. After you have fixed the top ten problems, your database will run smoothly.

   D. Gathering baseline statistics is essential to the performance tuning process.

   E. It precludes the involvement of the end users.

   F. The focus is on scalability.

3. **Which of these are legitimate performance tuning goals? (Choose three.)**

   A. Reduce throughput.

   B. Increase SQL run times.

   C. Lower hit ratios.

   D. Decrease sorts to disk.

   E. Eliminate lock contention.

   F. Optimize connection management.

4. **Which of these tuning efforts should occur first?**

   A. Tune the OS.

   B. Tune database I/O.

   C. Tune memory.

    D. Tune the network.

    E. Tune the application.

    F. Tune the design.

5. **An SLA, in the context of performance tuning, is best described as _____?**

    A. A wish list of database features from the application development team

    B. Tuning specifications

    C. An agreement between the DBAs about how they will tune rollback segments

    D. An agreement between the stakeholders in an application about expected performance

    E. A set of tuning methods that the DBA should follow

6. **Which one of these performance tuning opportunities should you investigate first?**

    A. An end user informs you that a report that usually takes four hours took at least four hours and five minutes last Thursday.

    B. You notice that the buffer cache hit ratio has dropped from 99.9 to 99.5 percent over the past two weeks.

    C. End users report that the new self-service web application has slowed down considerably since the last module was added.

    D. You notice that there are many more disk reads in the files that comprise the APP_INDEX tablespace than in the APP_DATA tablespace.

Answers to Chapter Questions

1. F.   Pizza delivery person

Explanation   This is an easy one. Although pizza delivery personnel may be essential contributors to a performance tuning emergency, they don't have an official role. The Oracle DBA is ultimately responsible for the performance of the database. He or she is responsible for monitoring all facets of the database, monitoring user query statistics, and modifying database configuration and instance parameters.

2. B, D, F.   Performance tuning is iterative and continuous. Gathering baseline statistics is essential to the performance tuning process. The focus is on scalability.

Explanation   The Oracle Performance Tuning Methodology focuses on scalability as the goal of performance tuning. To achieve scalability, you will need to continuously gather statistics and resolve the performance problems that have the greatest impact. The end users will help you identify the most important tuning problems.

   3. D, E, F.   Decrease sorts to disk. Eliminate lock contention. Optimize connection management.

Explanation   Answer A is incorrect because we want to increase throughput. We also want to decrease SQL run times and raise hit ratios. Answer D is correct because sorts to disk are significantly slower than sorts in memory. We also want to reduce or eliminate lock contention so that user processes are not waiting. We also want to optimize connection management because poor connection management creates unnecessary overhead on the network and the database server.

   4. F.   Tune the design.

Explanation   Tuning the design is the first step in the application development phase of the Performance Tuning Model. Tuning the application should follow this step during the coding phase. The remaining tuning opportunities are usually the DBA's responsibility and occur later in the design and implementation process.

   5. D.   An agreement between the stakeholders in an application about expected performance

Explanation   An SLA is a contract between those who need a service and those who provide it. In this context, it specifically describes agreed-upon expectations about system performance.

   6. C.   End users report that the new self-service web application has slowed down considerably since the last module was added.

Explanation   As with most tuning exercises, you need to prioritize the data you've gathered and determine which to address first. I don't consider A to be a problem until I can see upward trends in run times. Note that there's a five-minute increase over a 240-minute process, and then gather run-time information when the report runs again. B may or may not be a problem, but we should note the downward trend and see if it continues. Answer D would indicate that the indexes are being read more often than the table, which is probably a good thing, not an indicator of poor performance. If the opposite were true, you might want to investigate FTSs on the tables in the APP_DATA tablespace. Answer C seems to be the most visible performance problem, but one that isn't quantified. You need to gather information, analyze, and propose a remedy.

CHAPTER
3

Diagnostic and
Tuning Tools

n this chapter, you will learn about diagnostic and tuning tools, and will learn specifically to

- Describe the data dictionary and dynamic performance views related to tuning.

- Use the ANALYZE command, DBMS_UTILITY package procedures, and DBMS_STATS package procedures to gather statistics.

- Describe statistics in the dynamic performance views.

- Describe how Statspack collects statistics.

- Collect statistics using Statspack.

- List and describe other tools that can be used for tuning.

- Describe the use of the alert log and trace files.

This chapter focuses on the tools that you will use to gather statistics about the Oracle instance and database, events occurring in the database, and individual sessions working with the database. The most fundamental tools you will use include the data dictionary and dynamic performance views. We will then discuss Statspack and other tools that can be used to gather information. Finally, we will review the alert log and trace files created by the Oracle instance, and how we can use them to performance tune.

Diagnostic and Tuning Tools

Before you can tune your database application, you need to get comfortable with the tools of performance tuning. Fundamental to performance tuning is the information gathering phase. Fortunately, Oracle has a built-in set of performance tuning views that we can simply query to gain some information about our database. No third-party tool is required to gather this information. But simple one-time views of the database aren't enough to tune; we need to take snapshots of the statistics and compare them over some time interval. This will give us an indication of how the database performs over a given time. This makes sense because we really want to measure our database as it is used, not at some singular point in time. Oracle provides several tools that we can use to gather and compare snapshots of performance data; we will introduce and discuss them in this chapter.

The Data Dictionary and Dynamic Performance Views Related to Tuning

There are two distinct categories of views that we will query to gather information about the state of the instance, database, and sessions. The first category is data dictionary views, the names of which start with DBA_*, followed by a descriptive name. These data dictionary views are owned by the SYS schema and provide detailed information about objects in the database. For example, DBA_*TABLES lists the owner, table name, and data storage information of each relational table in the database. The second category is the set of dynamic performance views, which are also owned by the SYS schema, but begin with V$ and are then followed by a descriptive name. For example, V$LOCKED_OBJECT lists the database objects that currently have a lock held on them.

Data Dictionary Views

The DBA_* dictionary views are actual views against tables owned by the SYS schema. The DBA_*TABLES view mentioned previously is a query that joins SYS.user$, SYS.tab$, and several other SYS tables. There is also a public synonym for each DBA_* view. The DBA_* views are created by scripts in $ORACLE_HOME/rdbms\admin, so which DBA_* views are in the database depends on which scripts have been run. For the purpose of gathering performance tuning information, we will describe some of the DBA_* views that you will need to become familiar with. For the sake of brevity, we will not include each column and associated description of a view.

DBA_SEGMENTS

DBA_SEGMENTS describes storage allocated for all database segments. The columns that are most useful for tuning purposes are as follows:

- **SEGMENT_TYPE** The type of segment, such as table, index, and so on
- **BYTES** The size of the segment in bytes
- **BLOCKS** The size of the segment in blocks
- **HEADER_FILE** The ID of the file containing the segment header
- **HEADER_BLOCK** The ID of the block containing the segment header

Additional columns in DBA_SEGMENTS are also referenced in the associated DBA_TABLES, DBA_INDEXES, and the other views for each type of segment.

DBA_TABLES

As mentioned previously, this view describes each of the relational tables in the database. For performance tuning, these are some of the important columns, with text describing the column queried from DBA_COL_COMMENTS. The first group of columns are storage related and initially populated when the table is created.

- **PCT_INCREASE** The percentage increase in extent size when allocating new extents
- **PCT_FREE** The minimum percentage of free space in a block
- **PCT_USED** The minimum percentage of used space in a block
- **MAX_TRANS** The maximum number of transactions
- **FREELISTS** The number of process freelists allocated in this segment
- **FREELIST_GROUPS** The number of freelist groups allocated in this segment
- **CACHE** Whether the table is to be cached in the buffer cache
- **BUFFER_POOL** The default buffer pool to be used for table blocks

The following columns are NULL when the table is created and are updated when the table is analyzed.

- **LAST_ANALYZED** The date of the most recent time this table was analyzed
- **NUM_ROWS** The number of rows in the table
- **CHAIN_CNT** The number of chained rows in the table
- **BLOCKS** The number of used blocks in the table
- **EMPTY_BLOCKS** The number of empty (never used) blocks in the table
- **AVG_SPACE** The average available free space in the table
- **AVG_ROW_LEN** The average row length, including row overhead
- **NUM_FREELIST_BLOCKS** The number of blocks on the freelist
- **AVG_SPACE_FREELIST_BLOCKS** The average freespace of all blocks on a freelist

The value of these columns is set to NULL when you delete statistics for the table.

DBA_TAB_COLUMNS

Used in conjunction with DBA_TABLES, this view gives more detailed information about each column that comprises a table. The DBA_TAB_COL_STATISTICS view contains a subset of the columns in DBA_TAB_COLUMNS. Here are some of the columns that we look at in both views:

- **LOW_VALUE**   The low value in the column
- **HIGH_VALUE**   The high value in the column
- **AVG_COL_LENGTH**   The average length of the column in bytes
- **DENSITY**   The density of the column
- **NUM_DISTINCT**   The number of distinct values in the column
- **NUM_NULLS**   The number of nulls in the column
- **NUM_BUCKETS**   The number of buckets in the histogram for the column
- **LAST_ANALYZED**   The date of the most recent time this column was analyzed
- **SAMPLE_SIZE**   The sample size used in analyzing this column

DBA_CLUSTERS

This is the description of all clusters in the database. Some of the important tuning columns are as follows, with descriptions from DBA_COL_COMMENTS:

- **PCT_FREE**   The minimum percentage of free space in a block
- **PCT_USED**   The minimum percentage of used space in a block
- **MAX_TRANS**   The maximum number of transactions
- **PCT_INCREASE**   The percentage of increase in the extent size
- **FREELISTS**   The number of process freelists allocated in this segment
- **FREELIST_GROUPS**   The number of freelist groups allocated in this segment
- **AVG_BLOCKS_PER_KEY**   The average number of blocks containing rows with a given cluster key
- **CLUSTER_TYPE**   The type of cluster: B-Tree index or hash
- **CACHE**   Whether the cluster is to be cached in the buffer cache
- **BUFFER_POOL**   The default buffer pool to be used for cluster blocks

DBA_INDEXES

This is a description of each of the indexes in the database. As with tables, we want to focus on storage-related and performance statistics, so we will look closely at these columns:

- **UNIQUENESS**   The uniqueness status of the index: UNIQUE, NONUNIQUE, or UNDEFINED

- **INDEX_TYPE**   The type of index: NORMAL, BITMAP, FUNCTION-BASED NORMAL, FUNCTION-BASED BITMAP, or DOMAIN

- **MAX_TRANS**   The maximum number of transactions

- **PCT_INCREASE**   The percentage of increase in the extent size

- **FREELISTS**   The number of process freelists allocated in this segment

- **FREELIST_GROUPS**   The number of freelist groups allocated to this segment

- **PCT_FREE**   The minimum percentage of free space in a block

- **BLEVEL**   The B-Tree level

- **LEAF_BLOCKS**   The number of leaf blocks in the index

- **DISTINCT_KEYS**   The number of distinct keys in the index

- **LAST_ANALYZED**   The date of the most recent time this index was analyzed

- **SAMPLE_SIZE**   The size of the sample used to analyze the index

- **PARTITIONED**   Is this index partitioned? YES or NO

- **GLOBAL_STATS**   Are the statistics calculated without merging underlying partitions? YES or NO

- **BUFFER_POOL**   The default buffer pool to be used for index blocks

- **FUNCIDX_STATUS**   Is the function-based index DISABLED or ENABLED?

DBA_IND_COLUMNS

This view shows each column and its associated description that is indexed in the database. This view doesn't contain detailed information like we see in DBA_TAB_COLUMNS, but the one column presented here is very important:

- **DESCEND**   The value is DESC if this column is sorted in descending order on disk; otherwise, it is ASC.

DBA_TAB_HISTOGRAMS

This view describes histograms on tables. Besides columns for OWNER and TABLE, we're interested in the following:

- **COLUMN_NAME** The column name or attribute of the object type column

- **ENDPOINT_NUMBER** The histogram bucket number

- **ENDPOINT_VALUE** The normalized endpoint value for this bucket

- **ENDPOINT_ACTUAL_VALUE** The actual string value of the endpoint for this bucket

INDEX_HISTOGRAM

This view stores information from the last ANALYZE INDEX . . . VALIDATE STRUCTURE command issued. Its columns are as follows:

- **REPEAT_COUNT** The number of times that one or more index key(s) is repeated in the table

- **KEYS_WITH_REPEAT_COUNT** The number of index keys that are repeated that many times

How the ANALYZE Command Is Used with Data Dictionary Views

The ANALYZE command is used to gather statistics for the DBA_* views mentioned previously. For example, when the ANALYZE command is used on a table, these columns are updated to reflect the current optimizer statistics gathered about that table: NUM_ROWS, BLOCKS, EMPTY_BLOCKS, AVG_SPACE, CHAIN_CNT, AVG_ROW_LEN, AVG_SPACE_FREELIST_BLOCKS, NUM_FREELIST_BLOCKS, SAMPLE_SIZE, and LAST_ANALYZED. You can analyze tables, clusters, and indexes with the ANALYZE TABLE, ANALYZE CLUSTER, or ANALYZE INDEX SQL commands.

You can use the DBMS_UTILITY.ANALYZE_SCHEMA procedure to gather statistics for all the objects in a schema. The ANALYZE_DATABASE procedure can be used to gather statistics for the entire database.

Additionally, you can use the DBMS_STATS package to gather statistics. The DBMS_STATS package is preferred over the ANALYZE command or the DBMS_UTILITY procedures. DBMS_STATS has procedures for gathering, deleting, exporting, and importing statistics for schemas, objects, and the entire database. You can also gather statistics in parallel with DBMS_STATS.

Dynamic Performance Views

The dynamic performance views, or V$ views, are the most important Oracle-supplied views available to you for gathering performance data. The V$ views are actually synonyms on V_$ views. The V_$ views are based on the sys.X$ tables, which are actually memory structures that are populated at instance startup and cleared at instance shutdown. The X$ tables have cryptic names that aren't easily deciphered and should not be queried directly unless you have a really good reason to. The X$ tables are undocumented and may change from release to release.

The X$ tables are updated continuously; therefore, the V$ views reflect the current state. The V$ views are designed as a level of abstraction above the X$ tables and provide almost all the performance tuning information you will ever need. As the DBA, you must understand which V$ views to look at to gather and analyze data about your instance. The view V$FIXED_TABLE lists the X$ tables and V$ views. Also, if you want to collect timing information in the V$ views, you'll need to set the init.ora parameter TIMED_STATISTICS=TRUE before startup or set the parameter with the ALTER SYSTEM command after the instance is started. Depending on which document or performance tuning book you read, the V$ views are grouped into a few basic categories.

Current State Views

These views indicate what is currently happening in the instance: V$LOCK, V$LATCH_HOLDER, V$OPEN_CURSOR, V$SESSION, or V$SESSION_WAIT.

Accumulator Views

These views record how many times something has happened since instance startup. It is important to remember that the V$ views are reset when the instance goes through a shutdown and startup cycle. These views are used to collect information between two different points in time (while the database is up) and to compare the activity that has occurred. These views include V$MYSTAT, V$SESSION_WAIT, V$SESSTAT, V$DB_OBJECT_CACHE, V$FILESTAT, V$LATCH, V$LATCH_CHILDREN, V$LIBRARYCACHE, V$ROLLSTAT, V$ROWCACHE, VSQL, VSQLAREA, V$SYSSTAT, V$SYSTEM_EVENT, V$UNDOSTAT, and V$WAITSTAT.

Informational Views

These views contain information that is updated dynamically, but usually not as often as the current state views: V$PARAMETER, V$SYSTEM_PARAMETER, V$SQLTEXT, V$PROCESS, and V$SQL_PLAN.

Statistics in the Dynamic Performance Views

Another way to categorize the dynamic performance views is by the components of the Oracle database that they measure. The categories of instance and database views show information regarding the entire instance or database and all the events or processes that are occurring within. Memory views show information about cache performance and objects that are cached. Disk performance views contain statistics about disk input/output (I/O). Contention views show when processes are waiting for resources, and session-related views enable us to see exactly what is happening in a user session.

Instance/Database Performance Views

These are systemwide views that give an overview of occurrences within the database. In general, these views indicate at a high level where you can begin to analyze potential problems.

V$SYSTEM_EVENT

The V$SYSTEM_EVENT view shows summary information about each wait event since system startup. The view has columns for the number of waits, the timeouts, the total time waited, and the average wait. This is a good place to start when you don't know exactly where waits are occurring in your database.

V$WAITSTAT

This view summarizes buffer waits and is useful in determining the general class of buffer waits. An analysis of V$WAITSTAT will help you determine if you have enough rollback segments, if you have full table scans (FTSs) or index range scans on sparse segments, or if you have freelist contention.

V$PROCESS

Each process in the instance has a row in the V$PROCESS view. One of the most important functions of the V$PROCESS view is to relate an operating system (OS) process ID (PID) to an Oracle session ID (SID). When troubleshooting a process that is using considerable OS resources, you can use the OS PID to query this view and join it with V$SESSION.

Here's an example query joining V$PROCESS with V$SESSION:

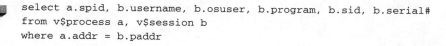

```
select a.spid, b.username, b.osuser, b.program, b.sid, b.serial#
from v$process a, v$session b
where a.addr = b.paddr
```

```
and a.spid = 44
/
SPID    USERNAME    OSUSER     PROGRAM        SID    SERIAL#
----    --------    -------    ------------   ---    --------
44      SYSTEM      OraUser    SQLPLUSW.EXE   8      26
```

Also, trace files created for a process use the value represented in the SPID column in the V$PROCESS view as part of their name. For example, issuing the ALTER SESSION SET SQL_TRACE=TRUE command in the previous session will create the file ora00044.trc in the USER_DUMP_DEST directory.

V$SYSSTAT

The V$SYSSTAT view shows system statistics and is the primary place to look for system performance and resource usage information. Hit ratios, cumulative logons, total CPU usage, parse counts, total physical reads and writes, and in-memory and to-disk sorts are just a few of the vital statistics that are available in this view.

The V$SYSSTAT view CLASS column must be decoded to make sense. Here's a sample query; see Table 3-1 as a reference for the CLASS column.

```
SELECT * FROM V$SYSSTAT
WHERE value > 0
ORDER BY name
/
STATISTIC# NAME                             CLASS      VALUE
---------- ------------------------------   --------   ---------
        90 CR blocks created                   8           4
...
       179 table scan rows gotten             64      129549
       175 table scans (long tables)          64          67
       174 table scans (short tables)         64          53
         6 user calls                          1         102
```

V$PX_PROCESS_SYSSTAT

This view concerns system statistics for parallel query operations. It indicates the number of parallel query servers in use, available, and started. It also shows memory chunk and buffer statistics.

Memory

As you learned in previous discussions about the Performance Tuning Method, tuning memory is the first exercise a tuner should undertake after the design and

1	General instance activity
2	Redo log buffer activity
4	Locking
8	Database buffer cache activity
16	OS activity
32	Parallelization
64	Table access
128	Debugging

TABLE 3-1. *The Meaning of the CLASS Column on V$SYSSTAT*

application are tuned. There are several views that help the performance tuner gather information about the usage of the memory structures. The V$SYSSTAT view described previously is also an excellent source for memory statistics such as consistent gets, DB block changes, DBWR buffers scanned, free buffers inspected, and physical reads and writes.

V$SGASTAT
This view contains statistics for SGA components. The statistics, indicated in bytes, represent the size allocated to each SGA component and cumulative totals for each SGA component since startup.

V$LIBRARYCACHE
This view shows hit ratios and other valuable statistics for the different classes of objects that are in or have been in the library cache of the shared pool.

V$DB_OBJECT_CACHE
Whereas the V$LIBRARYCACHE view provides statistics at the class level, the V$DB_OBJECT_CACHE provides detailed information about individual objects in the library cache. The name and type of object, whether the object is pinned, and how many sessions are executing the object are some of the important statistics available in this view.

V$ROWCACHE

This view is analogous to the V$LIBRARY_CACHE view, providing summary statistics for the row cache. It is also referred to as the data dictionary cache. This view is most beneficial in determining whether the shared pool (and data dictionary cache) is properly sized.

V$BUFFER_POOL_STATISTICS

This view shows summary statistics about each of the configured buffer pools. Waits for free buffers, blocks changed, physical reads, and physical writes are some of the important statistics viewed here.

V$DB_CACHE_ADVICE

This view is used to estimate the impact on the number of physical reads caused by decreasing or increasing the size of the buffer cache. The value of the dynamically configurable parameter DB_CACHE_ADVICE determines if this view is populated and updated. We will discuss this in detail in Chapter 5.

V$PGASTAT

New to Oracle9*i*, this view indicates memory usage statistics for the Program Global Area (PGA). The NAME column indicates the statistic, and the VALUE column indicates the current value of the statistics.

Disk

There are two categories of disk files in the Oracle9*i* database: datafiles and tempfiles. The V$FILESTAT view shows physical read and write statistics about each datafile in the database. The V$TEMPSTAT view shows similar information for files of type temporary. These views are essential when searching for disk I/O bottlenecks. When TIMED_STATISTICS=TRUE for the instance, these views show the total read and write times. You can then calculate the average read and write time for each datafile.

Contention

Contention is best described as two or more processes competing for the same resource. These particular views deal with contention for system resources such as latches on memory structures and rollback segments. The V$WAITSTAT view mentioned previously is also used to measure contention.

V$LATCH, V$LATCH_CHILDREN, and V$LATCH_PARENT

V$LATCH shows summary information about each type of latch. With this view, you can identify which latches have a high miss rate or an unusually high number of requests. You can't tune latches, but you can identify latch contention and investigate what is causing it. V$LATCH_CHILDREN is a detailed view of latch children for latches that have children. If a latch has children, you can look to this view for more detailed information about which latch children may be the source of the problem. You can then refer back to V$LATCH_PARENT to see the parent latch for the children.

V$ROLLSTAT

This view shows summary information about rollback segment activity. This information is useful in determining whether rollback segments are undersized or if the optimal size is set correctly. This view is available for both Automatic Undo Management and Manual Undo Management (conventional rollback segments).

V$UNDOSTAT

This view tracks undo and transaction information in ten-minute intervals since startup. Valuable information includes the total number of transactions, the maximum concurrent transactions, and ORA-1555 Snapshot Too Old errors during the interval. This view is available for both Automatic Undo Management and Manual Undo Management (conventional rollback segments). Also, this view can be used in determining space issues and UNDO_RETENTION settings.

Session-Related

These views help the performance tuner identify specific activity within an active session. It is important to distinguish these views from the previous ones, in that these views only contain information about active sessions. Once a session is gone, the session statistics are no longer available. To analyze a specific user session, query these views for that session's SID.

V$SESSION

This view is important for gathering basic session information; it is where you will find the user name, program name, machine name, serial number, and SID for each session in the database. Each Oracle background process has a record in V$SESSION; the number of rows in V$SESSION is one of your first general indicators of system load.

V$SESS_IO

This view is a good indicator of individual session activity. Columns for block gets, block changes, consistent gets, consistent changes, and physical reads are updated when activity occurs.

V$LOCK

The V$LOCK view keeps track of each lock currently held and each queued request for a lock. This view shows the SID for the session that is holding or requesting the lock, the type of lock, and whether the session is holding or requesting the lock.

V$SESSTAT

V$SESSTAT shows statistics for individual session events and must be joined with the V$STATNAME view to make sense. Use the following query to join the two views:

```
select b.name, a.value
from v$sesstat a, v$statname b
where sid=1
and a.statistic# = b.statistic#
/
NAME                                                              VALUE
-----------------------------------------------------------  ----------
logons cumulative                                                    1
...
sorts (disk)                                                         0
sorts (rows)                                                         0
```

V$SESSION_EVENT

This view contains the number of times waited, the number of timeouts, and the total time waited statistics for each type of event that occurs in a session.

V$SESSION_WAIT

This view shows the resources that a session is currently waiting on. Query this view without specifying the SID to determine if there are waits for any currently connected sessions.

V$SORT_USAGE

This is populated when a session creates temporary segments. The CONTENTS column shows whether the segment was created in a temporary or permanent tablespace. Because this view contains the address of the session that is creating the sort segments, you can join V$SORT_USAGE with the V$SESSION and V$SQLTEXT views to determine which user is performing disk sorts and which Structured Query Language (SQL) they're executing.

V$OPEN_CURSOR

V$OPEN_CURSOR is used to view all cursors opened by a session and the first 60 characters of the SQL text. Use this query in conjunction with V$SQLTEXT to view the complete SQL statement if longer than 60 characters. Join it with V$SQLAREA and V$SQL to view statistics about the individual SQL statements.

V$PX_SESSTAT
This view shows parallel query operations for each session.

It is important to remember that these are just a few of the views that you will use to performance tune. We will use these and other views in subsequent chapters. Also remember that V$ views are cleared at shutdown. If you want to measure performance over time, you'll need to capture data from the V$ views at a start and end time, and then subtract the values to obtain the delta.

What Is Statspack?

Statspack is an Oracle-supplied tool for gathering, storing, and reporting information about the performance of an Oracle database. It is comprised of SQL and PL/SQL scripts (the Statspack package), tables, indexes, constraints, sequences owned by the PERFSTAT schema, and public synonyms for the PERFSTAT objects. Statspack was introduced in Oracle8*i* version 8.1.6 and is the evolution of the UTLBSTAT and UTLESTAT scripts that you may be familiar with from previous Oracle versions. We will discuss UTLBSTAT/UTLESTAT later in this chapter, but here are some of the advantages of Statspack over BSTAT/ESTAT:

- Statspack gathers more statistics and calculates many ratios.

- Statspack data is stored in permanent tables owned by the PERFSTAT schema.

- Data collection is separated from report generation and is easily automated with the $ORACLE_HOME/rdbms/admin/spauto.sql script.

- Statspack includes both rollbacks and commits when it calculates the number of transactions.

Central to the Statspack design is the snapshot. This is in no way associated with the snapshot database object used with Oracle8*i* replication.

A Statspack snapshot is a point-in-time collection of data. Each snapshot has a unique identifier based on SNAP_ID, DBID, and INSTANCE_NUMBER. After you collect at least two snapshots, you can run the Statspack performance report to analyze the activity between the two points in time.

Installing and Configuring Statspack
Before you install Statspack, it's a good idea to create a tablespace specifically for the Statspack tables and indexes, or use the TOOLS tablespace. You'll need

approximately 75MB of disk space for the install, but I recommend at least 100MB to start. Your storage needs may increase, depending on the number of snapshots you generate and keep. For more information on the proper usage of this feature and how to interpret the generated reports, read the Statspack document, $ORACLE_HOME/rdbms/admin/spdoc.txt.

By default, the PERFSTAT user is created with the password PERFSTAT; for security reasons, change the password immediately following a successful installation.

Interactive or Batch Installations

You can install Statspack interactively by connecting as a user with the SYSBA privilege and running the $ORACLE_HOME/rdbms/admin/spcreate.sql script. You will be prompted for the default and temporary tablespaces for the new PERFSTAT user. Do not use the SYSTEM tablespace for either, or the installation script will abort with an error message indicating that this is the problem.

The spcreate.sql script runs three scripts: spcusr.sql, spctab.sql, and spcpkg.sql. Each script generates an output file in the current directory with the same prefix, but it uses .lis for the suffix instead of .sql. If the spcreate.sql script fails, you can determine the problem from the output files, fix the problem, drop Statspack by running the $ORACLE_HOME/rdbms/admin/spdrop.sql script, and then reinstall using spcreate.sql. The spdrop.sql script actually runs two scripts, spdtab.sql and spdusr.sql, and generates two output files with the same naming convention mentioned previously.

To install Statspack in batch mode, simply create an SQL script that defines variables for the default_tablespace and temporary_tablespace before executing spcreate.sql.

Statspack Maintenance

Eventually, you'll need to remove snapshots that are no longer needed. The sppurge.sql script enables you to delete a range of snapshots, and the sptrunc.sql script can be used to truncate the performance tables in the PERFSTAT schema. The spuexp.par export parameter file can be used to export the PERFSTAT schema. Also, if you've upgraded the database from an Oracle8*i* version, you'll need to upgrade the PERFSTAT schema too. Look for the spup816.sql or spup817.sql script, depending on the version you upgraded from.

Configuring Statspack Statistics Gathering

The amount of data gathered by Statspack is configurable. The snapshot level, which is set to 5 by default, can be changed to 6 to gather information on SQL plans for high-resource-usage SQL statements.

This is beneficial when generating a baseline snapshot or after collecting optimizer statistics. However, using higher snapshot levels can also be very resource intensive, so they should be used infrequently.

Collect Statistics Using Statspack

Gathering statistics with Statspack is easy, and Oracle has supplied a script that we can use to schedule the process to run automatically. If you want to collect timing information, make sure the database initialization parameter TIMED_STATISTICS is set to TRUE, or issue the command ALTER SYSTEM SET TIMED_STATISTICS=TRUE.

Take a Snapshot

To take a snapshot, connect to the database using SQL*Plus with the PERFSTAT userid, and execute the statspack.snap procedure. It's that simple. To take a snapshot in an Oracle Real Application Clusters (RAC) environment, simply connect to the instance that you wish to gather information about. Repeat for each instance you wish to take a snapshot of.

Automating Snapshots

Oracle provides a script that we can use to automate the snapshot process. The script $ORACLE_HOME/rdbms/admin/spauto.sql can be used to run the snapshot process every hour on the hour. The script uses DBMS_JOB to schedule the snapshot, so you will need to set the init.ora parameter JOB_QUEUE_PROCESSES to a value greater than 0 if you want the job to run. You can use the DBMS_JOB .INTERVAL procedure to change the frequency of snapshot collection.

Another method is to schedule the statspack.snap procedure to run in a batch job scheduled with the Windows NT at command or with the Unix cron command.

Producing a Performance Report

To produce a Statspack performance report, you will need to have created at least two snapshots because the report calculations are based on the deltas. Remember that the statistics gathered by Statspack are based on the V$ views; therefore, if you shut down the instance between the two snapshots you've chosen, the report will be invalid. Logged on as PERFSTAT, execute the $ORACLE_HOME/rdbms/admin/ spreport.sql script. You will be shown a list of all completed snapshots, and then you will be prompted for the beginning snapshot ID, ending snapshot ID, and the name of the output file for the report. The report generated is the general instance health report.

The other report that you can generate is the SQL report, generated by the script $ORACLE_HOME/rdbms/admin/sprepsql.sql. This report can be used to get more detailed information about a single SQL statement. In addition to the report name and beginning and ending snapshot IDs, you will be prompted for the hash value of the offensive SQL.

Contents of the Statspack Performance Report

The Statspack report begins with a summary of information about the instance and database, and follows with more detailed information about different subject areas:

- **General information**   Database name, DB_ID, instance name, DBMS version, hostname, beginning and ending snapshot IDs, and times

- **Cache sizes**   Current db_block_buffers, log_buffer, and shared_pool_size

- **Load profile**   Instance events per second and per transaction

- **Instance efficiency percentages**   Buffer cache and shared pool

- **Top five wait events**   Waits such as the library cache pin, based on total wait time in seconds

- **Complete list of wait events**   As it is written, the complete list with waits, timeouts, the total wait time, the average wait time, and waits per transaction

- **SQL statements currently in the shared pool**   Ordered by buffer gets, in descending order

- **Instance activity stats**   From V$SYSSTAT between snapshots

- **Tablespace and file I/O**   Listed by tablespaces first, and then a detailed file report

- **Buffer pool stats**   General pool, instance recovery stats, wait statistics, and PGA memory stats

- **Rollback or UNDO segment activity**   Per rollback or UNDO segment

- **Rollback segment storage statistics**   Bytes written, wraps, shrinks, and extends

- **Enqueue activity**   table (TM) and transaction (TX) locks

- **Latch activity**   Get, get miss, sleep, and nowait statistics for each latch

- **Dictionary cache stats**   Gets, misses, and SGA percent

- **Library cache stats**   Gets, misses, pins, reloads, and invalidations

- **SGA stats**   By region and by individual statistic within each region
- **Init.ora parameters at startup**   Name, beginning value, and end value if different

Other Tools That Can Be Used for Tuning

Statspack is considered a foundation tool for gathering performance information. However, there are other tools that the performance engineer may prefer to use in different circumstances. As mentioned previously, UTLBSTAT/UTLESTAT is similar to Statspack except that trending or historical data storage is not part of the tool. Oracle Enterprise Manager (OEM) has two optional packs that can be used to performance tune. Last but not least, each DBA should have their own toolkit of performance-gathering scripts.

UTLBSTAT/UTLESTAT

UTLBSTAT/UTLESTAT is similar to Statspack in that you take a beginning and ending snapshot and evaluate the performance of the instance between snapshots. Start the data collection by running the $ORACLE_HOME/rdbms/admin/utlbstat.sql script. The script creates several tables and populates them with initial statistics. At some time later, run the script $ORACLE_HOME/rdbms/admin/utlestat.sql, which ends the data collection and generates the report file report.txt in the current directory. The utlestat.sql script also drops the tables used to collect and store the data, so there is no continuity between executions.

Statspack and UTLBSTAT/UTLESTAT both use a table called STATS$WAITSTAT, so be aware of potential conflicts. Statspack is a better tool, so you really should only use UTLBSTAT/UTLESTAT for backward compatibility with third-party tuning applications.

Oracle Enterprise Manager (OEM) Performance Manager

If you use OEM, you can purchase the optional Performance Manager pack. Performance Manager is a graphic user interface (GUI) real-time performance monitor. It enables the performance engineer to see events as they occur in the database. It contains several predefined performance charts for I/O, contention, database and instance statistics, load, cache hit ratios, top resource consumers, performance overview, and throughput overview. The performance engineer can also define charts to meet specific performance monitoring needs.

OEM Oracle Expert

Another OEM optional pack is Oracle Expert, which provides a step-by-step implementation of the Oracle Performance Tuning Methodology described in Chapter 2. It automates the collection and analysis of instance information, and then generates recommendations and scripts that the DBA can use to implement the recommendations.

Custom Tools

As a DBA and performance engineer, you will gather useful scripts from performance tuning books, magazine articles, web sites, and professional peers. You may find that some of these scripts are particularly useful for one or more systems that you support. You may also discover that Statspack and other Oracle-supplied performance tools do not gather all the statistics that you need. One good place to start looking for additional scripts is in $ORACLE_HOME/rdbms/admin. Also, Oracle's Metalink web site and Revealnet's web site are good sources. Several vendors also have product offerings in the Oracle monitoring realm. Download and evaluate their software, and see if it meets your needs.

The Alert Log and Trace Files

The Oracle instance generates system messages to the alert log, located in the directory specified in the BACKGROUND_DUMP_DEST init.ora parameter. Background process trace files are written to the same directory and contain information about specific background process events and errors. If you enable SQL_TRACE for the instance or for a session, SQL information for each process is written to a trace file in the USER_DUMP_DEST directory.

Instance Alert Log

A performance engineer can use the instance alert log to determine the time between log switches and the recovery time following a crash. If the init.ora parameter LOG_CHECKPOINTS_TO_ALERT is set to TRUE, then checkpoint performance can be measured.

Trace User SQL

We will look at user trace files in more detail in a later chapter; for now, you need to know that you can generate a trace file of the SQL executed in your SQL*Plus session by entering the ALTER SESSION SET SQL_TRACE=TRUE command. The DBA can turn tracing on or off in a user session with the DBMS_SYSTEM.SET_SQL_TRACE_IN_SESSION procedure. Once a session has been traced and the output file located, use the TKPROF utility to generate a legible report.

Chapter Summary

In this chapter, you learned about the tools used to gather and analyze information essential to the Performance Tuning Method. You learned about several of the important data dictionary views and the importance of using the ANALYZE command or the DBMS_STATS package to update the storage information for tables and indexes.

You learned about the different categories of dynamic performance views and that these views are cleared when the instance is shut down and are populated when the instance is up. You learned about Statspack, an extremely useful diagnostic and performance tuning tool supplied by Oracle with the RDBMS. You learned how to install, configure, and collect snapshot statistics with Statspack. You also learned how to run a Statspack performance report and gained an introduction to the different components of the report. You learned about additional tools such as UTLBSTAT/UTLESTAT and OEM optional packs that you can use to diagnose and tune. Finally, you learned that you can trace a user session and generate a file that contains information about the SQL he or she has executed.

Two-Minute Drill

- There are two basic classes of views that we will use to gather diagnostic information about our database: data dictionary views and dynamic performance views.

- The data dictionary views DBA_TABLES, DBA_TAB_COLUMNS, DBA_INDEXES, and DBA_SEGMENTS are views on SYS tables and contain important storage information about the objects.

- The ANALYZE command or the DBMS_STATS package can be used to gather storage statistics for the data dictionary tables.

- Dynamic performance views, also known as the V$ views, are based on the SYS-owned X$ tables, which are memory structures in the instance.

- V$ views are updated continuously while the instance is up; they are cleared when the instance is shut down.

- There are five basic categories of V$ views: instance/database, memory, disk I/O, contention, and user session.

- Important instance/database V$ views include, V$SYSSTAT, V$WAITSTAT, V$PROCESS, V$SYSTEM_EVENT, and V$PX_PROCESS_SYSSTAT.

- Important memory V$ views include V$LIBRARYCACHE, V$ROWCACHE, V$BUFFER_POOL_STATISTICS, V$SGASTAT, and V$DB_OBJECT_CACHE.

- Important disk I/O V$ views include V$FILESTAT and V$TEMPSTAT.

- Important contention V$ views include V$ROLLSTAT, V$LATCH, V$LATCH_CHILDREN, and V$UNDOSTAT.

- Important user session V$ views include V$SESSION, V$LOCK, V$SESSTAT, V$SESS_IO, V$SESSION_EVENT, V$SESSION_WAIT, V$SORT_USAGE, V$OPEN_CURSOR, and V$PX_SESSTAT.

- Statspack is the Oracle-supplied diagnostics tool used to gather and store snapshots of performance data. Use it instead of UTLBSTAT/UTLESTAT.

- Statspack is easily installed with one script, and installation requires approximately 75MB of free space in the database.

- Statspack objects are installed in the PERFSTAT schema.

- Set TIMED_STATISTICS=TRUE if you want to gather timing information.

- A Statspack snapshot is created by running the stastpack.snap procedure.

- You can automatically generate snapshots by running the spauto.sql script, which uses the DBMS_JOB package to run stastpack.snap every hour.

- Use the spreport.sql script to generate the Statspack performance report. Use the sprepsql.sql script to run the Statspack SQL report.

- The Statspack performance report is organized into several sections: general information, cache sizes, load profile, instance efficiency stats, wait events, shared pool contents, instance activity, I/O, cache stats, latch activity, rollback and undo stats, SGA information, enqueue activity, and init.ora parameters.

- Other tools that you can use to diagnose and tune include UTLBSTAT/UTLESTAT, custom scripts, OEM optional performance tuning packs, and third-party tools.

- The alert log has limited information that can be used to diagnose performance problems.

- You can trace user sessions, and use TKPROF to analyze the SQL.

Chapter Questions

I. **A user executes a procedure from his desktop and notices that the process is taking significantly longer than expected. Which of these steps should you take to determine which SQL statements in the procedure are potentially causing a performance problem?**

A. Connect to the user's session and issue the SQLTRACE=TRUE command.

B. Alter the system and set SQL_TRACE=TRUE.

C. Execute the DBMS_SYSTEM.SET_SQL_TRACE_IN_SESSION procedure to create a user trace file.

D. Print the last 100 lines of the instance alert log.

E. Run a Statspack report from the most recent snapshot.

2. **You want to update the NUM_ROWs column of DBA_TABLES; therefore, you should do which of the following? (Choose two.)**

A. Execute the DBMS_SYSTEM.STATS procedure.

B. Execute statspack.snap.

C. Execute the DBMS_SYSTEM.SET_SQL_TRACE_IN_SESSION procedure to create a user trace file.

D. Use the ANALYZE command to gather statistics for selected tables.

E. Use the DBMS_UTILITY.ANALYZE_SCHEMA procedure to gather statistics for all the tables in a schema.

3. **The best place to start looking for general resource usage statistics is in which V$ view?**

A. V$INSTANCE

B. V$INSTANCE_STATS

C. V$SYSSTAT

D. V$PROCESS

E. V$WAITSTAT

4. **You've decided to use Statspack to gather performance information and want to collect statistics every hour on the hour. Which of the following describes a valid way to do this?**

A. Set the init.ora parameter JOB_QUEUE_RESOURCES to a value greater than 0, and execute the $ORACLE_HOME/rdbms/admin/spauto.sql script.

B. Set the init.ora parameter JOB_QUEUE_PROCESSES to a value greater than 0, and execute the $ORACLE_HOME/rdbms/admin/spauto.sql script.

    C. Set the init.ora parameter JOB_QUEUE_RESOURCES to a value greater than 0, and execute the $ORACLE_HOME/rdbms/admin/statspack.snap script.

    D. Use the Unix cron command to run the Statspack UTLBSTAT script every hour.

5. **Your senior DBA tells you to start diagnosing a performance problem in a particular database and tells you to look at the instance alert log first. What evidence of a performance problem might you find in the instance alert log?**

    A. Frequent checkpointing, if the LOG_CHECKPOINTS_TO_ALERT parameter is set to TRUE

    B. Unusual amounts of recursive SQL

    C. Frequent buffer cache misses

    D. An unusually high number of invalidations in the SQL area of the library cache

    E. Excessively high file read times

6. **One of your DBA peers hands you the report generated from a UTLBSTAT/UTLESTAT snapshot and asks your help in diagnosing the performance problems. What compelling arguments can you use to convince your peer to begin using Statspack instead? (Choose two.)**

    A. Statspack can be used to gather and store multiple snapshots of information.

    B. UTLBSTAT/UTLESTAT is easier to use.

    C. The Statspack spreport output has more detailed and easier-to-read information.

    D. Statspack doesn't create tables in the database, so it doesn't impact performance.

    E. Statspack doesn't report detailed statistics like the UTLESTAT report.

7. **It appears that several user processes are at a standstill, that is, no throughput. However, other user processes seem to be working fine. Which dynamic performance view could you look at to ascertain the cause?**

    A. V$LIBRARYCACHE

    B. V$LOCK

   C. V$PARAMETER

   D. V$INSTANCE

   E. V$DB_OBJECT_CACHE

8. Which of these statements most accurately describes how Statspack works?

   A. Statspack gathers information from each of the data dictionary tables and stores it in dynamic performance views.

   B. Statspack gathers information from the dynamic performance views and stores it in replication snapshots.

   C. Statspack gathers information from the dynamic performance views and stores it in tables in the PERFSTAT schema.

   D. Statspack creates reports of DBMS_STATS activity.

   E. Statspack is an OEM optional package and stores performance data in the repository.

9. Which of these statements does not describe Statspack snapshots?

   A. A Statspack snapshot is a point-in-time collection of statistics from the dynamic performance views.

   B. Statspack snapshots can be deleted with a script when they are no longer needed.

   C. Statspack snapshots can be exported with the exp utility.

   D. From one instance in an Oracle RAC, you can take Statspack snapshots across multiple instances.

10. Which of these statements accurately describes Oracle Expert?

   A. It is a real-time GUI for gathering diagnostics.

   B. It is not an optional component of the OEM.

   C. It works directly with Statspack.

   D. It aids and assists performance tuning by making instance configuration recommendations.

Answers to Chapter Questions

1. C. Execute the DBMS_SYSTEM.SET_SQL_TRACE_IN_SESSION procedure to create a user trace file.

Explanation Turn tracing on in the session by executing this procedure from SQL*Plus: DBMS_SYSTEM.SET_SQL_TRACE_IN_SESSION('sid','serial#',TRUE). Answer E might show the poorly performing SQL, but it's not the most direct way to find it. Answer A isn't possible, and answer B would create a trace for each session in the instance. Answer D wouldn't give you any information useful to this problem.

2. D, E. Use the ANALYZE command to gather statistics for selected tables. Use the DBMS_UTILITY.ANALYZE_SCHEMA procedure to gather statistics for all the tables in a schema.

Explanation Analyzing the tables, either individually with the ANALYZE command or for a schema with the DBMS_UTILITY.ANALYZE_SCHEMA procedure, will update the statistics in the DBA_TABLES view for the tables or schema analyzed. Answer A is incorrect because it is not a valid procedure; B is incorrect because statspack.snap doesn't generate statistics for tables.

3. C. V$SYSSTAT

Explanation V$SYSSTAT is the view that shows general resource usage statistics for the instance. Answer A, V$INSTANCE, simply shows the state of the current instance. B is incorrect because the V$INSTANCE_STATS view doesn't exist. D is incorrect because V$PROCESS has a row for each process in the instance, but doesn't indicate resource usage. E is incorrect because V$WAITSTAT is specific to buffer wait events, not general resource usage.

4. B. Set the init.ora parameter JOB_QUEUE_PROCESSES to a value greater than 0, and execute the $ORACLE_HOME/rdbms/admin/spauto.sql script.

Explanation JOB_QUEUE_PROCESSES must be set to a value greater than 0 so that jobs scheduled via DBMS_JOB will actually run. Answers A and C are misleading because they have incorrect script or parameter names. Answer D is incorrect because UTLBSTAT isn't a Statspack component.

5. A. Frequent checkpointing, if the LOG_CHECKPOINTS_TO_ALERT parameter is set to TRUE

Explanation The instance alert log is useful in determining whether there is a problem with checkpoint performance; either it works too often or too slowly. Answers B, C, D, and E are incorrect because none of this information is available in the alert log.

6. A, C. Statspack can be used to gather and store multiple snapshots of information. The Statspack spreport output has more detailed and easier-to-read information.

Explanation Statspack enables the performance engineer to gather and store multiple snapshots of information in the database, and to generate an easy-to-read performance report. Answers B and D are subjective, but not arguments in favor of Statspack. Answer E is incorrect because Statspack *does* report detailed statistics.

7. B. V$LOCK

Explanation Of the choices, V$LOCK should be the first place to look if some processes appear to be frozen while other processes are working without problems. If you see locked objects and sessions waiting on the locked objects, take action. Answers A and E are incorrect because they specifically show the state of the library cache and the objects cached there. Although these are good performance views to look at, they don't apply in this case. Answers C and D are incorrect; these views are informational only and won't help you resolve the locking conflict described in the question.

8. C. Statspack gathers information from the dynamic performance views and stores it in tables in the PERFSTAT schema.

Explanation Answers A and B are meant to confuse you. Answer D is incorrect because Statspack doesn't specifically report DBMS_STATS usage. Answer E is incorrect because Statspack is not an optional component of OEM.

9. D. From one instance in an Oracle RAC, you can take Statspack snapshots across multiple instances.

Explanation It is not possible to take a Statspack snapshot of other instances in a RAC from one instance. You must connect to each instance that you wish to take a snapshot of. In a RAC, the snapshots from the different instances are stored in the same database. Answers A, B, and C are each true statements about Statspack snapshots.

10. D. It aids and assists performance tuning by making instance configuration recommendations.

Explanation Oracle Expert, an optional component of OEM, is a tool that you can use to properly configure a database. Oracle Expert offers recommendations and generates scripts to implement the recommendations. Answer A accurately describes Oracle Performance Manager, also an optional component of OEM. Answer B is incorrect; Oracle Expert *is* an optional component of OEM. Answer C is incorrect; Oracle Expert and Statspack are two completely separate tools.

CHAPTER
4

Sizing the Shared Pool

n this chapter, you will learn how to size the shared pool for performance, and specifically to

- Measure and tune the library cache hit ratio.
- Size and pin objects in the shared pool.
- Tune the shared pool reserve space.
- Measure and tune the dictionary cache hit ratio.
- Describe UGA and session memory considerations.
- Describe other tuning issues related to the shared pool.
- Setting the large pool.

The Shared Pool is one of the major components of the Oracle System Global Area (SGA). We will review shared pool concepts, and then you will learn how to gather and interpret key performance statistics related to the different elements of the shared pool. We will discuss how the User Global Area (UGA) is related to the shared pool, and also discuss the relationship between the shared pool and the large pool.

Sizing the Shared Pool

When we talk about performance tuning the shared pool, we're primarily referring to determining an adequate size for the shared pool. But simply allocating a big shared pool shouldn't be our goal. We want to adequately size the shared pool so that we can cache and reuse SQL and PL/SQL, as well as data dictionary information. Shared pool misses and reloads are more costly than buffer cache reloads, so always tune the shared pool. With this in mind, our performance tuning goal is to adequately size the shared pool so that the caches within the pool have enough space to fulfill requests without performance degradation. The shared pool size is determined by the init.ora parameter SHARED_POOL_SIZE.

Shared Pool Concepts

The shared pool is one of the fundamentally important memory areas of the SGA. The major components of the shared pool are the library cache, the dictionary cache, and—under certain configurations—the UGA. The dictionary cache is sometimes referred to as the row cache, but in this book we will refer to it as the dictionary cache. The UGA is only a shared pool component when using the shared server feature and the large pool is not configured. We will discuss the UGA issues in detail later in this chapter in the section entitled "Describing UGA and Session Memory Considerations."

The Library Cache

The library cache stores actual SQL statement text, execution plans, and executable forms of SQL cursors, Java classes, and PL/SQL blocks (functions, procedures, triggers, packages, and anonymous PL/SQL blocks). Once parsed and placed in the library cache, application code can be shared and reused by database sessions. In addition to this shared SQL area, the library cache also contains control structures such as locks.

If a user submits a statement that has already been parsed and is in the cache, then Oracle doesn't have to reparse the statement. This is preferred, since parsing is a relatively expensive task. Ideally, the majority of your user code is already cached and can be reused. When a piece of code is reused, we call that a *library cache hit* or *soft parse*. If the executable code is not found in the cache and Oracle must create a new executable, we have a *library cache miss* or *hard parse*. To determine if an SQL statement is already in the cache, Oracle calculates the numeric value of the ASCII text, and then uses a hashing algorithm to find the matching SQL cursor. A least recently used (LRU) algorithm determines which statements in the cache will be aged out and replaced by new statements.

Because the cache is dynamic, code can be aged out between application calls. A hard parse can occur during a parse call if the SQL statement does not exist in the library cache, or during an execute call if the executable code has been aged out.

When tuning the library cache, the two primary tuning goals are to minimize reparsing and to avoid memory fragmentation.

Minimize Reparsing   As mentioned in the previous section, one of the conditions that causes a hard parse or library cache to miss is when an application makes a parse call for an SQL statement and Oracle can't find the parsed version of it in the shared SQL area. You can minimize reparsing by using sharable and reusable code. Use bind variables instead of constants, use coding standards that lead to more generic code, and avoid large numbers of ad hoc queries. Another condition that causes hard parses is when an application makes an execute call for an SQL statement and the executable version of the code has been aged out. You can remedy this type of situation by increasing the size of the shared pool.

If you modify a schema object, executable versions of code stored in the library cache that reference the objects become invalid, causing a hard parse for the next execute call. This invalidation is because the executable code is dependent on data dictionary information about the schema object that is stored in the dictionary cache, which is no longer valid when the schema object is modified.

Avoid Memory Fragmentation   The library cache can become fragmented if objects are frequently aged out. The key to avoiding memory fragmentation is to keep often-used large objects in the cache. One mechanism to reduce fragmentation is to pin large SQL and PL/SQL blocks in memory, so that the LRU process does not age them out. You can convert large PL/SQL anonymous blocks into smaller packaged functions. Configuring the large pool in a shared server environment also reduces fragmentation. Also, you can reserve memory in the shared pool for large objects by configuring the SHARED_POOL_RESERVED_SIZE parameter.

The Dictionary Cache

The dictionary cache stores information from the data dictionary tables. This includes metadata about schema objects such as tables, columns, and indexes. The dictionary cache also stores information about segments, usernames, sequence numbers, privileges, profiles, and tablespaces. This data is used for fast lookup when parsing SQL statements or compiling PL/SQL code. At instance startup, the dictionary cache contains no data dictionary information. Initially, user queries take longer because data dictionary information must be read from disk into the cache. As more user statements are processed, dictionary cache information begins to populate the dictionary cache. Once the instance has been up for a sufficient amount of time, the dictionary cache performance will stabilize.

Measure and Tune the Library Cache Hit Ratio

The V$LIBRARYCACHE dynamic performance view is our primary repository for library cache statistics. The more important columns in the view include the following:

- **NAMESPACE**   Identifies the library cache item
- **GETS**   Identifies the number of requests or lookups for objects in the namespace
- **GETHITS**   The number of times an object's handle was found in memory
- **PINS**   The number of reads or executions of the object in the namespace
- **RELOADS**   The number of lookups that failed, either because the parsed SQL statement has been aged out, or because the object was modified and therefore invalidated
- **INVALIDATIONS**   The number of object invalidations in the namespace
- **GETHITRATIO**   The ratio of GETHITS to GETS

Querying V$LIBRARYCACHE

Query V$LIBRARYCACHE after the instance has been up and running for awhile:

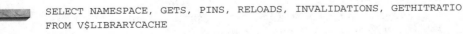

```
SELECT NAMESPACE, GETS, PINS, RELOADS, INVALIDATIONS, GETHITRATIO
FROM V$LIBRARYCACHE
/
```

NAMESPACE	GETS	PINS	RELOADS	INVALIDATIONS	GETHITRATIO
SQL AREA	4492	14831	15	0	.937444346
TABLE/PROCEDURE	5741	3263	0	0	.834001045
BODY	18	17	0	0	.555555556
TRIGGER	6	6	0	0	.5
INDEX	31	31	0	0	0
CLUSTER	204	246	0	0	.970588235
OBJECT	0	0	0	0	1
PIPE	0	0	0	0	1
JAVA SOURCE	0	0	0	0	1
JAVA RESOURCE	2	2	0	0	.5
JAVA DATA	1	6	0	0	0

```
/
```

From this query you can see that our GETHITRATIO for the SQL AREA is 93.7 percent, indicating that SQL cursors are being shared a high percentage of the time. This isn't too bad for a data warehouse or decision support system, but we should strive for a GETHITRATIO in the upper-90 percentile for OLTP systems.

Measuring the Overall Library Cache Hit Ratio

After the instance has been up and running for awhile, you can get the overall library cache hit ratio with the following query:

```
SELECT SUM(PINS-RELOADS)/SUM(PINS)*100 "Library Cache Hit Ratio"
FROM V$LIBRARYCACHE
/
Library Cache Hit Ratio
-----------------------
            99.9206349
```

In this case at 99.9+ percent, we have little room for improvement!

You should also become familiar with interpreting the inverse of the hit ratio statistic; that is, the reload ratio.

If the RELOADS to PINS ratio is greater than 1 percent, increase the value of SHARED_POOL_SIZE.

```
SELECT SUM(PINS) "EXECUTIONS", SUM(RELOADS) "MISSES",
SUM(RELOADS)/SUM(PINS) "RELOAD RATIO"
FROM V$LIBRARYCACHE
/
EXECUTIONS    MISSES RELOAD RATIO
---------- ---------- ------------
     18448        15   .000813096
```

This ratio is less than 1 percent, so our objects have not been aged out of the cache at an unacceptable rate. Again, if the reload ratio is greater than 1 percent, the objects are being aged out of the cache more often than they should; therefore, increase SHARED_POOL_SIZE.

Invalidations   Invalidations occur when an object is referenced in a cached SQL statement, and then the object is modified in some way. The INVALIDATIONS column indicates the number of invalidations that occur in the namespace.

Other Important Dynamic Performance Views
In addition to the V$LIBRARYCACHE view, there are several views that we use to monitor the library cache.

V$SGASTAT   The V$SGASTAT view shows the size of each of the SGA cache areas. From this view you can see the size of the SQL Area, the library cache, table definitions, and all of the other structures.

V$SQLAREA   The V$SQLAREA view has the first 1000 characters of the SQL statement and all of the statistics about the shared cursor.

V$SQLTEXT   The V$SQLTEXT view contains the full SQL text, broken down into 64-character strings.

V$DB_OBJECT_CACHE   The V$DB_OBJECT_CACHE view shows the objects that are currently cached, including packages, tables, and synonyms. We will look at this view in more detail later in this chapter in the section entitled "Size and Pin Objects in the Shared Pool."

Statspack Report
You can use a section in the Statspack report to analyze the performance of the library cache for the time period between two snapshots. It's important to use a beginning snapshot that occurs well after the instance has been up for awhile.

```
Library Cache Activity for DB: OR9I   Instance: or9i   Snaps: 1 -2
->"Pct Misses"  should be very low
```

Namespace	Get Requests	Pct Miss	Pin Requests	Pct Miss	Reloads	Invali- dations
BODY	13	15.4	10	20.0	0	0
CLUSTER	50	0.0	47	0.0	0	0
INDEX	14	50.0	7	100.0	0	0

SQL AREA	4,270	10.0	13,184	5.4	0	0
TABLE/PROCEDURE	1,370	24.4	2,133	44.7	1	0
TRIGGER	1	0.0	1	0.0	0	0

In this report, the SQL AREA Get Pct Miss is 10 percent, or a 90-percent hit ratio. The SQL AREA Pin Pct Miss is 5.4 percent. As mentioned earlier, this may be acceptable for many systems, but we should work toward a lower Get Pct Miss on OLTP systems.

You should also look at the section of the report on Instance Activity Statistics—specifically at the open cursors and parse counts and times.

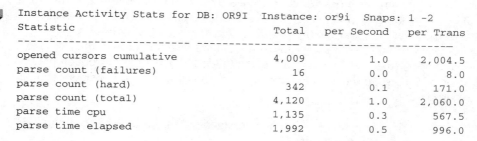

```
Instance Activity Stats for DB: OR9I  Instance: or9i  Snaps: 1 -2
Statistic                               Total   per Second   per Trans

opened cursors cumulative               4,009      1.0         2,004.5
parse count (failures)                     16      0.0             8.0
parse count (hard)                        342      0.1           171.0
parse count (total)                     4,120      1.0         2,060.0
parse time cpu                          1,135      0.3           567.5
parse time elapsed                      1,992      0.5           996.0
```

Cached Execution Plans

In Oracle9*i*, as long as a SQL statement is in memory, the execution plan for that statement will remain in memory. When the SQL statement is aged out of the library cache, the execution plan is also aged out. In previous versions of Oracle, we could capture the SQL statement and explain the execution plan, but it was never guaranteed that the actual execution plan for the SQL statement would be the same as the one returned by the EXPLAIN PLAN command. With Oracle9*i* we have the actual execution plan as long as the SQL statement is in the cache.

V$SQL_PLAN and V$SQL   The V$SQL_PLAN view contains the actual execution plan for SQL statements that are stored in V$SQL. We can see the execution plan for an SQL statement by joining the two views on the V$SQL.PLAN_HASH_VALUE and the V$SQL_PLAN.HASH_VALUE columns.

Sizing the Library Cache

To determine the optimal size for the library cache, you'll need to

- Calculate the total space needed for stored objects such as views, triggers, and procedures.

- Calculate how much memory your application SQL statements will use.

In upcoming sections, we discuss the following important practices that can lead to better library cache performance:

- Pinning oft-used and large PL/SQL objects in memory
- Using the reserved pool, the shared pool reserved space for large memory requirements
- Converting anonymous PL/SQL blocks

Size and Pin Objects in the Shared Pool

As mentioned previously, blocks of code are aged out of the shared pool according to their place on the LRU list. A large block of code can be swapped out if smaller blocks need to be loaded. When the large block is needed again it must be reloaded. This constant loading and unloading causes fragmentation and performance degradation. One way to prevent this is to keep large or frequently used objects in the shared pool. Here are some objects you should consider keeping in the shared pool:

- Cached sequence numbers (if they are aged out of the cache, the cached sequence numbers are lost)
- Large objects such as DBMS_STANDARD
- Oft-used application triggers

These large and oft-used objects should be pinned immediately after startup, so as to reduce fragmentation.

Using the command ALTER SYSTEM FLUSH SHARED_POOL does not flush pinned objects.

V$DB_OBJECT_CACHE   The V$DB_OBJECT_CACHE dynamic performance view shows which objects are cached in the shared pool. We can reduce the search to the objects that we've discussed pinning, and further reduce the list to only those objects that are larger than 10,000 bytes. From this list, you can determine which objects are candidates to keep. The EXECUTIONS column is also helpful at determining which objects to keep.

```
SELECT OWNER, NAME, TYPE, SHARABLE_MEM, EXECUTIONS
FROM V$DB_OBJECT_CACHE
WHERE SHARABLE_MEM > 10000
AND TYPE IN ('PACKAGE','PACKAGE BODY','PROCEDURE','FUNCTION','TRIGGER')
AND KEPT='NO'
ORDER BY SHARABLE_MEM DESC
/
```

OWNER	NAME	TYPE	SHARABLE_MEM	EXECUTIONS
SYS	LOGMNR_KRVRDLUID3	PROCEDURE	97377	1
SYS	DBMS_JAVA	PACKAGE	93509	2
SYS	DBMS_UTILITY	PACKAGE BODY	28952	1
SYS	DBMS_STANDARD	PACKAGE	28161	1
SYS	DBMS_JAVA	PACKAGE BODY	23721	2
HR	ADD_JOB_HISTORY	PROCEDURE	20770	1
SYS	DBMS_OUTPUT	PACKAGE	13291	1
HR	SECURE_DML	PROCEDURE	12989	1
SYS	DBMS_APPLICATION_INFO	PACKAGE	12653	1
SYSTEM	DBMS_SHARED_POOL	PACKAGE	11595	1
SYS	DBMS_SHARED_POOL	PACKAGE	10448	1

DBMS_SHARED_POOL   The DBMS_SHARED_POOL package is not automatically created when you build a database. You'll need to connect to the database as sys or sysdba and execute the $ORACLE_HOME/rdbms/admin/dbmspool.sql script, which invokes prvtpool.plb. The dbmspool.sql script is also called by spcusr.sql when configuring Statspack.

There is no public synonym for this package, so you must either be connected as SYS or use a qualifier both for the package you are executing and the package you are pinning. The KEEP procedure is used to pin objects in the shared pool as follows:

```
EXEC SYS.DBMS_SHARED_POOL.KEEP('SYS.STANDARD');
PL/SQL procedure successfully completed.
```

The KEPT column in the V$DB_OBJECT_CACHE will now show YES for the STANDARD package. Use the UNKEEP procedure to change the status of the pinned object; this does not remove the now unpinned object from the shared pool.

It is important to remember that an object must be read into the shared pool before it can be pinned. Before attempting to pin a large object that is not already in the shared pool, reference the object in a query, query the V$DB_OBJECT_CACHE to verify that the object is now in the shared pool, and then pin it with DBMS_SHARED_POOL.KEEP. Verify that the pin worked by querying on the KEPT column. You may need to flush the shared pool before you attempt to keep a large object.

You can also use the DBMS_SHARED_POOL.SIZES procedure, which takes one NUMBER parameter, to discover which objects in the shared pool are greater than that number in K. For instance, SIZES(150) will return those objects that are larger than 150KB. The three columns returned are SIZE(K), KEPT, and NAME.

```
set serveroutput on
EXEC SYS.DBMS_SHARED_POOL.SIZES(150)
/
```

```
SIZE(K) KEPT    NAME
------- ------  ------------------------------------------
371             SYS.STANDARD                 (PACKAGE)
166             SYS./5ee89977_NamespaceRDBMS (JAVA CLASS)
PL/SQL procedure successfully completed.
```

Pinning Anonymous Blocks   If you have large anonymous PL/SQL blocks, you can either convert them into smaller blocks that call packaged functions and procedures, or identify the PL/SQL block in the V$SQLAREA view and then use DBMS_SHARED_POOL to pin it. In the following query, we identify anonymous PL/SQL blocks that are larger than 100 characters:

```
SELECT ADDRESS, HASH_VALUE, SQL_TEXT FROM V$SQLAREA
WHERE COMMAND_TYPE =47
AND LENGTH(SQL_TEXT) > 100
/
ADDRESS  HASH_VALUE
-------  ----------
SQL_TEXT
673EFC54 2199871176
DECLARE       opstring_in VARCHAR2(31) := :1;      session_num_in NUMBER
:= :2;
    logmnr_uid_inout BINARY_INTEGER := :3;  BEGIN
sys.logmnr_krvrdluid3(ops
tring_in, session_num_in, logmnr_uid_inout);       :3 :=
logmnr_uid_inout;  END;
```

Once you have identified the code that you wish to keep, use the address and hash value of the code with the following KEEP procedure:

```
EXEC SYS.DBMS_SHARED_POOL.KEEP('address,hash_value');
```

Tune the Shared Pool Reserve Space

Memory allocation in the shared pool occurs in small chunks. Requests for large chunks of memory are broken down into smaller chunks. Some operations require large contiguous memory allocations, such as compiling PL/SQL or temporarily storing Java objects. If you have these types of operations, Oracle recommends configuring the reserved pool by setting the initialization parameter SHARED_POOL_RESERVED_SIZE to 10 percent of the SHARED_POOL_SIZE if the shared pool is already tuned. By default, this parameter is set to 5 percent of SHARED_POOL_SIZE.

This memory is allocated from the shared pool. It is not additional memory outside the shared pool; therefore, increasing the size of the reserved pool decreases the size of the unreserved part of the shared pool. Oracle does not allow you to make it larger than 50 percent of SHARED_POOL_SIZE. Small objects are not loaded into the reserved pool, thereby reducing fragmentation. Once the operation is through with reserved pool memory, it is returned to the reserved pool.

Oracle attempts to allocate large chunks according to this decision process:

1. From the unreserved section of the shared pool.

2. If there's not enough space there and the allocation is large, look in the reserved pool for available space.

3. If there's still not enough free space, begin freeing memory chunks, then retry the unreserved and reserved.

V$SHARED_POOL_RESERVED   The V$SHARED_POOL_RESERVED dynamic performance view contains statistics about reserved pool performance. Our tuning goal is to minimize REQUEST_MISSES and REQUEST_FAILURES. Ideally, they're both = 0. If REQUEST_FAILURES is greater than zero and increasing, then the reserved pool is too small and possibly the shared pool as well.

Tuning the Reserved Pool   If you have determined that the reserved pool is too small and you have enough free real memory, then you can increase the size of the shared pool and the reserved pool until REQUEST_FAILURES stops increasing. If you increase the size of the reserved pool without increasing the size of the shared pool, then other requests on the unreserved part of the shared pool may be affected.

DBMS_SHARED_POOL.Aborted_Request_Threshold Procedure   The DBMS_SHARED_POOL.Aborted_Request_Threshold procedure is used to limit the amount of shared pool cache to flush before an ORA-04031 error occurs. This is particularly useful if the attempt to load a large object causes too much shared pool cleanout.

Measure and Tune the Dictionary Cache Hit Ratio

As mentioned previously, definitions of data dictionary objects is stored in the dictionary cache. Query the V$ROWCACHE dynamic performance view to gather information about the performance of the dictionary cache. Each row has cumulative data since instance startup for a specific dictionary cache item. The columns that we will use for performance tuning are as follows:

- **PARAMETER**   The name of the data dictionary item.
- **GETS**   The cumulative total of requests for information on the item.

■ **GETMISSES** The cumulative total of requests that were not met by the cache, also referred to as a cache miss. A cache miss requires I/O.

■ **MODIFICATIONS** The cumulative number of times data about this item has been updated.

Querying V$ROWCACHE

We should query the V$ROWCACHE view to determine the hit ratio for each item in the dictionary cache. Run the following query after the instance has been up and running for awhile:

```
SELECT PARAMETER, GETS, GETMISSES, 100*(GETS-GETMISSES)/(GETS) HIT_RATE,
MODIFICATIONS
FROM V$ROWCACHE
WHERE GETS > 0
/
```

PARAMETER	GETS	GETMISSES	HIT_RATE	MODIFICATIONS
dc_free_extents	42	1	97.6190476	0
dc_segments	88	51	42.0454545	0
dc_tablespaces	15	2	86.6666667	0
dc_users	713	26	96.3534362	0
dc_rollback_segments	1057	11	98.9593188	31
dc_objects	1232	834	32.3051948	55
dc_object_ids	641	78	87.8315133	55
dc_sequences	1	1	0	1
dc_usernames	94	7	92.5531915	0
dc_histogram_defs	13	11	15.3846154	11
dc_profiles	1	1	0	0
dc_user_grants	28	12	57.1428571	0

From the results of this query, we can see that the HIT_RATE calculated column shows us that the hit ratio for the dc_objects parameter is very low. This would indicate that the definition of the objects queried on had not been loaded into the cache yet. In this case, the instance had been up for several hours, but with little user activity; therefore, we should probably run the query after the database has had some more activity. If we had noticed a high number of misses and updates in the extents and segments parameters, we might suspect a large amount of dynamic extent allocation, which could be reduced by more accurately sizing the objects in the design phased. Our tuning goal should be less than 2 percent misses for most of the parameters. Generally, we accomplish this goal by increasing the value of SHARED_POOL_SIZE.

Measuring the Cumulative Dictionary Cache Hit Ratio

You can calculate the overall dictionary cache hit ratio with the following simple query:

```
SELECT (SUM(GETS - GETMISSES )) / SUM(GETS) "Dictionary Cache Hit Ratio"
FROM V$ROWCACHE
/
Dictionary Cache Hit Ratio
--------------------------
              .911266809
```

Our tuning goal should be to keep the overall dictionary cache hit ratio at or above 85 percent; therefore, we should see less than 15 percent misses for the entire cache. If you run this query immediately after instance startup, you'll see a much higher percentage of misses than you'll see after the cache has reached a steady state. You'll never see a 100-percent hit ratio, because object definitions are not in the cache at startup, but must be loaded into the cache the first time they're needed. Also keep in mind that the statistics are cumulative since startup, so the hit ratio will smooth out over time.

Statspack Report

You can use a section in the Statspack report to analyze the performance of the dictionary cache for the time period between two snapshots. It's important to use a beginning snapshot that is relevant—that is, after the cache has reached a steady state. This report was taken from an end snapshot shortly after the queries in the previous section were run:

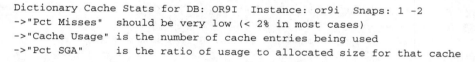

```
Dictionary Cache Stats for DB: OR9I   Instance: or9i   Snaps: 1 -2
->"Pct Misses"  should be very low (< 2% in most cases)
->"Cache Usage" is the number of cache entries being used
->"Pct SGA"     is the ratio of usage to allocated size for that cache
```

Cache	Get Requests	Pct Miss	Scan Reqs	Pct Miss	Mod Reqs	Final Usage	Pct SGA
dc_free_extents	13	0.0	0		0	2	8
dc_histogram_defs	188	93.1	0		0	186	97
dc_object_ids	1,536	33.6	0		0	871	99
dc_objects	794	40.6	0		1	1,547	99
dc_profiles	1	0.0	0		0	1	50
dc_rollback_segments	310	0.0	0		0	12	67
dc_segments	1,108	67.1	0		0	899	99

dc_tablespaces	14	0.0	0	0	8	80
dc_user_grants	942	0.0	0	0	16	31
dc_usernames	746	2.5	0	0	31	78
dc_users	1,665	0.8	0	0	41	95

It is important to note that the Statspack report has a Pct Miss column for Get Requests, and another Pct Miss column for Scans; in previous queries we looked at the hit ratio instead of the miss ratio. As indicated in the report section heading, the Get Pct Miss should be less than 2 percent in most cases. If we compare the Statspack report to our previous query of the V$ROWCACHE view, and specifically look at the dc_free_extents item, you can see that the hit ratio is within the less than 2-percent preferred threshold for the period.

Improving Dictionary Cache Performance

You can do a few things to improve the performance of the dictionary cache.

Sequence Numbers   If you do not use the CACHE option on a sequence, each call to NEXTVAL creates a get in the dc_sequences dictionary cache item. If you use the CACHE option when you create or alter a sequence, a get is registered each time you must repopulate the sequence cache. For example, if you use the CACHE 10 clause, every ten calls to NEXTVAL will create a get in the dc_sequences item. Not caching or caching too few sequence numbers can artificially inflate your cache hit ratio, and also increase the number of dictionary cache locks. Reducing the number of dictionary cache locks improves scalability.

Reduce DDL Activities   Data Definition Language (DDL) commands are essential tools of the DBA. Gathering statistics for schema objects and modifying schema objects are necessary events; however, modifying an object invalidates the information about the object in the dictionary cache. To reduce the impact on performance, both in the Dictionary and library cache, do not perform DDL on heavily used objects when they are usually accessed the most.

Sizing the Dictionary Cache   The dictionary cache increases or decreases in size as needed, within the boundaries of the SHARED_POOL_SIZE. The algorithm that manages data in the shared pool prefers to keep dictionary cache data over library cache data. Therefore, if the library cache statistics indicate that the shared pool is sized correctly, then the dictionary cache is usually sized satisfactorily.

Describe UGA and Session Memory Considerations

The User Global Area (UGA) consists of user session data and cursor state information. If you are using dedicated servers, then the UGA exists in private user memory, known as the Program Global Area (PGA) as shown in Figure 4-1.

In a shared server environment, the user session data and cursor state information are moved into the shared pool, as seen in Figure 4-2. The session stack space remains in the PGA regardless of server configuration. The sort areas and private SQL areas are included in the session data, so the size of this component can vary greatly. Oracle recommends using the shared server environment because it reduces overall memory and CPU consumption; fewer processes are used than in the dedicated server environment, so less PGA memory is used. You may need to increase the value of SHARED_POOL_SIZE, thereby increasing the overall size of the SGA, but total memory consumption by the instance and server processes will be less.

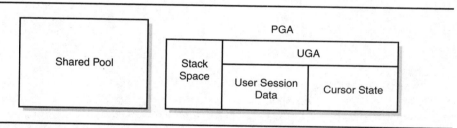

FIGURE 4-1.   *UGA in the Dedicated Server environment*

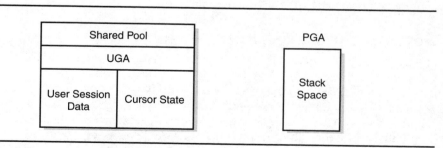

FIGURE 4-2.   *UGA in the Shared Server environment*

Querying UGA Statistics   The V$SESSTAT, V$MYSTAT, and V$STATNAME views are joined to report on session UGA memory usage. V$MYSTAT shows the information for the current session; V$SESSTAT shows the information for all sessions. Here are some sample queries (Substitute V$MYSTAT for V$SESSTAT if you want to see just your session information):

```
SELECT SUM(VALUE) "Total sessions UGA memory"
FROM V$SESSTAT A, V$STATNAME B
WHERE NAME = 'session uga memory'
AND A.STATISTIC#=B.STATISTIC#
/
Total sessions UGA memory
--------------------------
                   499744

SELECT SUM(VALUE) "Total session UGA memory max"
FROM V$SESSTAT A, V$STATNAME B
WHERE NAME = 'session uga memory max'
AND A.STATISTIC#=B.STATISTIC#
/
Total session UGA memory max
--------------------------
                   529396
```

These queries do not differentiate between shared server or dedicated processes. If you're running in dedicated server mode, you can use the two numbers in this sample to estimate the additional memory to allocate to the shared pool when configuring the shared servers. The first query indicates the current memory consumption; the second indicates the maximum that each session has used. Somewhere between these numbers you'll probably find the optimal increase in the shared pool size. In the next section, we'll discuss configuring the large pool for UGA structures in a shared server environment.

Setting the Large Pool

The large pool is not part of the shared pool, but is a separate and optional memory component within the SGA. The large pool is set by the initialization parameter LARGE_POOL_SIZE; the minimum value is 300KB and the maximum value is 2000MB, but may be higher depending on your operating system.

The large pool does not have an LRU list or mechanism. The large pool is useful for parallel executions, Recovery Manager (RMAN) processes, and if you have configured the Oracle shared server feature. If the large pool is not configured, the shared pool contains the memory structures needed by these operations.

Large Pool and Parallel Query   If PARALLEL_AUTOMATIC_TUNING is TRUE, the value for the LARGE_POOL_SIZE is automatically computed and parallel execution message buffers are allocated from the large pool.

If PARALLEL_AUTOMATIC_TUNING is set to FALSE, the LARGE_POOL_SIZE parameter must be configured in the init.ora file, and parallel execution message buffers will be allocated from the shared pool.

Oracle recommends that you let Parallel Automatic Tuning set the value of large pool for you. However, sometimes the size calculated is too large and the size of the SGA ends up larger than real memory. If you set PARALLEL_AUTOMATIC_TUNING to TRUE and the instance fails to startup due to not enough memory, then set the LARGE_POOL_SIZE parameter to a low value, such as 1 M and startup the instance. If you start to see ORA-04031 errors in the alert log and the message specifies the large pool, then you can then query V$SGASTAT and adjust the size of the large pool.

```
SELECT NAME, BYTES
FROM V$SGASTAT
WHERE POOL='large pool'
/
NAME                              BYTES
-------------------------  ----------
free memory                      124416
PX msg pool                      122880
```

For detailed information about configuring the large pool for use with parallel executions, refer to the Oracle9*i* Data Warehousing Guide.

Large Pool and RMAN   When the large pool is configured, RMAN uses the large pool to cache buffers for I/O slaves during backup and restore operations. These buffers are a few hundred kilobytes. Oracle recommends that you use the large pool for RMAN only if the instance is unable to allocate memory from the shared pool for I/O slaves, indicated by a message in the alert log. When RMAN needs I/O buffers for slaves, Oracle goes through the following decision tree to determine where to get the buffers from:

1. If the large pool is configured, Oracle attempts to get the buffers there.

2. If the large pool is configured but not large enough to allocate the buffers, then Oracle does not attempt to use the shared pool.

3. If the large pool is not configured, then Oracle tries to allocate the buffers from the shared pool.

4. If Oracle cannot allocate the buffers it needs from the large pool or the shared pool based on the previous rules, then it uses local process memory

for the buffers and writes a message to the alert log stating that synchronous I/O is used for this operation. If synchronous I/O is used, backup slaves are not used.

If you plan to use the large pool for RMAN I/O buffers, here's the formula to follow when determining how much space to add to the LARGE_POOL_SIZE:

- If BACKUP_TAPE_IO_SLAVES is TRUE, then allocate 4MB per channel.

- If BACKUP_DISK_IO_SLAVES is TRUE, then allocate 512KB per channel times the value of MAXOPENFILES.

For more details, see the Oracle9*i* Recovery Manager User's Guide.

Large Pool and Shared Server   If you configure shared servers but do not have the large pool configured, then Oracle moves the User Global Area (UGA) into the shared pool. If you configure the large pool, then most of the UGA memory structures are allocated from the large pool instead. About 10KB per session is still allocated from the shared pool. Oracle recommends that you configure the large pool for use with shared servers to reduce the amount of fragmentation due to session memory in the shared pool, and to reduce the shrinking the shared SQL cache to make room for session memory.

There is not a specific value to set the LARGE_POOL_SIZE to that will optimize shared server performance. You should calculate the shared server requirements of the large pool by determining the per-session memory utilization, and multiply that number by the peak number of concurrent users or session high water mark.

Describe Other Tuning Issues Related to the Shared Pool

In addition to setting the optimal value for SHARED_POOL_SIZE, we need to consider a few initialization parameters and application design topics for optimal shared pool performance.

CURSOR_SPACE_FOR_TIME   If the library cache hit ratio is 100 percent—that is, no misses—then consider setting CURSOR_SPACE_FOR_TIME to TRUE. If set to TRUE, then the cursor cannot be deallocated from memory while an application cursor that is associated with it is open. The default value of FALSE indicates that a cursor can be deallocated even if application cursors associated with it are open.

Setting the value to TRUE improves performance on execution calls because Oracle doesn't have to verify that the cursor still exists in the library cache. You should only set this parameter to TRUE if there are no library cache misses on execution calls, indicating that the library cache is sized sufficiently to store all concurrently open cursors.

CURSOR_SHARING   By default, CURSOR_SHARING=EXACT, which means a SQL statement text must match a cached statement text exactly if it is to be reused. By modifying the setting to SIMILAR or FORCE, similar statements can use the same SQL area.

SIMILAR causes the statements to share the SQL area, but parse checks are still used to determine whether the executable SQL area can be shared; FORCE causes the statements to use the same executable SQL area. FORCE can therefore cause less than optimal execution plans.

Using other than EXACT reduces hard parsing and can benefit applications where the queries are similar but may differ in literal values, or where the library cache hit ratio is very low. CURSOR_SHARING=SIMILAR or FORCE should not be used in DSS systems or with Star transformation queries.

SESSION_CACHED_CURSORS   Setting the SESSION_CACHED_CURSORS initialization parameter to a positive integer, or using the ALTER SESSION command to do the same will cache up to that number of session cursors. Setting this parameter improves the performance of repeated parse calls to the same SQL statements. If Oracle detects that more than three parse calls have been made to the same SQL, it moves the cursor to the session cursor cache. An LRU mechanism manages the session cursor cache. Query V$SYSSTAT where the value of NAME is like the string session cursor% to evaluate the effectiveness of the session cursor cache.

OPEN_CURSORS   This value is the number of cursors that a user process is allowed to use to reference private SQL areas. Increasing this number allows the session to open more cursors simultaneously. The trade-off is that more open cursors means more memory consumption. The application code should be written to close cursors when unneeded.

Chapter Summary

In this chapter, we discussed the major components of the shared pool, diagnosing performance issues with the components, and tuning the components. The major components of the shared pool are the library cache and the dictionary cache. The dictionary cache is also referred to as the row cache. The User Global Area (UGA) is also part of the shared pool in the shared server environment when the large pool is not configured. The large pool is not part of the shared pool, but when configured is home to several of the buffers that would otherwise be in the shared pool.

The size of the shared pool is configured at startup by the init.ora parameter SHARED_POOL_SIZE. The sizes of the major components of the shared pool are not DBA configurable, but they are managed dynamically by the Oracle instance.

The library cache is responsible for storing SQL statement text, execution plans for the SQL statements, and executable forms of the statements. The library cache also stores PL/SQL blocks and Java classes. The library cache improves application performance by keeping compiled application code in memory, and allowing the code to be shared between sessions. The V$LIBRARYCACHE dynamic performance view is queried to determine the library cache hit ratios, which measure overall cache effectiveness. Ideally, the GETHITRATIO should be in the high-90 percentile for OLTP systems. Also, the ratio of RELOADS to PINS should be less than 1 percent. Invalidations occur in the library cache when an object that is referenced by a cached SQL is modified. The library cache hit ratio is the sum of pins minus the sum of reloads, divided by the sum of pins, and multiplied by 100.

The dictionary cache stores information from the data dictionary. SQL statements use the dictionary cache to retrieve information about the objects they need to query. This cache improves performance by reducing the number of data dictionary lookups that cause I/O when not cached. The V$ROWCACHE view is our primary tool to measure dictionary cache effectiveness—ideally, less than 2 percent GETMISSES.

Both the library cache and the dictionary cache are sparsely populated immediately after startup. Wait until the instance has been up for awhile before you measure cache effectiveness.

We can improve the performance of the shared pool by pinning large and oft-used PL/SQL blocks in memory. The DBMS_SHARED_POOL.KEEP procedure is used to pin a specific block. We can also improve the performance by caching sequence numbers. You may need to flush the shared pool before attempting to pin a large object. Also, pinning should occur shortly after startup to avoid fragmentation.

The shared pool reserve space, also known as the reserved pool, can be configured to store large objects in an area that will not become fragmented by smaller objects. Set the init.ora parameter SHARED_POOL_RESERVED_SIZE to modify the default size of the reserved pool.

In the dedicated server environment, the UGA is part of the PGA. In a shared server environment, user session data and cursor state information is moved into the shared pool or large pool. Although the size of the shared pool should be increased in the shared server environment, overall memory consumption is reduced.

The large pool is used to alleviate some of the fragmentation that can occur in the shared pool. The large pool can store parallel execution message buffers, RMAN I/O slave buffers, and UGA structures if the shared server environment is configured.

The four init.ora parameters that influence cursor caching are CURSOR_SPACE_FOR_TIME, CURSOR_SHARING, OPEN_CURSORS, and SESSION_CACHED_CURSORS. These parameters should only be changed from the default if a specific performance problem has been identified.

Two-Minute Drill

- The shared pool is one of the primary components of the Oracle SGA.
- The init.ora parameter SHARED_POOL_SIZE determines the size of the shared pool.
- The major components of the shared pool are the library cache, the dictionary cache, and the User Global Area (UGA) (for shared server environments only).
- The library cache stores SQL text, parsed executable code, and execution plans in memory.
- The library cache is managed by an LRU mechanism that ages out objects to make space for user requests.
- The V$LIBRARYCACHE view is queried to determine library cache performance.
- A section in the Statspack report shows library cache performance between snapshots.
- The library cache GETHITRATIO should be in the upper-90 percentile for OLTP systems.
- The V$LIBRARYCACHE RELOADS to PINS ratio should be less than 1 percent.
- Our primary tuning goals for the library cache are to minimize reparsing and avoid memory fragmentation.
- Library cache performance can be improved by pinning large PL/SQL blocks, reusing code, and using bind variables.
- Use the V$DB_OBJECT_CACHE view to determine which pieces of code are cached in memory, and if they are pinned.
- Use the DBMS_SHARED_POOL.KEEP procedure to pin an object.
- The shared pool reserve space or reserved pool is configured by setting the SHARED_POOL_RESERVED_SIZE init.ora parameter. It is set to 5 percent of the shared pool size by default.

- The reserved pool is used to store large objects so that fragmentation is reduced in the shared pool.

- The dictionary cache stores data dictionary information in memory.

- The V$ROWCACHE view is used to measure dictionary cache performance.

- The GETMISSES column of V$ROWCACHE should be less than 2 percent of GETS for most of the cache parameters.

- The performance of the dictionary cache is improved by caching sequence numbers, reducing DDL activities, and adequately sizing the shared pool.

- The algorithm that allocates space in the shared pool favors the dictionary cache; therefore, tune the library cache, and the dictionary cache will probably be sufficiently tuned also.

- shared pool misses and reloads are more costly than buffer cache reloads, so always tune the shared pool.

- The UGA consists of user session data and cursor state information.

- The UGA resides in the PGA in a dedicated server environment.

- The UGA resides in the shared pool in a shared server environment, unless the large pool is configured; then the majority of the UGA resides in the large pool.

- The large pool is an optional memory component that is set automatically if the init.ora parameter is PARALLEL_AUTOMATIC_TUNING=TRUE. If FALSE, then the LARGE_POOL must be configured in the init.ora.

- RMAN uses the large pool for I/O slave buffers. If the large pool isn't available, either the shared pool is used or no I/O slaves are used.

- CURSOR_SPACE_FOR_TIME=TRUE means that cursors will not be aged out of the shared pool until all associated cursors are closed.

- CURSOR_SHARING=SIMILAR or FORCE can improve the library cache performance by not forcing an exact match on SQL; therefore, similar queries can use the same cursor and even the same execution plan.

- SESSION_CACHED_CURSORS=integer improves the performance of repeated parse calls to the same SQL.

- OPEN_CURSORS=integer is the number of open cursors allowed by a process.

Chapter Questions

1. **You query V$LIBRARYCACHE and record an overall GETHITRATIO of 75 percent. What is the best course of action?**

   A. Decrease the SHARED_POOL_SIZE parameter value.

   B. In an OLTP environment, increase the SHARED_POOL_SIZE parameter value.

   C. Increase the LIBRARY_CACHE_SIZE parameter value.

   D. Investigate which parts of the library cache have poor ratios.

   E. Increase the value of the LARGE_POOL parameter.

2. **You query V$DB_OBJECT_CACHE and see the following results:**

```
OWNER      NAME                                TYPE            SHARABLE_MEM KEP
---------- ----------------------------------- --------------- ------------ ---
HR         SECURE_DML                          PROCEDURE             12989 NO
SYS        STANDARD                            PACKAGE              371020 NO
```

   What should you do?

   A. Use the DBMS_LOB_INFO.KEEP procedure to pin the STANDARD package.

   B. Use the DBMS_BUFFER_POOL.UNKEEP procedure to pin the STANDARD package.

   C. Nothing; the STANDARD package is already pinned.

   D. Use the DBMS_BUFFER_POOL.KEEP procedure to pin the STANDARD package.

3. **You query V$ROWCACHE and record an overall GETMISS ratio of 5 percent. What should you do?**

   A. Decrease the SHARED_POOL_SIZE parameter value.

   B. Increase the SHARED_POOL_SIZE parameter value.

   C. Increase the ROW_CACHE_SIZE parameter value.

   D. Investigate which parts of the dictionary cache have poor ratios.

   E. Increase the value of the LARGE_POOL parameter.

4. **Which of these columns are used to calculate the library cache Hit Ratio?**

   A. GETS and PINS

   B. PINS and PINHITS

   C. PINS and RELOADS

   D. GETMISSES and GETS

   E. GETS and RELOADS

5. **Which of these methods can you use to reduce fragmentation in the shared pool? (Choose three.)**

   A. Pin large PL/SQL blocks.

   B. Configure the SHARED_POOL_RESERVED_SIZE.

   C. Rewrite large anonymous blocks to be smaller blocks that call packaged functions.

   D. Increase the value of CURSOR_SPACE_FOR_TIME.

   E. Pin PL/SQL objects in the large pool.

6. **You execute the following command:**

   ```
   EXEC DBMS_SHARED_POOL.SIZES(150)
   ```

   What does this tell you?

   A. The cached objects that are less than or equal to 150KB in size.

   B. The uncached objects in the database that are larger than 150KB and should be cached.

   C. The cached objects that are greater than 150KB in size.

   D. This command sets the threshold value for cached objects at 150KB.

   E. This command removes objects from the cache that are greater than 150KB.

7. **In the shared server environment, cursor state information resides in which pool? (Choose two.)**

   A. The reserved shared pool

   B. The large pool if it is configured

   C. The PGA

D. The shared pool if the large pool is not configured

E. The large pool if the shared pool is not configured

8. **In the dedicated server environment, user session data resides in which pool?**

   A. The shared pool

   B. The large pool if it is configured

   C. The PGA

   D. The shared pool if the large pool is not configured

   E. The large pool if the shared pool is not configured

9. **How is fragmentation in the shared pool reduced by configuring the reserved pool?**

   A. Large memory allocations are segregated from the rest of the shared pool.

   B. Objects are pinned in the reserved pool until the instance is shut down.

   C. Small objects are pinned in the reserved pool, keeping them out of the way of large objects.

   D. The reserved pool LRU algorithm is very effective at aging small objects out.

   E. UGA memory structures are moved to the reserved pool when it is configured.

10. **Immediately after startup, you query V$ROWCACHE and note a bad hit ratio. What should you do?**

    A. Wait until the library cache reaches a steady state, and then measure the hit ratio again.

    B. In an OLTP environment, increase the SHARED_POOL_SIZE parameter value.

    C. Flush the shared pool and pin the data dictionary using DBMS_SHARED_POOL.

    D. Wait until the dictionary cache reaches a steady state, and then measure the hit ratio again.

    E. Increase the value of the LARGE_POOL parameter.

11. **You note that the library cache hit ratio is 100 percent and want to improve the performance of execution calls. Which of the following is probably a good option?**

    A. Increase the SHARED_POOL_SIZE parameter value.

    B. Set CURSOR_SPACE_FOR_TIME=FALSE.

    C. Set CURSOR_SPACE_FOR_TIME=TRUE.

    D. Set OPEN_CURSORS=50.

    E. Set CURSOR_SHARING=FORCE.

12. **Which of these are good coding practices that can improve shared pool performance?**

    A. Do not use bind variables. Instead, use literals and set CURSOR_SHARING=FORCE.

    B. Use large anonymous PL/SQL blocks.

    C. Generate ad hoc queries as often as possible.

    D. Between queries in your application code, analyze the referenced tables.

    E. Use generic code that is easily reused.

Answers to Chapter Questions

1. D.   Investigate which part of the library cache has poor ratios.

Explanation   Your first thought may be to increase the SHARED_POOL_SIZE, but the problem may be that the application is not coded properly. Investigate further and determine what is causing the low GETHITRATIO. You may need to increase the SHARED_POOL_SIZE, but do not do so until you have investigated the individual hit ratios to determine where the performance problems are. Answer A is incorrect because decreasing the shared pool size will probably not improve performance. Answer B is probably our eventual course of action, but we need to investigate before we modify the value. Answer C is incorrect because there is no LIBRARY_CACHE_SIZE parameter. Answer E is not a primary course of action, but should be considered after tuning the shared pool size.

2. D.   Use the DBMS_BUFFER_POOL.KEEP procedure to pin the STANDARD package.

Explanation   Pin the STANDARD package. It is already cached, but it is not pinned as indicated by the NO in the KEPT column. Answer A is not a valid procedure. Answer B is what we would execute to unkeep the object. Answer C is incorrect because of the previously stated value of the KEPT column.

3. D.   Investigate which parts of the dictionary cache have poor ratios.

Explanation   As in Question 1, we need to investigate further. We may eventually increase the value of SHARED_POOL_SIZE, but we should find out what has caused the low hit ratio. Answer A is incorrect. We probably will not decrease the SHARED_POOL_SIZE. ROW_CACHE_SIZE is not a valid parameter. Answer E is not the first choice, but may be considered if there are opportunities to use the large pool instead of the shared pool.

4. C.   PINS and RELOADS

Explanation   The library cache hit ratio is calculated as the sum of PINS minus the sum of RELOADS, divided by the sum of PINS, and multiplied by 100.

5. A, B, C.   Pin large PL/QL blocks, configure the SHARED_POOL_RESERVED_SIZE, rewrite large anonymous blocks to be smaller blocks that call packaged functions.

Explanation   Each of these is a good method that the DBA can implement to reduce fragmentation in the shared pool. Pinning large PL/SQL blocks reduces fragmentation caused by aging out small and large blocks. Configuring the SHARED_POOL_RESERVED_SIZE to a larger than default value reduces fragmentation caused by large memory requests. If the DBA or user applications use large anonymous blocks, then the applications should be rewritten.

6. C.   The cached objects that are greater than 150KB in size.

Explanation   The DBMS_SHARED_POOL.SIZES procedure is used to report the objects cached in memory that are larger than the passed NUMBER value in kilobytes. In SQL*Plus, issue the SET SERVEROUTPUT ON command before you execute the procedure.

7. B, D.   The large pool if it is configured, and the shared pool if the large pool is not configured.

Explanation   In the shared server environment, UGA cursor state information and user session data are stored in the large pool if it is configured; otherwise, it is stored in the shared pool. This configuration uses less overall memory than the dedicated server environment.

8. C.   The PGA

Explanation   In the dedicated server environment, UGA cursor state information and user session data resides in the PGA. The previously mentioned shared server configuration is preferred because less memory is used than with dedicated servers and the private PGA memory.

   9. **A.**   Large memory allocations are segregated from the rest of the shared pool.

Explanation   The reserved pool is specifically designed to handle requests for large chunks of memory. Since smaller memory allocations are handled in the non-reserved part of the shared pool, the reserved pool helps to reduce fragmentation that would be caused by large memory requests forcing smaller memory chunks out of the pool.

   10. **D.**   Wait until the dictionary cache reaches a steady state.

Explanation   The dictionary cache is not fully populated at startup. As user SQL processing requires data dictionary information about objects, information about those objects is loaded into the dictionary cache. Answer B—Increase the value of the shared pool—may turn out to be the eventual solution, but we should not make that decision based on poor hit ratios at startup. Wait until the cache is at a steady state, and then query.

   11. **C.**   Set CURSOR_SPACE_FOR_TIME=TRUE.

Explanation   CURSOR_SPACE_FOR_TIME=TRUE tells Oracle that it cannot age out a cursor until all associated cursors have been relinquished. This reduces the amount of hard parsing that occurs. If the hit ratio is less than 100 percent, then you already have cursors being swapped out, so you don't want to exacerbate the problem. Since the library cache hit ratio is already 100 percent, increasing the size of the shared pool will probably not improve the performance of the library cache. Answer B is the default value—CURSOR_SPACE_FOR_TIME=FALSE—and does not improve performance if the library cache hit ratio equals 100 percent. Answer D—OPEN_CURSORS=50—simply sets the maximum open cursors for a session to 50. Answer E is incorrect because CURSOR_SHARING to FORCE will force similar statements to share the executable SQL area at the risk of deteriorating execution plans. We already know that cursors are being shared, so there's no need to set this parameter value to FORCE.

   12. **E.**   Use generic code that is easily reused.

Explanation   Using generic code may sound odd, but the point is to use code that is easily repeatable. Stick with coding standards so that SQL statements are written the same. Answer A is incorrect because we should use bind variables, and should only use CURSOR_SHARING=FORCE under special conditions. Don't use large anonymous PL/SQL blocks, as they are not reusable and can clutter and fragment the shared pool. Ad hoc queries are by nature not reusable. Analyzing a table, or modifying the data dictionary information for a table, will invalidate the shared SQL that references the objects and cause a hard parse.

CHAPTER
5

Sizing the Buffer Cache

n this chapter, you will learn how to diagnose, tune, and accurately size the buffer cache, and specifically to

- Describe how the buffer cache is used by different Oracle processes.
- Describe the tuning issues related to the buffer cache.
- Set the DB_CACHE_ADVICE parameter.
- Implement Dynamic SGA Allocation.
- Monitor the use of the buffer cache, and the different pools within the buffer cache.
- Create and size multiple buffer pools.
- Make appropriate use of table caching.
- Diagnose LRU latch contention and diagnose freelist contention.
- List deprecated initialization parameters associated with the buffer cache.

This chapter focuses on diagnosing and tuning the database buffer cache. The buffer cache is one of the major components of the Oracle System Global Area (SGA) and is responsible for holding copies of data blocks that have been read from disk by server processes. These blocks are then sharable between server processes. We will first review buffer cache concepts, and then you will learn how to gather and interpret key performance statistics related to the buffer cache. We will then discuss dynamically sizing the buffer cache, caching specific objects, using multiple buffer pools within the buffer cache, and latching issues.

Sizing the Buffer Cache

Since the buffer cache is used to hold blocks of data in memory while Oracle processes perform operations on them, it makes sense that we want a block to be in memory when it is needed. Therefore, an adequately sized buffer cache is one that already contains the data blocks that we need when we need them. At the extreme, we could cache every block of every segment that we might potentially need; however, as databases grow larger, it is often too expensive to build a server with enough real memory to cache an entire database. Our focus should then be to adequately size the buffer cache so that the majority of the data blocks that we need are cached, and also to properly design and tune the application so that the buffer cache is used effectively.

Describe How the Buffer Cache Is Used by Different Oracle Processes

The buffer cache is used by Oracle to cache blocks of data read from disk; Oracle processes share the blocks of data in the buffer cache. Operations that bypass the buffer cache include sorts and parallel reads. The first time an Oracle server process needs a block of data, it looks for the data in the Database buffer cache. If the block of data is in the cache (a *cache hit*), the server process can read the data from the cache memory. If the data is not in the cache (a *cache miss*), the block of data must be read into the cache from a datafile on disk before the process can use the data. Obviously, accessing data in the cache is faster than accessing data on disk. Also, at any given time, multiple copies of the same data block may exist in the cache for read-consistency. Only one of these copies is considered current. A DBWn process writes blocks from the buffer cache back to disk.

How the Buffer Cache Is Organized

The buffers in the buffer cache are organized into two lists: the least recently used (LRU) list and the dirty list.

Buffer Cache LRU List   The LRU list keeps free buffers, pinned buffers, and dirty buffers that have not been moved to the dirty list. Free buffers are the same in memory as they are on disk, and are available for use. Pinned buffers are currently being accessed. Dirty buffers contain changed data that has not been written to disk.

When an Oracle process accesses a buffer, the process moves the buffer toward the most recently used (MRU) end of the LRU list. As buffers are moved toward the MRU end of the LRU list, dirty buffers and less-often used buffers age toward the LRU end of the list. Before a data block is read into the cache, there must be a free buffer where it can fit. The Oracle process starts searching the LRU list at the least recently used end, searching until it finds a free buffer or it has searched a number of buffers up to a threshold limit. Any dirty buffers discovered in the search are moved to the dirty list, since they must be written to disk before the buffer can be reused. When a free buffer is found, the data block is read from disk into the free buffer and the buffer is moved higher in the LRU list.

Buffer Cache Dirty List   This list is also referred to as the Write List. As described previously, dirty buffers are moved to the dirty list before they are written to disk. If an Oracle user process is searching for a free buffer and reaches the threshold limit, the process signals the DBWn background process to write some of the dirty buffers to disk.

Full Table Scans and the LRU Algorithm

During normal process block reads, data blocks are read from disk and placed at the MRU end of the LRU list. During a full table scan, blocks of data are read from disk and placed into the LRU list at the LRU end. This is a measure taken by Oracle because blocks in a full table scan are usually only accessed briefly, therefore the blocks should be moved out of the buffer cache as soon as they are not needed anymore. This leaves room in the cache for more frequently used blocks.

Buffer Cache Sizing Parameters

Oracle9*i* supports multiple block sizes in the same database—from 2KB to 32KB. The buffer cache can also be configured for multiple block sizes. The standard or default block size, specified by the DB_BLOCK_SIZE init.ora parameter, determines the default for the system tablespace and also is the block size of the standard block size buffer cache. The size of the default buffer cache is determined by the DB_CACHE_SIZE init.ora parameter in bytes, kilobytes, or megabytes. The nonstandard block size buffers are configured by setting a valid size for the following init.ora parameters:

- DB_2K_CACHE_SIZE

- DB_4K_CACHE_SIZE

- DB_8K_CACHE_SIZE

- DB_16K_CACHE_SIZE

- DB_32K_CACHE_SIZE

You cannot set the nonstandard block size buffer cache for the same size as your standard block size buffer cache. For example, if the value of DB_BLOCK_SIZE is 4096, then you cannot set the value for DB_4K_CACHE_SIZE.

Also, the size of each cache can be modified with the command ALTER SYSTEM SET <cache_name> = <new_value>.

Describe the Tuning Issues Related to the Buffer Cache

Earlier we described (in a general way) how the buffer cache is used by server processes. In this section, we'll go into greater detail so that you can understand some of the performance issues related to the buffer cache.

Managing the Database Buffer Cache

Server processes are responsible for reading the buffer cache to see if needed data blocks are present. Here are the general steps that the server processes go through when using the buffer cache:

1. The server process uses a hash function to determine if the needed block is in memory. If found, the block is moved up to the MRU end of the LRU list

and a logical read occurs. If the block is not found, the server process searches the LRU list for a free buffer.

2. The server process moves dirty buffers to the dirty list as it searches the LRU list for a free buffer.

3. If the dirty list exceeds its threshold or the server process cannot find a free buffer within its search threshold, the server process signals DBWn to flush the dirty buffers from the buffer cache.

4. Once a free buffer is found, the server process reads the block from its datafile and places it in the free buffer. The buffer is then moved away from the LRU end of the LRU list, and the server process can then read the contents of the buffer or perform its data changes.

5. If the block contains data that is too recent for the query, the server process rebuilds the earlier version of the block from rollback segments and the current block.

As mentioned, the DBWn process writes dirty blocks from the buffer cache to the data files. So as server processes are adding to and modifying the buffers in the buffer cache, DBWn processes keep the buffer cache clean. Here are the DBWn activities associated with the buffer cache:

- When a server process determines that the dirty list exceeds its size threshold, it signals DBWn to write the blocks from the dirty list.

- When a server process cannot find a free block on the LRU list, it signals DBWn to flush dirty blocks; in this case, DBWn writes dirty blocks from the LRU list.

- DBWn checks the dirty list every three seconds for blocks to write. It will move blocks from the LRU list to the dirty list so that the write buffer is full, and then write from the dirty list to datafiles.

- When LGWR signals a checkpoint, DBWn copies dirty blocks from the LRU list to the dirty list and writes the blocks to datafiles.

- If you ALTER a tablespace to begin a hot backup, or take the tablespace OFFLINE TEMPORARY, DBWn copies the dirty blocks for the tablespace from the LRU list to the dirty list and writes the blocks to datafiles.

- When an object is dropped, DBWn flushes the object's dirty blocks to disk before the object is dropped.

- During a Normal, Immediate, or Transactional shutdown, DBWn writes dirty blocks to datafiles.

Tuning Goals

The buffer cache is designed to hold oft-needed data blocks in memory. Physical I/O causes increased CPU demands and takes longer time than memory reads and writes. The performance of the Oracle server improves when it finds most of the data blocks it needs in memory. Performance worsens when the buffer cache is too small and blocks must be read from disk. To determine our relative effectiveness at finding data blocks in memory, we use the buffer cache hit ratio.

Diagnostic Tools

You can use several tools to determine the effectiveness of the buffer cache. You can measure the hit ratio using V$SYSSTAT, run the Statspack report, run UTLBSTAT/UTLESTAT report, and also query the V$DB_CACHE_ADVICE view. The V$DB_CACHE_ADVICE view is covered in the section entitled "Getting Advice about the Buffer Cache Size," and the hit ratio is covered in the section entitled "Measuring the Cache Hit Ratio." Since the Statspack report provides more information than the UTLBSTAT/UTLESTAT report, we will only discuss the Statspack report instead of both reports.

The Statspack Report   As you learned in previous chapters, the Statspack report displays performance information about the instance between two snapshots. Starting on the first page of the Statspack report, look for a few key items:

- **Cache Sizes**   Buffer cache size in MB.

- **Instance Efficiency Percentages**   Buffer Nowait% and Buffer Hit% should both approach 100 percent.

Toward the end of the report, you'll find the Buffer Pool Statistics section. The key number to look for is the Cache Hit%, which is the buffer cache hit ratio:

```
Buffer Pool Statistics for DB: OR9I   Instance: or9i   Snaps: 1 -2
-> Standard block size Pools  D: default,  K: keep,  R: recycle
-> Default Pools for other block sizes: 2k, 4k, 8k, 16k, 32k


                                                  Free    Write  Buffer
                                                Buffer Complete   Busy
         Number of Cache    Buffer   Physical  Physical  Waits    Waits   Waits
  P      Buffers Hit %      Gets     Reads     Writes
  ---   ---------- -----  ---------- --------- --------- ------- -------- ------
  D      7,864  96.9       35,160     1,095       205       0        0       0
        --------------------------------------------------------------
```

Tuning Techniques
Based on the hit ratio and other gathered statistics, you may need to make some changes to improve the performance of the buffer cache. There are a few techniques that you can implement to improve the performance of the buffer cache.

Increase the Size of the Buffer Cache   If the hit ratio is low, increasing the size of the buffer cache will generally improve the buffer cache performance, but not always. If the application performs mostly full table scans—as in data warehouse or decision support systems—then adding buffers will probably not improve performance. If the cache hit ratio is less than 90 percent and there is adequate real memory for other processes, consider increasing the size of the buffer cache.

Use Multiple Buffer Pools   You can configure multiple buffer pools for segments with different usage profiles. We will discuss this in detail in an upcoming section.

Cache Tables in Memory   Caching is a good strategy for small tables that generally are accessed with full table scans. This topic will be discussed in detail in the upcoming section entitled "Make Appropriate Use of Table Caching."

Getting Advice about the Buffer Cache Size
When you first configure an Oracle instance, there's really no way to know an accurate value for DB_CACHE_SIZE. You can set the value too low, resulting in too much I/O and poor performance. You can set the value too high, resulting in poorly utilized real memory.

To assist in the proper configuration of the default buffer cache, Oracle has provided us with an init.ora parameter to set, and a view to query. When you set the DB_CACHE_ADVICE parameter value to ON, either dynamically or in the init.ora file, Oracle begins collecting statistics about cache utilization and projects the physical I/O for 20 cache sizes, ranging from 10 percent of the current size to 200 percent.

Dynamic Buffer Cache Advisory Parameter
The DB_CACHE_ADVICE parameter has three possible values: ON, OFF, and READY. If ON or READY, about 100 bytes per buffer is allocated from the shared pool.

■ **OFF**   Disables advice statistics gathering and does not allocate memory from the shared pool. If the value was ON or READY, memory is deallocated.

■ **READY**   If set at instance startup, the shared pool memory is preallocated, but statistics are not gathered. If altered to READY while the system is running, the memory is allocated.

■ **ON** Memory is allocated and statistics are gathered. This causes a small increase in CPU utilization.

View to Support Buffer Cache Advisory
The V$DB_CACHE_ADVICE view is used to determine potential physical I/O that would result from using a different sized buffer cache.

Using V$DB_CACHE_ADVICE
Use this simple query to display the estimated physical I/O for 20 different buffer cache sizes:

```
SELECT SIZE_FOR_ESTIMATE "Cache Size (Mb)",
BUFFERS_FOR_ESTIMATE "Buffers",
ESTD_PHYSICAL_READ_FACTOR "Read Factor",
ESTD_PHYSICAL_READS "Estimated Reads"
FROM V$DB_CACHE_ADVICE
ORDER BY BUFFERS_FOR_ESTIMATE
/
```

Cache Size (Mb)	Buffers	Read Factor	Estimated Reads
30	3,840	20.20	206,026,022
60	7,680	12.10	123,411,627
90	11,520	8.20	83,634,326
120	15,360	5.30	54,056,332
150	19,200	3.50	35,697,578
180	23,040	2.70	27,538,132
210	26,880	1.70	17,338,824
240	30,720	1.30	13,259,100
270	34,560	1.10	11,219,239
300	38,400	1.00	10,199,308
330	42,240	0.94	9,587,350
360	46,080	0.88	8,975,391
390	49,920	0.85	8,669,412
420	53,760	0.81	8,261,439
460	58,880	0.79	8,057,453
490	62,720	0.77	7,853,467
520	66,560	0.73	7,445,495
550	70,400	0.71	7,241,509
580	74,240	0.69	7,037,523
610	78,080	0.67	6,833,536

If DB_CACHE_ADVICE has not been previously set to ON, the Read Factor and Estimated Reads column will be NULL. You'll note that as the projected size of the cache increases, the performance increases measured in expected physical reads come at a decreasing rate. From the preceding query, we can see that increasing the buffer cache from 300MB to 390MB reduces the physical reads by nearly the same amount as increasing the size of the cache from 390MB to 580MB. That's a great deal more memory for nearly the same reduction in physical reads.

Implement Dynamic SGA Allocation

New with Oracle9*i*, the Dynamic SGA Allocation feature allows the DBA to change the SGA configuration without shutting down the instance. The DBA can grow and shrink the SGA with an SQL command. In previous versions of the Oracle RDBMS, the SGA was a static allocation of memory. With Oracle9*i*, the buffer cache, shared pool, and large pool can be resized without changing init.ora parameters and restarting the instance. With the dynamic SGA infrastructure, limits on physical SGA memory can be set at run time; you can set the maximum amount of memory allowed, and then allow the SGA to grow as you need it to.

Unit of Allocation in the Dynamic SGA: The Granule

In Oracle9*i*, SGA components are allocated and deallocated in units of contiguous memory called granules. The size of a granule depends on the estimated size of the SGA. If the SGA is less than 128MB, then a granule is 4MB. If the SGA is larger than 128MB, then a granule is 16MB.

Allocating Granules at Startup

The minimum number of granules allocated at startup is 1 for the buffer cache, 1 for the shared pool, and 1 for the fixed SGA, which includes redo buffers. So according to these requirements, the minimum configurable SGA is 3 granules or 12MB. When the instance starts up, Oracle allocates granule entries to support SGA_MAX_SIZE bytes of address space. Each SGA component gets as many granules as it needs. Also, the buffer cache, redo buffers, Java pool, large pool, shared pool, and reserved shared pool all must fit inside the SGA_MAX_SIZE limit.

Adding Granules to Components

You can add granules to or take granules away from a component with the ALTER SYSTEM command. You can only deallocate unused granules. If you attempt to add granules to a component and there aren't enough free granules available, the attempt will fail. The value of SGA_MAX_ SIZE determines the upper limit on how many granules can be added to all caches. Here's an example where we shrink the buffer cache, attempt to add more granules than are allowed by SGA_MAX_SIZE, shrink the shared pool, and then retry growing the buffer cache:

```
SHOW PARAMETER SGA_MAX_SIZE
NAME                                     TYPE        VALUE
------------------------------------- ----------- ---------
```

```
sga_max_size                              big integer 126644216

SHOW PARAMETER DB_CACHE_SIZE
NAME                                 TYPE          VALUE
------------------------------------ ----------- --------
db_cache_size                             big integer 33554432

ALTER SYSTEM SET DB_CACHE_SIZE = 28 M
/
System altered.
SHOW PARAMETER DB_CACHE_SIZE
NAME                                 TYPE          VALUE
------------------------------------ ----------- --------
db_cache_size                             big integer 29360128

ALTER SYSTEM SET DB_CACHE_SIZE = 36 M
/
ALTER SYSTEM SET DB_CACHE_SIZE = 36 M
*
ERROR at line 1:
ORA-02097: parameter cannot be modified because specified value is invalid
ORA-00384: Insufficient memory to grow cache

SHOW PARAMETER SHARED_POOL_SIZE
NAME                                 TYPE          VALUE
------------------------------------ ----------- --------
shared_pool_size                          big integer 46137344
ALTER SYSTEM SET SHARED_POOL_SIZE = 40 M
/
System altered.
ALTER SYSTEM SET DB_CACHE_SIZE=36 M
/
System altered.
```

Dynamic Buffer Cache Size Parameters

As demonstrated previously, the buffer cache can be resized dynamically with the ALTER SYSTEM SET DB_CACHE_SIZE command. The cache cannot be set to zero, it must be a multiple of the granule size, and it cannot be set to a number that will cause the total SGA size to exceed MAX_SGA_SIZE. Each SGA component is sized independently, and the size increase or decrease will be set to the next granule boundary.

```
ALTER SYSTEM SET DB_CACHE_SIZE = 33 M
/
System altered.
```

```
SHOW PARAMETER DB_CACHE_SIZE

NAME                                   TYPE        VALUE
------------------------------------   -----------  --------
db_cache_size                          big integer 37748736

SELECT 37748736/1024/1024 MB FROM DUAL
/
        MB
----------
        36
```

Monitor the Use of the Buffer Cache and the Different Pools Within the Buffer Cache

As mentioned previously when we discussed tuning goals for the buffer cache, there are several dynamic performance views that we can use to monitor buffer cache performance. The primary tool is the buffer cache hit ratio. Information gathered from other diagnostics tools can augment the buffer cache hit ratio diagnostics tool.

Measuring the Cache Hit Ratio

Oracle gathers statistics about buffer cache performance and stores it in the V$SYSSTAT dynamic performance view. These are the values of the NAME column in V$SYSSTAT that we're most interested in:

- **Physical reads**   Number of blocks read from disk
- **Physical reads direct**   Number of blocks read from disk that did not require the cache
- **Physical reads direct (lob)**   Number of direct reads of large binary objects
- **Session logical reads**   Total number of read requests for data

Session logical reads includes requests that found data blocks in memory and those requests that required physical reads. Direct reads and LOB reads do not use the buffer cache.

Here's the formula to calculate the buffer cache hit ratio from the V$SYSSTAT view:

$$1 - (\text{physical reads} - \text{physical reads direct} - \text{physical reads direct (lob)})/\text{session logical reads}$$

Here's the query you use to calculate the hit ratio:

```
SELECT 1-(PHY.VALUE - LOB.VALUE - DIR.VALUE)/SES.VALUE "CACHE HIT RATIO"
FROM V$SYSSTAT SES, V$SYSSTAT LOB,
V$SYSSTAT DIR, V$SYSSTAT PHY
```

```
WHERE SES.NAME = 'session logical reads'
AND   DIR.NAME = 'physical reads direct'
AND   LOB.NAME = 'physical reads direct (lob)'
AND   PHY.NAME = 'physical reads'
/
CACHE HIT RATIO
---------------
    .907196824
```

As always, gather the buffer cache hit ratio after the instance has been up for awhile and the buffer cache is populated and in use.

Statspack Report   In the Statspack report, look for these parameters in the Instance Activity Stats section:

```
Instance Activity Stats for DB: OR9I  Instance: or9i  Snaps: 1 -2
Statistic                              Total    per Second    per Trans
------------------------------- ------------------ ------------- -----------
physical reads                         1,095          0.3         547.5
physical reads direct                      0          0.0           0.0
session logical reads                183,011         44.1      91,505.5
```

Guidelines to Use the Cache Hit Ratio and Increase the Cache Size

The buffer cache hit ratio can be greatly affected by full table scans, application design, large tables with random access, and uneven distribution of cache hits. Large full table scans drive the ratio lower. Poorly designed SQL can sometimes result in a high hit ratio even though performance is bad. Random access on large tables causes blocks to be used sparsely, driving the ratio lower. Scheduled batch processes that perform full table scans can temporarily drive the ratio lower.

You should consider increasing the size of the buffer cache if the buffer cache hit ratio is less than 90 percent on an OLTP system, there is little or no system page faulting, and the previous buffer cache increase was effective. If the previous increase didn't improve the hit ratio, then look to the application design for solutions.

You can add buffers to the buffer cache dynamically if there is enough space within SGA_MAX_SIZE to increase the value of DB_CACHE_SIZE. You can also increase the values of these parameters in the init.ora file if you wish to wait until the next startup to increase the size of the buffer cache. Once the new buffer cache size is established and in use, reevaluate performance by checking the buffer cache hit ratio.

Other Cache Performance Indicators

In addition to the hit ratio, there are other statistics that you can use to evaluate buffer cache performance.

V$BUFFER_POOL   The V$BUFFER_POOL view shows which buffer pools are configured, the number of buffers assigned to each (BUFFERS), and the block size. The columns for number (SET_COUNT) and range (LO_SETID, HI_SETID) of LRU latches are obsolete since DB_BLOCK_LRU_LATCHES is obsolete in Oracle9*i*.

V$BUFFER_POOL_STATISTICS   Whereas V$BUFFER_POOL shows us how buffer pools are configured, V$BUFFER_POOL_STATISTICS show us information about buffer pool usage. Important columns include FREE_BUFFER_WAIT, DIRTY_BUFFERS_INSPECTED, CONSISTENT_GETS, PHYSICAL_READS, and PHYSICAL_WRITES. Possible values for the NAME column are DEFAULT, KEEP, and RECYCLE; there is one row for each configured buffer pool. All nonstandard block size pools are listed as DEFAULT.

Wait Statistics   Query the V$SYSSTAT.VALUE where name equals free buffer inspected. This value indicates the number of dirty or pinned buffers that were skipped before a free buffer could be found. An excessively high number indicates that more buffers might improve performance.

Wait Events   Query the EVENT column in the V$SYSTEM_EVENT view to determine if there are any of the following wait events:

- **Buffer busy waits**   If there are waits of this type, query V$WAITSTAT and diagnose the data block, segment header, undo header, and undo block rows. A buffer busy wait is a wait while trying to access a particular buffer.

  Data block waits indicate a wait for the current copy of a data block in memory, due to unselective indexes, index keys that may be potential candidates for REVERSE KEY indexes, or free list contention on inserts. Undo header waits indicate a wait on the rollback segment transaction table. If you are not using automatic undo management, and you see a large number of undo header waits, consider adding more rollback segments; if you see a large number of undo block waits, consider increasing the size of your rollback segments.

- **Free buffer inspected**   A measure of the number of buffers on the LRU list that are inspected when looking for a free buffer before triggering DBWn to flush dirty buffers.

- **Free buffer waits**   Number of waits for DBWn to write buffers to disk. This indicates that DBWn is not keeping up with the number of dirty buffers that must be written to make room for new blocks. It's possible that the I/O system isn't keeping up. Also, a high number may indicate that the buffer cache is too small; refer back to the buffer cache hit ratio and increase the size of the buffer cache if necessary. It could also be that the buffer cache is too large for the number of DBWn processes. In this case, you have two possible remedies. You can increase the number of DBWn processes by increasing the value of DB_WRITER_PROCESSES or DBWR_IO_SLAVES, depending on your system; or you may consider decreasing the size of the buffer cache if the hit ratio is acceptable.

Create and Size Multiple Buffer Pools

Most databases perform well when the default buffer cache is configured properly. However, there are some cases where you may want to configure multiple buffer pools to meet specific application needs. If a segment is used frequently, you want the blocks kept in the buffer cache as much as possible. If a segment is used rarely and almost never reused, then you want blocks from that segment aged out as soon as possible to make room for oft-used blocks. Oracle provides us with the KEEP and RECYCLE buffer pools for these two purposes.

Using Multiple Buffer Pools

The DEFAULT buffer pool is always configured. It is the same thing as the standard block size buffer cache. The KEEP buffer pool—as the name suggests—is used to keep buffers in the pool as long as possible for data blocks that are likely to be reused. The RECYCLE buffer pool is used to temporarily host blocks from segments that you don't want to interfere with blocks in the default buffer pool. The KEEP and RECYCLE buffer pools are separately defined memory areas from the default buffer pool; they are not a subset of the DEFAULT pool.

Defining Multiple Buffer Pools

The KEEP buffer pool is configured with the init.ora parameter DB_KEEP_CACHE_SIZE; the RECYCLE buffer pool is configured with DB_RECYCLE_CACHE_SIZE. These parameters are dynamically configurable. Oracle automatically allocates latches for the pools.

Assigning Segments to Buffer Pools

You can assign a segment to a specific pool when you create or alter the segment. Here are some examples:

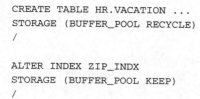

```
CREATE TABLE HR.VACATION ...
STORAGE (BUFFER_POOL RECYCLE)
/

ALTER INDEX ZIP_INDX
STORAGE (BUFFER_POOL KEEP)
/
```

If you don't specify the BUFFER_POOL, the DEFAULT pool is used. If you create an object and assign it to a pool, the entire segment is not automatically loaded into the pool; only as blocks are read are they loaded into the assigned pool. If you change the buffer pool of an object while blocks are loaded in the previously assigned pool, those blocks do not move over to the newly assigned pool. Newly read blocks are loaded into the newly assigned pool. For objects with multiple segments (partitioned tables, for example), you can assign blocks from the different segments to different pools.

KEEP Buffer Pool Guidelines

The tuning goal for the KEEP buffer pool is to keep needed objects in memory, thereby reducing I/O. Frequently accessed segments should be placed in the KEEP pool. If the segment size is less than 10 percent of the DEFAULT pool size and blocks are accessed repeatedly, consider placing them in the KEEP pool. Calculate the size needed for the KEEP pool by summing the size of all of the objects you intend to place there.

Determine the Size Needed for KEEP Objects

Use the ANALYZE ... ESTIMATE STATISTICS command to collect the number of blocks below the high water mark for each object you intend to place in the KEEP pool. Query DBA_TABLES, DBA_TAB_PARTITIONS, DBA_OBJECT_TABLES, and DBA_CLUSTERS for the objects you want; then sum the BLOCKS column to determine the total number of BLOCKS required. Add to this the number of LEAF_BLOCKS from DBA_INDEXES for the indexes you want to keep. It is not necessary to cache all the blocks in the KEEP pool to improve performance. Be aware that growing objects need to be reevaluated often to determine if they might cause buffers to be aged out of the KEEP pool.

RECYCLE Buffer Pool Guidelines

The tuning goal for the RECYCLE pool is to get a block out of memory as soon as the transaction that is using it no longer needs it. If the segment size is greater than twice the size of the DEFAULT pool, and blocks in the segment are not used outside of the current transaction, consider using the RECYCLE pool.

Using V$CACHE to Determine the RECYCLE Pool Size   Use the V$CACHE view to assist with sizing the RECYCLE pool. The V$CACHE view is built by running the $ORACLE_HOME\rdbms\admin\catparr.sql script. During peak system usage, query the V$CACHE view and sum the BLOCKS column for all objects that you intend to place in the RECYCLE pool. Divide the total by 4; this is an assumption that one-fourth of the blocks are active at any given time.

```
SELECT USERNAME, NAME, COUNT(*) "BLOCKS"
FROM V$CACHE, DBA_USERS
WHERE OWNER#=USER_ID
AND USERNAME = 'HR'
GROUP BY USERNAME, NAME
/
USERNAME                          NAME                               BLOCKS
------------------------------    ------------------------------    ----------
HR                                EMPLOYEES                              4
```

You can also use SQL trace with TKPROF, Oracle Trace Manager, or query current session I/O in V$SESS_IO to see the number of physical reads caused by a user session and its SQL. If you are accessing an object that has been assigned to the RECYCLE pool, expect to see a higher ratio of physical reads on that object than you would if the object were assigned to the KEEP or DEFAULT pool.

Calculating the Hit Ratio for Multiple Pools

Use the V$BUFFER_POOL_STATISTICS dynamic performance view to calculate the buffer cache hit ratio for each of the buffer pools.

```
SELECT NAME, 1-(PHYSICAL_READS/(DB_BLOCK_GETS + CONSISTENT_GETS)) "Hit Ratio"
FROM V$BUFFER_POOL_STATISTICS
WHERE DB_BLOCK_GETS + CONSISTENT_GETS > 0
/
NAME                 Hit Ratio
-------------------- ----------
KEEP                 .998467311
RECYCLE              .498124372
DEFAULT              .927135331
```

The results of this query indicate that our DEFAULT pool has a respectable hit ratio. The RECYCLE pool is lower than the others, as we would expect. The KEEP pool is high, which was our intent—greater than 99 percent of the read requests found the needed block in the KEEP pool.

Views that Indicate the Buffer Pool Assignment

As mentioned in a previous section, you can assign a segment to a buffer pool when you create the segment, or ALTER the segment later to change the buffer pool. The data dictionary keeps track of the assigned buffer pool for an object. You can query the BUFFER_POOL column from any of the following data dictionary views to determine which pool objects are assigned to:

DBA_ALL_TABLES	DBA_LOB_SUBPARTITIONS
DBA_CLUSTERS	DBA_OBJECT_TABLES
DBA_INDEXES	DBA_SEGMENTS
DBA_IND_PARTITIONS	DBA_TABLES
DBA_IND_SUBPARTITIONS	DBA_TAB_PARTITIONS
DBA_LOB_PARTITIONS	DBA_TAB_SUBPARTITIONS

Most of these views have an associated ALL_ or USER_ view.

Make Appropriate Use of Table Caching

When a table is read using a full table scan, blocks are read into the LRU end of the LRU list. Blocks read in this fashion are aged out quickly. If you have a need to keep tables that are accessed mostly via full table scans, you can change this default LRU list behavior on a per-table basis.

Caching Tables

Use the CACHE clause when you CREATE or ALTER a table or cluster, and blocks of the object will be placed at the MRU end of the list during a full table scan. This is a good idea for small tables that are repeatedly accessed by full table scans. For larger tables, you may want to reconsider your indexing strategy. Remember that the point of caching tables is to reduce I/O; if you notice that larger objects are CACHED and I/O is increasing, then investigate removing the objects from the cache with the NOCACHE option. If you have placed an object in the KEEP buffer pool, the NOCACHE clause has no effect on it.

The CACHE SQL Hint   You can also code in a CACHE hint into an SQL statement to force blocks to the MRU end of the LRU list. Here's an example:

```
SELECT /*+ CACHE (EMPLOYEES) */
* FROM HR.EMPLOYEES
/
```

Diagnose LRU Latch Contention

We'll want to monitor two types of latches on the buffer cache for potential problems: the cache buffer LRU chain and the cache buffer chain.

Cache Buffer LRU Chain

This latch protects the lists of buffers in the cache. A latch must be obtained when dirty blocks are written to disk or when a server process is searching for a block to write to. A single latch of this type is sufficient for a uniprocessor machine; for multiprocessor machines, Oracle sets the number of cache buffer LRU chain latches to one-half the number of CPUs. Query V$SYSTEM_EVENT to see if there is any appreciable contention on this latch.

Cache Buffer Chains

These latches are used to protect a buffer list in the cache and are used when searching for, adding, or removing a buffer. The buffer cache actually consists of chains of blocks, and each of the chains is protected by a child of this latch when it needs to be searched.

Contention on this latch usually indicates a buffer that is heavily contended for. Query V$LATCH_CHILDREN for a particular cache buffer chains latch that has a high number of GETS, MISSES, and SLEEPS. Use the ADDR column and query the SYS.X$BH table to get the associated FILE# and DBABLK. Repeat the queries and look for repeat FILE# and DBABLK. Then query DBA_EXTENTS to determine the segment that is contended for. Use the following example queries to find the block, and segment.

```
SELECT File# , dbablk, class, state
FROM x$bh
WHERE hladdr='&ADDR_OF_CHILD_LATCH'
/

SELECT SEGMENT_NAME, SEGMENT_TYPE
FROM dba_extents, x$bh
WHERE dba_extents.FILE_ID = x$bh.FILE#
AND dba_extents.BLOCK_ID =x$bh.DBABLK
AND x$bh.hladdr = '&ADDR_OF_CHILD_LATCH'
ORDER BY SEGMENT_TYPE, SEGMENT_NAME
/
```

Diagnose Freelist Contention

A freelist on an object keeps track of blocks that are available for inserts. If multiple processes attempt to insert into the same object at the same time, freelist contention can occur. The number of freelists for an object is set at object create time or can be altered dynamically. In a single-CPU system, multiple freelists can be used, but may not be necessary because the CPU manages one process at a time. Our tuning goal for freelists is to make sure that there are enough of them to minimize waits caused by multiple processes attempting to insert into the same object at the same time.

Automatic Segment-Space Management eliminates freelist contention because free and used segment space is stored in a bitmap in the datafile. This is only available for locally managed tablespaces.

Diagnosing Freelist Contention

We use three dynamic performance views and one data dictionary view to diagnose freelist contention:

- **V$WAITSTAT**   Query COUNT and TIME for the segment header CLASS.

- **V$SYSTEM_EVENT**   Query TOTAL_WAITS for the EVENT buffer busy waits.

- **V$SESSION_WAIT**   For server process wait events, join with DBA_SEGMENTS as specified in the query below.

- **DBA_SEGMENTS**   Can be used to determine the name of the segment waited on in V$SESSION_WAIT; you can then determine if the free lists should be increased for this segment. Use this query to determine the segment in question:

```
SELECT S.SEGMENT_NAME, S.SEGMENT_TYPE, S.FREELISTS, W.WAIT_TIME,
W.SECONDS_IN_WAIT, W.STATE
FROM DBA_SEGMENTS S, V$SESSION_WAIT W
WHERE W.EVENT='buffer busy waits'
AND W.P1=S.HEADER_FILE
AND W.P2=S.HEADER_BLOCK
/
```

Resolving Freelist Contention

To resolve data block waits, you can increase the value of INITRANS, and/or modify the values of PCTUSED and PCTFREE. If you identify a segment header that has freelist contention, you can increase the number of freelists for the segment just like this:

```
ALTER TABLE HR.EMPLOYEES
STORAGE (FREELISTS 2)
/
Table altered.
```

If you're using Oracle Real Application Clusters, then you might also want to increase the number of FREELIST_GROUPS assigned to the segment.

Auto-Management of Free Space

You should also consider using tablespace Automatic Segment-Space Management. With this feature of Oracle9*i*, free space is automatically managed inside database segments; a bitmap is used to track free and used space, instead of using freelists. Advantages include better space utilization, better multi-instance performance and space utilization, and better adjustments to concurrent access. Auto-management of free space is designated at the tablespace create time; all segments subsequently created within the tablespace then use auto-management. Also, your choice of method cannot be subsequently altered. Only permanent, locally managed tablespaces can specify Automatic Segment-Space Management.

Deprecated Buffer Cache Parameters

The following buffer cache related parameters are deprecated in Oracle9*i*; the first three have been kept in Oracle9*i* for backward compatibility.

- **DB_BLOCK_BUFFERS** In previous versions, the buffer cache size was determined by the product of DB_BLOCK_SIZE and DB_BLOCK_BUFFERS. This has been replaced by the DB_CACHE_SIZE parameters.

- **BUFFER_POOL_KEEP** Replaced by DB_KEEP_CACHE_SIZE. You can only use one of these parameters at a time.

- **BUFFER_POOL_RECYCLE** Replaced by DB_RECYCLE_CACHE_SIZE. You can only use one of these parameters at a time.

- **DB_BLOCK_LRU_LATCHES** Now an obsolete init.ora parameter.

Chapter Summary

In this chapter you learned about the buffer cache, how to measure relative buffer cache effectiveness with the buffer cache hit ratio, and how to tune the buffer cache. You learned how to use the buffer cache advisory feature, separate segments into multiple buffer pools, cache tables, and avoid freelist contention. You also learned factors that contribute to buffer cache performance. You learned that we want to achieve a buffer cache hit ratio of 90 percent or greater.

We reviewed the different components of the buffer cache. You learned how Oracle server processes search the buffer cache for free buffers, and how DBWn processes write dirty buffers to disk. You learned how to set the DBA_CACHE_ADVICE parameter and use the V$DB_CACHE_ADVICE view to determine the effects of resizing the buffer cache.

You learned about the Dynamic SGA Allocation infrastructure that is new to Oracle9*i*. You learned that we can resize the DB_CACHE_SIZE parameter as long as it fits within the SGA_MAX_SIZE parameter value and no other SGA structures require the space.

You learned how to create multiple buffer pools. The KEEP buffer pool is used for segments that are HOT—that is, used often. The RECYCLE pool is used for segments that are rarely or never reused. The DEFAULT buffer pool is always configured. You also learned how to assign segments to a specific pool.

The V$SYSSTAT dynamic performance view is used to calculate the buffer cache hit ratio; the ratio of nonphysical reads to total reads. You also learned that there is a Statspack report section for the buffer cache statistics.

You can also use the CACHE option when creating or altering a table. This moves segment blocks to the MRU end of the LRU list, effectively keeping the segment blocks in memory. NOCACHE has no effect on objects assigned to the KEEP pool.

You learned about the causes and cures for LRU latch contention and freelist contention. Finally, we listed and described deprecated init.ora parameters that are related to the buffer cache.

Two-Minute Drill

- The buffer cache is one of the major components of the SGA.

- The buffer cache is responsible for keeping data blocks in memory so that processes don't have to perform physical reads.

- An adequately sized buffer cache can greatly improve database performance.

- The buffer cache consists of the least recently used (LRU) list and the dirty list.

- Oracle server processes read data blocks from data files and place them in the LRU list.

- Once in the LRU list, subsequent server processes can use them.

- Most recently used (MRU) blocks are moved up the LRU list towards the MRU end of the list.

- Unused buffers and buffers in memory that are the same as the data blocks on disk are called free buffers.

- Buffers that are in use are called pinned buffers.

- Blocks in the buffer cache that have been changed are called dirty buffers.

- Dirty buffers are moved to the dirty list and written to data files by DBWn processes.

- Blocks from full table scans of tables that are not cached are placed at the LRU end of the LRU list, so they are aged out quickly.

- The DB_CACHE_SIZE parameter determines the size of the DEFAULT buffer pool for the default block size.

- There are also configurable caches for blocks of size 2KB, 4KB, 8KB, 16KB, and 32KB using the DB_*n*K_CACHE_SIZE. You cannot configure this type of cache for the default block size. Up to four DB_*n*K_CACHE_SIZE initialization parameters can be specified.

- The buffer cache hit ratio is our primary diagnostics tool for the buffer cache.

- The ratio is calculated as: 1 − [physical reads − physical reads direct − physical reads direct (lob)]/session logical reads.

- On OLTP systems, the ratio should be greater than 90 percent.

- You can improve buffer cache performance by increasing the size of the buffer cache, using multiple buffer pools, and by caching tables in memory.

- The DB_CACHE_ADVICE when set to ON causes the Oracle instance to set aside a small amount of space in the shared pool and begin collecting information about the effects of different buffer cache sizes.

- The V$DB_CACHE_ADVICE view is queried to show projected physical I/O impact caused by resizing the buffer cache.

- You can dynamically increase the size of the SGA components up to the size of SGA_MAX_SIZE.

- You can increase the DB_CACHE_SIZE parameter as long as there is unallocated space within SGA_MAX_SIZE.

- The granule is a unit of contiguous memory. If your SGA is smaller than 128MB, then the granule is defined as 4MB. If the SGA is equal to or larger than 128MB, the granule is 16MB.

- V$BUFFER_POOL_STATISTICS contains read, scan, and write information about each buffer pool. Use it to monitor the activity of each buffer pool.

- Wait events like buffer busy waits, free buffer inspected, and free buffer waits can indicate performance problems with the buffer cache.

- Multiple buffer pools can be used to segregate objects with different usage patterns.

- The KEEP buffer pool can be used for objects that are often used, such as lookup tables. The init.ora parameter DB_KEEP_CACHE_SIZE is used to configure the KEEP pool.

- The RECYCLE buffer pool should be configured for large objects that are seldom reused. The init.ora parameter DB_RECYCLE_CACHE_SIZE is used to configure the RECYCLE pool.

- The DEFAULT buffer pool is always configured; DB_CACHE_SIZE cannot be 0.

- The KEEP and RECYCLE pools are not allocated from memory assigned to the DEFAULT pool.

- You can assign a segment to a buffer pool when you create or alter the segment by using the BUFFER_POOL option in the STORAGE clause.

- Use the V$BUFFER_POOL_STATISTICS view to determine hit ratios for multiple buffer pools.

- DBA_TABLES, DBA_SEGMENTS, and other data dictionary views with a BUFFER_POOL column indicate the buffer pool assignment of an object.

- You can CACHE a table to improve performance and the hit ratio if the table is accessed via full table scans, and used often.

- Query V$SYSTEM_EVENT to see if there is contention for the cache buffer LRU chain latch.

- Query V$LATCH_CHILDREN to see if there is contention for a cache buffer chain latch.

- Freelist contention causes waits during inserts into segments.

- Freelist contention is more prevalent on multiprocessor machines because multiple processes may be competing for the same freelist.

- Automatic Segment-Space Management can be used in a tablespace to eliminate the need for freelists on the objects within the tablespace.

- DB_BLOCK_BUFFERS, BUFFER_POOL_KEEP, and BUFFER_POOL_RECYCLE have been replaced with new init.ora parameters, but have been kept for backward compatibility.

- DB_BLOCK_LRU_LATCHES is now obsolete.

Chapter Questions

1. **Which one of the following does not describe the buffer cache?**

   A. Is dynamically configurable.

   B. Consists of the MRU list and the dirty list.

   C. Can be segmented into KEEP, RECYCLE, and DEFAULT pools.

   D. The size of the buffer cache is set by DB_CACHE_SIZE.

   E. DB Writer processes move dirty blocks from the buffer cache to data files.

   F. Can contain pinned buffers, which are buffers currently being used.

2. **Which one of the following accurately describes how an Oracle server process interacts with the buffer cache?**

   A. Reads blocks from the dirty list and writes them to datafiles

   B. Scans the LRU list for free blocks and reads them into datafiles

   C. Scans the MRU list for free blocks and writes them to the dirty list

   D. Scans the LRU list for free blocks before reading a data block from disk

   E. Scans the LRU list for pinned blocks and writes them to disk

3. **Which one of the following describes how DBWn interacts with the buffer cache?**

   A. Reads blocks from the dirty list and writes them to datafiles

   B. Scans the LRU list for free blocks and reads them into datafiles

   C. Scans the MRU list for free blocks and writes them to the dirty list

   D. Scans the LRU list for free blocks before reading a data block from disk

   E. Scans the LRU list for pinned blocks and flushes them from the pool

4. **Which of the following describes a good candidate segment for the KEEP pool? (Choose two.)**

   A. Larger than the buffer cache

   B. Less than 10 percent of the buffer cache

   C. Used often

D. Mostly accessed with full table scans

E. Seldom used

5. **You have just used the ALTER command to set the DB_CACHE_ADVICE parameter to READY. What is now happening in the instance?**

   A. Memory has been allocated in the shared pool for cache advice buffers.

   B. CPU utilization will significantly increase because Oracle is collecting more detailed statistics about the buffer cache.

   C. The buffer cache hit ratio will now increase.

   D. The V$DB_CACHE_ADVICE view is now populated.

6. **Which of the following parameters sets the maximum amount of memory that can be dynamically allocated to the SGA components?**

   A. SGA_SESSION_MAX

   B. MAX_SGA_SIZE

   C. The product of DB_CACHE_SIZE and SHARED_POOL_SIZE

   D. SGA_MAX_SIZE

   E. SGA_DYNAMIC_SIZE

7. **You notice that Statspack snapshots taken over the weekend and at night indicate a low buffer cache hit ratio. What should you do? (Choose two.)**

   A. Increase the size of the buffer cache by modifying DB_CACHE_SIZE.

   B. Determine which application components were running between the snapshots, and investigate further.

   C. Use the DB_CACHE_ADVICE option to determine by how much you should increase the size of the buffer cache.

   D. Query V$BUFFER_POOL and compare the statistics to the Statspack report.

   E. Deallocate granules from the Shared Pool and add them to the buffer cache during these hours.

8. **Which of these accurately describes granule sizes?**

   A. Are dynamically configurable between 2KB and 32KB

   B. Are set to 4MB if your SGA is larger than 128MB

    C. Are set to 16MB if your SGA is larger than 128MB

    D. Are the same size as the default or standard block size (system tablespace block size)

    E. Are only configurable at startup with the DB_GRANULE_SIZE parameter

9. **Which of the following are possible solutions to freelist issues? (Choose two.)**

    A. Decrease the number of freelists.

    B. Increase the number of freelists on a multiprocessor system.

    C. Use dictionary-managed tablespaces.

    D. Use automatic management of free space on the tablespace.

    E. Increase the number of freelist groups on a uniprocessor nonclustered system.

10. **You notice that write times for dirty blocks are exceptionally slow. Which of these is a likely explanation of the problem? (Choose two.)**

    A. There are too many server processes competing for pinned blocks.

    B. There are too few DBWn processes for the size of the buffer cache.

    C. There are too many DBWn processes for the size of the buffer cache.

    D. The disk I/O subsystem is not sized properly for the workload.

    E. LGWR isn't signaling checkpoints often enough for the DBWn processes.

11. **You just set the DB_CACHE_ADVICE parameter to OFF. What just happened? (Choose two.)**

    A. The V$DB_CACHE_ADVICE view was truncated.

    B. Oracle stops gathering statistics for buffer cache size estimates.

    C. The shared pool buffers for the Advice feature were freed.

    D. The instance must be restarted to begin gathering these statistics again.

    E. The value of DB_CACHE_SIZE was increased according to the advice.

12. **You have decided that a table is a good candidate for the RECYCLE pool. Which of these factors convinced you of that? (Choose two.)**

    A. The table is small and used often.

    B. The table is greater than twice the size of the DEFAULT pool.

    C. The table is large and seldom reused.

    D. The table is used often, but accessed solely with full table scans.

    E. The table is already CACHED.

    F. The table is less than 10 percent the size of the DEFAULT pool.

13. **Which one of the following formulas describes the buffer cache hit ratio?**

    A. Physical reads − physical reads direct + session logical reads − 1

    B. 1 − (session logical reads) / [(physical reads direct − physical reads direct (lob) − physical reads)]

    C. 1 − (physical reads − physical reads direct (lob) − physical reads direct) / (session logical reads)

    D. (physical reads direct − physical reads direct (lob) − physical reads) / (session logical reads) − 1

    E. (buffer gets − buffer busy gets) / (buffer waits) × 100

14. **Which views can be used to determine the segment that is causing cache buffer chains contention? (Choose one.)**

    A. V$BH, DBA_SEGMENTS, V$LATCH

    B. XBH, VLATCH_CHILDREN, DBA_EXTENTS

    C. V$BUFFER_CACHE, V$LATCH_CONTENTION

    D. XBH, VBUFFER_CACHE

    E. V$SYSTEM_EVENT

Answers to Chapter Questions

1. B.   Consists of the MRU list and the dirty list.

Explanation   The buffer cache consists of the LRU list and the dirty list. The LRU list has an MRU end and an LRU end. Each of the other answers correctly describes the buffer cache.

2. D.   Scans the LRU list for free blocks before reading a data block from disk

Explanation   When an Oracle server process needs to read a block of data, it first scans the LRU list of the buffer cache for free buffers before it reads from disk. Answer A is incorrect because DBWn reads from the dirty list and writes to datafiles. Answer B is incorrect because blocks are read into the buffer cache, not into datafiles. Answer C is incorrect for multiple reasons. Answer E is incorrect because pinned blocks are currently in use.

3. A.   Reads blocks from the dirty list and writes them to datafiles

Explanation   DB Writer processes are responsible for reading dirty blocks from the buffer cache dirty list, and writing the dirty blocks to disk. Answers B, C, and E do not accurately describe any Oracle process. Answer D describes what an Oracle server process does when searching for a free buffer.

4. B, C.   Less than 10 percent of the buffer cache, and used often.

Explanation   The Objects in the KEEP pool should be less than 10 percent of the buffer cache size, and often used. Rarely used objects will be aged out soon. If the object is in the KEEP pool and the pool is configured large enough, blocks are rarely aged out. Answers A, D, and E are criteria for the RECYCLE pool.

5. A.   Memory has been allocated in the shared pool.

Explanation   When DB_CACHE_ADVICE is set to ready, memory for the advice collection is configured in the shared pool. CPU utilization will not increase because no data gathering occurs until you set the value to ON. Answer C is not correct because DB_CACHE_ADVICE makes no changes to the buffer cache size; it merely forecasts physical I/O changes to the instance if the buffer cache is configured smaller or larger. Answer D is not correct because the V$DB_CACHE_ADVICE view remains unpopulated until the advice parameter is set to ON.

6. D. SGA_MAX_SIZE

Explanation The parameter SGA_MAX_SIZE determines the largest value that the SGA can be expanded into. You cannot grow the DB_CACHE_SIZE infinitely; it reaches an upper bound within SGA_MAX_SIZE. Answers A, B, and E are not valid initialization parameters. Answer C is not correct; it does not include the Java pool, large pool, and redo buffers.

7. B, C. Determine which application components were running between the snapshots, and investigate further, and use the DB_CACHE_ADVICE option to determine by how much you should increase the size of the buffer cache.

Explanation Answer B is a good practice before modifying the instance. Determine what processes occur during weekend and off hours. You may discover that the majority of the processes that performed full table scans never reuse data. These would be good candidates for the RECYCLE pool. Answer C is also correct, because this method can be used to estimate the new size of the buffer cache. Answer A may be your eventual solution, but not before investigating the cause of the low hit ratio. Answer D is incorrect because the V$BUFFER_POOL view does not give us the cache hit ratio. Answer E is not correct because we don't know that the Shared Pool is oversized during the stated hours.

8. C. Are set to 16MB if your SGA is larger than 128MB

Explanation If your SGA is smaller than 128MB, the granule size is 4MB; otherwise, the granule size is 16MB. Answer A is incorrect; the values are not dynamically configurable. Answer B conflicts with answer C. Answer D is incorrect because granules are specified in megabytes, while the standard block size is in kilobytes.

9. B, D. Increase the number of freelists, or use Automatic Segment-Space Management.

Explanation If you're in a multiprocessor environment, consider increasing the number of freelists for specific segments. Also, Automatic Segment-Space Management saves a tremendous amount of overhead because free space is managed using bitmaps instead of freelists. Answer A is the opposite of one of the correct answers. Answer C does not apply, since extent management at the dictionary-level is a separate issue. Answer E is incorrect because freelist groups apply to clustered systems.

10. B, D.   Too few DB Writer processes for the size of the buffer cache, or the disk I/O subsystem is not sized properly for the workload.

Explanation   This can happen if the DBWn process spends a great deal of time searching the LRU list for dirty buffers. If the buffer is exceptionally large, one DBWn process may not be able to keep up with write demands. Answer D is also correct because a slow or undersized I/O system would cause slow DBWn write times. Answer A is not related to the problem. Answer C would not slow down write times. Answer E is the opposite of what we would expect: If LGWR is signaling checkpoints too fast for DBWn processes to keep up, we would expect performance problems.

11. B, C.

Explanation Setting DB_CACHE_ADVICE to OFF stops gathering DB_CACHE_ADVICE statistics, and also the shared pool buffers are freed. The V$DB_CACHE_ADVICE view is not truncated; it remains intact. The instance doesn't need to be restarted to begin gathering statistics again. Answer E is incorrect because the DB_CACHE_SIZE parameter is not modified by the value of DB_CACHE_ADVICE.

12. B, C.

Explanation   Recycle pool candidates have almost the exact opposite access pattern as KEEP pool candidates. A good candidate will be large and infrequently used. Answers A and F are more like a KEEP object. Answers D and E apply to cached objects.

13. C.   1 − (physical reads − physical reads direct (lob) − physical reads direct) / (session logical reads)

Explanation   This formula, used to calculate the buffer cache hit ratio, is very important. Remember that we want to subtract the reads from the total logical reads when we calculate the hit ratio.

14. B.   XBH, VLATCH_CHILDREN, DBA_EXTENTS

Explanation   V$LATCH_CHILDREN will contain rows for cache buffer chains; look for a high number of GETS, MISSES, and SLEEPS. Use the ADDR column and query the X$BH table to determine the FILE# and DBABLK (file number and block number), which can be decoded with DBA_EXTENTS.

CHAPTER
6

Sizing Other
SGA Structures

n this chapter, you will learn how to size the remaining SGA structures and will learn specifically to

- Monitor and size the redo log buffer.
- Monitor and size the Java pool.
- Limit the amount of Java session memory used by a session.
- Configure I/O slaves.
- Configure multiple database writer (DBW) processes.

This chapter focuses on diagnosing and tuning the remaining Shared Global Area (SGA) structures: specifically, the redo log buffer and the Java pool. We will also discuss configuring I/O slave processes and multiple DBWn. In previous chapters, we discussed the larger SGA structures: the shared pool and the buffer cache. We also discussed the large pool, the User Global Area (UGA), and how to use DBWn processes. In this chapter, we will finalize our discussion on the SGA.

Sizing Other SGA Structures

At this point in our tuning methodology, we have already diagnosed and tuned the largest SGA structures. However, we have not completed our task of tuning memory and processes. The redo log buffer is very small compared to the buffer cache and shared pool, but it is very important to instance performance. The Java pool is used by the Oracle9*i* Enterprise Java Engine (EJE) to cache session state in memory, thus improving the performance of Java stored procedures and Java applications that run in the database. Properly sizing these two SGA objects leads to better system performance.

Also in this chapter, we will discuss both the use of I/O slaves to help the DBWn process and the configuration of multiple DBWn processes. These may not appear to be related to sizing the SGA, but they do impact system waits; we have added them here to complete the discussion on SGA and instance performance monitoring, diagnostics, and improvement.

Monitor and Size the Redo Log Buffer

When a user makes changes to the database with INSERT, UPDATE, DELETE, CREATE, ALTER, or DROP commands, the information required to reconstruct or redo the changes is written from the user's memory space into redo log buffer entries by the Oracle server process. The redo log buffer is used to cache redo entries before they are written to redo log files. Redo entries in the log buffer take up continuous, sequential space.

The redo entries in the redo log files are used for database recovery. The log writer (LGWR) process begins writing from the redo log buffer to the online redo log file or members of the active redo log group if the log buffer becomes one-third full, a DBWn process tells LGWR to write, or a server process performs a COMMIT or ROLLBACK. LGWR writes all redo entries that have been copied to the redo log buffer since the last write, so the buffer is flushed.

After LGWR writes redo entries from the redo log buffer to the online redo log file, the space in the redo log buffer for the redo entries that were written to disk becomes available for user processes to begin copying new redo entries into the redo log buffer. The buffer is circular; new entries are written over old entries that have been written to disk.

Sizing the Redo Log Buffer

The default value for the redo log buffer is OS-specific, but generally 500KB. The minimum size is 64KB. Increasing the size of the redo log buffer reduces the number and frequency of I/Os if the buffer is usually flushed by reaching the one-third rule instead of by frequent COMMITs. If the buffer is too small, then large transactions will force LGWR to continuously flush the buffer and write to the online redo log file. For most systems, 1MB is a sufficient size for the redo log buffer. Some systems that perform many writes may benefit from a larger buffer. There is no real detriment to using a larger buffer, except that the memory might be better used by other SGA structures.

Diagnosing Redo Log Buffer Inefficiency

On systems that have fast processors and relatively slow disks, server processes may fill the redo log buffer faster than LGWR can write the redo entries to the online redo log file. Generally, LGWR writes often enough to keep up with the server processes; however, if the redo log files are on relatively slow disks or disks that are very busy, then LGWR may not be able to keep up. Increasing the size of the redo log buffer will decrease the likelihood that server processes will have to wait for redo entry space and potentially reduce the frequency of writes to the online redo log file.

Our tuning goal then is to size the redo log buffer so that server processes do not have to wait for space to create redo entries. We can gather several statistics to help us diagnose inefficiencies and help us reach our tuning goal.

Redo Buffer Allocation Retries   To determine the number of waits for space in the redo log buffer, query the V$SYSSTAT view where the value of the NAME column is equal to redo allocation buffer retries. This value is the number of times user processes have had to wait for space in the redo log buffer to copy new entries.

```
SELECT NAME, VALUE
FROM V$SYSSTAT
WHERE NAME = 'redo buffer allocation retries'
/
NAME                                                                 VALUE
------------------------------------------------------------------ ----------
redo buffer allocation retries                                           6
```

Our tuning goal is for the value of redo retries to be near 0; and it should not be more than 1 percent of the redo entries. Use the following query to determine the redo allocation buffer retries ratio:

```
SELECT 100*(A.VALUE/B.VALUE) "redo buffer retries ratio"

FROM V$SYSSTAT A, V$SYSSTAT B
WHERE A.NAME = 'redo buffer allocation retries'
AND B.NAME = 'redo entries'
/

redo buffer retries ratio
-------------------------
                2.6315789
```

Waits may be due to the small size of the log buffer, log switching, or checkpointing. Because this value is greater than 1 percent, we should consider increasing the size of the redo log buffer. We may also look at tuning the checkpointing or redo log file archiving processes.

Log Buffer Space Waits   You can query V$SESSION_WAIT to determine if any sessions are waiting for log buffer space.

```
SELECT SID, EVENT, SECONDS_IN_WAIT, STATE
FROM V$SESSION_WAIT
WHERE EVENT = 'log buffer space'
/
SID        EVENT                          SECONDS_IN_WAIT STATE
---------- ------------------------------ --------------- -----------
        18 log buffer space                           120 WAITING
        41 log buffer space                           150 WAITING
```

Our tuning goal is to have no log buffer space waits. Waiting sessions indicate that the server process is waiting for space in the redo log buffer, which tells us that server processes are writing redo entries into the log buffer faster than LGWR can write to the redo log file. Basically, LGWR isn't keeping up. If the session is currently waiting, the value of the WAIT_TIME column is 0, the STATE column will have the value WAITING; the value of SECONDS_IN_WAIT indicates how long the session has waited for this event. If the session is no longer waiting, then the WAIT_TIME column indicates the length in seconds of the last wait.

If log buffer space waits exist, consider increasing the size of the redo log buffer or moving the redo log files to faster disks.

Redo Log Space Requests   The V$SYSSTAT view is also used to indicate that the online redo log file is full and that the server is waiting for the next redo log file to become available. LGWR can't write redo log entries to the online redo log file until the log switch completes.

```
SELECT NAME, VALUE
FROM V$SYSSTAT
WHERE NAME = 'redo log space requests'
/

NAME                                                                    VALUE
------------------------------------------------------------------ ----------
redo log space requests                                                     3
```

Digging Deeper

If LGWR isn't keeping up, we should investigate to see if there is I/O contention on the redo log files, if checkpointing can be improved, or if the archiving process can be improved. Also, DB_BLOCK_CHECKSUM=TRUE causes some minor performance overhead that may contribute to LGWR not keeping up; however, Oracle highly recommends we keep it set to TRUE.

Redo Log File I/O Contention   Verify that the redo log files are on separate and fast devices. Also verify that no other database files are causing contention for the redo log files. Query V$SYSTEM_EVENT for log file switch completion waits, which indicates the time waited for log switches. Also consider increasing the size of the redo log files to reduce the frequency of log switches.

Checkpointing   LGWR may be waiting because DBWn has not completed checkpointing the file. The following are a few items to investigate:

- Check the alert log for "Checkpoint not complete" messages.

- Query V$SYSTEM_EVENT for the log file switch (checkpoint incomplete) event. This indicates log file switch waits due to incomplete checkpoints.

- Verify the frequency of checkpoints and review the initialization parameters LOG_CHECKPOINT_INTERVAL and LOG_CHECKPOINT_TIMEOUT.

- Investigate the size and number of redo log groups.

Archiving   If you're running the database in archivelog mode, then it's possible that the archive process (ARCn) is not fast enough or is unable to write to the archived redo log file. If ARCn cannot write to the archived redo log file, it will prevent LGWR from overwriting the online redo log file that is waiting to be archived.

This can occur if you're archiving to significantly slower devices, such as tape. Check the V$SYSTEM_EVENT view for the log file switch (archiving needed) event, which indicates log file switch waits due to archiving. You can increase the number of ARCn processes by increasing the value of the initialization parameter LOG_ARCHIVE_MAX_PROCESSES; the default is 1.

Reducing Redo Operations

There are a few ways to decrease redo log activity during bulk load operations. Using the direct path option with SQL*Loader and using NOLOGGING can significantly reduce redo log entries.

SQL*Loader Redo Generation   When you use SQL*Loader to bulk load data into the database, you have a choice between conventional and direct path loads. Conventional path loads cause redo log entries. With direct path loads, redo log entries are not generated if the database is in noarchivelog mode. If the database is in archivelog mode and you're using direct path, you can use the UNRECOVERABLE clause in the loader control file or use the NOLOGGING option on the database table to avoid logging redo.

You can use the NOLOGGING clause when you CREATE or ALTER a table, tablespace, or index. When you set NOLOGGING for a tablespace, objects created in the tablespace will have the NOLOGGING attribute set by default, unless you specifically override the default.

Setting this significantly reduces the amount of redo that is written to the redo log buffer. Some minimal logging still occurs, but data changes are not recorded in the redo log buffer. After the bulk load completes, you can use the LOGGING clause to begin generating redo log entries for the object.

SQL Statements and NOLOGGING   If the NOLOGGING attribute is set for a table or index, only certain SQL statements will be affected.

Use the NOLOGGING clause with CREATE TABLE, CREATE TABLE . . . AS SELECT, CREATE INDEX, and ALTER INDEX . . . REBUILD to significantly reduce redo log activity and improve the performance of the statement. UPDATE, DELETE, conventional path INSERT, and other Data Definition Language (DDL) statements will still create redo entries even if the table is created with NOLOGGING specified.

Query the LOGGING column in DBA_TABLES, DBA_TABLESPACES, and DBA_INDEXES to determine if the NOLOGGING attribute has been set. LOGGING=NO indicates NOLOGGING was specified for the object.

Monitor and Size the Java Pool

The Oracle9*i* Java Virtual Machine (JVM), also known as the Oracle9*i* EJE, uses memory from the shared pool and the Java pool. If you are using the Oracle9*i* JVM, you should monitor memory usage in both pools.

Java and the Shared Pool

Shared pool memory is used by the EJE class loader, which uses on average about 8KB for each loaded class. Memory in the shared pool is used when loading and resolving Java classes into the database, when compiling source code in the database, or when using Java resource objects in the database. If you use the initjvm.sql script to create the Java binaries in a database, or load large JAR files, the SHARED_POOL_SIZE should be set to at least 50MB. Shared pool memory is consumed when you use the loadjava utility, when you create call specifications, and when the system tracks dynamically loaded Java classes at run time.

Java Pool Usage

The Oracle9*i* EJE memory manager allocates all other Java state memory from the Java pool during run-time execution. This memory includes the shared in-memory representation of the Java method and class definitions, and the Java objects that are migrated to the Java session space at end-of-call. Documentation states that the default size of the Java pool is 20MB; however, the default on my Oracle9*i* test instance is 24MB.

The default size is appropriate for most Java stored procedure usage. The JAVA_POOL_SIZE parameter is not dynamically configurable. If performance problems exist, you compile code on the server side, compilations fail, you use large applications, or distribute Enterprise Java Beans (EJB), then you should consider increasing JAVA_POOL_SIZE from the default value. For medium-sized Java applications, 50MB should be sufficient; increase the pool size for larger applications. The Java pool memory is used differently for dedicated servers and shared servers.

Java Pool and Dedicated Servers   Dedicated servers use Java pool memory for the shared part of each Java class used per session, which can on average consume between 4KB and 8KB for each class. The per-session Java state of each session is stored in the UGA within the Program Global Area (PGA), not in the Java pool within the SGA.

Java Pool and Shared Servers   As in dedicated servers, the shared server uses Java pool memory for the shared part of each Java class used per session. Java pool memory is also used for some of the UGA used for the per-session state of each session. To estimate the JAVA_POOL_SIZE required in the shared server environment, estimate the total memory requirement for the applications and multiply by the number of concurrent sessions.

Monitoring Java Pool Memory

The V$SGASTAT view is used to monitor Java pool free memory and memory in use.

```
SELECT * FROM V$SGASTAT
WHERE POOL LIKE '%java%'
/
POOL          NAME                               BYTES
-----------   --------------------------------   ----------
java pool     free memory                        28311552
java pool     memory in use                       5242880
```

The sum of free memory and memory in use equals the value of JAVA_POOL_SIZE. In addition to the V$SGASTAT view, the Statspack report SGA statistics section shows Java pool usage:

```
SGA breakdown difference for DB: OR9I   Instance: or9i   Snaps: 1 -2

Pool    Name                              Begin value        End value   % Diff
------  --------------------------------  ----------------   ----------------  -------
java    free memory                       27,934,720         27,934,720   0.00
java    memory in use                      5,619,712          5,619,712   0.00
```

Please note the value of JAVA_POOL_SIZE was 24MB when we queried V$SGASTAT; the Statspack report was from an earlier configuration in which the JAVA_POOL_SIZE was set to 32MB.

If you observe that the free memory is always low or zero, increase the value of the JAVA_POOL_SIZE init.ora parameter. Again, the parameter is not dynamic; an instance restart is required for the new Java pool size to take effect.

Limit the Amount of Java Session Memory Used by a Session

Java session space is memory that holds Java state from one database call to another. There are two initialization parameters that enable the DBA to limit the amount of memory used by a Java session.

JAVA_SOFT_SESSIONSPACE_LIMIT

This parameter enables you to specify a soft limit, or warn limit, on Java memory usage in a session. When memory is allocated in a session, the amount allocated is checked against this warn limit. When a session's session-duration Java state surpasses this limit, the Oracle9*i* EJE writes a warning message to the trace file. The warning has no impact on your application, but it helps you identify possible memory usage problems in your deployed classes.

JAVA_MAX_SESSIONSPACE_SIZE

This parameter places a hard limit on the amount of session space made available to a Java program executing in the server. This is useful for Java applications that are not self-limiting in their memory consumption. When a session's session-duration Java state attempts to allocate memory beyond this size, an out-of-memory error occurs, an ORA-29554 error message is displayed, and the session is killed. The default value for this parameter is set to a very high value, 4GB, so that it is normally not an issue.

Configuring I/O Slaves

If your OS doesn't support asynchronous I/O, you can simulate that behavior by configuring I/O slave processes for the DBW0 process and for Recovery Manager (RMAN) tape backup processes. The I/O slave processes only perform I/O. The initialization parameters DISK_ASYNC_IO and TAPE_ASYNC_IO indicate whether or not to use asynchronous I/O, if your OS supports it. Both parameters are set to TRUE by default; you can disable asynchronous I/O by setting the parameter values to FALSE.

You can configure I/O slaves for RMAN backup tape processes by setting the parameter BACKUP_TAPE_IO_SLAVES value to TRUE. RMAN only uses I/O slaves if asynchronous I/O is disabled (either your platform does not support asynchronous I/O or DISK_ASYNCH_IO is set to FALSE).

You can configure I/O slaves for DBW0 by setting an integer value for DBWR_IO_SLAVES. You do not have to turn off asynchronous I/O to use I/O slaves with DBW0. If asynchronous I/O is enabled and you configure I/O slaves, the I/O slaves will use asynchronous I/O. This is especially useful in database environments with very large I/O throughput.

I/O slaves for DBW0 are allocated when the first I/O request is made immediately after the database is opened.

The following lists the process that DBW0 uses to activate and utilize I/O slaves:

1. DBW0 looks for an idle I/O slave; if one is available, it will be used.

2. If there are no idle I/O slaves, the DBW0 process spawns one.

3. If the maximum of I/O slaves has been reached, determined by the value of DBWR_IO_SLAVES, DBW0 waits and then tries to find an idle I/O slave.

While this process is occurring, DBW0 continues to gather dirty buffers into a batch and prepares them for write. Then the I/O slave is called to perform the write on behalf of the DBW0 process.

The writing of the batch is parallelized between I/O slaves, so write performance improves in a write-intensive environment.

Configuring Multiple DBW Processes

By default, the instance is configured with one database writer process, referred to as DBW0.

Multiple DBWn processes can be configured by setting the DB_WRITER_PROCESSES initialization parameter to a value greater than 1 and less than or equal to 10. A maximum of ten processes, DBW0 through DBW9, can be configured. Because DBWn processes gather dirty buffers and write them to disk, configuring multiple DBWn processes is more effective than using an equivalent number of I/O slaves with one DBWR process. This parallelization of DBWn processes is useful on symmetric multiprocessing (SMP) systems with many central processing units (CPUs). Multiple DBWn processes cannot be used concurrently with I/O slaves.

Tuning DBWn Processes   The V$SYSTEM_EVENT view can be used to determine if you need to configure multiple DBWn processes. Query for the free buffer waits event:

```
SELECT EVENT, TOTAL_WAITS
FROM V$SYSTEM_EVENT
WHERE EVENT = 'free buffer waits'
/
EVENT                                                              TOTAL_WAITS
------------------------------------------------------------------ -----------
free buffer waits                                                           31
```

If you see a high number of TOTAL_WAITS, then consider increasing the number of DBWn processes. The DB_WRITER_PROCESSES parameter is not dynamically configurable, so an instance restart is required for the change to take effect.

Chapter Summary

In this chapter, we discussed tuning the redo log buffer and the Java pool and configuring I/O slaves and multiple DBWn processes. This chapter finalizes our discussion about tuning the SGA.

The redo log buffer is responsible for caching redo entries in memory until the entries can be written to the online redo log file. The redo log buffer is relatively small compared to the other SGA structures, but it is extremely important to write performance. Increasing the size of the redo log buffer from the default of 500KB to 1MB is generally sufficient for most systems.

The Java pool is used by the Oracle9i Enterprise Java Engine (EJE) to store shared in-memory representations of Java method and class definitions and the Java objects that are migrated to the Java session space at end-of-call. The default value for the Java pool is 20MB; you may need to increase it to 50MB or more depending on the size of your Java applications.

To improve the performance of dirty buffer writes to data files, you can enlist I/O slaves or multiple DBWn processes. I/O slaves can be used by the DBW0 process to parallelize writes to disk. Multiple DBWn processes also parallelize the dirty buffer gathering and batching process, so this option is more effective than using I/O slaves.

Multiple DBWn processes are incompatible with I/O slaves.

Two-Minute Drill

- The redo log buffer is used to cache redo entries before they are written to the online redo log file.

- The size of the redo log buffer is set by the LOG_BUFFER initialization parameter. It is not dynamically configurable.

- The default size of the redo log buffer is 500KB. Increasing the value to 1MB will usually improve the redo log buffer performance. Larger increases are usually not needed.

- The contents of the redo log buffer are written to disk when the redo log buffer is one-third full, a COMMIT or ROLLBACK is issued, or DBWn tells LGWR to write.

- The redo log buffer is circular, so new redo entries overwrite old entries that have been written to disk.

- Redo log buffer inefficiency is detected by querying V$SYSTAT for redo buffer allocation retries. The value should be near 0 and less than 1 percent of redo entries.

- V$SESSION_WAIT can be used to detect log buffer space wait events, which indicates the length of time server processes are waiting for space to be made available in the log buffer.

- LGWR may not be able to keep up with redo requests because of redo log file I/O contention, suboptimal checkpointing, or suboptimal archiving.

- Redo log file I/O contention can be caused by slow devices, redo log files existing on the same disk, data files existing on the same disk as the redo log files, or even undersized redo log files.

- Log file switch waits due to incomplete checkpoints can be remedied by modifying the size and number of redo log groups or by tuning the LOG_CHECKPOINT_INTERVAL and LOG_CHECKPOINT_TIMEOUT initialization parameters.

- If the database is in archivelog mode, you may need to increase the number of ARCn processes by setting the LOG_ARCHIVE_MAX_PROCESSES initialization parameter or by moving the archived redo log file destination to a faster device.

- You can reduce redo log entry generation by using SQL*Loader direct path loads instead of conventional path loads and by using the NOLOGGING clause.

- The shared pool and the Java pool are both used by Java processes in the database.

- The Java pool is used to store Java per-session Java state.

- In the shared server environment, the Java pool is also used for some of the per-session Java state.

- In the dedicated server environment, the per-session Java state is stored in the UGA within the PGA.

- The default value for JAVA_POOL_SIZE is 20MB.

- You may need to increase the Java pool size if you use EJE.

- Query V$SGASTAT for Java pool free memory and memory in use.

- The JAVA_SOFT_SESSIONSPACE_LIMIT initialization parameter places a soft limit on the amount of memory used by a Java session. If the session-duration Java state surpasses this value, a warning message is written to the trace file.

- The JAVA_MAX_SESSIONSPACE_SIZE is a hard memory limit, which is set artificially high at 4GB. When this value is reached, the session is killed with an out-of-memory error.

- I/O slaves are configured by setting the init.ora parameter DBWR_IO_SLAVES for disk I/O and BACKUP_TAPE_IO_SLAVES for RMAN tape I/O slaves.

- DBWn I/O slaves assist the DBWn process by writing dirty blocks to disk in parallel.

- I/O slaves start up immediately after the database is open and the first I/O request is made.

- You can configure up to ten DBWn processes (DBW0 through DBW9) by setting the initialization parameter DB_WRITER_PROCESSES to a positive integer value less than or equal to 10. The default value is 1.

- DBWn processes are more effective than the same number of I/O slaves because they gather dirty buffers and write them to disk in parallel with each other, whereas I/O slaves simply perform the I/O for a single DBWn process that performs all the dirty block gathering.

- Query V$SYSTEM_EVENT for the free buffer waits event. If the TOTAL_WAITS is high, consider increasing the number of DBWn processes.

Chapter Questions

1. **You notice that the redo buffer retries ratio is 5 percent. Which of the following is a viable remedy?**

   A. Move the archive redo log file destination to a slower device.

   B. Decrease the size of the redo log buffer.

   C. Increase the size of the redo log buffer.

   D. Decrease the size of the redo log files.

2. **What happens when a Java session's session-duration Java state surpasses the value of JAVA_SOFT_SESSIONSPACE_LIMIT?**

   A. The session is killed.

   B. An ORA-29554 error message is written to the alert log.

   C. An out-of-memory error occurs.

   D. The Java pool dynamically expands to meet the Java session's memory requirements.

   E. A warning message is written to the trace file.

3. Which of the following would *not* lead you to increase the size of the Java pool?

   A. The shared server environment is used with the Oracle9*i* EJE.

   B. The Oracle9*i* EJE is not used.

   C. New Java stored procedures are being added to your application.

   D. The Java application is considered large.

   E. V$SGASTAT indicates a low percentage of Java pool free memory.

4. Your server has multiple CPUs and the OS supports asynchronous I/O, and you note that the free buffer waits event is high and increasing. Which of the following is a viable solution?

   A. Dynamically increase the number of LGWR processes.

   B. Increase the value of the DB_WRITER_PROCESSES initialization parameter and restart the instance.

   C. Dynamically add more I/O slaves.

   D. Increase the size of the redo log buffer.

   E. Increase the size of the Java pool.

5. Which of the following will *not* benefit from the NOLOGGING attribute? (Choose two.)

   A. CREATE INDEX

   B. Conventional path data loads

   C. Direct path data loads when the database is in noarchivelog mode

   D. CREATE TABLE ... AS SELECT

   E. Direct path data loads when the database is in archivelog mode

6. Which of the following would lead you to configure multiple DBWn processes? (Choose three.)

   A. Your server is a uniprocessor system.

   B. Your server is an SMP system.

   C. Free buffer waits are high.

   D. Your application is write-intensive.

   E. All of the database files are on one disk.

Answers to Chapter Questions

1. C. Increase the size of the redo log buffer.

Explanation When the number of redo buffer allocation retries is greater than 1 percent of the number of redo entries, then we should consider increasing the size of the redo log buffer. The redo buffer allocation retries are indicators of waits for space in the redo log buffer. Answer A will not improve the waits; it will increase waits for the redo log switch. Answer B is not correct because that will more than likely increase the number of retries. Answer D is not correct because that will cause more frequent log switching and contribute to waits.

2. E. A warning message is written to the trace file.

Explanation Because this is a soft limit, only a warning is written to the trace file. The session itself is not interrupted. Answers A, B, and C occur when the JAVA_MAX_SESSIONSPACE_SIZE parameter value is surpassed. Answer D is incorrect because the Java pool does not dynamically expand to meet session state needs.

3. B. The Oracle9*i* EJE is not used.

Explanation If you do not use the Oracle9*i* EJE, then the Java pool is not needed, and you can set the JAVA_POOL_SIZE to 0. All of the other answers would lead you to increase the size of the Java pool. If you are using shared servers with the EJE, then you'll need more memory allocated to the Java pool. Adding more Java stored procedures or supporting a large Java application at the server requires a larger Java pool. If V$SGASTAT indicates a low percentage of free memory in the Java pool, then you should increase the size of the Java pool. The JAVA_POOL_SIZE parameter is not dynamically configurable.

4. B. Increase the value of the DB_WRITER_PROCESSES initialization parameter and restart the instance.

Explanation Free buffer waits are indicators that the DBWn process is not keeping up with demand, so increasing the number of DBWn processes should be our solution. The DB_WRITER_PROCESSES parameter determines the number of DBWn processes that will be configured for the instance. This parameter is not dynamically configurable, so a restart is required for it to take effect. Answer A is not correct because there is only one LGWR process. Answer C is not correct; I/O slaves would not be our optimal choice because our system has multiple CPUs and supports asynchronous I/O. With a single CPU system, we might consider I/O slaves instead of multiple DBWn processes. Answer D is not correct because free buffer waits are related to the buffer cache, not the redo log buffer. Answer E is incorrect because the problem is not related to the Java pool.

5. B, C.   Conventional path data loads, and direct path data loads when the database is in noarchivelog mode

Explanation   Conventional path data loads generate redo logging just like other Data Manipulation Language (DML) statements, so the NOLOGGING attribute has no effect. When the database is in noarchivelog mode, direct path data loads do not generate redo; therefore, the NOLOGGING attribute is irrelevant. Answers A, D, and E all benefit from the NOLOGGING attribute. Answers A and D are two SQL statements that utilize NOLOGGING to improve performance.

6. B, C, D.   Your server is an SMP system, free buffer waits are high, or your application is write-intensive.

Explanation   Multiple DBWn processes can alleviate performance bottlenecks if your system has multiple CPUs and the application is write-intensive. If you have a single-CPU system, processes are not running in parallel and must wait for each other; therefore, multiple DBWn processes wouldn't help with I/O. If free buffer waits are high, then processes are waiting for free buffers; this is an indicator that DBWn isn't keeping up with the dirty buffers that need to be written to disk. Answer E is incorrect because if all of the database files are on one disk, then having multiple DBWn processes attempting to write to the same disk will cause contention.

CHAPTER
7

Database Configuration
and I/O Issues

n this chapter, you will learn how to diagnose and optimally configure database I/O and will learn specifically to

■ Describe reasons for distributing different Oracle file types.

■ Describe reasons for partitioning data in tablespaces.

■ Diagnose inappropriate use of tablespaces.

■ Tune full table scan (FTS) operations.

■ Describe how checkpoints work.

■ Monitor and tune checkpoints.

■ Monitor and tune redo logs.

This chapter focuses on configuring the database so that I/O problems are minimized. We will first discuss the reasons for distributing different Oracle file types, and then demonstrate ways to diagnose I/O-related performance problems. We will discuss the inappropriate use of tablespaces and learn how to tune FTSs. We complete the chapter by discussing how checkpoints impact performance and how to tune redo logs.

Database Configuration and I/O Issues

During the database configuration phase of the application development process, the DBA is responsible for determining an optimal layout for the database files. It is important for you to get the physical database configuration correct, so that I/O is balanced and problems are minimized. It is also important at this time to understand the expected I/O volume and frequency, or average load. With that information, you can determine optimal checkpoint frequency and redo log file size.

Describe Reasons for Distributing Different Oracle File Types

Each of the Oracle processes in an instance has different responsibilities, and therefore each has different interactions with files:

■ Archiver (ARCn) reads and writes control files, reads from redo log files, and writes to archived redo log files.

■ Checkpoint (CKPT) writes to datafile headers and control files.

■ Database writer (DBWn) writes dirty buffers to datafiles.

- Log writer (LGWR) writes redo entries into redo log files.

- Server processes read from datafiles; sort direct write server processes write to datafiles.

Because we know that each process reads or writes to a different type of file associated with the Oracle database, we can build a plan to place the different types of files on different disks, so that contention is kept to a minimum.

The performance guidelines for database configuration are straightforward: keep disk I/O to a minimum, balance the disk load across multiple disk drives and controllers, and use locally managed tablespaces when possible.

Distributing Files Across Devices

To help balance the I/O and prevent contention between Oracle processes, Oracle recommends a few simple guidelines to follow when you design the database.

Keep Heavily Accessed Files on Separate Disks   Database files that are continuously read or written to should be kept separate from each other to reduce contention. If a disk is overloaded, move one or more of the datafiles from that disk to a less-utilized disk. If one or more tables in a tablespace are heavily used, consider striping the tables across datafiles that are kept on separate disks.

Keep Redo Log Files on Their Own Devices   Redo log files, which are covered in detail in the "Monitor and Tune Redo Logs" section in this chapter, should be kept on fast devices separate from other types of files. The reason for this is that redo log files are written sequentially and almost continuously by the LGWR process, and contention can occur if the I/O subsystem has to meet requests for other files on the same device. Use of RAID-5 for redo logs is discouraged because of traditionally slower write times.

Keep Non-Oracle Data on Disks Separate from Oracle Files   Because most organizations strive to keep costs down, your Oracle database server may be responsible for other tasks, such as application or web serving. Although it is optimal to keep the server dedicated to running Oracle databases, you may have to share resources. In the case where you have to share your database server with other processes, make sure that you keep all of your Oracle files on separate disks from other applications' files.

Consider Using Raw Devices   On Unix and Windows NT, raw devices can offer I/O performance improvements. A system that has a high write rate may benefit from using raw devices or third-party software that is able to perform reads directly to disk. Generally, raw devices are not as easy for the DBA to manage as cooked devices; there are administrative trade-offs with using raw devices.

Striping

I/O balance can be achieved by striping datafiles across multiple disks. For tables that are heavily used, you should consider striping the tables across multiple datafiles that are on separate disks. Striping is beneficial in Online Transaction Processing (OLTP) systems because random access becomes more balanced and in Decision Support Systems (DSS) because parallel operations can read large volumes of data more quickly.

We will discuss two basic types of striping: OS striping and object striping.

OS Striping and RAID　In OS striping, a file appears to exist on one disk, but is actually spread across multiple disks. If your OS supports a logical volume manager, you can use it to optimally configure striping. Some of the criteria that go into stripe configuration include the following:

- **DB_BLOCK_SIZE**　The size of a single-block I/O request

- **DB_FILE_MULTIBLOCK_READ_COUNT**　The maximum number of blocks read in a single I/O request during an FTS

- **OS block size**　I/O size for redo log file and archive log file operations

- **SORT_AREA_SIZE**　I/O size for sort operations

- **HASH_AREA_SIZE**　I/O size for hash operations

- **Type of system**　OLTP or DSS

- **Low versus high concurrency of datafile usage**

A redundant array of inexpensive disks (RAID) improves reliability and safety, and different levels of RAID offer striping options. The following are general descriptions of some of the more popular RAID configurations:

- **RAID 0**　Files are striped across multiple physical disks. Read and write performance is good, but there is no file mirroring. Oracle recommends that you do not use RAID 0 for production database files.

- **RAID 1**　Mirroring, but no striping. It has a high safety factor, but has none of the benefits of file striping.

- **RAID 0+1**　Striping and mirroring. It has good reliability and read/write times.

- **RAID 5**　Striping and redundancy. RAID 5 does not use mirroring as in RAID 1, but achieves recoverability by using parity disks. RAID 5 is very popular because of the combination of safety, striping, and lower cost due to fewer disks required than mirroring. The striping is similar to RAID 0.

Read performance is very good, but write performance is affected because of the parity checking.

Your choice of RAID depends on your unique combination of cost, risk, and performance requirements.

Object Striping   One of the drawbacks of RAID is that you cannot control the physical location of an object or extents within a segment. If you manually stripe an object, you can specify which disks its extents reside on. With or without OS striping, you can manually stripe objects within the database across multiple disks. In order to manually stripe, you'll need to create a tablespace that consists of datafiles on different disks and build the object within the tablespace. You can then manually stripe the object by allocating extents to the object in the different datafiles, as shown in the following:

```
CREATE TABLESPACE APP_DATA
DATAFILE 'D:\ORACLE\ORADATA\OR9I\APP_DATA01.DBF' SIZE 10 M,
         'E:\ORACLE\ORADATA\OR9I\APP_DATA02.DBF' SIZE 10 M,
         'F:\ORACLE\ORADATA\OR9I\APP_DATA03.DBF' SIZE 10 M,
         'G:\ORACLE\ORADATA\OR9I\APP_DATA04.DBF' SIZE 10 M
/
ALTER TABLE RAILCARS
ALLOCATE EXTENT (DATAFILE 'E:\ORACLE\ORADATA\OR9I\APP_DATA02.DBF' SIZE 5 M)
/
```

You can also manually stripe an object by creating the object with MINEXTENTS greater than 1 and making the extent size too large for two extents to fit into one datafile. Manually striping can become an administrative burden, especially if you manage thousands of objects in many databases.

The Oracle Partitioning Option

With the Oracle Partitioning option, you can simplify the administration of object striping and benefit from the many other features of partitioning. With the Oracle Partitioning option, you can decompose a table or index into its own partition that is stored in its own segment, and even in its own tablespace, which can consist of multiple datafiles on different disks. When the table or index grows and new extents are allocated, they occur within the partition that grows; the remaining partitions are unaffected. You won't need to allocate extents manually to achieve striping as you did in the previous example.

In addition to specifying the tablespace for each partition, you can also specify other storage parameters, such as INITIAL, NEXT, and MAXEXTENTS for individual partitions. The following are some of the benefits of partitioning:

- Very large table scans can be reduced to the scanning of fewer partitions based on a range of values.

- Data can be loaded by adding a partition and purged by dropping a partition.

- The cost-based optimizer can find a more efficient access path by pruning unneeded partitions from a query execution plan.

- A partition can be taken offline while remaining partitions are kept online.

As mentioned, Oracle Partitioning is an optional feature. The following is a sample Data Definition Language (DDL) to create a partitioned table:

```
CREATE TABLE RAILCARS
(CAR_ID                 NUMBER,
 CAR_TYPE               VARCHAR2(10),
 HEIGHT_INCHES          NUMBER,
 LENGTH_INCHES          NUMBER,
 CONSTRUCTION_DATE      DATE)
PARTITION BY RANGE (CAR_ID)
(PARTITION P1 VALUES LESS THAN (250) TABLESPACE APP_DATA01,
 PARTITION P2 VALUES LESS THAN (500) TABLESPACE APP_DATA02,
 PARTITION P3 VALUES LESS THAN (750) TABLESPACE APP_DATA03,
 PARTITION P4 VALUES LESS THAN (9999) TABLESPACE APP_DATA04)
/
Table created.
```

Diagnostics

Oracle has supplied us with the V$FILESTAT view to monitor and diagnose I/O issues. We can also use the File I/O monitor in Oracle Enterprise Manager (OEM) and view the I/O sections of the Statspack report. It is crucial that you enable timed statistics in the database by setting the initialization parameter TIMED_STATISTICS = TRUE or issuing the ALTER SYSTEM SET TIMED_STATISTICS=TRUE command; otherwise, the reports will not indicate the time required to complete an I/O request, which is crucial information in our tuning effort. Use the views and the Statspack report to help you with a plan to balance I/O.

V$FILESTAT, V$DATAFILE, and DBA_DATA_FILES V$FILESTAT contains information about I/O for each database file. We can join V$FILESTAT with V$DATAFILE or DBA_DATA_FILES to get the datafile name. We are most interested in the following columns in V$FILESTAT:

- **File#** Join with V$DATAFILE file# or DBA_DATA_FILES file_id to get the datafile name

- **Phyrds**   The number of physical reads since database startup
- **Phywrts**   The number of physical writes since database startup
- **Phyblkrd**   The number of physical blocks read
- **Phyblkwrt**   The number of physical blocks written
- **Readtim**   Cumulative time spent reading, in milliseconds
- **Writetim**   Cumulative time spent writing, in milliseconds
- **Avgiotim**   The average time spent on I/O, in milliseconds
- **Maxiortm**   The maximum time spent doing a single read
- **Maxiowtm**   The maximum time spent doing a single write

Again, the timing columns will be 0 if TIMED_STATISTICS = FALSE. The following is a sample query:

```
SELECT FILE_NAME, PHYRDS, PHYWRTS, READTIM, WRITETIM
FROM V$FILESTAT A, DBA_DATA_FILES B
WHERE A.FILE#=B.FILE_ID
/
FILE_NAME                                    PHYRDS     PHYWRTS    READTIM    WRITETIM
------------------------------------------ ---------- ---------- ---------- ----------
D:\ORACLE\ORADATA\OR9I\SYSTEM01.DBF            2820        148       4381        278
D:\ORACLE\ORADATA\OR9I\UNDOTBS01.DBF             25        199         36        270
...
D:\ORACLE\ORADATA\OR9I\APP_DATA01.DBF             3         42          7         40
D:\ORACLE\ORADATA\OR9I\APP_DATA02.DBF             0         23          0         22
```

From these columns, we can determine the read and write hot spots. We can modify the query to calculate average read and write times, which will help us determine how to load balance our I/O.

Statspack   The Statspack report is an excellent tool to use because we can sample I/O behavior over a peak usage period, such as during a large payroll run or during month-end closing. The following is an excerpt from the report:

```
File IO Stats for DB: OR9I  Instance: or9i  Snaps: 1 -2
->ordered by Tablespace, File

Tablespace               Filename
------------------------ -------------------------------------------------
                Av      Av    Av                      Av      Buffer Av Buf
          Reads Reads/s Rd(ms) Blks/Rd    Writes Writes/s  Waits Wt(ms)
```

| -------------- | ------- | ------ | ------- | ------------- | -------- | ---------- | ------ |
CWMLITE				E:\ORACLE\ORADATA\OR9I\CWMLITE01.DBF			
	54	0	15.7	1.1	0	0	0
DRSYS				F:\ORACLE\ORADATA\OR9I\DRSYS01.DBF			
	73	0	12.6	1.0	0	0	0
EXAMPLE				G:\ORACLE\ORADATA\OR9I\EXAMPLE01.DBF			
	231	0	25.8	2.0	0	0	0
SYSTEM				D:\ORACLE\ORADATA\OR9I\SYSTEM01.DBF			
	332	0	18.4	1.4	8	0	0

From this report, you can see that the average read time for the EXAMPLE01.DBF datafile is considerably longer than for the others. You should investigate the cause: Are other Oracle datafiles on the same disk, or are there other non-Oracle processes running against files on the same disk? Is the physical device slower technology?

You'll also see the Tablespace I/O Stats section in the report just above the File I/O Stats section. Use the two sections to compare the tablespace average times to the average times for the individual files within a tablespace.

Diagnose Inappropriate Use of Tablespaces

From the beginning as a DBA, you've been told to keep user objects out of the SYSTEM tablespace and to keep tables and indexes in separate tablespaces. We'll take this opportunity to expand on these rules of thumb and add a few more reasons to keep different types of segments in their own tablespaces. We'll complete this section with a guideline for separating or grouping types of tablespaces.

Tablespace Usage Guidelines

We keep different segment types in different tablespaces not only to ease our administrative tasks, but also to keep performance problems to a minimum. Also keep in mind that if all of your tablespaces consist of files that are on the same disk, then performance will probably not be optimized. When we discuss performance tuning, the phrase "separate tablespaces" implies separate physical disks. Otherwise, the only real gains from distinct tablespaces are administrative.

The SYSTEM Tablespace   The SYSTEM tablespace is for data dictionary objects owned by SYS and some objects owned by SYSTEM only. No user objects should exist in the SYSTEM tablespace, and no user should have the ability to create objects there. Stored procedures are stored in the data dictionary, and therefore in the SYSTEM tablespace. Also remember that by default, a new user's DEFAULT tablespace is SYSTEM; therefore, you should always specify a different DEFAULT tablespace when you create a new user. If you do not specify a DEFAULT TEMPORARY TABLESPACE when you create the database, the SYSTEM tablespace will be defined as the temporary tablespace for each new user. If you define a default temporary tablespace and then later drop it, the SYSTEM tablespace becomes the default temporary tablespace. Query DBA_USERS for users whose DEFAULT_TABLESPACE or TEMPORARY_TABLESPACE = 'SYSTEM'; also, query DBA_SEGMENTS for segments that are in the SYSTEM tablespace and owned by a user other than SYS or SYSTEM.

Table and Index Segments   Keep index segments separate from their associated table segments. You've heard it mentioned that if both the index and its associated table were on the same disk, then contention problems would occur when performing index lookups. Some counter that because the index block is read first and then the table, it is OK to keep both segments on the same disk. However, contention can still occur when reading and writing because they are closely associated. Other reasons for separating tables and indexes include parallel query operations and updating tables with indexes defined on them through a cursor (combines reads and writes). It's a good idea to keep indexes and tables in separate tablespaces, and keep the underlying datafiles separated. Consider it another form of striping or load balancing.

Rollback and UNDO Tablespaces   Keep rollback segments in their own tablespaces, separate from other segments. Because of the dynamic nature of rollback segments, creating other objects in the same tablespace will probably lead to fragmentation.

In automatic undo management mode (initialization parameter UNDO_MANAGEMENT = AUTO), each instance is assigned one and only one UNDO tablespace for undo management. UNDO segments can only exist in an UNDO tablespace, so no other type of segment can be created in an UNDO tablespace.

We will discuss tuning rollback and UNDO in great detail in Chapter 10.

Large Segments, LONG, and LOB   Keep tables that have LONG columns in their own tablespace. Also, keep large object (LOB) segments in separate tablespaces from the table data. Regular tables, indexes, and clusters should be stored in their own tablespace. If you have a table that is 40GB in size, it's best to partition it into its own tablespace or tablespaces.

Temporary Tablespaces   Create temporary tablespaces to store temporary segments for sort operations. As mentioned previously, you can define a default temporary tablespace for users when you create the database; this is not the same as creating a temporary tablespace. When you define the default temporary tablespace, new users will use the default temporary tablespace rather than SYSTEM, as was the case in previous releases.

A user's temporary tablespace can be any tablespace, permanent or temporary. However, a temporary tablespace can only be used for sort segments. No permanent objects can exist in a temporary tablespace. Operations that use sorts include joins, index builds, queries with the ORDER BY or GROUP BY clause, and the ANALYZE statement. Each of these benefits from using a temporary tablespace. Chapter 8 describes tuning sort operations.

Locally Managed Tablespaces

Use locally managed tablespaces to reduce the amount of data dictionary updates and therefore I/O on the system tablespace caused by space operations. Locally managed tablespaces use bitmaps instead of data dictionary tables to track used and free space. The performance and manageability of locally managed tablespaces is so much better than dictionary managed that beginning in Oralcle9*i*, it is now the default for non-SYSTEM permanent tablespaces.

Guidelines for Grouping Files on the Same Disk   In the ideal DBA world, we would have separate fast and cheap devices for each of our tablespaces and database files. This is rarely the case. We usually have to compromise and put files of different types on the same disk. The following are some general guidelines to follow when you have to spread datafiles across a limited number of disks:

- Put redo log files, control files, and dump destinations on the same disk.

- Put all UNDO or rollback segments on the same disk.

- Put table-only datafiles with index-only datafiles if the indexes are not associated with the tables (noncontending).

To avoid inefficient groupings of datafiles, use the following guidelines:

- Rollback and redo should not be on the same devices.

- Index, SYSTEM, UNDO, or rollback should not be on the same devices as data tablespaces.

- Do not place temporary tablespaces on the same disks as datafiles.

Tune Full Table Scan Operations

Full table scans (FTSs) are usually performance killers. If unintentional, they cause too many reads and contribute to other I/O problems. In V$FILESTAT or the Statspack report File I/O section, look for many I/O on one tablespace or datafile; this is usually an indicator that you have one or more untuned queries that perform FTSs.

V$SYSSTAT   Query V$SYSTAT to determine how many FTSs have taken place in the database since startup:

```
SELECT NAME, VALUE
FROM V$SYSSTAT
WHERE NAME LIKE '%table scan%'
/
NAME                                                             VALUE
---------------------------------------------------------- ----------
table scans (short tables)                                         208
table scans (long tables)                                          125
table scans (rowid ranges)                                           0
table scans (cache partitions)                                       0
table scans (direct read)                                            0
table scan rows gotten                                          570294
table scan blocks gotten                                         49044
7 rows selected.
```

The values for table scans (long tables) and (short tables) are what we're interested in. Long table scans are the total number of FTSs performed on tables with more than five db_blocks. Indexes should be used on long tables if more than 10 to 20 percent of the rows from the table are returned. Short table scans are the number of FTSs performed on tables with less than five db_blocks. It is optimal to perform FTSs on short tables rather than using indexes.

Monitoring Full Table Scans   You can query the V$SESSION_LONGOPS view to monitor FTSs on tables that exceed 10,000 formatted blocks and estimate their completion time.

```
SELECT SID, SERIAL#, OPNAME, TO_CHAR(START_TIME, 'HH:MI:SS') "START TIME",
SOFAR/TOTALWORK "% COMPLETE"
FROM V$SESSION_LONGOPS
/
SID     SERIAL# OPNAME                        START TI % COMPLETE
----- ---------- ---------------------------- -------- ----------
   47         121 TABLE SCAN                   03:58:39     .7581
```

You can join the SQL_ADDRESS column from V$SESSION_LONGOPS with the ADDRESS column of V$SQLTEXT to get the complete SQL statement that is executing.

DB_FILE_MULTIBLOCK_READ_COUNT   The DB_FILE_MULTIBLOCK_READ_COUNT initialization parameter determines the maximum number of database blocks read in one I/O during an FTS. This value can improve the performance of FTSs by reducing the number of I/O calls needed. The Oracle server process is constrained by OS limits on the number of OS blocks or bytes that can be read in a single I/O call.

DB_FILE_MULTIBLOCK_READ_COUNT is dynamically configurable for the instance and each session, so batch work can be tuned. You can control the number of I/O calls required to read a table in an FTS by setting the parameter. The tuning goal for setting DB_FILE_MULTIBLOCK_READ_COUNT is to perform fewer, larger I/O requests and improve the performance of FTSs.

The cost based optimizer is influenced by DB_FILE_MULTIBLOCK_READ_COUNT; if the estimated cost of an FTS is lower than the estimated cost of an index scan, then the optimizer will prefer the FTS. Because setting DB_FILE_MULTIBLOCK_READ_COUNT higher contributes to fewer I/O calls, FTSs may be preferred to index scans.

Describe How Checkpoints Work

The Oracle server uses a checkpoint to synchronize the modified data blocks in memory with the datafiles on disk and to ensure the consistency of data modified by transactions. When a redo log file is filled, Oracle must perform a checkpoint before switching to the next redo log file. At checkpoint time, the checkpoint process (CKPT) is responsible for signaling DBWn to write all or part of the dirty buffers in the database buffer cache to the datafiles. CKPT also updates the datafile headers and the control files to indicate the most recent checkpoint—that is, the highest system change number (SCN) for data block consistency written to the datafiles. A checkpoint generates many disk writes and thus causes a performance hit; the more datafiles in the database, the greater the impact.

There are five database events that cause a checkpoint:

- A redo log file switch

- Issuing the ALTER SYSTEM CHECKPOINT command

- Issuing the ALTER SYSTEM SWITCH LOGFILE command

- When LOG_CHECKPOINT_TIMEOUT is reached

- When (LOG_CHECKPOINT_INTERVAL × (multiplication sign) size of I/O OS blocks) bytes of data is written to the current redo log file

It is important to remember that a redo log switch triggers a *complete* checkpoint, whereas LOG_CHECKPOINT_INTERVAL or LOG_CHECKPOINT_TIMEOUT are used to configure *incremental* checkpoints, which don't signal a redo log switch. This means that there will most likely be redo entries in the redo log file after an incremental checkpoint. The most recent entry in the redo log specifies the end of the redo log file. The amount of redo between the checkpoint and the end of the redo log file influences recovery time following a failure.

Checkpointing Trade-off Between Performance and Recovery Time

There is a trade-off between performance and recoverability with checkpoints. More frequent checkpoints reduce the time needed for recovery following a failure because less redo must be applied to reach a consistency point. However, more frequent checkpoints can cause database slowdowns because DBWn must write to datafiles and CKPT must write to datafile headers and control files. Less frequent checkpoints may help performance, but may increase recovery time.

Monitor and Tune Checkpoints

You can monitor checkpoint activity by setting an initialization parameter and viewing the alert log, and also by querying V$SYSTEM_EVENT. By setting the value of LOG_CHECKPOINTS_TO_ALERT to TRUE, dynamically or in the init.ora file, Oracle will create an alert log entry for each checkpoint. You can then compare the timestamp for each checkpoint to determine checkpoint frequency. The following is an excerpt from the alert log:

```
Mon Nov 12 17:21:00 2001
Beginning global checkpoint up to RBA [0x1e.2.10], SCN: 0x0000.000cdfab
Completed checkpoint up to RBA [0x1e.2.10], SCN: 0x0000.000cdfab
Mon Nov 12 17:21:43 2001
Beginning global checkpoint up to RBA [0x1e.5.10], SCN: 0x0000.000cdfb0
Completed checkpoint up to RBA [0x1e.5.10], SCN: 0x0000.000cdfb0
```

Also check the alert log for error messages indicating that LGWR had to wait for the checkpoint to complete:

```
Checkpoint not complete: unable to allocate file
```

Another way to check on the frequency of log switches is to use the elapsed time listed at the beginning of a Statspack report and the DBWR checkpoints statistic under the Instance Activity Stats section. For example, DBWR checkpoints equals 9 and elapsed time equals 57 minutes, so the checkpoint frequency is about one every 6 minutes.

V$SYSSTAT   You can also query V$SYSSTAT for checkpoint process activity:

```
SELECT NAME, VALUE
FROM V$SYSSTAT
```

```
WHERE NAME LIKE 'background check%'
/
NAME                                                          VALUE
------------------------------------------------------------ ----------
background checkpoints started                                    6
background checkpoints completed                                  6
```

If the value of started is greater than the value of completed by more than 1, then checkpoints are not completing between log file switches; therefore, increase the size of the redo log files. Also, you can compare the number of blocks written by DBWn to the number of checkpoints by querying the same view:

```
SELECT NAME, VALUE
FROM V$SYSSTAT
WHERE NAME LIKE 'DBWR check%'
/
NAME                                                          VALUE
------------------------------------------------------------ ----------
DBWR checkpoint buffers written                                 162
DBWR checkpoints                                                  6
```

You can also view the Instance Activity section of the Statspack report for DBWR checkpoint statistics.

Initialization Parameters That Influence Checkpointing

As mentioned previously, the initialization parameter LOG_CHECKPOINTS_TO_ALERT tells Oracle to generate a message in the alert log each time a checkpoint occurs, which you can then use to determine the frequency of checkpoints. A checkpoint must occur when a redo log switch occurs. If you determine that checkpoints occur too often and are causing performance problems, you can decrease the checkpointing frequency by increasing the size of the redo log files, unless the frequent checkpointing is triggered because you have set LOG_CHECKPOINT_TIMEOUT too low.

If you have negotiated a recovery time service level agreement (SLA) with your business that requires faster recoveries from failure, then you may want to increase the checkpointing frequency by setting one or both of the LOG_CHECKPOINT_* initialization parameters.

LOG_CHECKPOINT_TIMEOUT　　LOG_CHECKPOINT_TIMEOUT is an integer value that specifies the maximum amount of time in seconds a dirty buffer can remain in the database buffer cache before DBWn must write it to disk. It is also the amount of time that the checkpoint position will lag behind the redo activity in the redo log. The default value is 1,800, or 30 minutes.

LOG_CHECKPOINT_INTERVAL LOG_CHECKPOINT_INTERVAL is an integer value that specifies the maximum number of redo blocks that the checkpoint position will lag behind the redo activity in the redo log. Redo blocks are the same size as OS blocks. The value of LOG_CHECKPOINT_INTERVAL cannot exceed 90 percent of the number of redo blocks in the smallest redo log file. This guarantees that the checkpoint position will be in the current redo log file before the log file fills up and a log switch occurs.

Checkpoint Tuning Guidelines

Checkpointing frequency is dependent on the transaction volume and frequency of data change in the database. Some OLTP systems may experience checkpoints every few seconds, whereas other systems have checkpoints several hours apart. The key thing to remember is that we should reduce the amount of performance impact caused by checkpointing, but still maintain a recovery window that is acceptable to our customers.

Fast-Start Checkpointing You can configure fast-start checkpointing to reduce the amount of time required for instance recovery by limiting the number of dirty buffers and the lag between the checkpoint and the end of the redo log. Older dirty blocks are written first to ensure that the checkpoint moves forward and stays close behind the end of the redo log. The initialization parameter FAST_START_MTTR_TARGET specifies the number of seconds for the expected mean time to recover (MTTR) the instance following a crash. Oracle will then vary the checkpointing processes to keep up with the MTTR. The maximum value for this parameter is 3,600, or 1 hour.

The FAST_START_IO_TARGET is similar to the MTTR setting except that you specify the upper bound on the number of dirty buffers. This has been deprecated in favor of FAST_START_MTTR_TARGET. Don't use LOG_CHECKPOINT_INTERVAL, LOG_CHECKPOINT_TIMEOUT, or FAST_START_IO_TARGET when FAST_START_MTTR_TARGET is set.

The V$INSTANCE_RECOVERY view contains information about expected MTTR, actual and target redo blocks for recovery, and estimated I/Os for recovery. This view can be used to help you determine realistic settings for SLAs and FAST_START_MTTR_TARGET.

Monitor and Tune Redo Logs

As we've discussed previously, redo log files are used by Oracle to keep track of redo entries and are used during instance recovery to recover committed transactions. A redo log group consists of one or more redo log file members. All of the members in a group are mirrored, so their size and content are identical. A database must have at least two redo log groups; three or more redo log groups are recommended. LGWR writes to the redo file members in a group sequentially and almost continuously, so for performance (and safety) reasons, you should place redo log file members in the same group on different fast disks that are dedicated to online redo log files. If you follow this simple guideline, then there will be very little performance overhead associated with mirroring redo log files.

When a redo log file switch occurs, LGWR begins writing to members of the next redo log file group. When a log switch occurs at the end of the last group, LGWR begins writing to members of the first redo log file group. Figure 7-1 shows one acceptable way to segregate redo log file groups and members.

Small log files can increase checkpoint activity and reduce performance. Therefore, you should size redo logs to minimize frequent log switches and contention.

Monitoring Redo Log File Information

There are basically six places to find out information about the redo log files: four dynamic performance views, the Statspack report, and the OS.

V$LOGFILE, V$LOG, and V$LOGHIST   These three views are used to monitor the redo log files. V$LOGFILE lists each redo log file member, the group each

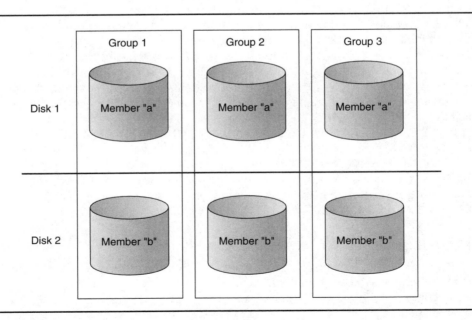

FIGURE 7-1.   *Redo log file placement*

belongs to, and the file status. V$LOG provides more detail, specifically the size of each group's members, the first system change number (SCN) in each group, and the status of each group.

V$LOGHIST has a row for each log switch, read from the control file. You can use this view to determine historical log switch frequency. This view indicates the date of the log switch and the first and last change numbers in the log file. The length of time that such information is retained in the control file is determined by the MAXLOGHISTORY clause of the CREATE CONTROLFILE (or DATABASE) command.

V$SYSTEM_EVENT   Query the V$SYSTEM_EVENT view for the log file parallel write event. Waits indicate a possible I/O problem:

```
SELECT EVENT, TOTAL_WAITS, TIME_WAITED
FROM V$SYSTEM_EVENT
WHERE EVENT = 'log file parallel write'
/
EVENT                                                            TOTAL_WAITS
TIME_WAITED
------------------------------------------------------------ ----------- -----------
log file parallel write                                              230
42
```

Statspack   The Instance Activity section of the Statspack report has entries for redo size statistics; look in the Event section for log file parallel write wait events.

OS Measurement of Redo Log File I/O   Within the Oracle database, there is no view that indicates I/O rates for the redo log files. Depending on your OS, you'll need to use tools outside of Oracle to determine I/O rates. On Unix systems, the IOSTAT and SAR commands are both useful for monitoring I/O on the devices that host the redo log files.

Archiving Redo Logs

If archiving is enabled in the database, be sure that you make the archive log destination some disk other than the disks used for the online redo logs. To make sure LGWR isn't writing to the same disk that ARC0 is reading from, consider moving redo log groups and members to different disks between redo log groups, as shown in Figure 7-2.

Information about Archived Log Files   If you're archiving, the V$ARCHIVE view contains information about redo log files that need to be archived; V$LOG has the same information, and Oracle recommends that you use it instead. V$ARCHIVE_DEST describes all the archive log destinations for the current

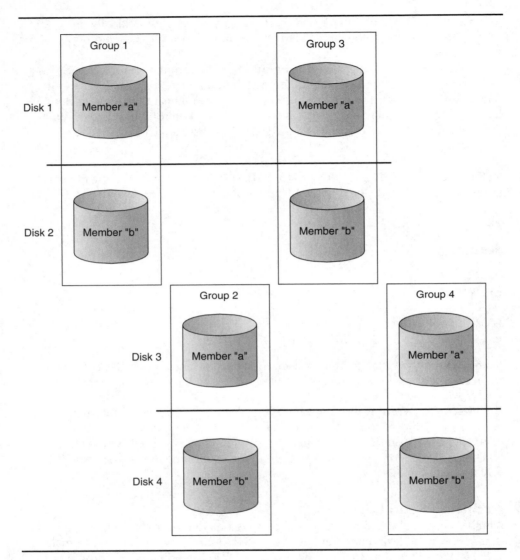

FIGURE 7-2. *Redo log file placement when archiving*

instance. V$ARCHIVED_LOG view displays archived log information from the control file. A record is added when an online redo log is successfully archived or cleared, an archive log is restored from a backup, or a copy of a log is made by RMAN.

The V$ARCHIVE_PROCESSES view gives us information about the ARCn processes for the instance. The STATE column value of IDLE or BUSY indicates if the ARCn process is active. The STATUS column indicates if the ARCn process is STOPPED, SCHEDULED, STARTING, ACTIVE, STOPPING, or TERMINATED. On busy systems, a single ARCn process may not be sufficient. With Oracle9*i*, you can configure multiple ARCn processes by setting the initialization parameter LOG_ARCHIVE_MAX_PROCESSES to an integer value between 1 and 10. If DBWR_IO_SLAVES is set to a value greater than 0, then 4 ARCn processes are automatically used.

You can start up additional ARCn processes by issuing the following command:

```
ALTER SYSTEM ARCHIVE LOG ALL TO 'directory name'
/
```

When V$ARCHIVE_PROCESSES or V$ARCHIVE indicates that two or more logs need to be archived, use the ARCHIVE LOG ALL command to spawn an additional archive process.

Chapter Summary

Because the Oracle database is dependent on datafiles that reside on disk, it is important for performance that we balance the I/O across multiple disk drives. Different Oracle processes create different I/O patterns, so we need to segregate the files that they use based on I/O balancing and reducing contention. We want to keep heavily used files on separate disks or at least away from each other. We want to put non-Oracle files on disks separate from Oracle. We want to keep redo log files and archive log files on their own disks. One way to balance database I/O is through the use of striping.

We discussed the process of OS striping datafiles by using RAID, striping database objects manually by explicitly allocating extents in different datafiles, and using the Oracle Partitioning option to improve query performance and ease the administration of object striping.

We can use the V$FILESTAT view to diagnose I/O performance problems for datafiles. The V$FILESTAT view does not contain the name of the datafile; we must join it with V$DATAFILE or DBA_DATA_FILES to look up the filename. You can also read the File I/O Stats section of the Statspack report to view I/O performance between two snapshots.

There are several guidelines for placing appropriate objects into correct tablespaces. The SYSTEM tablespace is reserved for objects owned by SYS or SYSTEM—the data dictionary, which includes all stored procedures. Users should never create their own objects or temporary segments in the SYSTEM tablespace. Temporary tablespaces should be used for SORT segments. Rollback segments should have their own tablespace, whereas UNDO segments are exclusively in the UNDO tablespace.

Tables and indexes should be kept apart. Also, LOBs that are stored out of line with the table data should be in their own tablespace, and tables containing LONG columns should be created in separate tablespaces.

Finally, locally managed tablespaces should be used to reduce data dictionary I/O due to space management requests.

You should be aware of the I/O contention that can be caused by putting table and index tablespaces on the same device and putting redo on the same device as any other database file or archive log file.

FTS activity is monitored by querying the V$SYSTAT view for a NAME like table scan%. Long table scans indicate that the optimizer probably can't find a usable index for a query and so it chooses to perform an FTS. FTS I/O can be improved by setting the initialization parameter DB_FILE_MULTIBLOCK_READ_COUNT to a sufficiently high number. This number is the upper bound for blocks that can be read with one OS I/O. You can monitor FTS operations with the V$SESSION_LONGOPS view.

The checkpoint is used to synchronize the modified data blocks in memory with the datafiles on disk and to ensure the consistency of data modified by transactions. The checkpoint process (CKPT) signals DBWn to write dirty buffers to disk, and then CKPT updates the datafile headers and the control files to indicate the SCN of the synchronization point. A checkpoint occurs when a redo log file fills up and must switch, when the ALTER SYSTEM CHECKPOINT command is entered, when a logfile is manually switched, when LOG_CHECKPOINT_TIMEOUT is reached, or when LOG_CHECKPOINT_INTERVAL is surpassed. You can observe checkpoint frequency by setting the parameter LOG_CHECKPOINTS_TO_ALERT to TRUE, and then monitor the timestamp for each checkpoint. V$SYSSTAT indicates if checkpoints are not completing between log switches.

LOG_CHECKPOINT_TIMEOUT specifies the maximum time in seconds that a dirty buffer can remain in the database buffer cache. LOG_CHECKPOINT_INTERVAL specifies the maximum number of redo blocks that the checkpoint will lag behind the end of the redo log file.

Redo logs are written to sequentially and almost continuously by LGWR, so they should be on separate fast disks. However, it should preferably not be done with RAID-5, as RAID-5 is not optimally configured for write performance. Query V$LOGFILE to list each redo log file group member; query V$LOG for more specific tuning information. V$LOGHIST has a row for each log file switch. The system event log file parallel write is used to analyze redo log performance.

Archive redo log files should be kept on their own separate device. If there are problems with the ARCn process not keeping up with demand, you can specify the use of more ARCn processes by setting the initialization parameter LOG_ARCHIVE_MAX_PROCESSES to a value between 1 and 10.

Two-Minute Drill

- The tuning goal for disk I/O performance is to balance I/O and reduce I/O contention.

- Keep heavily used files separate from each other.

- Keep non-Oracle files on disks separate from Oracle files.

- File striping can be achieved at the OS or hardware level with a logical volume manager or RAID.

- Object striping can be achieved within Oracle by manually allocating extents for a segment in separate datafiles.

- Object striping can also be achieved by using the Oracle Partitioning option to automatically allocate extents to partitions.

- Oracle Partitioning greatly improves the administrative functions required for manual striping.

- Oracle Partitioning also improves the performance of queries against large tables.

- Use V$FILESTAT or the Statspack report File I/O section to diagnose file I/O problems.

- Do not place nonsystem objects in the SYSTEM tablespace.

- Use temporary tablespaces for sort segments.

- Keep table and indexes segments in separate tablespaces.

- Use locally managed tablespaces to reduce system tablespace I/O and fragmentation.

- Use the V$SESSION_LONGOPS view to monitor long running queries.

- Set the DB_FILE_MULTIBLOCK_READ_COUNT parameter to improve I/O when performing full table scans (FTSs).

- A checkpoint is a synchronization point for the database.

- The CKPT process signals DBWn to write dirty buffers to disk.

- If checkpoints occur too frequently, there can be performance issues.

- Diagnose checkpoint frequency problems by setting the LOG_CHECKPOINTS_TO_ALERT initialization parameter, and then checking the alert log; or by using the elapsed time in a Statspack report and the DBWR checkpoints statistic.

- LOG_CHECKPOINT_INTERVAL is used to keep the checkpoints close behind redo log entries by a certain number of redo blocks.

- LOG_CHECKPOINT_TIMEOUT is used to regulate the length of time a dirty buffer can remain in the buffer cache.

- Redo log files should be sized large enough so that redo log switches do not happen so often that performance is affected.

- Redo log files should be kept on separate fast devices.

- If the ARCn process can't keep up with archiving requirements, you can specify additional ARCn processes by setting the LOG_ARCHIVE_MAX_ PROCESSES parameter to a value between 1 and 10.

Chapter Questions

1. **Which one of the following is *not* true about checkpointing?**

   A. A checkpoint occurs each time a redo log switch occurs.

   B. A redo log switch occurs each time a checkpoint occurs.

   C. CKPT signals DBWn to write dirty buffers to disk.

   D. Checkpointing causes significant disk I/O.

   E. A checkpoint occurs when LOG_CHECKPOINT_TIMEOUT is reached.

   F. ALTER SYSTEM SWITCH LOGFILE causes a checkpoint.

2. **You can monitor checkpoint frequency by which of the following methods?**

   A. Query V$SYSTEM_EVENT for EVENT = 'checkpoint frequency'.

   B. Query V$CHECKPOINT_HISTORY.

   C. Query V$LOG_HISTORY.

   D. Query V$SYSSTAT for 'checkpoint frequency'.

   E. View the alert log for completed checkpoint messages.

3. **Which of these scenarios describes an optimal configuration of the online redo log files when the database is in archivelog mode?**

   A. One disk drive for online and archived redo log files

   B. Two disk drives: one for archived redo log files and one for online

   C. Three disk drives: one for each redo log file group and one for archived redo log files

   D. Four disk drives: one for each redo log file member and one for archived redo log files

   E. Five disk drives: one for each current mirrored online redo log file member, one for each in the next group, and one for archived redo log files

4. What is an acceptable method for estimating an appropriate redo log file size? (Choose two.)

   A. Not so small that checkpointing occurs too frequently

   B. Not so large that checkpointing occurs too frequently

   C. Sized so that V$SYSTEM_EVENT indicates no log file parallel write wait events

   D. Product of LOG_BUFFER ×(multiplication sign) DB_BLOCK_SIZE initialization parameters

   E. Product of LOG_BUFFER ×(multiplication sign) DB_FILE_MULTIBLOCK_READ_COUNT

5. Which of the following is true about the initialization parameter LOG_CHECKPOINT_INTERVAL?

   A. The value of LOG_CHECKPOINT_INTERVAL cannot exceed 90 percent of the number of blocks in the database buffer cache.

   B. The value of LOG_CHECKPOINT_INTERVAL cannot exceed 90 percent of the number of redo blocks in the largest redo log file.

   C. The value of LOG_CHECKPOINT_INTERVAL cannot exceed 90 percent of the number of redo blocks in the smallest redo log file.

   D. The value of LOG_CHECKPOINT_INTERVAL cannot exceed 90 percent of the number of redo entries in the log buffer.

6. Which one of the following accurately describes the relationship between recovery time and normal operations performance depending on how checkpointing is configured?

   A. More frequent checkpoints improve operational performance, but slow down recovery following a crash.

   B. More frequent checkpoints improve recovery time and also improve operational performance.

    C. Less frequent checkpoints improve both operational performance and recovery time.

    D. Less frequent checkpoints degrade operational performance, but improve recovery time.

    E. More frequent checkpoints improve recovery time following a crash, but can degrade operational performance.

7. **Which of the following is an indicator of inappropriate tablespace usage? (Choose three.)**

    A. HR objects are stored in the SYSTEM tablespace.

    B. UNDO segments and rollback segments are in separate tablespaces.

    C. User sort segments are created in a tablespace of type TEMPORARY.

    D. Rollback segments and user sort segments are in the same tablespace as user data.

    E. Indexes and tables are in the same tablespace.

    F. Stored procedures are in the SYSTEM tablespace.

8. **Given this information about a table in your database:**

    ■ You have estimated it will grow to over 500GB in the next six months.

    ■ Once it has grown to full size, new data will be added and old data will be purged every month, based on the value of a YYYYMM key.

    ■ Users will query the table on specific date-range criteria.

    Which of the following strategies would help you optimize performance?

    A. Use manual striping within Oracle, creating datafiles for each date range.

    B. Use the Oracle Partitioning option to create partitions based on the date key.

    C. Use RAID-5 to stripe the table across multiple datafiles.

    D. Use RAID-1 to purge unneeded data.

    E. Put each month's data into a separate table and allow user access to all the tables with a UNION ALL view.

    F. Set DB_FILE_MULTIBLOCK_READ_COUNT high enough so that the entire table can be read in one I/O.

9. **Which one of the following is an indicator of a performance problem in a particular datafile?**

   A. The Statspack report indicates that I/O averages for each datafile in a tablespace are comparable.

   B. V$FILESTAT indicates very high AVGIOTIM compared to other datafiles.

   C. DBA_DATA_FILES indicates very high AVGIOTIM compared to other datafiles.

   D. You note a higher than normal number of physical reads in the Statspack report.

   E. All the nonsystem rollback segments are in one tablespace.

10. **Which of these is *not* an advantage of Oracle partitioning over manual striping? (Choose two.)**

    A. Each partition can be assigned to its own tablespace and datafiles.

    B. Extent allocation is manual with the Oracle Partitioning option.

    C. The cost-based optimizer can choose better-performing execution plans by pruning partitions that aren't needed by the query.

    D. RAID-5 isn't compatible with manual striping, but it is compatible with partitioning.

    E. The administration of manual striping is labor-intensive.

Answers to Chapter Questions

   1. B. A redo log switch occurs each time a checkpoint occurs.

Explanation The checkpoint process does not signal a log switch. However, when a log switch occurs, a checkpoint also occurs. The checkpoint process (CKPT) signals DBWn to write dirty buffers to disk when a checkpoint occurs. This is a synchronization point for the database. Checkpointing causes disk I/O; DBWn must update the data blocks, and CKPT must update the datafile headers and the control files. When the value of LOG_CHECKPOINT_TIMEOUT is reached, or when the ALTER SYSTEM SWITCH LOGFILE command is entered, a checkpoint occurs.

   2. E. View the alert log for completed checkpoint messages.

Explanation If you set the initialization parameter LOG_CHECKPOINTS_TO_ALERT to TRUE, then an entry is written to the alert log each time a checkpoint occurs. You can compare the timestamps for each checkpoint logged to determine the checkpointing frequency. There is no system event called checkpoint frequency. There is no dynamic performance view called V$CHECKPOINT_HISTORY. The V$LOG_HISTORY view tells us about the frequency of log file switches, but it does not indicate how many checkpoints occurred. There is no system statistic named checkpoint frequency.

3. E.   Five disk drives: one for each current mirrored online redo log file member, one for each in the next group, and one for archived redo log files

Explanation   To minimize contention between LGWR writing to the current online redo log and ARCH reading from the previous one, we need to keep log file members in adjacent groups on separate disks. Because we need a minimum of two log file members in a group for safety, and Oracle requires at least two redo log file groups, we reach the four-disk minimum. Add in another separate disk for archive log files, so that ARCH is not reading from and writing to the same disk, to make a total of five disks. If we're in noarchivelog mode, then a minimum of two disks is preferred.

4. A, C.   Not so small that checkpointing occurs too frequently, and Sized so that V$SYSTEM_EVENT indicates no log file parallel write wait events

Explanation   We want to size the redo log files so that log switches, and therefore checkpoints, do not occur too frequently and impact performance. We also want to make sure that there are no log file parallel write waits in V$SYSTEM_EVENT. Answer B is incorrect because larger redo logs imply fewer checkpoints due to log switches. Answers D and E are not useful calculations.

5. C.   The value of LOG_CHECKPOINT_INTERVAL cannot exceed 90 percent of the number of redo blocks in the smallest redo log file.

Explanation   LOG_CHECKPOINT_INTERVAL determines how far behind the checkpoint can remain from the end of the redo log file. The 90 percent maximum ensures that the checkpoint will be in the current redo log file when the log file is ready to switch. The other answers are incorrect because they base the 90 percent rule on a database object that is not used for this measurement.

6. E.   More frequent checkpoints improve crash recovery time following a crash, but can degrade operational performance.

Explanation   Frequent checkpointing reduces the number of redo blocks that must be applied after a crash to get the database to a synchronization point. At the checkpoint, all datafiles and the control files are synchronized. However, frequent checkpointing causes DBWn to write frequently, possibly causing I/O issues. The other answers are incorrect because they contradict the correct answer.

7. A, D, and E.   HR objects are stored in the SYSTEM tablespace, Rollback segments and user sort segments are in the same tablespace as user data, and Indexes and tables are in the same tablespace.

Explanation   Objects owned by users other than SYS should not be in the SYSTEM tablespace because they can cause fragmentation and contention. Rollback and sort segments should not be in the same tablespaces as user data; rollback and temporary segments should be in separate tablespaces. Indexes and tables should not be in the same tablespace. Answer B is appropriate; UNDO cannot share a tablespace with other types of segments, and Rollback segments should be in their own tablespace. Answer C is an appropriate tablespace recommendation, and Answer F is a fact.

8. B.   Use the Oracle Partitioning option to create partitions based on the date key.

Explanation   Because this table is so large, it makes sense to use the Oracle Partitioning option to help with both performance and administration. Also, because data will be rolled off and added in on a regular basis, date-range partitioning makes sense. Answer A is not possible, as we cannot guarantee that data for a particular data range will end up in a particular datafile without partitioning. Answer C is incorrect; RAID-5 does not enable us to directly stripe Oracle objects, but instead it stripes the datafiles across multiple disks. Answer D is nonsense. Answer E is sometimes referred to as poor man's partitioning; it does not guarantee performance gains, and administration cannot be simplified as it is with the Oracle Partitioning option. Answer F would not be possible because we probably don't have the technology to read 50GB with one I/O.

9. B.   V$FILESTAT indicates very high AVGIOTIM compared to other datafiles.

Explanation   A higher than normal average I/O time on one datafile indicates that there may be a problem. You can also calculate the average read time and write times separately. Answer A is not correct because we want to balance the I/O across datafiles in a tablespace. Answer C is incorrect because DBA_DATA_FILES does not contain I/O information. Answer D is incorrect because a high number of physical reads does not necessarily equate to performance problems; it is an indicator of high usage, but performance may not be affected. Answer E is not correct because all nonsystem rollback segments should be in their own tablespace.

10. B, D. Extent allocation is manual with the Oracle Partitioning option, and RAID-5 isn't compatible with manual striping, but it is compatible with partitioning.

Explanation Answers B and D are not advantages of using the Oracle Partitioning option. Extent allocation is automatic with the Oracle Partitioning option, and the extents will end up in the partition's tablespace. You do not need to manually allocate an extent. RAID-5 is compatible with both manual striping and the Oracle Partitioning option. Answers A, C, and E are advantages of partitioning over manual striping.

CHAPTER
8

Optimize Sort
Operations

n this chapter, you will learn how to optimize sort operations and will learn specifically to

- Describe how sorts are performed in Oracle.

- Set old and new sort parameters.

- Describe the operations that cause sorting.

- Differentiate between disk and memory sorts, and determine the number of sorts performed in memory.

- Create and monitor TEMPORARY tablespaces.

- Describe ways to reduce total sorts and disk sorts.

This chapter focuses on diagnosing and tuning sort operations. We begin the chapter with a discussion on how Oracle performs sorts and discuss the initialization parameters that affect sorting. Following our discussion about operations that cause sorts, we'll query our dynamic performance views to determine if we sort to disk too frequently. After we describe the use of sort segments and temporary tablespaces, we'll complete our discussion by describing options that reduce the sorting requirements of some common operations.

Optimize Sort Operations

Sorting is the process of ordering a list. Sorting is a way to make logical sense out of an unordered list of records, rows, or column values. We usually think of sorting in the sense of alphabetizing an employee list, listing checks or vouchers by sequential number, or listing budget items by dollar amount.

Internal sorts are those sorts that work on data entirely in memory. External sorts use work areas external to memory, usually on disk. Within the Oracle database, sort operations occur quite frequently and can cause performance problems if not tuned properly. Obviously, we want to tune our sorts to occur primarily in memory.

Describe How Sorts Are Performed in Oracle

Since internal sorts are greatly preferred over external sorts, Oracle server processes will sort as much as they can in memory before utilizing external work areas.

The Sorting Process

If the parameter WORKAREA_SIZE_POLICY is set to MANUAL, each Oracle server process will use up to the value of SORT_AREA_SIZE in bytes to perform a sort operation in memory. The value of the initialization parameter SORT_AREA_SIZE sets the size of the sort area. If there is too much data to be sorted entirely in memory, then the sort is split into phases and processed according to the following:

- The data to be sorted is split into smaller pieces called sort runs.

- Each sort run is sorted independently.

- When a sort run is complete, the sorted data is written to temporary segments in the user's temporary tablespace. Temporary segments hold intermediate sort run data while the server process continues to work on another sort run.

- After all the data has been sorted by this method, the server process merges the partially sorted data from the sort runs to produce the final sorted output.

- If the sort area is not large enough to merge all the runs at once, it will merge the partially sorted data in several passes to produce the final sorted output.

Set Old and New Sort Parameters

With Oracle9*i*, we have the option to configure the sort area size used by each server process, as in previous versions. In addition, we have two new parameters that enable us to configure an aggregate Program Global Area (PGA) that can be shared by dedicated server processes.

Sort Area and Parameters

The sort area is a component of the User Global Area (UGA), which is part of the PGA in the dedicated server process. The UGA and sort area are part of the shared pool when using an Oracle shared server process. You should not use shared server processes for operations that require large sorts; instead, use dedicated server processes to avoid shared pool fragmentation and space problems.

SORT_AREA_SIZE and SORT_AREA_RETAINED_SIZE   As mentioned in the previous section, if the WORKAREA_SIZE_POLICY parameter is set to MANUAL, then the value of SORT_AREA_SIZE determines how much space will be allocated to each server process for in-memory sorts. A single-server process needs SORT_AREA_SIZE for an active sort, and each server in a parallel execution needs SORT_AREA_SIZE bytes of memory.

SORT_AREA_RETAINED_SIZE indicates the size the sort area will shrink to or the lower bound of memory retained when a sort is complete. It is the amount of memory used by each cursor for the duration of a fetch. In a dedicated server process, the freed memory is not returned to the operating system (OS), but is retained by the server process. If you are using a shared server connection, the freed memory is returned to the shared pool; therefore, setting the SORT_AREA_RETAINED_SIZE to a value lower than SORT_AREA_SIZE is beneficial in a shared server configuration, but not so important for a dedicated server process.

When a query requires more than one sort, such as when you have sort-merge join and then a sort based on an ORDER BY clause, the server process needs a sort area for each sort. The operation will use SORT_AREA_SIZE memory for the current sort and memory equal to SORT_AREA_RETAINED_SIZE for each completed sort run that is still needed.

For parallel query processes, each server process needs SORT_AREA_SIZE memory. Parallel operations use a parent-child architecture to process the data. Parent operations can begin consuming rows as soon as the child operations have produced rows, so two sets of servers can be working at the same time. Calculate the memory requirements using these guidelines:

- SORT_AREA_SIZE $\times$ 2 $\times$ degree of parallelism for each active sort.

- SORT_AREA_RETAINED_SIZE $\times$ degree of parallelism $\times$ (total number of sorts-2). Because Oracle9*i* can automatically manage the PGA working memory, Oracle does not recommend using the SORT_AREA_SIZE and SORT_AREA_RETAINED_SIZE parameter unless you're using the shared server option. These parameters are retained for backward compatibility.

New Sort Area Parameters

If you're using dedicated servers, Oracle recommends that you configure PGA_AGGREGATE_TARGET and WORKAREA_SIZE_POLICY to enable automatic PGA memory management. When running in automatic PGA memory management mode, the sizing of Structured Query Language (SQL) work areas for all dedicated server sessions becomes automatic. To automatically manage the sort area size for dedicated servers, configure PGA_AGGREGATE_TARGET and WORKAREA_SIZE_POLICY; the settings for SORT_AREA_SIZE and SORT_AREA_RETAINED_SIZE will be ignored for all dedicated server processes.

PGA_AGGREGATE_TARGET   The initialization parameter PGA_AGGREGATE_TARGET specifies the target aggregate PGA memory available to all dedicated server processes. Set this parameter to a value between 10MB and 4,000GB to set the upper bound for PGA structures such as SQL work areas, which includes the sort area. When WORKAREA_SIZE_POLICY is set to AUTO, Oracle adapts the size of the sort areas to meet private memory needs.

When using automatic PGA memory management, sort operations are more likely to run completely in memory. An upper-bound starting point for determining the value of PGA_AGGREGATE_TARGET is to subtract the total size of the System

Global Area (SGA) from the total memory on your system that is available to the Oracle instance. If you have multiple instances running on the same server, be careful not to size the PGA_AGGREGATE_TARGET and SGA of the instances larger than real memory.

WORKAREA_SIZE_POLICY   When PGA_AGGREGATE_TARGET is defined, setting the WORKAREA_SIZE_POLICY to AUTO causes work areas used by memory-intensive operators to be sized automatically. The size of the work areas is based on the PGA memory used by the system, the value of PGA_AGGREGATE_TARGET, and the requirement of each individual operator.

When WORKAREA_SIZE_POLICY is set to MANUAL, the size of the sort area is equal to SORT_AREA_SIZE. This same rule applies to other work areas defined by the following initialization parameters: BITMAP_MERGE_AREA_SIZE, CREATE_BITMAP_AREA_SIZE, HASH_AREA_SIZE, and SORT_AREA_SIZE. MANUAL configuration can lead to suboptimal performance and poor PGA memory utilization if it is not configured properly for your system.

Statistics to Diagnose PGA Memory   If you're using automatic PGA memory management, then the V$PGASTAT view can be used to diagnose PGA memory utilization. The Statspack report also has a section for PGA Memory Stats. You can also monitor user memory by tracking the statistics *session uga memory* and *session pga memory* in the V$SESSTAT and V$STATNAME views.

Describe the Operations That Cause Sorting

The Oracle server process is responsible for sorting data during several types of common operations.

Index Creation   The purpose of an index is to provide a means to quickly find requested rows of data. Because the underlying table data in a relational database is not constrained by order, the index must be ordered to provide a quicker search mechanism. The server process, or processes if the index is created in parallel, must sort the indexed values before building the index. Sorting occurs when building both normal (B-Tree) and bitmap indexes.

Queries with DISTINCT, ORDER BY, GROUP BY, UNION, MINUS, INTERSECT, CONNECT BY, and CONNECT BY ROLLUP   A SELECT statement that includes any of the mentioned clauses requires a sort operation. A subquery will also generate a sort if it contains one of the clauses. For the ORDER BY, CONNECT BY, GROUP BY, or CONNECT BY ROLLUP clause, the server process must sort on the value or condition specified in the clause. For queries that include the DISTINCT keyword or the UNION, INTERSECT, or MINUS operators, the server process must eliminate duplicates.

Execution Plans with Sort-Merge Joins If there are no indexes available when making an equijoin request in a query with two or more tables, the server process may perform a sort-merge join. If the optimizer chooses a sort-merge join, the server process will perform a full table scan (FTS) of each table, sort each table separately by the value of the join column, and then merge the tables together based on matching the values in the join condition. The following is an example where neither table has an index:

```
SELECT NAME, VALUE FROM V$SYSSTAT WHERE NAME LIKE 'sorts (rows)'
/
NAME                                                              VALUE
----------------------------------------------------------- ----------
sorts (rows)                                                      10422

SELECT D.DEPARTMENT_ID, EMPLOYEE_ID
FROM MY_DEPT D, MY_EMPLOYEES E
WHERE E.DEPARTMENT_ID = D.DEPARTMENT_ID
/
...
...
106 rows selected.

SELECT NAME, VALUE FROM V$SYSSTAT WHERE NAME LIKE 'sorts (rows)'
/
NAME                                                              VALUE
----------------------------------------------------------- ----------
sorts (rows)                                                      10556
```

Even though only 106 rows were returned by the query, the number of rows sorted is 134 because there are 27 rows in MY_DEPT and 107 rows in MY_EMPLOYEES. An FTS was performed on each table, and the result was set for each table sorted and joined to satisfy our query.

Collecting Statistics: The ANALYZE Command and DBMS_STATS

Sorts happen when gathering statistics with the ANALYZE command, DBMS_UTILITY.ANALYZE_SCHEMA (or database) procedures, or with DBMS_STATS procedures. Data is sorted to provide summary information.

Differentiate Between Disk and Memory Sorts

When the internal sort process is too large for the in-memory sort area and has to use an external work area, the server process uses sort segments in the tablespace designated as the user's temporary tablespace. To monitor how many sorts occur in memory, how many occur to disk, and how many total rows are being sorted, query the V$SYSSTAT view and read the Statspack report.

Where Have Sorts Occurred?

V$SYSTAT tracks the number of in-memory and to-disk sorts, as well as the total number of rows sorted. To determine the cumulative sort statistics since startup, query V$SYSSTAT:

```
SELECT NAME, VALUE
FROM V$SYSSTAT
WHERE NAME LIKE 'sorts%'
/
NAME                                                                    VALUE
----------------------------------------------------------------  ----------
sorts (memory)                                                           2657
sorts (disk)                                                                3
sorts (rows)                                                             5495
```

The value of sorts (memory) represents the number of sorts that occurred entirely in memory; that is, no temporary sort segments were used. The value of sorts (disk) is the number of sorts that were too large to fit entirely in memory, so input/output (I/O) occurred when temporary sort segments were written to disk.

Determine the Number of Sorts Performed in Memory

To determine the ratio of in-memory versus to-disk sorts, use the following query:

```
SELECT 100*(A.VALUE-B.VALUE)/(A.VALUE) "In-memory Sort Ratio"
FROM V$SYSSTAT A, V$SYSSTAT B
WHERE A.NAME = 'sorts (memory)'
AND B.NAME = 'sorts (disk)'
/
In-memory Sort Ratio
--------------------
          99.8870907
```

In-memory sorts are greatly preferred; the ratio of in-memory sorts to disk sorts should be greater than 95 percent. If it is less than 95 percent, consider increasing the value of SORT_AREA_SIZE if you are not using automatic PGA memory management. Increasing SORT_AREA_SIZE will increase the size of each sort run and decrease the number of sort runs and merges required to complete a sort.

If you are using automatic PGA memory management, increasing the value of PGA_AGGREGATE_TARGET will indirectly increase the memory allotted to work areas. Consequently, more memory-intensive operations will be able to run fully in memory and fewer sorts will be performed on disk. Setting this parameter too large may result in paging at the OS level and poor performance within the database.

Sort Statistics in the Statspack Report

The Statspack report shows the total sort numbers as in the V$SYSSTAT view, but it also calculates the in-memory sort ratio. When you study the report, look at the Instance Efficiency Percentages section and the Instance Activity Stats section.

```
Instance Efficiency Percentages (Target 100%)
~~~~~~~~~~~~~~~~~~~~~~~~~~~~~~~~~~~~~~~~~~~~~~~~~~
          Buffer Nowait %:    99.08    Redo NoWait %:   100.00
          Buffer  Hit   %:    99.40    In-memory Sort %:  100.00
...
...
...
Instance Activity Stats for DB: OR9I  Instance: or9i  Snaps: 1 -2
Statistic                            Total    per Second    per Trans
-----------------------------------  --------  -----------  ----------
sorts (disk)                               3      0.0          0.3
sorts (memory)                           323      0.1         32.3
sorts (rows)                          18,095      5.3      1,809.5
```

Create and Monitor Temporary Tablespaces

There are basically two types of tablespaces: those that can contain permanent objects and those that cannot. The latter is called a temporary tablespace, because we cannot build permanent objects there. The temporary tablespace is designed for sort segments and therefore has performance and administrative advantages over normal tablespaces for sort operations. You create a temporary tablespace by issuing the following command:

```
CREATE TEMPORARY TABLESPACE TEMP_BIG
TEMPFILE 'D:\ORACLE\ORADATA\OR9I\TEMP_BIG01.DBF'
SIZE 1000 M
/
Tablespace created.
```

By using a temporary tablespace for external sorts, you eliminate the serialization of space management operations when allocating and deallocating sort space. You'll note that we used a TEMPFILE instead of a DATAFILE. A temporary tablespace must use a temporary file. One of the advantages of this is that the tempfile is not required for database recovery, therefore you do not need it in your database backup. Query the V$TEMPFILE or DBA_TEMP_FILES views to get information about the temporary files. You should also consider striping the tempfiles in a temporary tablespace. If you do not create a temporary tablespace, then the SYSTEM tablespace is used by default, as mentioned in the previous chapter.

The Sorting Process and Temporary Space Segments

Temporary tablespaces are exclusively designated for sort operations. The only types of segments allowed in a temporary tablespace are sort segments and temporary table segments.

A sort segment is created when the first sort operation uses the tablespace and is dropped when the database is closed. The sort segment grows as needed and is made up of extents that can be used by different sort operations. When a process needs sort space, it looks in the SGA Sort Extent Pool (SEP) to determine if there are free extents in the sort segment. The temporary tablespace contains a single sort segment per instance for Oracle Real Application Clusters.

It's important to remember that the default storage parameters for the temporary tablespace apply to the sort segment extents, and that sort segments have unlimited extents. Set PCTINCREASE to zero. Also, all true temporary tablespaces have locally managed extents, and all extents have the same uniform size. If you want to specify a uniform size other than the default, do so by using the UNIFORM clause and the SIZE clause.

In the previous version of Oracle, the practice was to set the initial and next extents to an integer multiple of SORT_AREA_SIZE plus one block for the segment header. This is no longer necessary when using temporary type tablespaces, which are locally managed. Make the initial and next extents an integer multiple of the DB_BLOCK_SIZE and an integer divisor of the SORT_AREA_SIZE. This practice of keeping sort extents smaller will not degrade performance and will make room for temporary table segments that may also exist in the same tablespace.

Monitoring Temporary Tablespaces

We monitor sort segments in temporary tablespaces by querying the V$SORT_SEGMENT view. We can also monitor the current active disk sorts for user sessions by joining V$SORT_USAGE and V$SESSION.

V$SORT_SEGMENT   Query V$SORT_SEGMENT to view information about every sort segment in the temporary tablespaces. The columns we're most interested in are

- **Tablespace_name**   The name of the temporary tablespace
- **Current_users**   The number of active users in the segment
- **Total_extents**   The number of extents in the segment
- **Used_extents**   The number of extents currently allocated to sorts
- **Free_extents**   The number of extents not allocated to any sorts
- **Extent_hits**   The number of times an unused extent was found in the pool

- **Max_size** The maximum number of extents ever used
- **Max_used_size** The maximum number of extents used by all sorts
- **Max_sort_size** The maximum number of extents used by an individual sort

We're most interested in extent usage; there are also columns that contain information about block usage. The following is a sample query:

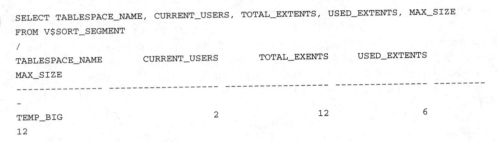

```
SELECT TABLESPACE_NAME, CURRENT_USERS, TOTAL_EXTENTS, USED_EXTENTS, MAX_SIZE
FROM V$SORT_SEGMENT
/
TABLESPACE_NAME       CURRENT_USERS        TOTAL_EXENTS      USED_EXTENTS
MAX_SIZE
--------------- -------------------- ------------------- ---------------- ---------
-
TEMP_BIG                        2                   12                6
12
```

Using V$SORT_USAGE and V$SESSION V$SORT_USAGE describes user sorting activities such as the extents allocated and the type of segment created. We're mostly interested in the following columns:

- **Username** The user who requested temporary space
- **Session_addr** The address of shared SQL cursor
- **Session_num** The serial number of session
- **Sqladdr** The address of SQL statement
- **Tablespace** The tablespace in which space is allocated
- **Extents** The extents allocated to the sort
- **Blocks** The extents in blocks allocated to the sort
- **Segtype** DATA for temporary table segments and SORT for sort segments

Join V$SORT_USAGE with V$SESSION to see which user sessions are using sort extents.

```
SELECT S.USERNAME, S.SID, S.SERIAL#, U.TABLESPACE, U.EXTENTS, U.BLOCKS
FROM V$SESSION S, V$SORT_USAGE U
WHERE U.SESSION_ADDR = S.SADDR
AND U.CONTENTS='TEMPORARY'
/
```

USERNAME	SID	SERIAL#	TABLESPACE	EXTENTS	BLOCKS
HR	13	227	TEMP_BIG	8	400

One thing to note: When creating a temporary table, an entry will be created in V$SORT_USAGE, and the SEGTYPE column will have the value DATA. After the sorting is done and the temporary table has been created, you'll see an entry in the V$TEMP_EXTENT_POOL view, indicating that temp extents have been allocated.

If you see patterns in V$SORT_USAGE where some users require larger disk sorts, you should consider moving them to another temporary tablespace with an extent size tailored to their sort needs.

Describe Ways to Reduce Total Sorts and Disk Sorts

Our tuning goal for sorts is to reduce or avoid sorts when possible. Reducing or eliminating disk sorts is our primary goal because disk sorts are much more expensive than in-memory sorts. We should strive to perform all sorts in memory. Set SORT_AREA_SIZE to a large enough value so that over 95 percent of sorts occur in memory, but not so large that paging and swapping occur. Our final goal is to reduce extent allocation issues by using temporary tablespaces instead of permanent tablespaces for sort segments.

Avoiding Sorts

There are several options we can use with our daily tasks to help avoid sorts.

NOSORT Index Builds   If the column values you intend to index are in ascending order, either because a bulk load was presorted or rows were inserted with ascending key values, you can use the NOSORT clause when you build the index to eliminate the sort phase of the index build.

UNION ALL Instead of UNION   The UNION ALL clause does not eliminate duplicates, so no sort is needed during the union phase of the query.

Use Index Access for Table Joins   Previously in this chapter, we discussed the sort-merge join, which required FTSs and a sort-merge of the result set. The nested-loop join based on index access offers performance benefits by reducing FTSs and eliminating sorts.

Create Indexes on Columns Referenced in the ORDER BY Clause   Create indexes on columns that are frequently used in the ORDER BY clause. Oracle will use the index to impose order instead of sorting.

Also, there is no need to use the DISTINCT or UNIQUE clause with a SELECT on a primary key, since by definition the primary key is unique.

Select Specific Columns to Analyze   Only generate statistics for columns that you intend to use in join conditions. Use the ANALYZE . . . FOR ALL INDEXED COLUMNS, or ANALYZE . . . FOR COLUMNS column1, column2, and so on. Also, there's no need to generate histograms for columns with primary key or unique constraints.

Use ESTIMATE Instead of COMPUTE   When you COMPUTE statistics, you use more sort space. Use ESTIMATE instead. For small tables you probably won't notice a difference, but you definitely will for larger tables. In addition to using more sort space, COMPUTE will lock the table. Also, be aware that ESTIMATE behaves like COMPUTE if you specify that more than 50 percent of the table should be used to estimate the statistics.

Chapter Summary

In this chapter, we discussed how Oracle performs sorts. A sort operation takes an unordered list and produces an ordered list. Some of the operations that rely on sorts are index builds, the gathering of statistics, aggregate operations such as GROUP BY, and of course, using the ORDER BY clause in a SELECT statement.

Oracle server processes attempt to perform sort operations in memory. The parameter SORT_AREA_SIZE is used to configure the amount of memory used for sorting by a server process. For a dedicated server, the SORT_AREA_SIZE is in the PGA; for a shared server, the sort area is in the shared pool. If you use automatic PGA memory management with dedicated servers, you can specify an aggregate pool to use for sort areas and other PGA work areas.

If the sort operation can't fit entirely into memory, the process must use sort segments on disk. We measure the ratio of in-memory to disk sorts by querying V$SYSSTAT or reading the Instance Efficiency Percentages section of the Statspack report. Oracle has designed the temporary tablespace type specifically for sort segments. The temporary tablespace type is more efficient at processing sort segments and does not allow permanent segments to be built in the tablespace. We can monitor temporary tablespace usage by querying V$SORT_SEGMENT and also view user session sort operations by joining V$SORT_USAGE and V$SESSION.

We can reduce total sorts by using the NOSORT option when building indexes on presorted table data. The UNION ALL operator eliminates the sort step of the UNION operator because duplicate rows are not removed. Use index access for table joins and also columns referenced in the ORDER BY clause. When analyzing tables, eliminate unneeded histograms, and use ESTIMATE instead of COMPUTE to reduce sorts.

Two-Minute Drill

■ A sort operation takes an unordered list as input and creates an ordered list as output.

■ The Oracle server process is responsible for performing sort operations.

■ The SORT_AREA_SIZE initialization parameter determines the in-memory sort area for each server process.

■ The SORT_AREA_RETAINED_SIZE parameter determines the size of the sort area when the sort operation is complete.

■ For shared servers, the sort area is in the shared pool.

■ For dedicated servers, the sort area is in the UGA section of the PGA.

■ For dedicated servers, we can configure automatic PGA memory management by setting WORKAREA_SIZE_POLICY to AUTO and PGA_AGGREGATE_TARGET to a value between 10MB and 4,000GB.

■ Automatic PGA memory management does not apply to shared servers.

■ In automatic PGA memory mode, SORT_AREA_SIZE is ignored for dedicated servers.

■ In automatic PGA memory mode, the sort area is within the memory allocated by PGA_AGGREGATE_TARGET.

■ Automatic PGA memory management enables larger internal sorts.

■ When the sort process requires more memory than can be met with SORT_AREA_SIZE or automatic PGA memory management, sort runs must be written to disk.

■ Sort runs are written to a sort segment in the user's temporary tablespace.

■ The tablespace type temporary is optimally designed for sort segments.

■ No permanent objects are allowed in a temporary tablespace.

■ A temporary tablespace uses TEMPFILES, which are not required for database recovery.

■ Monitor in-memory versus to-disk sorts by querying V$SYSSTAT where name like sorts%.

■ Sorts should occur in memory more than 95 percent of the time; if not, increase SORT_AREA_SIZE, configure automatic PGA memory management, or increase the value of PGA_AGGREGATE_TARGET, if feasible.

- Monitor sort segments by querying V$SORT_SEGMENT and by joining V$SORT_USAGE and V$SESSION.

- The Oracle SQL operations that use sorts include CREATE INDEX and queries with DISTINCT, UNIQUE, ORDER BY, GROUP BY, CONNECT BY, CONNECT BY ROLLUP, UNION, MINUS, and INTERSECT.

- Gathering statistics with ANALYZE and DBMS_STATS generates sorts.

- Query execution plans that perform sort-merge joins can generate large sorts.

- Our tuning goal is to reduce overall sorts and eliminate or avoid disk sorts.

- Use NOSORT on index builds where the key column data is already ordered in the table.

- Use UNION ALL instead of UNION if duplicate rows are not an issue.

- Use indexes for nested-loop table joins.

- Create indexes on columns referenced in the ORDER BY clause.

- Analyze on the columns that you'll join on, excluding primary and unique keys.

- Use ESTIMATE instead of COMPUTE for statistics gathering.

Chapter Questions

1. **Which of these SQL statements cause a sort operation? (Choose two.)**

   A. CREATE TABLE

   B. GROUP BY

   C. UNION

   D. UNION ALL

   E. SORT BY

2. **Which of these are valid reasons for using a tablespace of type temporary for sort segments? (Choose two.)**

   A. A temporary tablespace increases the allocation and deallocation of sort segments.

   B. Temporary files, required for temporary tablespaces, are automatically recovered in case of media failure.

    C. All extents within a temporary tablespace are uniform.

    D. No permanent objects are allowed in a temporary tablespace, so sort segment space allocation is optimized.

    E. Temporary sort segments should be allocated from the SYSTEM tablespace.

    F. The tempfiles are automatically striped, leading to better sort performance.

3. **From the following list, select the valid methods to reduce sort operations. (Choose two.)**

    A. Use the NOSORT option when building indexes on empty tables.

    B. Use UNION instead of UNION ALL.

    C. Use UNION ALL instead of UNION.

    D. Use sort-merge joins instead of nested-loop joins.

    E. Use the DISTINCT keyword with primary key searches.

    F. Use the NOSORT option when building indexes on presorted data.

4. **You're running your database in shared server mode, and note that the in-memory sorts ratio is 85 percent. What should you do?**

    A. Use automatic PGA memory management to help your shared server processes.

    B. Increase the value of SORT_AREA_SIZE, and also consider lowering SORT_AREA_RETAINED_SIZE.

    C. Increase the value of PGA_AGGREGATE_TARGET to help shared pool memory.

    D. Set WORKAREA_SIZE_POLICY to AUTO.

5. **Which one of the following queries will most likely require a sort-merge join?**

    A. Two-table equijoin with no indexes

    B. Two-table equijoin with one index

    C. Two-table equijoin in which both tables are indexed on the join column

    D. SELECT DISTINCT on a single table

6. **Which of the following accurately describe the sort area? (Choose two.)**

   A. The sort area is in the PGA in a shared server environment.

   B. The sort area is in the PGA for a dedicated server process.

   C. The sort area is in the shared pool when using automatic PGA memory management.

   D. SORT_AREA_SIZE is used to size the shared pool in automatic PGA memory management.

   E. SORT_AREA_SIZE is ignored for dedicated server processes when automatic PGA memory management is configured.

Answers to Chapter Questions

1. B, C.   GROUP BY and UNION

Explanation   The GROUP BY clause explicitly directs Oracle to aggregate the result set, which requires the atomic data to be sorted. The UNION operator requires a sort because duplicate values are eliminated. Answer A is incorrect—the exception would be the CREATE TABLE . . . AS SELECT when a primary key is specified. Answer D is incorrect because UNION ALL does not eliminate dupiicates. Answer E is not a valid SQL statement clause.

2. C, D.   All extents within a temporary tablespace are uniform, and the tempfiles are automatically striped, leading to better sort performance.

Explanation   A temporary tablespace is specifically designed to contain temporary sort segments. No permanent object is allowed in a temporary tablespace. All extents within a temporary tablespace are UNIFORM sized. Answer A is not correct, as frequent allocation and deallocation of temporary segments is a trait of permanent tablespaces. Answer B is not correct because temporary tablespaces are not recovered in case of a media failure, because no permanent objects exist in the tablespace. Answer E is wrong; we should never allocate sort segments from the SYSTEM tablespace. Answer F is incorrect; tempfiles should be striped for better performance.

3. C, F.   Use UNION ALL instead of UNION, and use the NOSORT option when building indexes on presorted data.

Explanation   Answer C is correct because UNION ALL does not require a sort, but UNION does require one. Answer F is correct because the sort phase of the index creation can be skipped if the data is already sorted on the index key value. Answer

A will save us nothing; no sort is needed because there is no data in the table. Answer B is the opposite of answer C, so it's wrong. Answer D is the opposite of what we want; nested-loop execution plans do not use sorts, but sort-merge plans do use them. Answer E is incorrect because the DISTINCT keyword is not needed with a primary key search; therefore, there are no savings.

    4. B.   Increase the value of SORT_AREA_SIZE and also consider lowering SORT_AREA_RETAINED_SIZE.

Explanation   Because we've specified that we're using shared servers, automatic PGA memory management will not be used. Increase the value of SORT_AREA_SIZE to increase the number of sorts that complete in memory. Answers A, C, and D are all related to dedicated servers using automatic PGA memory management.

    5. A.   Two-table equijoin with no indexes

Explanation   Because neither table has an index on the join column, Oracle must read and sort each table and then merge the two result sets together. Answers B and C will use a nested-loop join; Answer D will get a sort on the query, but no join will occur.

    6. B, E.   The sort area is in the PGA for a dedicated server process, and SORT_AREA_SIZE is ignored for dedicated server processes when automatic PGA memory management is configured.

Explanation   Answer B is correct because the sort area is in the UGA, which is part of the PGA in the dedicated server process memory. Answer E is also correct; when automatic PGA memory is configured by setting WORKAREA_SIZE_POLICY to AUTO and PGA_AGGREGATE_TARGET is set to a valid size, the SORT_AREA_SIZE is ignored for dedicated server processes. Answer A is incorrect because the sort area is in the UGA, which is part of the shared pool in a shared server connection. Answer C is incorrect because the sort area is allocated from the PGA aggregate when using automatic PGA memory management. Answer D is also wrong. SORT_AREA_SIZE is not used to size the shared pool.

CHAPTER
9

Diagnosing Contention for Latches

n this chapter, we will discuss identifying contention for latches, and you will learn specifically to

■ Describe the purpose of latches.

■ Describe the different types of latch requests.

■ Describe how to diagnose contention for latches.

■ Identify the resources to be tuned to minimize latch contention.

This chapter focuses on diagnosing contention for latches. We will begin the chapter with an introduction to latches—what they are, their purpose, and what latch contention indicates. We will discuss the two types of latch requests: immediate and willing to wait. We will then look at the tools for diagnosing latch contention: dynamic performance views and the Statspack report. Once we have learned how to identify the latches contended for, we will discuss ways to reduce contention for specific latches.

Diagnosing Contention for Latches

We know from previous chapters that database processes continuously access data structures in the System Global Area (SGA) and that different database processes are likely to attempt to access the same data structures at the same time. For example, server processes scan the buffer cache least recently used (LRU) list to find a free buffer. It is essential that a data structure can only be modified by one process at a time and that a data structure cannot be modified while another process is scanning it. To prevent two or more processes from modifying the same data structure at the same time, Oracle uses either locks or latches. We will discuss locks in a later chapter; we will discuss latches in this chapter.

Describe the Purpose of Latches

Latches protect shared data structures in the SGA and protect shared memory allocations. A server or background process requests a latch on a data structure and acquires a latch for a brief time (usually microseconds) while scanning or modifying the structure. For example, the LRU latch is used to protect the LRU list when server processes need to access the buffer cache. Latches also prevent the simultaneous execution of specific critical pieces of code.

What Are Latches?
Latches are simple and efficient low-level serialization mechanisms. They serialize access to data structures and shared memory allocations and serialize the execution

of specific code. Latches do not support queueing, so if a latch request fails because the latch is busy, the process simply retries until it succeeds.

The implementation of latches is operating system (OS) and platform specific. Because the requirements on a latch are simple, the latch structure and operations are simple. On most platforms, a latch needs only a single location in memory, and latch get operations require simple atomic instructions from the hardware's instruction set. Generally, the memory location has a nonzero value if the latch is busy and a value of zero if the latch is free.

Parent and Child Latches   Most data structures are protected by only one latch. There are exceptions, such as the library cache, which requires latches for different groups of objects within the cache. If multiple latches are used to protect different parts of a structure, we refer to these latches as *child* latches. For each of these child latches of the same type, there is one *parent* latch. Solitary latches with no children are also referred to as parent latches.

Tuning Latches in Oracle9*i*

We do not tune latches; instead, latch contention is an indicator that we need to tune some component of the SGA or the application. In Oracle versions previous to Oracle9*i*, the database administrator (DBA) could set the number of specific types of latches with initialization parameters. In Oracle9*i*, there are no supported initialization parameters that directly set the number of latches. The DBA has no need to control latch occurrence or duration, so the latch parameters are either hidden or obsolete. However, you can use latch statistics gathered from the dynamic performance views and Statspack reports to identify areas for tuning opportunities.

Waiting for a Latch

Depending on the number of CPUs, a process will behave differently when waiting for a latch. On single-CPU machines, the requesting process will release the CPU and "sleep" for a brief period of time and then try again. When a sleep occurs, it is a wait registered as a *latch free* wait event.

On multiprocessor systems, the process holding the latch may be running on a different CPU than the one requesting the latch. The requesting process does not release the CPU as in a single-CPU system; instead, it holds the CPU and counts to a specific number. This hold-and-count is called a *spin*; spin time and the number of spins are both OS and platform specific. If the latch is still unavailable after the first spin, the requesting process spins again until the latch becomes available or the allowed number of spins is reached. If the number of spins is surpassed and the latch is still unavailable, the requesting process releases the CPU and then sleeps. Releasing the CPU (context switch) and acquiring the CPU again at a later time is an expensive operation; therefore, spinning is preferred to releasing the CPU. However, excessive spinning can cause performance problems because spinning does consume CPU cycles. In single-CPU systems, spinning is not an option.

Describe the Different Types of Latch Requests

A process requests a latch in one of two modes: willing to wait or immediate (no wait). The difference between the two is the way the requesting process behaves when the requested latch is unavailable.

Willing-to-Wait Requests

When a latch is requested in willing-to-wait mode and the latch is unavailable, the process waits briefly (sleeps) and then requests the latch again. Sleeping and trying continues until the latch is obtained.

Immediate Requests

A process may need to hold several latches concurrently, so it is possible that deadlocks could occur between processes attempting to obtain several latches. To prevent deadlocks from occurring, every latch has a predefined level from 0 to MaxLevel (OS dependent, up to 15), and latches are always taken in a specific order.

Immediate requests, often referred to as no-wait requests, are used when the requesting process is holding a latch and needs to obtain a latch at the same latch level or lower. Everything is okay if the latch is obtained. However, if the process cannot obtain the latch requested in immediate mode, the potential exists for a deadlock. To prevent this, the process will release the higher-level latches, release the CPU, and then attempt to obtain the latches again.

In other cases, an immediate request will either fail and return an error code or continue with other processing. An example is when PMON is cleaning up following an abnormally terminated process. If the immediate latch request is not obtained, the process monitor (PMON) will continue processing other instructions.

Describe How to Diagnose Contention for Latches

As described previously, it is expected that a latch will be held briefly and intermittently. However, if many processes request the same latch at the same time, or if a latch is not held briefly, contention for the latch can occur. Our tuning goal is to minimize contention for latches, but first we need to understand how to identify latch contention. We will use our dynamic performance views and the Statspack report to help identify latch contention.

Dynamic Performance Views

The V$LATCH family of views will be used to identify which latches may be contended for; however, before we investigate individual latch issues, we need to understand the severity of latch contention in our instance.

V$SYSTEM_EVENT   Query the V$SYSTEM_EVENT view to determine the overall severity of latch contention. If the *latch free* event has a high value for the TIME_WAITED column, investigate further by querying V$LATCH.

V$LATCH   This view lists statistics for solitary latches and summary statistics for parent latches from their children. Columns SLEEP5 through SLEEP11 are deprecated and unused. These are the columns that we'll use in our diagnostics:

- **Addr**   The address of the latch object.
- **Latch#**   The latch number, which is used to join with child latches.
- **Level#**   The latch level.
- **Name**   The name of the latch.
- **Gets**   The number of times a willing-to-wait latch was requested and obtained successfully.
- **Misses**   The number of times an initial willing-to-wait request failed.
- **Sleeps**   The number of times a process slept after an initial willing-to-wait request.
- **Immediate_gets**   The number of times a no-wait request was obtained without a wait.
- **Immediate_misses**   The number of times a no-wait request failed to get without a wait.
- **Spin_gets**   The number of gets that missed on the first try, but succeeded on a spin.
- **SLEEP1 through SLEEP4**   The number of waits that slept 1 through 4 times, respectively.
- **Wait_time**   Time spent waiting for the latch; this is 0 if timed_statistics is not set to TRUE. Other OS-specific settings affect this column, so see your platform-specific Oracle documentation.

The following is a sample query that returns the five most often requested latches from V$LATCH:

```
SELECT * FROM
   (SELECT NAME, GETS, MISSES, SLEEPS, IMMEDIATE_GETS, IMMEDIATE_MISSES
    FROM V$LATCH
    ORDER BY GETS DESC)
WHERE ROWNUM < 6
/
```

NAME	GETS	MISSES	SLEEPS	IMMEDIATE_GETS	IMMEDIATE_MISSES
checkpoint queue latch	233248	0	0	0	0
cache buffers chains	153616	1	0	7412	1
library cache	73903	1	0	0	0
messages	59326	6	0	0	0
enqueues	53677	0	0	0	0

The results of this query show that an overwhelming percentage (99.9986 percent) of willing-to-wait latch requests (GETS) were obtained without misses or sleeps. The same holds true for immediate latch requests (IMMEDIATE_GETS), which have a 99.9865 percent immediate get ratio.

V$LATCH_PARENT   This view contains statistics about each parent latch. V$LATCH_PARENT has the same columns and a one-to-one row relationship with V$LATCH.

V$LATCH_CHILDREN   The V$LATCH_CHILDREN view contains statistics about child latches. It contains the CHILD# column, plus all the columns of V$LATCH. Child latches with the same LATCH# have the same parent latch. This query shows the number of child latches, grouped by parent latch:

```
SELECT LATCH#, NAME, COUNT(*)
FROM V$LATCH_CHILDREN
GROUP BY LATCH#, NAME
/
```

LATCH#	NAME	COUNT(*)
0	latch wait list	2

```
        5 session switching                                   4
...
       82 cache buffers lru chain                             8
...
       87 cache buffers chains                             1024
       99 redo copy                                           4
...
      141 shared pool                                         7
      142 library cache                                       3
...
```

The V$LATCH_CHILDREN view has the same columns as V$LATCH. When you discover that a latch in V$LATCH has a high number of misses, sleeps, or spin gets, use the LATCH# of the parent latch and query V$LATCH_CHILDREN to determine if the latch has child latches and if one of the child latches is contended for.

V$LATCHNAME   This view can be used to look up a latch name if you have the corresponding LATCH#. This view has a one-to-one relationship with the rows in V$LATCH.

V$LATCHHOLDER   This view contains information about the current latch holders. You can join V$LATCHHOLDER with either V$PROCESS or V$SESSION to get information about the session that is holding the latch. The PID column identifies the Oracle process holding the latch, the SID column identifies the session that owns the latch, and the NAME column identifies the latch being held. Because latches are held for such a short period of time, more often than not when you query this view, no rows will be returned.

V$LATCH_MISSES   This view contains cumulative statistics about missed attempts to acquire a latch. The PARENT_NAME column indicates the name of the parent latch. The NWFAIL_COUNT column indicates the number of times that no-wait requests failed. The SLEEP_COUNT column indicates the number of times that sleeps occurred because of willing-to-wait requests.

Statspack Report

Before we look at the latch sections of the Statspack report, look in the Top 5 Wait Events section for *latch free* wait events. This will indicate the relative severity of the latch contention problem.

```
Top 5 Wait Events
~~~~~~~~~~~~~~~~~                                          Wait      % Total
Event                                            Waits   Time (s)   Wt Time
------------------------------------------------ ------- ---------- -------
```

```
db file sequential read                      638     10   37.13
control file parallel write                1,348      8   32.59
db file scattered read                        83      5   18.08
control file sequential read                 442      2    9.27
latch free                                    26      1    1.57
```

If you don't find *latch free* wait events in the Top 5, look again in the Wait Events section of the report, which immediately follows the Top 5 Wait Events section.

The next section of the report to investigate is the Latch Activity section, followed immediately by the Latch Sleep section. The Latch Activity section has been abbreviated to save space.

```
Latch Activity for DB: OR9I  Instance: or9i  Snaps: 1 --2
->"Get Requests", "Pct Get Miss" and "Avg Slps/Miss" are statistics for
  willing-to-wait latch get requests
->"NoWait Requests", "Pct NoWait Miss" are for no-wait latch get requests
->"Pct Misses" for both should be very close to 0.0
-> ordered by Wait Time desc, Avg Slps/Miss, Pct NoWait Miss desc
```

| | | Pct | Avg | Wait | | Pct |
| | Get | Get | Slps | Time | NoWait | NoWait |
Latch	Requests	Miss	/Miss	(s)	Requests	Miss
checkpoint queue latch	33,041	0.0	0.0	0	0	
cache buffers chains	221,422	0.0		0	1,569	0.0
...						
redo copy	0			0	625	0.0
enqueues	7,978	0.0		0	0	
library cache	67,895	0.0		0	0	
cache buffers lru chain	4,617	0.0		0	0	
archive control	1	0.0		0	0	
cache buffer handles	169	0.0		0	0	
messages	8,247	0.0	3.0	0	0	
...						

```
Latch Sleep breakdown for DB: OR9I  Instance: or9i  Snaps: 1 --2
-> ordered by misses desc
```

| | Get | | | Spin & |
Latch Name	Requests	Misses	Sleeps	Sleeps 1->4
messages	8,247	1	3	0/0/0/1/0

Identify the Resources to Be Tuned to Minimize Latch Contention

As mentioned previously, we do not tune latches. Oracle9*i* automatically calculates and sets the number of latches required based on the instance initialization parameters and OS.

We use latch contention as an indicator that we need to tune some other process or processes, database or instance component, or the application. Latch contention is a symptom, and the type of latch contended for indicates the type of performance problem. When you see latch contention, investigate further to determine what is causing the contention. Latch contention is often reduced by modifying the user application. Also, latch contention may be the result of an undersized shared pool or buffer cache.

Important Latches and Tuning Approach

We've identified several latches that you may see as having contention. For each latch, we'll describe some steps you can take to reduce contention.

Shared Pool Latches   The shared pool latch protects memory allocation in the shared pool. Contention for the shared pool latch is an indicator that you may need to tune the application. The application cursor cache may be too small, or cursors may be closed explicitly too soon. Also, if you are using shared servers and you haven't configured the large pool or if you have frequent logon/logoff, you may see contention for the shared pool latch.

Library Cache Latches   The library cache latch is used to find matching Structured Query Language (SQL) in the library cache. Unshared SQL, reparsed sharable SQL, and an undersized library cache contribute to library cache latch contention. Consider using bind variables in the application, or tune the shared pool.

To investigate shared pool and library cache contention further, query V$SESSTAT for sessions with high parse time and parse count ratios. Also look in V$SQLAREA or V$SQL for a high ratio of parse calls to executions or a high number of reloads or invalidations.

Cache Buffers LRU Chain Latches   This latch protects the buffer cache LRU list. For single CPU machines, one latch is sufficient. For symmetric multiprocessing (SMP) systems, Oracle sets the number of latches to half the number of CPUs. Contention for this latch indicates that there is too much buffer cache activity. It is possible that the application SQL needs to be tuned so that large index range scans and full table scans (FTSs) are minimized. It is possible that the DBWn processes are not able to keep up with write requests; in this case, tune the number of DBWn processes and the buffer cache size.

Cache Buffers Chains Latches   This latch is used to protect data blocks in the buffer cache. These latches are used specifically when a block is searched for, added, or removed from the buffer cache. Contention usually indicates that a particular block is heavily requested. Identify the block, as described in Chapter 5.

Redo Copy and Redo Allocation Latches   The redo copy latch is used to write redo entries into the redo log buffer. When a process needs to write redo entries, it obtains a redo copy latch and then requests the redo allocation latch. The redo allocation latch manages the allocation of redo space in the redo log buffer to redo entries. After the redo allocation latch is obtained, space is allocated in the redo log buffer, and the redo allocation latch is released. Next, the server process uses the redo copy latch to write to the log buffer and then releases the redo copy latch.

In previous versions of Oracle, you could reduce redo copy latch contention by increasing the value of the initialization parameter LOG_SIMULTANEOUS_COPIES, which increases the number of redo copy latches. This parameter is obsolete in Oracle9*i*. However, you can increase the value of _LOG_SIMULTANEOUS_COPIES to have more latches available. The default is twice the numbers of CPUs.

In earlier releases, redo allocation latch contention could be reduced by lowering the value of the LOG_SMALL_ENTRY_MAX_SIZE parameter, which set the threshold value for redo log copies that could occur using the allocation latch without using the copy latch. Since Oracle8*i*, a redo copy latch is always required regardless of the redo size, so the check against LOG_SMALL_ENTRY_MAX_SIZE is no longer performed.

You can reduce redo allocation latch contention by using the NOLOGGING option to reduce the amount of redo log entries for certain operations or reduce the load on the latch by increasing the LOG_BUFFER parameter.

Chapter Summary

Oracle uses latches to protect memory structures from modification by more than one process at a time. A process requests a latch, and in most cases holds and uses the latch for a very brief time. Latches are very simple structures, using very small amounts of memory and atomic instructions from the underlying hardware's instruction set.

There are 16 levels of latches: 0 through 15. Also, child latches are used to protect a data structure that requires multiple latches. There is a one-to-many relationship between parent latches and child latches. A parent latch can be a solitary latch—that is, a latch with no children.

We do not tune latches in Oracle9*i*. Latch contention is a symptom of other performance problems and an indicator that we have tuning opportunities elsewhere.

There are basically two types of latch requests. Willing-to-wait latch requests, if they fail to obtain a latch on the first attempt, will wait and try again at a predetermined time. Immediate latch requests will either skip the latch request and continue with other instructions, or if the process has obtained additional latches, it will release the latches and try the request again later.

To diagnose contention for latches, we first query V$SYSTEM_EVENT for *latch free* waits or analyze the Top 5 Wait Events in the Statspack report. If we see that *latch free* waits are a significant contribution to system waits, then we should query V$LATCH to determine where the contention has originated from. If there is a corresponding LATCH# in V$LATCH_CHILDREN, then we can determine if a specific child latch is the culprit.

There are a few important latches that we need to be familiar with, and we need to understand how to reduce contention for them. Contention for the shared pool and library cache latches indicates that the library cache and shared pool may be sized inappropriately, that SQL statements are not being reused, and that the large pool might need to be configured. Contention for the cache buffers LRU chain latches indicates that the buffer cache is too active and that the number of DBWn processes and buffer cache size should be tuned. The cache buffers chains latches indicate that particular buffers are heavily used. You should identify the data block that is heavily used and determine a solution. Redo copy and redo allocation latches control how redo entries are written to the redo log buffer.

Two-Minute Drill

- Latches are small memory structures that protect SGA memory structures from being modified by more than one process at a time.

- Latches are simple and efficient, usually requiring a single memory location per latch and relying on atomic instructions to manage the latch state.

- Latch implementation is OS and platform specific.

- Generally, the memory location has a nonzero value if the latch is busy and a value of zero if the latch is free.

- When multiple latches are required to protect a data structure, we call the latches child latches.

- Latches with children and solitary latches are called parent latches.

- Access to child latches is controlled by a parent latch.

- Oracle automatically allocates the number of latches needed based on initialization parameter values.

■ We do not tune latches in Oracle9i; rather, latch contention is an indicator of other tuning problems that we should address.

■ On single-CPU systems, if a latch request fails, the requesting process will release the CPU, sleep, and try again later.

■ On multi-CPU systems, if a latch request fails, the requesting process will not release the CPU but will spin on the current CPU and try the request later instead.

■ A willing-to-wait latch request will, if the requested latch is unavailable, spin and request the latch again.

■ An immediate or no-wait latch request will release higher-level latches and release the CPU in order to prevent deadlocks.

■ If an immediate latch request fails, the process may skip the request, perform other duties, and try the request again later.

■ Diagnosing latch contention begins with the V$SYSTEM_EVENT view or the Statspack report Top 5 Wait Events section.

■ If latch contention exists in the form of *latch free* waits, then query the V$LATCH and V$LATCH_CHILDREN views to determine the latch contended for.

■ Shared pool latch and library cache latch contention is an indicator of unshared SQL, undersized cursor areas or an undersized shared pool.

■ Cache buffers LRU chain latch contention is an indicator that the buffer cache is too busy. Investigate untuned SQL statements that perform FTSs or large index range scans. Investigate tuning the number of DBWn processes and the size of the buffer cache.

■ Cache buffers chains latch contention indicates that specific buffers are being contended for.

■ The redo copy latches and redo allocation latch are responsible for protecting the process of placing entries into the redo log buffer.

Chapter Questions

1. **Select the statement that most accurately describes the function of a latch.**

    A. A latch is responsible for protecting database tables from concurrent changes by multiple processes.

B. A latch prevents two or more processes from modifying the same data structure at the same time.

C. The purpose of a latch is to prevent Oracle memory structures from growing too large for real memory.

D. The purpose of a latch is to coordinate which background process will be used to read data blocks from data files.

E. Latches are used to speed recovery following a database crash.

2. **Which of the following best describes latch request behavior on a multi-CPU server?**

A. If a requesting process cannot obtain a latch on the first try, it will release the CPU and request the latch later.

B. If the requesting process cannot obtain the latch on the first try, it will switch to the CPU that is running the process that holds the latch and force it to release the latch.

C. If a requesting process cannot obtain a latch on the first try, the requesting process will hold the CPU until the requested latch becomes available, and then it will obtain the latch immediately.

D. The requesting process will queue up behind existing latch requests and wait for them to complete.

E. If the request is made in high-priority mode, the requesting process will obtain the latch immediately.

F. If the requesting process cannot obtain the latch on the first try, it will hold the CPU, count to a predefined number, and then request the latch again.

3. **On a multi-CPU system, willing-to-wait latch requests differ from immediate requests in what way?**

A. Immediate requests, if not met, will spin indefinitely.

B. Willing-to-wait requests will skip a latch request if the latch is busy, whereas immediate requests will not.

C. Willing-to-wait requests will deadlock if the latch is not obtained.

D. Willing-to-wait requests will retry immediately and continuously if the latch is not obtained on the first try.

E. Willing-to-wait requests will sleep if they do not obtain the latch on the first try.

4. **As the DBA, you need to determine if you have latch contention in your database. Which of these accurately describes the latch contention diagnostic process?**

   A. Query V$LATCH for *latch free* waits, and then query V$LATCH_CHILDREN to determine where the contention occurred.

   B. Query V$SYSTEM_EVENT to determine if you have a significant *latch free* wait problem, and then query V$LATCH_WAITS to investigate specific latch problems.

   C. Query V$SYSTEM_EVENT to determine if you have a significant *latch free* wait problem, and then query V$LATCH and possibly V$LATCH_CHILDREN to find the specific latch contended for.

   D. Query V$SYSTEM_WAIT to determine if you have a significant *latch free* wait problem, and then query V$LATCH and possibly V$LATCH_CHILDREN to find the specific latch contended for.

5. **You discover contention for the cache buffers LRU chain latch. Which of the following describe a possible solution? (Choose two.)**

   A. Increase the number of LRU latches on the buffer cache by increasing the LRU_CHAIN_LATCHES parameter value.

   B. Decrease the number of LRU latches on the buffer cache.

   C. Tune the application SQL to reduce large index range scans and full table scans.

   D. Increase the number of DBWn processes.

   E. Increase the number of shared server processes.

   F. Increase the number of ARCn processes.

6. **Choose the order in which to search the Statspack report for latch contention problems.**

   A. Top 10 Wait Events, Wait Events, Latch Activity, Latch Sleep breakdown

   B. Top 5 Wait Events, Wait Events, Latch Activity, Latch Sleep breakdown

   C. Top 10 Wait Events, Latch Activity, Latch Sleep breakdown, Other Wait Events

   D. Latch Activity, Latch Sleep breakdown, Top 5 Wait Events, Other Wait Events

Answers to Chapter Questions

1. B.   A latch prevents two or more processes from modifying the same data structure at the same time.

Explanation   The function of a latch is to protect Oracle memory structures from being manipulated by more than one process at a time. Answer A more accurately describes a lock instead of a latch. Answer C is not the responsibility of a latch, but it is the responsibility of the DBA. Answers D and E are simply not functions associated with latches.

2. F.   If the requesting process cannot obtain the latch on the first try, it will hold the CPU, count to a predefined number, and then request the latch again.

Explanation   In a multi-CPU environment, it is more favorable to hold the CPU and wait for a few microseconds than it is to release the CPU and try the request again later. Answer A is the appropriate answer for a single-CPU machine. Answer B is incorrect because the process will not switch CPUs and will not force the release of a latch held by another process. Answers C, D, and E are incorrect because there is no guarantee that the latch will be obtained immediately by this requesting process, there is no queue for requests to wait in, and no request has priority over any other request.

3. E.   Willing-to-wait requests will sleep if they do not obtain the latch on the first try.

Explanation   If a willing-to-wait request does not obtain the requested latch on the first try, it will sleep and try again. Immediate requests do not spin. Answer A is incorrect because immediate requests spin only a predetermined number of times before giving up on the latch. Answer B is incorrect because immediate requests will skip a latch request if the latch is busy, whereas willing-to-wait requests will sleep. Answer C is incorrect because willing-to-wait requests do not deadlock because they do not hold multiple latches. Immediate requests, if they fail to obtain the latch, will release latches and the CPU to prevent deadlocks. Answer D is incorrect because willing-to-wait requests will not retry immediately and continuously, but will retry after a predetermined time.

4. C.   Query V$SYSTEM_EVENT to determine if you have a significant *latch free* wait problem, and then query V$LATCH and possibly V$LATCH_CHILDREN to find the specific latch contended for.

Explanation   Query V$SYSTEM_EVENT first to see if you have a significant *latch free* wait problem. If so, query V$LATCH to determine which parent latch has contention issues. Then query V$LATCH_CHILDREN using the parent LATCH# to determine if a child latch is causing the contention. Answer A incorrectly describes where to find the *latch free* wait events. Answer B is incorrect because there is no V$LATCH_WAITS dynamic performance view. Answer D is incorrect because there is no V$SYSTEM_WAIT dynamic performance view.

5. C and D.   Tune the application SQL to reduce large index range scans and full table scans, and increase the number of DBWn processes.

Explanation   Contention on the cache buffers LRU chain latch indicates that the buffer cache is very busy and has too much throughput. Investigate user SQL for FTSs or inefficient index range scans. Also, consider tuning the DBWn processes and buffer cache settings. Answer A is incorrect because LRU_CHAIN_LATCHES is not a valid initialization parameter. Answer B is incorrect because we cannot directly control the number of cache buffers LRU chain latches. Answers E and F are not relevant answers.

6. B.   Top 5 Wait Events, Wait Events, Latch Activity, Latch Sleep breakdown

Explanation   The correct approach is to evaluate if the *latch free* waits are in the Top 5 wait events for the instance first; if the *latch free* events aren't in the Top 5, look for them in the section with all the wait events to determine if further investigation of latch contention is needed. If so, then the next step is to diagnose individual latch activity, and then look at latch sleep statistics. Answers A and C are incorrect because they refer to the Top 10 wait events, which is not a valid report section in the Statspack report. Answer D is incorrect because the significance of the latch contention on the instance is not considered first.

CHAPTER
10

Tuning Rollback
or Undo Segments

n this chapter, you will learn about tuning the different methods for managing undo—that is, rollback segments and UNDO segments:

- Use the dynamic performance views to check rollback segment performance.

- Define the number and sizes of manual rollback segments.

- Appropriately allocate rollback segments to transactions.

- Understand and explain the concept of automatic undo management.

- Create and maintain automatic managed undo tablespace.

Manually configured rollback segments are not new to Oracle9*i*, but automatic undo management is. In this chapter we will discuss rollback segments, the traditional method of maintaining undo information, in detail. This is because many legacy Oracle systems will continue to use manually configured rollback segments, even after upgrading to Oracle9*i*. We will then introduce automatic undo management and discuss its advantages over manually configured rollback segments. Oracle strongly recommends that you use automatic undo management to eliminate many performance-tuning problems related to incorrectly configured rollback segments.

Tuning Rollback/Undo Segments

Oracle databases maintain undo information that can be used to roll back, or undo, changes to the database. Undo information mostly consists of the before image of data that is changed by a transaction. Undo space is required to keep information for read consistency, recovery, and rollback statements. Undo information is kept either in manually configured rollback segments or in automatic undo management tablespaces.

Previous to Oracle9*i*, manually configured rollback segments were the only method used to store undo information. Managing rollback segments is a tedious and often mistake-prone aspect of the DBA's work.

Oracle9*i* introduces another method of managing undo that alleviates the DBA of the responsibilities to manually configure and maintain undo, and enables the DBA to configure how long to retain undo before it can be overwritten.

If the database is configured to use the legacy method of manual rollback segments to manage undo, the database is running in *manual undo management* mode, also referred to as rollback segment undo (RBU). If the database is configured to use a system-managed undo tablespace, you are operating in *automatic undo management* mode, also referred to as system-managed undo (SMU). The mode is determined by the UNDO_MANAGEMENT initialization parameter.

Rollback and Undo Segment Usage

For the remainder of this section, we will discuss how undo works; this applies to both manual and automatic undo management. We will use the terms "rollback" and "undo" interchangeably. When we discuss a topic that is specific to one type of undo management, we will specify the undo management mode.

We will now discuss how undo segments are used. Undo segments are used for transaction rollback, transaction recovery, read consistency, and new to Oracle9i, the Flashback Query feature.

Transaction Rollback   When a transaction begins, there are two possible outcomes: the transaction is either committed or it is rolled back. When data is modified, Oracle uses an undo segment to keep a copy of the original image of the changed data. If the transaction is rolled back, the original image is restored from the undo segment to the modified row.

Transaction Recovery   If the Oracle instance fails while there are active transactions, undo segments are used to perform transaction recovery when the instance is opened. Uncommitted transactions are rolled back; modified rows are returned to their original values, deleted rows are put back into their table, and inserted rows are removed. Transaction recovery is only possible if the redo generated by the uncommitted transactions is available in the redo logs.

Read Consistency   When a transaction is in progress, other sessions in the database should not see the uncommitted changes. Also, a statement should not see data that is changed after the statement is executed. These are the two basic tenets of read consistency. A statement should see the original unchanged data as it existed at the time the statement was executed. Read consistency is made possible by using the original records, referred to as *undo*, in the undo segment.

Flashback Query   New to Oracle9i, the Flashback Query feature lets you query the database as of a certain system change number (SCN) or specified time in the past. If you're using automatic undo management, you specify how long undo information should be retained in the database. This retention period determines how far back in the past a Flashback Query can operate.

Rollback Segment Activity

In this section we will describe how Oracle writes undo information to rollback segments.

Transactions write to rollback segment extents in a circular fashion, advancing from one extent to the next after the current extent is full. A transaction writes a record to the current location in the rollback segment, and then advances the current pointer by the size of the record. Figure 10-1 illustrates this activity.

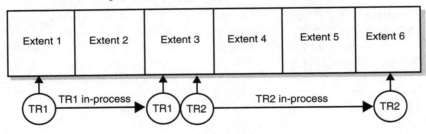

FIGURE 10-1. *Writing undo information to a rollback segment*

An extent of a rollback segment can contain information from more than one transaction, but a specific rollback segment block contains information from only one transaction.

If transactions are writing to an extent, that extent is active. If no transaction is writing to an extent, it is inactive.

In order for a transaction to write to a rollback segment, the undo data must be in the database buffer cache. Retaining large amounts of undo requires a large buffer cache, otherwise physical input/outputs (I/Os) can become a performance problem.

Rollback Segment Header Activity

Oracle uses a transaction table in the header of every rollback segment to keep track of the transactions that are currently writing undo data in that segment. The data structures in the rollback segment header manage the writing of changed data to the rollback segments.

The header is also a data block that is frequently modified, so it generally remains in the buffer cache. Therefore, gets of the rollback segment header block increase the buffer cache hit ratio; this artificial increase in the hit ratio can mislead you into thinking that you have allocated enough data blocks to the buffer cache.

Because every transaction must be able to update the rollback segment transaction table, contention can occur if multiple transactions try to update the same header block. Online Transaction Processing (OLTP) systems are notorious for this. With manually configured rollback segments, you may need to add more rollback segments to reduce or eliminate contention.

Growth of Rollback Segments

When a rollback segment extent becomes full, the current pointer moves to the next extent. When the last extent in the segment is full, the current pointer tries to move back to the beginning of the first extent. If the first extent is already in use, the pointer cannot skip to the next pointer. Instead, the rollback segment allocates a new extent and the pointer moves to it. This same approach applies if the current pointer attempts to move into any other active extent: The rollback segment allocates an additional extent and the current pointer moves into it. This method continues until Oracle is unable to allocate an extent, either because MAXEXTENTS has been reached or the tablespace runs out of free space.

The Impact of Rollback Segments Extending   As with other database objects, dynamic extent allocation (and deallocation) should be avoided, as it can result in performance problems. Rollback segments should not extend during normal operation. Make sure you allocate enough extents to your rollback segments so that dynamic extension doesn't occur. Monitor your rollback segments to make sure you haven't under- or overallocated.

Tuning Goals for Manually Managed Rollback Segments

The following are the basic goals for tuning manually managed rollback segments:

- Transactions should never wait for access to rollback segments.

- Rollback segments should never extend during normal operation.

- No transaction should ever run out of rollback segment space.

- Readers should always see the read-consistent images they need.

- Users and utilities should try to use less rollback.

Transactions will wait for access to rollback segments if you have too few rollback segments. The remedy is to increase the number of rollback segments. Rollback segments will not extend during normal operation if you have configured the appropriate number of extents, the correct size of extents, and the appropriate number of rollback segments. If rollback segments are sized properly, and overly large transactions are split into smaller transactions, you reduce the likelihood that a transaction will run out of rollback segment space. If you have configured the correct number and size of rollback segments, then readers will be able to see the read-consistent images that they need.

Use the Dynamic Performance Views to Check Rollback Segment Performance

Oracle has supplied us with a few dynamic performance views to directly monitor rollback segment activity. We can also view specific undo-related system event information. Additionally, there are sections in the Statspack report for diagnosing undo problems.

Dynamic Performance Views to Monitor Rollback Activity

The dynamic performance views are used to monitor manual and automatic managed undo. The undo segment number (USN) column is used universally to identify the undo segment number. The exception is the DBA_ROLLBACK_SEGS data dictionary view, which uses the SEGMENT_ID and can be joined with the USN in the dynamic performance views.

V$ROLLNAME   The V$ROLLNAME view has two columns: the USN column, which indicates the undo segment number, and the NAME column, which indicates the name of the undo segment. V$ROLLNAME contains one row for each undo segment that is currently online. If your instance is configured for manual undo management, you'll see something like this:

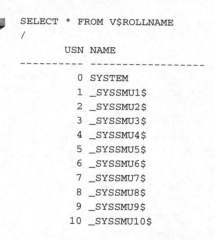

```
SELECT * FROM V$ROLLNAME
/
       USN NAME
---------- ------------------
         0 SYSTEM
        22 RB01
        23 RB02
        24 RB03
```

If you've configured your instance to run in automatic undo management mode, your query will instead look something like this:

```
SELECT * FROM V$ROLLNAME
/
       USN NAME
---------- ------------------
         0 SYSTEM
         1 _SYSSMU1$
         2 _SYSSMU2$
         3 _SYSSMU3$
         4 _SYSSMU4$
         5 _SYSSMU5$
         6 _SYSSMU6$
         7 _SYSSMU7$
         8 _SYSSMU8$
         9 _SYSSMU9$
        10 _SYSSMU10$
```

You'll note that the SYSTEM rollback segment, USN=0, is present whether your instance is configured for manual or automatic undo management.

V$ROLLSTAT   This view displays statistics of the activity for each of the rollback segments that are currently online. Columns of interest are

- **Xacts**   The number of active transactions.
- **Waits**   The number of header waits.

- **Hwmsize** High water mark of rollback segment size.
- **Shrinks** The number of times the size of a rollback segment decreases.
- **Wraps** The number of times rollback segment is wrapped; that is, when the last extent of the rollback segment becomes full, Oracle continues writing rollback data to the first extent in the segment.
- **Extends** The number of times rollback segment size is extended.
- **Aveshrink** The average shrink size.
- **Aveactive** The current size of active extents averaged over time.

Here's a sample query of the V$ROLLSTAT view, using manual undo management:

```
SELECT USN, XACTS, WAITS, HWMSIZE, SHRINKS, WRAPS,EXTENDS, AVESHRINK, AVEACTIVE
FROM V$ROLLSTAT
/
USN  XACTS  WAITS    HWMSIZE    SHRINKS   WRAPS    EXTENDS  AVESHRINK  AVEACTIVE
----- ------ ------ ---------- ---------- ------- ---------- ---------- ----------
    0     0     0     425984           0       1          0          0       6144
   22     0     0     126976           0       0          0          0          0
   23     1     0   35647488           0      48         47          0   40661928
   24     1     0     126976           0       0          0          0          0
```

V$TRANSACTION This view lists statistics about each currently active transaction. V$TRANSACTION contains several columns of interest to us. The XIDUSN indicates the USN of the undo segment that the transaction is using. Also, the USED_UBLK column indicates the number of undo blocks used by the transaction, and USED_UREC indicates the number of undo records used.

V$SYSTEM_EVENT The wait event *undo segment tx slot* indicates a wait for a transaction slot to become available within a rollback segment. This is an indicator of contention on rollback segment headers. If a wait event occurs, the transaction will continue waiting in one-second intervals until the slot is available.

The wait event *undo segment extension* indicates that the undo segment is being extended or shrunk. The transaction must wait, in centisecond increments, until the operation on the undo segment has finished.

In addition, there are wait events indicating that sessions or transactions are waiting for rollback activity to complete. The *undo segment recovery* wait event indicates that the Process Monitor (PMON) is rolling back a dead transaction. The session wait continues, in three-second increments, until the rollback finishes. The transaction wait event indicates that a session is waiting for a blocking transaction to be rolled back; it will continue waiting until the transaction has been rolled back.

V$WAITSTAT   The V$WAITSTAT view lists block contention statistics. This view indicates the class of block that is waited for, the number of waits by operation, and the sum of wait time. This view is only updated when TIMED_STATISTICS=TRUE.

```
SELECT * FROM V$WAITSTAT
WHERE CLASS LIKE '%undo%'
/
CLASS                 COUNT       TIME
------------------  ----------  ----------
...
system undo header        0           0
system undo block         0           0
undo header               2           0
undo block                5           0
```

V$SYSSTAT   Query the V$SYSSTAT to gather statistics for rollback and undo activity:

```
SELECT NAME, VALUE
FROM V$SYSSTAT
WHERE NAME LIKE '%roll%'
OR NAME LIKE '%undo%'
/
NAME                                                              VALUE
----------------------------------------------------------  ----------
user rollbacks                                                        0
DBWR undo block writes                                            24470
remote instance undo block writes                                    0
remote instance undo header writes                                   0
transaction tables consistent reads - undo records applied           0
transaction tables consistent read rollbacks                         0
data blocks consistent reads - undo records applied                247
rollbacks only - consistent read gets                              114
cleanouts and rollbacks - consistent read gets                      48
rollback changes - undo records applied                         457019
transaction rollbacks                                                1
```

Rollback Segment Header Contention

We detect contention for rollback segments by querying the dynamic performance views, looking for the following:

■ **V$ROLLSTAT** Nonzero value in the WAITS column. The sum of waits should be less than 1 percent of the sum of gets.

■ **V$WAITSTAT** The *undo header* row has a nonzero value in the COUNT column.

■ **V$SYSTEM_EVENT** The *undo segment tx slot* event indicates header contention when there is a nonzero value in the TOTAL_WAITS column or TIME_WAITED is greater than 0.

With manual undo management, rollback segment header contention is remedied by creating more rollback segments and placing them online.

Statspack Report—Rollback and Undo Segment Sections The Statspack report has four sections for rollback and undo: Rollback Stats, Rollback Storage, Undo Segment Summary, and Undo Segment Stats. The two rollback segment reports are relevant when using manual undo management. Each of the sections is relevant for automatic undo management, with certain caveats. Because undo segments are created and dropped as needed when using automatic undo management, rollback segment stats may not be accurate. We'll look at the Rollback Stats report to diagnose header contention:

```
Rollback Segment Stats for DB: OR9I  Instance: or9i  Snaps: 1 -2
->A high value for "Pct Waits" suggests more rollback segments may be required
->RBS stats may not be accurate between begin and end snaps when using Auto Undo
  managment, as RBS may be dynamically created and dropped as needed
```

RBS No	Trans Table Gets	Pct Waits	Undo Bytes Written	Wraps	Shrinks	Extends
0	15.0	0.00	0	0	0	0
1	29.0	0.00	138	0	0	0
2	35.0	0.00	138	0	0	0
3	132.0	0.00	115,220	2	2	0
4	21.0	0.00	276	0	0	0
5	35.0	0.00	276	0	0	0
6	64.0	0.00	276	0	0	0
7	23.0	0.00	260	0	0	0
8	29.0	0.00	1,452	0	0	0
9	32.0	0.00	1,842	0	0	0
10	19.0	0.00	138	0	0	0

In this report, we see that the PCT Waits is 0, so we have no rollback segment header contention. If we had observed greater than 1 percent waits, we should investigate adding more rollback segments.

Define the Number and Size of Manual Rollback Segments

The number and size of rollback segments that you should define in your database is dependent on the application. The type of application, the number of concurrent users, the number and size of concurrent transactions, and the types of transactions are all factors that should be evaluated to determine the optimal size and number of rollback segments.

The Number of Manual Rollback Segments

As we discussed in the previous section on monitoring rollback segment activity, rollback segment header contention, if present, is reduced by adding more rollback segments. Therefore, creating an appropriate number of rollback segments will prevent contention. Depending on the nature of your application and the types of transactions, there are a few general guidelines to practice.

OLTP   OLTP systems generally have a large number of concurrent users who each generate small transactions. A transaction may update an individual employee's address information or add a payment to a customer's payment history. The general guideline is to use relatively small rollback segments and allocate a rollback segment for every four concurrent transactions. So if you have 100 concurrent transactions during normal operations, make sure you have at least 25 rollback segments online.

Large Batch Transactions   Large transactions include SQL updates, deletes, or inserts, and large SQL*Loader conventional path data loads. Assign large batch transactions that modify large amounts of data to larger rollback segments. You define a larger rollback segment by specifying a large INITIAL and NEXT extent, by making MINEXTENTS large enough to accommodate most of the large transactions, and by making the MAXEXTENTS a very large number or UNLIMITED. The large rollback segment should exist in a large tablespace or a tablespace with the AUTOEXTEND automatic extension enabled. If you set MAXEXTENTS UNLIMITED and AUTOEXTEND, beware that you may fill up a file system; therefore, you should be cautious about what you place on the same file system with the rollback segment datafiles.

Also, keep in mind that the large rollback segments should be reserved for large transactions. The goal is to prevent large transactions from running out of space and prevent dynamic extent allocation. If your application has large batch transactions, you should create at least one large rollback segment per concurrent job.

Sizing Manual Rollback Segments

The size of the rollback segments can have a significant impact on performance. The performance-tuning goal when sizing rollback segments is to minimize dynamic extent allocation. Also, we want to find undo blocks in the buffer cache when they're needed, instead of reading from disk.

Previously, we discussed two categories of rollback segments: those used for OLTP sessions and those used for large batch transactions. We will refer to them as general purpose (OLTP) and large rollback segments in this section.

Storage Parameters There are a few guidelines to setting the appropriate size for your rollback segments. In general, we want all rollback segment extents to be the same size; therefore, you should set the INITIAL and NEXT storage parameters to the same value within the same category of rollback segments. For example, all of your general-purpose rollback segments should have the same storage parameters, but your large rollback segments may be tailored for specific transactions. You should use separate tablespaces to keep general-purpose rollback segments separate from large rollback segments. Also, keep your large rollback segments offline until they are needed.

To reduce the likelihood of dynamic extent allocation, set MINEXTENTS to 20. This is merely a guideline; your system will probably benefit from a larger or smaller number. The goal is to reduce dynamic extension, so whatever value works for your database is the right number.

Choose a multiple of the standard DB_BLOCK_SIZE for the INITIAL and NEXT storage parameters. Choose 8-, 16-, 32-, or 64KB for smaller transactions. Choose larger values, such as 128-, 256-, or 512KB, or 1-, 2-, 4-, 8MB, or even larger values for large batch-type transactions. The minimum value that you can set for INITIAL is two times the block size of the tablespace that will hold the rollback segment. My personal experience is that a very small INITIAL will not improve performance. Monitor the V$ROLLSTAT view for EXTENDS; if you see that EXTENDS occur frequently, then you should re-create the rollback segments with larger values for INITIAL and NEXT. If you see a large number of SHRINKS, then you should consider increasing the OPTIMAL setting. If the value for WRAPS is high and *snapshot too old* (discussed in the section "ORA-01555: snapshot too old (rollback segment too small)") error messages occur, consider increasing the size of the rollback segments.

Dynamic extent allocation causes performance problems, but larger-than-normal transactions may occur and cause a segment to extend. Make sure you have enough space in the rollback segment tablespace to accommodate larger-than-normal transactions. The OPTIMAL setting, used when creating or altering a rollback segment, determines the size the rollback segment will shrink to following an extend. Set OPTIMAL to shrink the rollback segments to the same size when not in use.

Appropriately Allocate Rollback Segments to Transactions

Different types of transactions require different amounts of rollback. The amount of rollback generated by a transaction is dependent on the number of rows affected by the transaction and the type of transaction being performed. We will also discuss assigning a specific rollback segment to a transaction.

Transaction Statements

There are three transaction statements: delete, insert, and update. Deletes generate the most rollback because the entire before image must be written to the rollback segment. Inserts generate the least rollback because we only need to write the ROWID to the rollback segment. With updates, the amount of rollback written is dependent on the number and size of the columns modified. If an indexed column is updated, Oracle must store the before image of the data and index column and the new index value.

Assigning a Rollback Segment to a Transaction

You assign a rollback segment to a transaction by issuing the SET TRANSACTION USE ROLLBACK SEGMENT <rollback_segment_name> command or by executing the DBMS_TRANSACTION.USE_ROLLBACK_SEGMENT('<rollback_segment_name>') procedure as the first statement in a transaction. SET TRANSACTION must be the first statement of a transaction otherwise an error message will be generated.

Before assigning a transaction to a rollback segment, perform a commit or rollback to end any previous transaction. Any Data Definition Language (DDL) implicitly commits a transaction, and any commit ends the transaction. A complete rollback, that is, not a rollback to a previously defined SETPOINT, will also end a transaction.

Estimating Rollback Segment Space Required by a Transaction

To accurately size your rollback segments, you should test your transactions in the development and test environment before sizing the production rollback segments. The following are two methods you can use to determine the volume of rollback required for a benchmark transaction. The assumption is that the test transaction is the only transaction running in the test environment.

Using V$TRANSACTION and V$SESSION to Determine Transaction Size

By joining V$TRANSACTION and V$SESSION, you can determine the number of blocks used by a benchmark transaction:

```
SELECT S.USERNAME, T.USED_UBLK
FROM V$TRANSACTION T, V$SESSION S
WHERE T.ADDR = S.TADDR
/
USERNAME                              USED_UBLK
------------------------------------ ----------
HR_USER                                      16
```

This query indicates that the HR_USER is the only current session with an active transaction, and the transaction is using 16 blocks of rollback.

You should run this query at the end of your longest transaction, before a commit or rollback. Base your rollback segment size on the value of USED_UBLK.

Using V$ROLLSTAT to Determine Transaction Size

Another method to determine the size of a transaction is to query the WRITES column of V$ROLLSTAT, run your benchmark transaction, and then query the view again. The WRITES column indicates the number of bytes written to the rollback segment.

```
SELECT USN, WRITES FROM V$ROLLSTAT
/
       USN      WRITES
---------- ----------
         0       40724
        23    49268532


DELETE FROM MY_EMPLOYEE
WHERE EMPLOYEE_ID = 1
/
5920 rows deleted.


SELECT USN, WRITES FROM V$ROLLSTAT
/


USN      WRITES
---------- ----------
         0       40724
        23    50559262


SELECT 50559262 - 49268532 "Bytes Written" FROM DUAL
/
Bytes Written
----------------
        1290730
```

This process reveals that the transaction wrote 1,290,730 bytes to the rollback segment; size the rollback segment so that the transaction will fit in the segment without causing an extend.

How to Reduce Rollback
There are some simple guidelines to follow that will reduce the amount of rollback generated or reduce contention for rollback segment space.

- Users should commit their work regularly.

- Developers should not code unnecessarily long transactions. A transaction should make good business sense. For example, a batch of receipts from the same vendor or a batch of checks from the same bank customer makes a transaction, rather than all receipts or all checks in a single transaction.

- When using the Oracle Import utility, set COMMIT=Y. The BUFFER value determines the size of the buffer Oracle will commit at once. Set the value of BUFFER based on the average row size and the number of rows you want to commit at once.

- When using the Oracle Export utility, setting CONSISTENT=Y creates a read-consistent export. That is, the export is consistent to a single point in time. This requires the retention of rollback segments if transactions modify the data while the export is in progress. Set CONSISTENT=N if you don't need a read-consistent export or if a large volume of the data will be modified during the export. Also, schedule exports during off-peak hours.

- Set the ROWS parameter with conventional path SQL*Loader data loads to specify the number of rows you want to read from the datafile before performing a commit.

Problems That Occur When Rollback Segments Are Too Small
There are basically two things that can happen if a rollback segment is too small: either the transaction is too big and it fails because the rollback segment cannot extend to a size large enough to contain the transaction or blocks needed for read consistency are overwritten too soon.

Transactions Too Large   If a transaction is too large for the rollback segment, it may fail because the MAXEXTENTS value for the rollback segment has been reached or because there is no space left in the tablespace for the segment to extend. A variant of the latter is when the tablespace cannot extend because there is no space left on the device.

Before you add space to the rollback segment tablespace or increase the MAXEXTENTS value, investigate the offending transaction. Maybe the transaction is a long-running batch job that should be assigned to a large rollback segment.

ORA-01555: snapshot too old (rollback segment too small)   After a transaction completes, the information in the rollback segment may still be needed by other sessions for read consistency. If the read-consistent information is not available, an ORA-01555: snapshot too old (rollback segment too small) error message is generated. There are three possible causes for this error:

- The undo information in the rollback segment has been overwritten after a commit, and Oracle is unable to undo the changes made by a committed transaction when constructing a read-consistent version of a data block in memory.

- The transaction slot in the rollback segment's transaction table has been overwritten, and Oracle cannot roll back the rollback segment header block or transaction table enough to get the original rollback segment transaction slot. Changes to the rollback segment headers are also stored in the rollback segments since they are Oracle blocks.

- The Interested Transaction List (ITL) in the block being queried has been reused, and the SCN in the block being queried is newer than the SCN at the start of the query.

Here's a simplified example to illustrate how the error can occur:

- A transaction has committed and the rollback segment blocks are released.

- A query needs to read the before image of the modified data from the rollback segment.

- Another transaction modifies the undo header (transaction table slot) or the actual redo block; now the query cannot read the required read-consistent image.

Again, this is a simplified series of events. The remedy for ORA-01555 errors is to increase the size of the rollback segments, which reduces the likelihood that undo information will be overwritten too soon. You should also consider adding more rollback segments for the same fundamental reason—reducing the likelihood that undo information will be overwritten while still needed. Still another good practice is to not run large batch jobs while OLTP work is significant.

Understand and Explain the Concept of Automatic Undo Management

New to Oracle9*i*, automatic undo management completely automates undo data management. An instance running in automatic undo management mode creates and manages undo segments without intervention by the DBA. In auto mode, the DBA doesn't need to specify the number, size, and location of the undo segments.

Manually tuning rollback segments is no longer a DBA issue with automatic undo management. Oracle recommends using automatic undo management instead of manual. Manual configured rollback segments are supported for compatibility reasons.

To run an instance in automatic undo management mode, set the undo management initialization parameter to AUTO, determine the maximum retention time for undo data, and create an undo tablespace.

Automatic Undo Management Initialization Parameters

There are four initialization parameters that you use to configure the behavior of automatic undo management for the instance.

UNDO_MANAGEMENT   Specifies which undo space management mode the system will use. When set to AUTO, the instance starts in automatic undo management mode. When set to MANUAL, the instance starts in manual undo management mode, which uses manually configured rollback segments. MANUAL is the default value; this parameter is not dynamically configurable.

UNDO_TABLESPACE   Names the undo tablespace that will be used when the instance starts up. This parameter is incompatible with UNDO_MANAGEMENT =MANUAL; an error will occur and startup will fail. If UNDO_MANAGEMENT= AUTO and the UNDO_TABLESPACE parameter are not set, the first available undo tablespace in the database will be used. If no undo tablespace is available, user transactions will use the SYSTEM rollback segment for undo. This parameter is dynamically configurable, so you can switch to a different undo tablespace while the instance is running.

UNDO_SUPPRESS_ERRORS   Setting this initialization parameter to TRUE suppresses error messages caused by references to manually configured rollback segments when the instance is running in automatic undo management mode. If your application makes references to manually configured rollback segments, as with the SET TRANSACTION USE ROLLBACK SEGMENT statement, you can set this parameter to suppress errors that would cause application failure. You can set this parameter dynamically for the instance with the ALTER SYSTEM command or for the current session with the ALTER SESSION command. If you plan to run in automatic undo management mode, update your applications and tools so that they no longer reference the manually configured rollback segments.

UNDO_RETENTION The dynamically configurable UNDO_RETENTION parameter specifies in seconds how long to retain committed undo information in the undo segment. The default value is 900 seconds (15 minutes). You can increase the value for UNDO_RETENTION when queries require older images of data blocks. The higher you set UNDO_RETENTION, the more space you'll need in the undo tablespace. If an active transaction needs undo space and free space is not available, the system will start reusing undo space, which can lead to the dreaded snapshot too old error. So, make sure you have plenty of undo space and monitor it closely.

Create and Maintain Automatically Managed Undo Tablespace

If you set UNDO_MANAGEMENT to TRUE in the init.ora file when you create an Oracle9*i* database, you can create an undo tablespace by specifying the tablespace name, block size, size, and datafile name for the undo tablespace with the CREATE UNDO TABLESPACE command.

If you set the UNDO_MANAGEMENT parameter to TRUE and don't specify an undo tablespace, a system default undo tablespace named SYS_UNDOTBS (depending on your OS and Oracle9*i* release) is created for you.

The system-generated datafile for the tablespace is $ORACLE_HOME/dbs/dbu1 <SID>.dbf, and AUTOEXETEND is set to ON. If you set the UNDO_TABLESPACE parameter in the init.ora file, and it doesn't match the name of the tablespace used in the CREATE DATABASE command, Oracle generates an error.

After the database has been created, you can also create an undo tablespace with the CREATE UNDO TABLESPACE command. Specify the default undo tablespace by setting the UNDO_TABLESPACE initialization parameter.

The following restrictions apply to undo tablespaces:

- You cannot create database objects in this tablespace.

- You can specify the extent_management_clause and datafile name only when creating the tablespace.

Tablespace Administration for Automatic Undo Management

Once you have created an undo tablespace, you can manage it much like you do other tablespaces. The same alter and drop commands apply. You can also switch undo tablespaces while the database is open.

Altering Undo Tablespaces   As with other tablespaces, you can add, rename, and take datafiles offline. You can also issue the BEGIN BACKUP and END BACKUP clauses if you're running the database in archivelog mode.

Switching Undo Tablespaces   You can switch from using one undo tablespace to another by issuing the ALTER SYSTEM SET UNDO_TABLESPACE=<another_ undo_tablespace>. You must have already created the new target undo tablespace. When this command is issued, all new transactions will begin using the newly activated undo tablespace. Existing transactions will continue to use the previous tablespace until they are complete.

As you already have learned, you designate one active undo tablespace with the UNDO_TABLESPACE initialization parameter. Only one active undo tablespace is allowed in the database. It is possible that more than one undo tablespace will have transaction undo in it, however.

Dropping an Undo Tablespace   You drop an undo tablespace the same way you drop an ordinary tablespace—with the DROP TABLESPACE command. You cannot drop the active undo tablespace or any undo tablespace that is currently being used by a transaction. You can drop an undo tablespace that is not the active tablespace and is not being used by a transaction, even if there is undo information in the tablespace required for read consistency. Sessions that need the read-consistent images will fail and return an error message.

Monitoring Undo Activity

You can use the V$UNDOSTAT view to monitor undo space. Each row in the view represents undo statistics for a ten-minute interval. The server uses this view to automatically tune undo space configuration. This view can also be used to estimate the undo space required, based on the workload represented during the captured ten-minute increments. The V$UNDOSTAT view is useful for both automatic and manual undo management.

There are two performance-related settings that you can control with automatic undo management: The size of the undo tablespace and the length of time undo blocks are retained before they can be overwritten. You can use the V$UNDOSTAT view and a few system parameters to determine the amount of undo needed to satisfy the UNDO_RETENTION requirement.

```
SELECT (UR * (UPS * OVERHEAD) + OVERHEAD) AS "Bytes"
FROM (SELECT VALUE AS UR FROM V$PARAMETER WHERE NAME = 'undo_retention'),
     (SELECT (SUM(UNDOBLKS) / SUM(((END_TIME - BEGIN_TIME) * 86400))) AS UPS FROM
V$UNDOSTAT),
     (SELECT VALUE AS OVERHEAD FROM V$PARAMETER WHERE NAME = 'db_block_size')
```

```
/
Bytes
----------
74454240.2
```

This query calculates the undo space required as a function of the undo activity per second, the block size, and the retention requirement. The result of this query shows that we need approximately 75MB of undo space to meet the undo retention requirement, which is set at the default 900 seconds.

Chapter Summary

In this chapter, you learned what rollback segments are used for, how to use the dynamic performance views to monitor undo activity, how to determine the number and size of manual rollback segments, how to allocate rollback segments to transactions, what automatic undo management is, and how to maintain automatic undo tablespaces.

With Oracle9*i*, the DBA has the option to manually configure rollback segments as in previous Oracle releases or to use the new automatic undo management feature to manage undo. Manual undo management, also known as rollback segment undo (RBU), requires the DBA to configure the number and size of rollback segments, and know when to use rollback segments for different types of transactions. It is very easy for the DBA to incorrectly configure rollback segments.

Automatic undo management relieves the DBA of the duties to configure the number and size of rollback segments. With automatic undo management, also known as system-managed undo (SMU), the DBA specifies the size of the undo tablespace and the retention period for undo information. This greatly simplifies undo management and also enables the DBA to reduce the likelihood of the occurrence of ORA-01555 errors.

Undo information is used for three basic functions: rolling back a transaction, recovering a transaction that was in progress when the Oracle instance or session failed, and providing read consistency for transactions.

Transactions write to rollback segments in a circular fashion. When an extent is full, the current pointer moves into the next extent. If the next extent is busy, a new extent is allocated. Dynamic extent allocation in a rollback segment can cause performance problems. More than one transaction may write to an extent, but a particular block within an extent can only contain information from one transaction.

The following are the basic tuning goals for manually configured rollback segments: keep dynamic extension to a minimum, transactions should never fail because they run out of rollback segment space, transactions should never wait for rollback segment resources, readers should always see the read-consistent images they need, and transactions should use as little undo as possible.

The V$ROLLNAME view is used to identify the rollback segment based on its unique undo segment number (USN). The USN is used as a unique identifier in the V$ROLLSTAT view, which contains the statistics that we use to diagnose rollback segment performance problems. The V$TRANSACTION view indicates which undo segment is in use by a transaction and statistics about the transaction. The undo segment tx slot system event indicates waits for transaction slots to become available in a rollback segment. If you see waits, increase the number of rollback segments. The V$WAITSTAT view indicates waits for undo headers and undo blocks. V$SYSSTAT indicates cumulative statistics for the undo segments. Also, use the Statspack rollback and undo reports to aid the diagnosis. Use these views and the Statspack reports to diagnose rollback segment header contention. If noted, the usual remedy is to add more rollback segments.

OLTP systems generally benefit from a large number of small rollback segments. The guideline is four transactions per rollback segment. Large batch transactions will benefit from having large rollback segments that are kept offline until needed.

Base the size of the rollback segments on the purpose they will serve. If your application has a large number of small transactions, then small storage parameters for the rollback segments will probably lead to better performance. Set the MINEXTENTS setting to the amount of undo generated by the largest normal transaction; that way, the likelihood of dynamic extension is decreased. Again, this is merely a guideline: Your system will need to be modified to fit your needs.

Assign a rollback segment to a transaction with the SET TRANSACTION USE ROLLBACK SEGMENT <rollback_segment_name> command. This is how you assign a large batch or long-running transaction to a specific rollback segment; this can be used with either manual or automatic undo management.

You can reduce rollback usage by committing transactions often, coding shorter transactions, using the COMMIT=Y parameter with the import utility, setting CONSISTENT=N with the export utility, and using the ROWS parameter with conventional path SQL*Loader data loads.

There are two common types of errors that transactions can encounter with rollback segments: running out of extents or space and ORA-01555: snapshot too old (rollback segment too small). The first type of error is caused by not configuring the MAXEXTENTS value high enough, by not configuring a large enough rollback segment tablespace, or by having too many rollback segments within the same tablespace. The ORA-01555 error occurs when users are not able to get read-consistent data from the rollback segment because it has already been overwritten. This problem is generally fixed by increasing the size and/or number of rollback segments.

Automatic undo management, new to Oracle9*i*, reduces the amount of work required of the DBA compared to using manually configured undo. The initialization parameter UNDO_MANAGEMENT=AUTO enables automatic undo management. The parameter UNDO_TABLESPACE specifies the undo tablespace to use for automatic undo management. The parameter UNDO_RETENTION determines how long, in seconds, to retain undo information after a transaction is complete.

Only one undo tablespace can be active at any given time. It is possible to have active transactions in more than one undo tablespace if a tablespace switch is signaled with the ALTER SYSTEM SET UNDO_TABLESPACE command while transactions are active in the previously defined tablespace. You cannot drop the active undo tablespace or an undo tablespace that has active transactions in it.

The V$UNDOSTAT view is used to determine the amount of undo space that is required to support the undo retention time specified with the UNDO_RETENTION initialization parameter.

Two-Minute Drill

- Oracle uses undo segments for read consistency, rollback, and transaction recovery.

- Read consistency means that queries will not see uncommitted changes, but they will see the unchanged data as it appeared at the time the query was executed.

- Undo is used to roll back transactions that are either explicitly or implicitly rolled back, restoring the original data.

- Undo is used to recover transactions that failed due to an instance crash, restoring the original data.

- There are two basic types of undo management: manual undo management and automatic undo management.

- Manual undo management is implemented with rollback segments that are created, configured, and managed by the DBA.

- Automatic undo management is new to Oracle9*i* and requires very little configuration or management by the DBA.

- Transactions write to rollback segments in a circular fashion, moving the current pointer to the end of each record that is added to the segment.

- If the current pointer reaches the end of the last extent, it will attempt to move to the beginning of the first extent.

- If the current pointer needs to move into the next extent and the next extent has active transaction records, then a new extent is added to the segment and the current pointer is moved into the new extent. The current pointer will not skip an extent.

- Manual rollback segments will extend as needed until they reach the value of MAXEXTENTS or until the rollback segment tablespace runs out of free space.

- The rollback segment header is a data block and generally will stay cached in the database buffer cache.

- These are the tuning goals for manually configured rollback segments:

  - Transactions should never wait for access to rollback segments.

  - Rollback segments should never extend during normal operation.

  - No transaction should ever run out of rollback segment space.

  - Readers should always see the read-consistent images they need.

  - Users and utilities should try to use less rollback.

- V$ROLLNAME contains the undo segment name and the USN of all online undo segments, manual or automatic managed.

- V$ROLLSTAT contains statistics about each online undo segment.

- V$TRANSACTION indicates the undo segment blocks in use by a particular transaction.

- The undo segment tx slot wait event, if present in the V$SYSTEM_EVENT view, indicates contention for the rollback segment header. The normal remedy is to add more rollback segments.

- V$WAITSTAT and V$SYSSTAT also indicate statistics for rollback and undo segment activity.

- The guideline for the number of rollback segments for OLTP systems is four concurrent transactions per rollback segment.

- If your application has large batch transactions, create at least one large rollback segment and keep it offline until it is needed.

- Small rollback segments should be used for small OLTP transactions.

- Large rollback segments should be used for large transactions.

- Assign a rollback segment to a transaction by using the SET TRANSACTION USE ROLLBACK SEGMENT command or by using the DBMS_TRANSACTION.USE_ROLLBACK_SEGMENT procedure.

- SET TRANSACTION must be the first statement of a transaction; otherwise, an error message will be generated.

■ You can determine the amount of rollback needed for a transaction by joining V$TRANSACTION and V$SESSION.

■ You can reduce rollback segment contention by committing frequently, coding shorter transactions, using the COMMIT=Y parameter with import, using the CONSISTENT=N parameter with export, and using the ROWS parameter with conventional path SQL*Loader.

■ If manual rollback segments are set too small, transactions can fail.

■ Add more space to the tablespace, and/or increase the value of MAXEXTENTS to prevent transactions from failing.

■ The ORA-01555 error message is generated when a query cannot get a read-consistent image that it needs. The usual remedy is to increase the size and/or number of rollback segments.

■ Setting the init.ora parameter UNDO_MANAGEMENT=AUTO and UNDO_TABLESPACE to a valid undo tablespace will enable automatic undo management.

■ With automatic undo management, the Oracle server determines the optimal size and number of undo segments. The DBA only needs to configure an appropriate size for the undo tablespace and the expected UNDO_RETENTION time.

■ UNDO_RETENTION determines the length of time undo information will stay in the undo segment before it is a candidate to be overwritten by new undo information.

■ Only one UNDO_TABLESPACE may be active at any given time. Use the ALTER SYSTEM SET UNDO_TABLESPACE command to switch undo tablespaces while the database is open.

■ Use the V$UNDOSTAT view to determine the amount of undo space required to keep enough undo blocks in the undo segment for the UNDO_RETENTION time.

■ If the undo tablespace is too small, transactions will fail.

■ If the UNDO_RETENTION time is too short, queries may experience ORA-01555 errors.

Chapter Questions

1. **Which of the following are advantages of automatic undo management over manual undo management? (Choose two.)**

   A. The DBA doesn't need to configure individual rollback segments.

   B. The DBA can set the length of time undo information is retained.

   C. The DBA can specify multiple active undo tablespaces.

   D. The end user can specify multiple active undo tablespaces.

   E. The DBA only needs to specify the number of undo segments required.

2. **Which of the following will correctly set the system so that read-consistent entries are kept for 30 minutes?**

   A. ALTER SYSTEM SET UNDO_CONTENTION=1800

   B. ALTER SYSTEM SET UNDO_TABLESPACE=1800

   C. ALTER SYSTEM SET REDO_RETAIN=1800

   D. ALTER SYSTEM SET UNDO_RETENTION=1800

   E. ALTER SYSTEM SET READ_CONSISTENT=1800

3. **You need to switch from one undo tablespace (active) to another (target). Which of the following conditions would prevent this action?**

   A. The target tablespace is smaller than the active tablespace.

   B. The target tablespace is defined as a temporary tablespace.

   C. There are transactions in the active tablespace.

   D. Queries need the undo images in the active tablespace for read consistency.

   E. The initialization parameter UNDO_MANAGEMENT is set to AUTO.

4. **When operating in automatic undo management mode, which of the following conditions will prevent the DBA from dropping the UNDO_01 undo tablespace? (Choose four.)**

   A. UNDO_01 is the currently active undo tablespace.

   B. UNDO_01 has no transactions assigned to it.

   C. There are active transactions in UNDO_01.

D. Queries need the undo images in UNDO_01 for read consistency.

E. There is no other UNDO tablespace.

F. Each of the other UNDO tablespaces is offline.

5. **Your database is configured to use manual undo management, and your application users regularly experience ORA-01555 errors. What can you do to reduce the likelihood of future errors if you continue to use manual undo management?**

A. Decrease the size of the rollback segments.

B. Increase the size of the rollback segments.

C. Decrease the number of rollback segments.

D. Configure an OPTIMAL value for each of the rollback segments.

6. **You're operating an OLTP database in manual undo management mode and notice that the query SELECT COUNT(*) from V$TRANSACTION is always less than or equal to 160 during peak transaction hours. How many rollback segments should you configure?**

A. 640

B. 40

C. 160

D. 50

E. 4

F. 20

7. **Which of the following would indicate an undo header performance problem? (Choose three.)**

A. V$ROLLSTAT—Nonzero value in the WAITS column.

B. V$WAITSTAT—The undo header row has a nonzero value in the COUNT column.

C. V$SYSSTAT—The undo header row has a nonzero value in the COUNT column.

D. V$SYSTEM_EVENT—The undo segment tx slot event shows that the nonzero value in the TOTAL_WAITS column or TIME_WAITED is greater than 0.

8. **You want to monitor the activity in current online undo segments. Which query would help you diagnose potential problems?**

   A. SELECT USN, XACTS, WAITS, HWMSIZE, SHRINKS, WRAPS,EXTENDS, AVESHRINK, AVEACTIVE, FROM V$ROLLSTAT

   B. SELECT USN, XACTS, WAITS, HWMSIZE, SHRINKS, WRAPS,EXTENDS, AVESHRINK, AVEACTIVE, FROM V$UNDOSTAT

   C. SELECT USN, XACTS, WAITS, HWMSIZE, SHRINKS, WRAPS,EXTENDS, AVESHRINK, AVEACTIVE, FROM V$TRANSACTION

   D. SELECT USN, XACTS, WAITS, HWMSIZE, SHRINKS, WRAPS,EXTENDS, AVESHRINK, AVEACTIVE, FROM V$ROLLBACK

9. **Which query would help you determine the volume of rollback created by a transaction and assist in determining the size of a manually configured rollback segment? (Choose two.)**

   A. SELECT USN, WRITES FROM V$ROLLNAME

   B. SELECT S.USERNAME, T.USED_UBLK,FROM V$TRANSACTION T, V$SESSION S, WHERE T.ADDR = S.TADDR

   C. SELECT USN, WRITES FROM V$ROLLSTAT

   D. SELECT USED_UBLK FROM V$ROLLSTAT

   E. SELECT USED_UBLK FROM V$UNDOTAT

10. **Which of the following sets of views can you use to determine the amount of undo space needed for automatic undo management?**

    A. V$TRANSACTION, V$ROLLSTAT, V$PARAMETER

    B. V$UNDOSTAT, V$PARAMETER, V$ROLLSTAT

    C. V$PARAMETER, V$ROLLSTAT

    D. V$PARAMETER, V$UNDOSTAT

    E. V$UNDOSTAT, V$ROLLNAME

    F. V$ROLLNAME, DBA_ROLLBACK_SEGS, V$SYSTEM_EVENT

Answers to Chapter Questions

1. A and B.   The DBA doesn't need to configure individual rollback segments, and the DBA can set the length of time to undo information is retained.

Explanation   The major advantage of automatic undo management over manual undo management is that the DBA doesn't need to configure individual rollback segments. Oracle does that for us automatically. The DBA sets the dynamically configurable UNDO_RETENTION parameter to the number of seconds that undo should be retained. Answers C and D are incorrect because only one undo tablespace can be the current UNDO_TABLESPACE. Answer E is incorrect because the number of rollback segments is not configurable with automatic undo management.

2. D.   ALTER SYSTEM SET UNDO_RETENTION=1800

Explanation   The correct parameter is UNDO_RETENTION, and the correct value is 30 minutes $\times$ 60 seconds / minute = 1,800. The other answers are incorrect because they do not reference the correct parameter.

3. B.   The target tablespace is defined as a temporary tablespace.

Explanation   The target tablespace must be defined as an undo tablespace, not a temporary tablespace. Answer A is incorrect because size doesn't matter. Answer C is incorrect because active transactions in the active tablespace will not prevent the switch to a new tablespace. The active transactions will continue, but no new transactions will begin in the tablespace. Answer D does not prevent the switch from occurring. Answer E is required for automatic undo management, so it will not prevent the switch from occurring.

4. A, C, E, and F.   UNDO_01 is the currently active undo tablespace, There are active transactions in UNDO_01, There is no other UNDO tablespace, Each of the other UNDO tablespaces is offline.

Explanation   Answers A, E, and F indicate the same thing—that the UNDO_01 tablespace is the currently active or only undo tablespace, and therefore cannot be dropped. Answer C is correct because you cannot drop an undo tablespace that has current transactions. Answers B and D, in and of themselves, will not prevent the DBA from dropping the tablespace.

5. B.   Increase the size of the rollback segments.

Explanation   ORA-01555 errors indicate read-consistency problems, usually due to undo information being overwritten in undersized rollback segments. Increase the size of the rollback segment to reduce the likelihood that an undo block will be overwritten. Answers A and C are incorrect because they will increase the probability that ORA-01555 errors will recur. Answer D can also contribute to the problem since rollback segments will shrink to the OPTIMAL setting if extents are no longer used by a transaction.

6. B.   40

Explanation   The general guideline is to configure the maximum number of concurrent transactions divided by 4. For this case, $160 \div 4 = 40$, so we should configure 40 rollback segments. Based on the guideline and the query, each of the other answers is an incorrect value.

7. A, B, and D.   V$ROLLSTAT—Nonzero value in the WAITS column, V$WAITSTAT—The undo header row has a nonzero value in the COUNT column, and V$SYSTEM_EVENT—The undo segment tx slot event shows that the nonzero value in the TOTAL_WAITS column or TIME_WAITED is greater than 0.

Explanation   Each of the Answers, A, B, and D, indicates undo header contention problems. Answer C is incorrect because the V$SYSSTAT view does not have a row for undo header contention, and the view does not have a COUNT column.

8. A.   SELECT USN, XACTS, WAITS, HWMSIZE, SHRINKS, WRAPS,EXTENDS, AVESHRINK, AVEACTIVE, FROM V$UNDOSTAT

Explanation   The requested statistics are in the V$ROLLSTAT view. The other answers are incorrect because they query the wrong views. Use V$ROLLSTAT to determine the cumulative statistics for online undo segments. You can use if for manual or automatic managed undo.

9. B and C.   SELECT S.USERNAME, T.USED_UBLK, FROM V$TRANSACTION T, V$SESSION S, WHERE T.ADDR = S.TADD; and, SELECT USN, WRITES FROM V$ROLLSTAT

Explanation   The query in Answer B will show us the username and number of used undo blocks for each transaction. We can use this to determine how much undo a benchmark transaction would require. Answer C indicates the number of undo bytes written to a rollback segment. You can run this before and after a benchmark transaction to determine how much undo the transaction will need. Answers A, D, and E are incorrect because they reference the wrong view or a nonexistent column.

10. D.   V$PARAMETER, V$UNDOSTAT

Explanation   Use the general formula:

Undo Space = (UNDO_RETENTION + (undo blocks per second ×
    DB_BLOCK_SIZE)) + DB_BLOCK_SIZE

The parameters db_block_size and undo_retention are stored in V$PARAMETER. The undo blocks per second statistic is obtained from the V$UNDOSTAT view. The specific query is supplied in the chapter, so there's no need to repeat it here. The other answers are incorrect because the wrong list of views is referenced.

CHAPTER
11

Monitoring and Detecting
Lock Contention

n this chapter, you will learn how to monitor and detect lock contention. The specific subjects that you will be tested on include

- Defining levels of locking
- Describing possible causes of contention
- Using Oracle utilities to detect lock contention
- Resolving contention in an emergency
- Preventing locking problems
- Recognizing Oracle errors arising from deadlocks

This chapter focuses on monitoring and detecting lock contention in the Oracle database server. First, you will learn about the Oracle locking mechanism, the different types of locks, and the different locking modes. You'll then learn about possible causes of lock contention. We'll then discuss how to detect locking and lock contention using different views and scripts. We'll show you how to resolve lock contention in an emergency and how to prevent further locking contention. Finally, we'll discuss deadlocks and how Oracle resolves them.

Monitoring and Detecting Lock Contention

Before we get into defining locking levels, we need to take some time to discuss the purpose of locks as well as the way Oracle manages locks and the locking mechanism. Once you have received a solid background in the various lock types and functions, we'll move on to locking levels.

The purpose of a lock is to protect resources that may be needed for a relatively long time, unlike latches, which are expected to be held only briefly. The locking mechanism enables sessions to wait in line for a resource if it is currently busy or being held in an incompatible mode. Database tables will be the focus of our discussion on locks, because most of the lock activity you'll see and need to tune relates to database tables.

Lock Management

The Oracle server automatically manages object locking, so most application development efforts do not need to focus on lock management. The default locking mechanism locks data at the lowest level of restrictiveness that will guarantee data consistency while enabling the highest degree of data concurrency. A lock is requested and then held on an object from the time the Data Manipulation

Language (DML) is executed until the transaction is complete, at which time all locks obtained during the transaction are released.

The DBA can modify the default locking mechanism by setting the ROW_LOCKING initialization parameter. The default value is ALWAYS; this causes default locking at the row level during DML statements. This is the least restrictive. You can also specify DEFAULT, which is synonymous with ALWAYS. Setting the value to INTENT causes default locking at the table level, except for SELECT . . . FOR UPDATE statements that cause row-level locking. In the remainder of this section, we will demonstrate how locks work between two transactions competing for the same resources.

Data Concurrency   The default Oracle locking mechanism is designed to enable a high level of data concurrency. Here's an example of DML locking, which occurs at the row level:

Transaction 1	Transaction 2
Update invoice	Update invoice
Set status='Closed'	Set status='Review'
Where nbr = '7651234';	Where nbr = '7651235';
1 row updated	1 row updated

In the previous example, the two sessions do not conflict because they are not attempting to update the same row or rows. Row-level locking is used, resulting in a high level of data concurrency.

A query holds no locks, unless the user specifies that it should with the SELECT . . . FOR UPDATE statement. Here's an example using an update and a normal query:

Transaction 1	Transaction 2
Update invoice	Select status
Set status='Closed';	From invoice
1250 rows updated	Where status='Review';
	654 rows returned

In this example, Transaction 1 locks rows for updates, but Transaction 2 is allowed to query without conflict.

Data Consistency The Oracle server also provides data consistency. The user sees a static picture of the data, even if other users are changing it. Data consistency is maintained with rollback or UNDO segments. If one transaction is in the process of modifying rows of data, other transactions will read the original unchanged data from the read-consistent view in the UNDO segments.

Data consistency also means that two transactions cannot change the same data at the same time. Once one transaction completes, another transaction can follow it and modify the same data.

Locking Modes An exclusive lock prevents a resource from being shared with other transactions until the exclusive lock is released. Here's an example that demonstrates an exclusive lock that is set at the row level for a DML transaction:

Transaction 1	**Transaction 2**
Update invoice	Update invoice
Set status='Closed'	Set status='Review'
Where nbr = '7651234';	Where nbr = '7651234';
1 row updated	Transaction 2 waits . . .

Transaction 2 will wait until Transaction 1 ends, either by rollback or commit. In share lock mode, several transactions can acquire locks on the same resource. So, two or more transactions can update different rows in the same table. Here's an example using shared locks, which are set at the table level for DML transactions:

Transaction 1	**Transaction 2**
Update invoice	Update invoice
Set status='Closed'	Set status='Review'
Where nbr = '7651234';	Where nbr = '7651235';
1 row updated	1 row updated

Because Transaction 1 and Transaction 2 update different rows, there is no locking conflict.

Lock Duration   Locks are held until a COMMIT or ROLLBACK statement executes, or a until a transaction is terminated. The Process Monitor (PMON) cleans up locks if a transaction terminates abnormally. Here's an example of lock duration:

Transaction 1	Transaction 2
Update invoice	Update invoice
Set status='Closed'	Set status='Review'
Where nbr = '7651234';	Where nbr = '7651234';
1 row updated	Transaction 2 waits . . .
commit;	1 row updated
Commit complete.	

Miscellaneous Locking Facts   Queries do not require table or row locks. Exclusive and shared lock modes are available for tables. In Oracle9*i*, the database administrator (DBA) can put the database in a quiesced state if there are no active transactions, queries, data fetches, Procedural Language/Structured Query Language (PL/SQL) activity, or shared resources held by a session.

Define Levels of Locking

In this section we'll describe the different types of locks, and within the types, the different levels of locks. The two basic types of locks that we will talk about are Data Manipulation Language (DML) or table locks and Data Definition Language (DDL) or dictionary locks.

DML or Data Locks

DML locks are designed to guarantee data integrity in a multiuser environment. DML locks prevent conflicting DML and DDL operations from destroying each other's data operations.

Table-Level Lock   A Type TM or table-level lock is set for a DML operation that modifies table data: INSERT, UPDATE, DELETE, SELECT . . . FOR UPDATE, or the explicit LOCK TABLE command. The table-level lock prevents DDL operations that would interfere with the transaction. Here's an example:

Transaction 1	**Transaction 2**
Update invoice	Drop table invoice;
Set status='Closed';	ERROR at line 1:
1250 rows updated	ORA-00054: resource busy and acquire with NOWAIT specified

Row-Level Lock A row-level lock is used to ensure that no two transactions modify the same row at the same time. When a transaction locks a row, all others that want to modify that row will wait in turn until the first transaction completes. A TX lock is acquired when a transaction starts, and there is only one TX lock per transaction. The TX lock signifies the rollback segment transaction's table header location that contains the transaction UNDO information. The TX lock is used to implement row locks for each row that the transaction is changing.

Here's an example:

Transaction 1	**Transaction 2**
Update invoice	Update invoice
Set status='Closed'	Set status='Review'
Where nbr = '7651234';	Where nbr = '7651234';
1 row updated	Transaction 2 waits until Transaction 1 completes.

DML Locks in Transactions When a transaction starts, it must acquire a slot in a rollback segment transaction table, which stores the location of the transaction's UNDO data. Each transaction has a unique identifier, which is the combination of a rollback segment number and a transaction table slot.

A DML lock gets at least two locks: a shared TM lock on the table and an exclusive TX lock that is used to implement row locks for each row that the transaction is changing.

The row lock is indicated by turning on a lock byte in the row header, which points to the interested transaction list (ITL) slot used by the transaction. The unique transaction identifier is stored in the ITL slots for each row locked by the transaction. The row-level lock mode can only be exclusive, and a transaction can hold an unlimited number of row locks.

If the table is a partitioned table, the transaction acquires a table lock and a table partition lock for each partition in which rows will be modified. The partition locks are TM locks against the table partitions being modified.

The following rules apply to DML row-level locks:

- Readers never wait for writers of the same row.

- Writers never wait for readers unless the reader uses the SELECT . . . FOR UPDATE statement.

- Writers wait for other writers only if they are attempting to update the same row.

Enqueue Mechanism   Oracle maintains locks as enqueues, shared memory structures that serialize access to a resource. To enqueue a lock request means to place that request on the queue for the lock. The enqueue mechanism keeps track of sessions waiting for locks, the lock mode requested, and the order in which locks were requested.

When several sessions need to update the same row at the same time, the first one gets the exclusive row lock, and each gets a shared table lock. The enqueue mechanism keeps track of which transaction holds the row lock, and an ordered list of which ones wait for it.

You can increase the overall number of locks available for an instance by increasing the parameters DML_LOCKS and ENQUEUE_RESOURCES. The value for DML_LOCKS specifies the maximum number of DML locks allowed in the instance. The value should be greater than the total number of locks that will be concurrently held on tables. The default value for DML_LOCKS is based on the values of other initialization parameters: four times the value of TRANSACTIONS, whose default is based on the SESSIONS parameter, whose default is based on the PROCESSES parameter, whose default is derived from the PARALLEL_MAX_SERVERS parameter, whose default is derived from the CPU_COUNT parameter and other PARALLEL_* parameters.

The default assumes an average of four tables per transaction. If transactions in your database on the average require more locks, then you'll need to increase DML_LOCKS. Oracle holds more locks during parallel DML than during serial execution, so if you have a lot of parallel DML, consider increasing the value of this parameter.

Setting the value of DML_LOCKS to 0 disables enqueues. This may improve performance slightly, but it prevents you from using commands that require exclusive locks, such as the DROP TABLE or CREATE INDEX statements. It also prevents the use of explicit lock statements such as LOCK TABLE IN EXCLUSIVE MODE.

The value of the ENQUEUE_RESOURCES initialization parameter sets the number of resources that can be concurrently locked within the database. You can check enqueue resource usage by querying V$RESOURCE_LIMIT where RESOURCE_NAME = 'ENQUEUE_RESOURCES'. Also, the V$ENQUEUE_STAT view displays statistics on the number of enqueue requests for each type of lock.

DML Locks in Blocks   Locking information is not cleared from the data block when the transaction commits, but when the next query reads the block. The term for this is *delayed block cleanout*. The query that does the cleanout checks the transaction's status and the SCN in the transaction table of the rollback segment header. The block header of the data block stores the lock byte for each row. The lock byte for each row stores the ITL slot, which contains the transaction ID of the transaction that has locked the row.

Automatic Table Lock Modes   The two TM table lock modes held by DML transactions are Row Exclusive (RX) and Row Share (RS). These table lock modes are automatically assigned for DML transactions. The table lock mode determines the modes in which other table locks on the same table can be obtained and held. The two table lock modes are detailed here:

- **RX**   This enables other transactions to query, insert, update, delete, or lock other rows concurrently, but it prevents others from manually locking the table for exclusive reading or writing.

- **RS**   The SELECT . . . FOR UPDATE statement causes a shared lock, so other transactions can still query, insert, update, delete, or lock other rows concurrently in the table. However, other transactions are not allowed to manually lock the table for exclusive write access.

Manual Table Lock Modes   The three other table lock modes are assigned explicitly with the LOCK TABLE command:

```
LOCK TABLE HR.EMPLOYEES IN EXCLUSIVE MODE;
```

There may be good reasons for the application to explicitly lock tables, but if you get lock contention, you may want to check with the developers. Often, developers from non-Oracle backgrounds use unnecessarily high locking levels, so it's important to educate them on Oracle's locking mechanism. The three other table lock modes are as follows:

- **Share (S)**   This lock mode permits other sessions to query the table and use the SELECT . . . FOR UPDATE statement, but S prevents any modification to the table. The SQL statements that implicitly get an S lock involve referential integrity constraints. In Oracle9*i*, the implementation of the referential integrity constraint has changed. The S lock against the parent table is held briefly, so therefore it does not require the index on the foreign key column of the child table to prevent the implicit table lock from being held for the duration of the transaction.

- **Share Row Exclusive (SRX)**   This is the next locking level above S. This prevents DML statements and manual share lock mode acquisition. The SQL statements that implicitly get an SRX lock involve referential integrity. As mentioned previously, you don't need to create an index on the foreign key column in the child table as you did in previous Oracle versions.

- **Exclusive (X)**   This is the highest and most restrictive level of table lock, which permits other sessions only to query the table. This lock prevents any type of DML statements and any manual lock mode.

Table Partition Locks   When DML transactions occur on partitioned tables, Oracle sets three levels of locks: table, partition, and row. Table locks are determined at parse time and are acquired at execution time. The need for a partition lock is determined, and acquired, when Oracle sees that it needs to modify a row in a specific partition.

DDL or Dictionary Locks

A DDL lock protects the definition of a schema object while the object is referenced in a DDL operation. Oracle automatically acquires a DDL lock to prevent other DDL operations from referencing or altering the same object. If a DDL lock is requested on an object that already has a DDL lock on it, the lock request will wait. DDL lock contention is rare because they are usually held only briefly. There are three types of DDL locks: exclusive, shared, and breakable parse locks.

Exclusive DDL Locks   Most DDL operations, including CREATE CLUSTER, DROP/ALTER TABLE, CREATE/ALTER/DROP INDEX, and CREATE/ALTER TABLESPACE, require an exclusive lock on the object they are working on. A user session can't get an exclusive lock on a table if any other user holds any level of lock on it. So any ALTER or DROP TABLE statement will fail if there is an uncommitted transaction using that table.

Shared DDL Locks   The following DDL statements need a shared DDL lock on the objects that they refer to: AUDIT, NOAUDIT, COMMENT, CREATE [OR REPLACE] VIEW/PROCEDURE/PACKAGE/PACKAGE BODY/FUNCTION/TRIGGER, and CREATE SYNONYM. Also, CREATE TABLE needs a shared DDL lock when the CLUSTER clause isn't specified. The shared DDL lock prevents other users from altering or dropping the object, but will not prevent similar DDL statements or any DML.

Breakable Parse Locks   An SQL statement or PL/SQL object in the library cache holds a breakable parse lock for each object that it references until the statement is aged out of the shared pool. The breakable parse lock is used to check if the statement should be invalidated if the object changes. This lock will never cause a wait or contention.

Describe Possible Causes of Contention

Oracle locks are designed to be inexpensive and efficient. Most applications do not experience lock contention problems. However, lock contention problems can occur in an Oracle database. Here are a few reasons why these problems can occur.

Unnecessarily High Locking Levels

Developers may have coded unnecessarily high locking levels. This would occur when a process holds an exclusive lock on a table, yet a less-restrictive lock would have worked, and other sessions want to modify rows in the table.

Long-Running Transactions

Developers may have coded unnecessarily long transactions. Remember that locks are held for the duration of a transaction, so the likelihood of contention increases with longer-running transactions.

Uncommitted Changes

Users are not committing changes when they should. The classic example is a user modifying data and then going to lunch without committing. The DBA is informed of this because other users are trying to complete their tasks before going to lunch. They are unable to because resources are locked, so they call the DBA and interrupt his lunch.

Other Products Imposing Higher-Level Locks

If you're developing applications in a multitier or multiplatform environment, you may be using tools that do not enable the developer to specify locking levels. The application programming interface (API) or database interface layer may explicitly lock database objects without the application developer's knowledge. Beware that other applications or interfaces used with the database may impose higher locking levels than needed.

Use Oracle Utilities to Detect Lock Contention

The DBA monitors and detects lock contention with the assistance of two dynamic performance views and several views that are created by Oracle-supplied scripts.

V$LOCK   The V$LOCK view lists the locks currently held within the Oracle server and the outstanding requests for a lock or latch. V$LOCK displays the type of lock held or requested, the lock mode, and the session holding or requesting the lock. The information V$LOCK contains is as follows:

- **SID**   The session ID of the holding or requesting session.

- **TYPE**   Either user or system locks. System locks are held very briefly; user locks are usually the ones causing contention, so we'll list them here:

  - **TX**   Transaction enqueue.

  - **TM**   DML enqueue.

  - **UL**   User supplied.

- **ID1**   If TYPE equals TM, this is the OBJECT_ID of the locked object. If TYPE equals TX, this is the transaction rollback segment and slot number.

Here's a query that shows information about locked objects:

```
SELECT O.OWNER, O.OBJECT_ID, O.OBJECT_NAME, O.OBJECT_TYPE, L.TYPE
FROM DBA_OBJECTS O, V$LOCK L
WHERE O.OBJECT_ID = L.ID1
/

OWNER        OBJECT_ID OBJECT_NAME            OBJECT_TYP TY
---------- ---------- -------------------- ---------- --
SYSTEM          32392 FOOBAR                 TABLE      TM
SYSTEM          32392 FOOBAR                 TABLE      TM
...
SYSTEM          32371 MY_DEPT                TABLE      TM
```

The V$ENQUEUE_LOCK view has the same columns as V$LOCK; it displays all locks owned by enqueue state objects. To determine all DML and user locks on the system, run this query:

```
SELECT * FROM v$lock
MINUS
SELECT * FROM v$enqueue_lock
/
```

V$LOCKED_OBJECT   The V$LOCKED_OBJECT view combines session, rollback, and locked object information for locks acquired by transactions in the system. Several columns can be joined with other views to gain more detailed information. The V$LOCKED_OBJECT view contains the following information:

- **XIDUSN** The undo segment number. Join this with the USN column in V$ROLLSTAT for more info. If the XIDUSN equals 0, then the session is requesting and waiting for a lock.

- **XIDSLOT** The slot number.

- **XIDSQN** The sequence number.

- **OBJECT_ID** The object ID being locked. Join this with OBJECT_ID column in DBA_OBJECTS.

- **SESSION_ID** The session ID. Join this with the SID column of V$SESSION for session details.

- **ORACLE_USERNAME** The Oracle user name.

- **OS_USER_NAME** The OS user name.

- **PROCESS** The OS process ID.

- **LOCKED_MODE** The locked mode.

Additional Views Used to Detect Lock Contention

Oracle gives us several scripts and a package to monitor lock contention. The Oracle script catblock.sql creates several views that assist in detecting and resolving lock contention. You only need to run catblock.sql once to create the DBA views, and it can be run after catproc.sql is run immediately after database creation.

DBA_BLOCKERS The DBA_BLOCKERS view has one column, HOLDING_SESSION, which indicates each session that is

- Not currently waiting on a locked object.

- Currently holding a lock on an object that another session is waiting for.

DBA_WAITERS The DBA_WAITERS view is the counterpart to DBA_BLOCKERS. It indicates which sessions are

- Currently waiting on a locked object.

- Not currently holding a lock on an object that another session is waiting for.

The WAITING_SESSION column indicates the SID of the waiting session, and the HOLDING_SESSION column indicates the SID of the holding session. The DBA_WAITERS view shows the lock type and the modes in which the lock is being held and requested.

Other Views Created by catblock.sql   In addition to the previously mentioned views, catblock.sql also creates the following views: DBA_DDL_LOCKS, DBA_DML_LOCKS, DBA_LOCK, and DBA_LOCK_INTERNAL. These views each have one row for each lock held and one row for each lock request.

Additional Monitoring Scripts

Once you have run catblock.sql and created the DBA views, you can run utllockt.sql to get a tree-based report of the blockers and waiters in the database.

Utllockt.sql   The $ORACLE_HOME/rdbms/admin/utllockt.sql script generates a report of the sessions holding and waiting for locks in a tree-structured fashion. The script creates the LOCK_HOLDERS table and then the DBA_LOCKS_TEMP table by selecting all rows from DBA_LOCKS. The script populates LOCK_HOLDERS by selecting and massaging the rows in DBA_LOCKS_TEMP; it then generates the locking report by querying LOCK_HOLDERS.

One of the downsides of running the script is that it must acquire locks when it creates the two tables, which could contribute to a locking problem.

Resolve Contention in an Emergency

In busy systems, it is inevitable that an occasional rogue user will lock other users out of required resources. This usually happens when a user begins a transaction and then leaves for a break, the end of the shift, or even vacation. If users are complaining that sessions are blocked, initiate your lock-monitoring tool and investigate. If you determine that a session is locking other essential sessions, you should attempt to contact the owner of the locking session and ask him or her to commit or rollback. If your efforts to resolve the lock condition civilly fail, you can kill the holding session to rollback the transaction and free the resource.

Killing Sessions

Your lock-detection script or utility will in the very least return the SID of the locking session. In order to kill the session, you'll also need the SERIAL# from the V$SESSION view. Here's one way to get the required information:

```
SELECT SID, SERIAL#
FROM V$SESSION
WHERE SID IN (SELECT HOLDING_SESSION FROM DBA_WAITERS)
/
    SID  SERIAL#
------ --------
    55     1876
```

Now that you have the required pieces of information, enter the following command to kill the session:

```
ALTER SYSTEM KILL SESSION '55,1876'
/
System altered
```

Row Wait Contention   Before you kill the offending session, you may want some more detailed information about the resource that other sessions are waiting on. V$SESSION has four columns that can help you trace lock contention down to the row level:

- **ROW_WAIT_OBJ#**   The object ID for the table containing the ROWID specified in ROW_WAIT_ROW#.

The following columns are only valid if the session is currently waiting for another transaction to commit, and the value of ROW_WAIT_OBJ# is not −1.

- **ROW_WAIT_FILE#**   The identifier for the data file containing the ROWID specified in ROW_WAIT_ROW#.

- **ROW_WAIT_BLOCK#**   The identifier for the block containing the ROWID specified in ROW_WAIT_ROW#.

- **ROW_WAIT_ROW#**   The current ROWID being locked.

Prevent Locking Problems

From the application development perspective, developers should keep in mind three basic considerations:

- Developers should write code so that all processes acquire locks in the same order.

- Always use the least restrictive mode of locking allowed for SELECT FOR UPDATE and UPDATE statements.

- In Online Transaction Processing (OLTP) systems, all long-running batch jobs should be scheduled outside regular business processing hours.

The DBMS_LOCK Package

With the DBMS_LOCK package, you can request a user-defined lock of a specific mode, change the lock mode, assign a unique name to it, and release it. These user-defined locks have all the functionality of Oracle locks, including deadlock detection. The difference is that DBMS_LOCK creates locks on abstract objects defined by the user, not on tables.

User locks never conflict with Oracle locks because user locks are identified with the prefix UL. User locks are automatically released when a session terminates.

Functions and Procedures in DBMS_LOCK   DBMS_LOCK offers the following capabilities:

- **Convert function**   Converts a user lock from one mode to another.

- **Allocate_unique procedure**   Allocates a unique lock ID to a named user lock.

- **Release function**   Releases a user lock.

- **Sleep procedure**   Puts a procedure to sleep for a specific time.

- **Request function**   Requests a user lock of a specific mode.

Using DBMS_LOCK   For the DBA, instead of killing a blocking session, you can alter a session's lock status or user lock mode. The DBMS_LOCK_ALLOCATED view describes user-allocated locks. The columns are NAME, LOCKID, and EXPIRATION date.

Recognize Oracle Errors Arising from Deadlocks

A deadlock can occur when two or more transactions wait for data locked by each other. A deadlock exists in the current session if the following conditions are met:

- Another session is holding a lock on a resource in an incompatible mode.

- The resource is required by the current session.

- The other session is waiting for a resource that is locked in an incompatible mode by the current session.

Oracle initiates deadlock detection when an enqueue wait times out, the type of resource is deadlock sensitive, and the lock state of the resource remains unchanged. Oracle automatically resolves deadlocks by rolling back the *statement* that detected the deadlock. The *transaction* is not rolled back, just the statement that caused the deadlock. An ORA-00060 error message is also returned to the session that detects the deadlock. At this point, the session should rollback the entire transaction. If the statement is part of a PL/SQL block, the error-handling routine should have been designed to clean up the transaction.

Please note that although the entire transaction is not rolled back, you are highly encouraged to do so. If the deadlock occurred once, the conditions may possibly still exist for it to recur if the transaction retries the statement that detected the deadlock. Deadlocks are most likely to occur when transactions are explicitly written to lock at too high a level, as in this example:

Sequence	Transaction #1	Transaction #2
1	Lock table my_dept In exclusive mode;	Lock table my_employees In exclusive mode;
2	Update my_employees Set employee_id = 199 Where employee_id = 100; T1 waits	Update my_dept Set department_id=1;
3	ORA-00060: deadlock detected while waiting for resource	

Here's an example of a set of otherwise innocuous statements that will cause a deadlock condition; you may encounter these in normal everyday activity:

Sequence	Transaction #1	Transaction #2
1	Update invoice Set status='Closed' Where nbr = '7651234'; 1 Row Updated	Update invoice Set status='Review' Where nbr = '7651235'; 1 Row Updated
2	Update invoice Set status='Closed' Where nbr = '7651235'; T1 waits	Update invoice Set status='Review' Where nbr = '7651234'; T2 waits
3	ORA-00060: deadlock detected while waiting for resource	

Information about Deadlocks   When the deadlock is detected, a trace file is created in the USER_DUMP_DEST directory. The name of the trace file includes the process ID number of the detecting server process, which correlates to the SPID column in V$PROCESS. The trace file contains the session_ids of the two sessions involved in the deadlock and the ROWIDs of the locked rows. The trace file also contains the SQL statement that was rolled back.

In addition to the trace file, the *enqueue deadlocks* statistic in V$SYSSTAT is incremented each time an enqueue deadlock is detected and resolved.

Chapter Summary

In this chapter, you learned about the locking mechanism, the types of locks, the levels of locks, lock modes, monitoring lock contention, preventing lock contention, resolving lock contention in case of an emergency, and how Oracle deals with deadlocks.

Oracle uses locks to protect resources from DML or DDL that may interfere with current transactions. Locks enable user requests to wait in line, or in the queue, until the resource becomes available. By default, Oracle locks data at the lowest level of restrictiveness that will guarantee data consistency while enabling the highest degree of data concurrency. Basically, multiple users will see consistent data.

There are two basic types of locks covered in this chapter: DML and DDL. DML locks protect data and can be either table-level or row-level. DDL locks protect the structure of data dictionary objects such as tables or views.

Every transaction acquires an exclusive TX lock when it initiates its first change and holds the lock until the transaction does a commit or rollback. Row-level DML locks prevent transactions from modifying rows that are held by other transactions. A row-level lock is always exclusive. Transactions can acquire an unlimited number of row-level locks. A table-level share lock is also acquired when a row-level DML lock is acquired. This prevents DDL or DML from acquiring an exclusive lock on the table.

Table-level, or TM locks, are used to provide various degrees of restrictiveness on table modifications. When an INSERT, UPDATE, DELETE, SELECT . . . FOR UPDATE, or explicit LOCK TABLE statement is issued, a lock is acquired on the specified table. The table-level lock prevents DDL operations that would interfere with the transaction. For example, the DROP TABLE command will fail if active transactions are accessing the table, because each active transaction holds a shared TM lock on the table.

There are several TM lock modes, some acquired automatically, others requested manually. RX locks are automatically acquired and prevent another transaction from acquiring an exclusive table lock. RS is automatically acquired when a user issues the SELECT . . . FOR UPDATE statement and prevents a manual exclusive write lock.

There are three manually requested TM lock modes: shared (S), shared row exclusive (SRX), and exclusive (X). S permits others to query and use SELECT . . . FOR UPDATE, while SRX prevents DML and manual share lock mode requests. Both S and SRX mode are implicitly acquired when enforcing referential integrity constraints on DML statements. Exclusive locks prevent all DML; only queries, which do not acquire table locks, are allowed.

A DDL lock protects the definition of a schema object while the object is referenced in a DDL statement. An exclusive DDL lock is acquired for the following operations: CREATE CLUSTER, DROP/ALTER TABLE, CREATE/ALTER/DROP INDEX, and CREATE/ALTER TABLESPACE. The following DDL statements need a shared DDL lock on the objects that they refer to: AUDIT, NOAUDIT, COMMENT, CREATE [OR REPLACE] VIEW/ PROCEDURE/ PACKAGE/PACKAGE BODY/FUNCTION/ TRIGGER, and CREATE SYNONYM. Also, CREATE TABLE needs a shared DDL lock when the CLUSTER clause isn't specified. The shared DDL lock doesn't prevent similar DDL or any DML.

A breakable parse lock is held for each object referenced in an SQL statement or a PL/SQL block until the statement is aged out of the shared pool; it is used to check if the statement should be invalidated if the object changes.

Contention for locks can occur if developers code unnecessarily high locking levels, create long-running transactions, leave changes uncommitted, or use products that lock at unnecessarily high levels.

You can monitor locks using the V$LOCK, V$LOCKED_OBJECT, V$ENQUEUE_LOCK, DBA_WAITERS, and DBA_BLOCKERS views. V$LOCK has an entry for each lock held and requested. V$LOCKED_OBJECT has an entry for each object locked as well as information about the transaction and session locking the object.

The DBA_BLOCKERS and DBA_WAITERS views are used to show the locking sessions and waiting sessions, respectively. Both views (and several others) are created by the catblock.sql script, which should be run after the database is created and catproc.sql has been run.

The utllockt.sql script can also be used to monitor lock activity. It provides a tree-based report showing blockers and waiters. Utllockt.sql reads from DBA_LOCKS, one of the views created by the catblock.sql script.

You may occasionally need to kill sessions that have locked objects required by other sessions. Use the ALTER SYSTEM KILL SESSION '<sid>, <serial#>' command to kill the offending session. You can obtain the SID as HOLDING_SESSION from DBA_WAITERS and the SERIAL# from V$SESSION.

You can prevent lock contention problems by enforcing several general guidelines on your application developers. If they manually acquire DML locks, make sure that they acquire locks in the same order of restrictiveness. They should always use the least restrictive mode of shared TM locks that will meet the application requirements. If they code long-running batch jobs, they should be scheduled to run when they will cause the fewest problems for other transactions.

Developers can use the DBMS_LOCK package to specify user-defined locks, request a lock, convert a lock to a different mode, release a lock, or let a procedure sleep for a specified time.

Deadlocks can occur when two or more transactions wait for data locked by each other. Oracle detects and resolves deadlocks automatically. When a session detects a deadlock, it rolls back the current statement (not the entire transaction), and the server process returns an ORA-00060 message to the session. At this point, the remainder of the transaction should be rolled back and/or managed by an error-handling routine.

Two-Minute Drill

- Oracle uses locks to protect objects from other transactions or DDL.

- Locks provide longer-duration protection than latches, and they also provide a queuing mechanism that enables transactions to wait for locks to be released.

- Oracle automatically uses the level and mode of lock that will enable the greatest amount of data consistency while still allowing data concurrency.

- Locks are held for the duration of a transaction until an implicit or explicit commit or rollback.

- DML locks guarantee the integrity of data that may be accessed concurrently by many transactions.

- Table-level DML locks are referred to as TM locks.

- There are different modes of TM locks; each provides a different mode of locking to control read and write activity.

- Manually acquired modes include, from the least to the most restrictive, shared (S), shared row exclusive (SRX), and exclusive (X).

- Automatically acquired locks include row exclusive (RX) and row shared (RS).

- DDL locks are used to protect the definition of objects that are currently referenced by DML.

- DDL locks are automatically acquired when a DDL statement is issued.

- Exclusive DDL locks are used during DROP and ALTER TABLE statements.

- An exclusive DDL lock request fails if uncommitted transactions are accessing the table.

■ Shared DDL locks prevent the definition of the locked object from being changed while the object is being defined.

■ A breakable parse lock is held for each object referenced by an SQL or PL/SQL statement in the shared pool.

■ The breakable parse lock is used to check if the statement should be invalidated if the object changes.

■ Lock contention can be caused by unnecessarily high locking levels coded by developers. Also, long-running transactions or uncommitted changes can lock objects that others need.

■ Use the V$LOCK view to gather detailed information about the types of locks being held and requested in the database.

■ Use the V$LOCKED_OBJECT view to determine which user sessions are locking which objects and which undo segment is being used to support the transaction.

■ Run the catblock.sql script after catproc.sql has completed. The script creates several views that you can use to monitor locking.

■ The DBA_BLOCKERS, DBA_WAITERS, and DBA_LOCKS views are just some of the views created by the catblock.sql script.

■ The DBA_BLOCKERS and DBA_WAITERS views are counterparts. DBA_BLOCKERS returns the SID of the session hold of a lock that others are waiting for. DBA_WAITERS gives detailed information about the sessions waiting for a lock to be released.

■ The utllockt.sql reads the DBA_LOCKS view, creates two tables, and generates a tree-based report of the current blockers and waiters. The script then removes the tables it created earlier.

■ In an emergency, you may need to kill a session that is locking an object that other users need. Use the ALTER SYSTEM KILL SESSION '<sid>, <serial#>' command to kill the session, roll back the transaction, and release the locks it held.

■ You can prevent unnecessary locking problems by not doing those things that we know cause lock contention: commit regularly, do not code long-running transactions, or run them after regular transaction hours. If you manually code lock requests, be consistent.

■ Use the DBMS_LOCK package to manage user-defined locks.

■ Oracle automatically detects and resolves deadlocks.

■ The session that detects the deadlock will roll back the current statement and return an ORA-00060 error message.

Chapter Questions

1. **As the DBA, you'll need to execute which script to create the DBA_BLOCKERS view?**

   A. Catproc.sql

   B. Utllockt.sql

   C. Utlblock.sql

   D. Catllock.sql

   E. Catblock.sql

   F. Dba_blockers.sql

2. **Users call you and complain that none of the OLTP transactions are moving. Which of these describes an appropriate course of action? (Choose two.)**

   A. Query V$SESSION to see if any sessions are ACTIVE.

   B. Execute utllockt.sql to display the list of locking and waiting transactions.

   C. Query the DBA_WAITERS view to determine if any sessions are waiting on locked resources.

   D. Query DBA_DEADLOCKS to diagnose the currently deadlocked sessions.

   E. Execute the catblock.sql script to populate the DBA_BLOCKERS view.

3. **You've determined the SID of a session that has a vital resource locked, and other critical sessions are waiting. Which of the following courses of action will resolve the current problem with minimal disruption?**

   A. Enter this query and then execute the resulting SQL statement:

```
SELECT 'ALTER SYSTEM KILL SESSION
'||''''||SID||''''||','||''''||PID||''''
FROM V$SESSION
WHERE SID IN (SELECT HOLDING_SESSION FROM DBA_BLOCKERS)
/
```

B. Issue the SHUTDOWN ABORT command.

C. Enter this query and then execute the resulting SQL statement:

```
SELECT 'ALTER SYSTEM KILL SESSION
'||''''||SID||''''||','||''''||SERIAL#||''''
FROM V$SESSION
WHERE SID IN (SELECT HOLDING_SESSION FROM DBA_WAITERS)
/
```

D. Enter this query and then execute the resulting SQL statement:

```
SELECT 'ALTER SYSTEM KILL SESSION '||''''||SID||','||SERIAL#||''''
FROM V$SESSION
WHERE SID IN (SELECT HOLDING_SESSION FROM DBA_BLOCKERS)
/
```

E. Issue the SHUTDOWN IMMEDIATE command.

4. **You determine that a long-running transaction has used an unnecessarily high-level user-defined lock and is causing contention. Which of these courses of action will eliminate the contention problem without disrupting the transaction?**

   A. Execute DBMS_LOCK.allocate_unique()

   B. Execute DBMS_LOCK.kill()

   C. Execute DBMS_LOCK.convert()

   D. Execute DBMS_LOCK.create()

   E. Execute DBMS_LOCK.release()

5. **When a deadlock occurs and is detected, what happens next?**

   A. The session that detected the deadlock rolls back, and an ORA-00600 message is returned to the session.

   B. The detecting session aborts, and PMON cleans up the uncommitted transaction.

   C. The detecting session rolls back the current statement, and an ORA-00600 message is returned to the session.

   D. The detecting session rolls back the current statement, and an ORA-00060 message is returned to the session.

   E. The detecting session commits the current statement, and an ORA-00060 message is returned to the other sessions that were affected by the deadlock.

6. **Which one of the following are good development practices to reduce the likelihood of lock contention? (Choose all that apply.)**

    A. Rely on the Oracle default locking levels.

    B. Do not code unnecessarily long transactions.

    C. Run long transactions during less busy hours.

    D. Explicitly code the locks that you think your application may need.

    E. Always explicitly code exclusive table locks when updating rows.

7. **Which of the following scenarios represents incompatible DML locking modes or levels in the same table?**

    A. Exclusive table lock and user queries

    B. Share table lock and user queries

    C. Row-level locks on different rows

    D. Share lock and DDL

8. **Choose the true statement from the following:**

    A. Table-level locks prevent DDL from disrupting DML operations.

    B. By default, Oracle exclusively locks an entire table to update rows.

    C. By default, Oracle sets DML_LOCKS equal to 0.

    D. Shared DDL locks prevent similar DDL statements and DML on resources they hold.

    E. Breakable parse locks prevent objects from aging out of the shared pool.

9. **During the application design phase, you are discussing locking strategies with the developer. Please indicate which of the following are examples of good advice. (Choose two.)**

    A. Do not explicitly lock tables unless it is essential to the application because Oracle will handle resource locking most efficiently without intervention.

    B. Explicitly lock tables in the application code whenever you modify data in a table because Oracle only locks at the row level.

    C. Code long transactions that commit infrequently.

    D. Rely on implicit commits.

    E. If you must use manual locking in the application code, make sure the lock levels are consistently implemented.

10. **When is a DML lock released by a transaction in the current session? (Choose all that apply.)**

    A. When a COMMIT occurs, implicitly or explicitly

    B. When a ROLLBACK occurs

    C. When a transaction ends abnormally

    D. When new DML is executed

    E. When another session detects a deadlock

Answers to Chapter Questions

    1. E.   Catblock.sql

Explanation   The catblock.sql script should be run shortly after the database is created and after the catproc.sql script is executed. Catblock.sql creates several views, one of which is the DBA_BLOCKERS view that the DBA can use to monitor locking issues. Answer A is a prerequisite, but does not create the DBA_BLOCKERS view. Answer B is a monitoring script that will not function until the catblock.sql script has been executed once in the database. Answers C, D, and F do not exist.

    2. B, C.   Execute utllockt.sql, and query DBA_WAITERS.

Explanation   The utllockt.sql script, which relies on views created by the catblock.sql script, displays a tree-like structure of the blocking and waiting transactions in the database. However, depending on the situation, you may not want to run utllockt.sql because it must request locks to create its tables. The DBA_WAITERS view displays users that are waiting on resources that are blocked by other users. Answer A does not give us enough information to act on. Answer D is not correct because the DBA_DEADLOCKS view does not exist. Answer E is incorrect because the catblock.sql script does not populate the dba_blockers view, but it does create the view.

    3. D.

Explanation   The query in answer D returns a string that you can copy and paste to the SQL*Plus command prompt. The query returns a string that includes the SID and the SERIAL# from V$SESSION for each HOLDING_SESSION in DBA_BLOCKERS. The string can be used to kill the offending session. Answers A and C do not return the correct information needed to kill the offending session. Answers B and E are extreme measures, and although they may kill the offending session, they will also disrupt all other sessions.

4. C.   Execute DBMS_LOCK.convert()

Explanation   The DBMS_LOCK.convert() function converts a lock from one mode to another. Answer B is incorrect because the kill() function is nonexistent. Answers A, D, and E are valid functions, but would not be used for this purpose. You may consider answer E, release(), but that would completely release the user-defined lock.

5. D.   The detecting session rolls back the current statement, and an ORA-00060 message is returned to the session.

Explanation   When Oracle detects the deadlock, the session that actually detects the deadlock will roll back the current statement. The entire transaction isn't rolled back unless it is just one statement. The ORA-00060 message is returned to the session that detected the deadlock. At this point, you should roll back the remainder of the transaction. Answer A is incorrect because it contradicts answer D. Answer B is incorrect because the session does not abort. Answer C is incorrect because the ORA-00600 error message is not the error message returned to the session. Answer E is incorrect because the detecting transaction is not committed.

6. A, B, and C.   Rely on the Oracle default locking levels, do not code unnecessarily long transactions, and run long transactions during less busy hours.

Explanation   To reduce the likelihood of users waiting unnecessarily long amounts of time for locked resources, the developer should let Oracle handle lock management with the default locking mechanism, code short, discrete transactions, and run longer transactions that may interfere with other sessions during low-traffic hours. Answer D is incorrect because manually coding lock requests can lead to unnecessarily high levels of locking, increasing the likelihood of contention and reducing concurrency. Answer E is incorrect because exclusive table locks are an extreme measure when updating rows.

7. D.   Share lock and DDL

Explanation   The Share (S) manual table lock prevents DDL against the table. The S mode enables queries and SELECT . . . FOR UPDATE, but no other exclusive lock may be placed on the table. Answers A, B, and C are incorrect because each combination represents a compatible combination.

8. A. Table-level locks prevent DDL from disrupting DML operations.

Explanation When a table lock exists, users are not allowed to drop a table or perform any disruptive DDL. DML locks prevent the DDL from occurring. Answer B is incorrect because the default behavior is to not lock the entire table to update rows. A shared lock is placed on the table, and exclusive locks are placed on the modified rows. Answer C is incorrect because the default value of DML_LOCKS is derived by multiplying the value of TRANSACTIONS by 4. Answer D is incorrect because shared DDL locks do not prevent similar DDL statements and DML on resources. Answer E is incorrect because breakable parse locks are used to invalidate shared SQL areas if a referenced object is altered or dropped.

9. A and E. Do not explicitly lock tables unless it is essential to the application and, if you must use manual locking in the application code, make sure the lock levels are consistently implemented.

Explanation Good advice to the developer includes the judicious use of manually coded lock requests. It is not necessary to code lock requests because Oracle detects what is needed automatically. If manual lock requests are coded, they should be implemented in a consistent manner with a standard process for requesting, acquiring, and releasing locks. Answer B is incorrect because Oracle places the necessary locks on tables when rows are modified. Answer C is incorrect on both accounts. Answer D is bad advice; the application should commit whenever a transaction is ready for it, and not rely on implicit commits that occur when a session ends normally or when DDL is executed.

10. A, B, and C. When a COMMIT, ROLLBACK, or abnormal end occurs.

Explanation Locks are held until the transaction ends whether through COMMIT or ROLLBACK. Whether the transaction completes normally or ends abnormally, the lock will be released. In case of an abnormal termination, PMON is responsible for cleaning up after the failed process and releasing any locks held. Answer D is incorrect because new DML does not cause a previous DML lock to release. Answer E is incorrect because if another session detects a deadlock, it will be the one that rolls back the current statement and releases the lock.

CHAPTER
12

Tuning Oracle
Shared Server

n this chapter, you will learn about tuning the Oracle shared server environment. This chapter is organized into three major sections:

- Identifying issues associated with managing users in a shared server environment

- Diagnosing and resolving performance issues with shared server processes

- Configuring the shared server environment to optimize performance

We'll start with a brief introduction to the shared server environment, comparing and contrasting it with the dedicated server environment. We'll then go into details on detecting, diagnosing, and tuning the shared server environment.

Tuning Oracle Shared Server

The Oracle shared server configuration is a low-overhead alternative to the dedicated server configuration. In the dedicated server environment, each user process or session in the database has its own server process. In the shared server environment, multiple user processes share a limited number of server processes.

When a dedicated server process is used, it may not be fully utilized because of what some refer to as "think time." This is the time when the server process is idle, waiting for the application to make another request. The dedicated server process is busy only when a user process submits a query or a change to the database. Unfortunately, the idle server process still consumes memory and even a small amount of the central processing unit (CPU). On systems that are limited in CPU or memory resources, too many dedicated server processes can lead to swapping. Dedicated servers are ideal for database-intense or batch processes, but are not the optimal solution for systems that support hundreds or thousands of interactive users.

In the shared server configuration, user processes are dynamically assigned to a server process, which is potentially shared by many user processes. User processes submit a request to a *dispatcher* process, which places the request on the *request queue* in the System Global Area (SGA). The shared server then processes the request and returns the results to the *response queue* in the SGA. Then the dispatcher returns the results from the response queue to the user process.

Identifying Issues Associated with Managing Users in a Shared Server Environment

The shared server configuration enables multiple user processes to share a smaller number of server processes. The performance goal is to improve scalability, not necessarily to improve the performance of server processes. Performance can improve over dedicated servers if too many dedicated servers were allocated and swapping or CPU starvation was noted. However, the primary goal is to greatly increase the number of concurrent sessions without having to add a linear amount of CPU and memory.

Shared Server Characteristics

In the shared server environment, users can share server processes. But in order to do this, Oracle Net must be configured. Here are some of the environment factors that may lead you to choose the shared server configuration over dedicated server processes:

■ The application supports a large number of interactive users.

■ Users are not local to the database server—that is, *n*-tier, client-server, or Web-based applications are using Oracle Net to connect to the database.

■ The database host OS is Unix or Windows NT.

■ A large amount of overhead has been identified and attributed to the dedicated server processes.

■ The server is approaching the limit on CPU and memory resources.

With the shared server configuration, you can take advantage of multiplexing with Oracle Connection Manager and also connection pooling; both extend the number of concurrent users that the current hardware can support.

Connection Manager   Oracle Connection Manager enables multiple client network sessions to be multiplexed through a single network connection to a database. Session multiplexing enables you to increase the number of network sessions that a server can handle without adding hardware. With multiple Oracle Connection Managers, you can connect thousands of concurrent users to a database server.

Connection Pooling   Connection pooling enables you to reduce the number of physical network connections to a dispatcher. With it, the database server can timeout an idle session and use the connection for an active session. The idle session remains open, and the connection is reestablished when the session makes a request. Thus, applications can allow larger numbers of concurrent users to be accommodated with existing hardware.

Configuring the Shared Server Environment

You must install and configure Oracle Net on your database server if you want to use shared servers. You'll need to configure at least the default listener. You'll also need to configure the *tnsnames.ora* file or use Oracle Names for instance name resolution. Once the Oracle Net configuration is proper, you can configure the initialization parameters to enable shared servers:

- **CIRCUITS** Specifies the total number of connections available through the shared server architecture for inbound and outbound network sessions.

- **DISPATCHERS** Specifies the PROTOCOL, ADDRESS, or DESCRIPTION. If you specify ADDRESS or DESCRIPTION, you can specify additional network attributes.

- **MAX_DISPATCHERS** Specifies the maximum number of dispatcher processes that can run simultaneously. Set it greater than or equal to the maximum number of concurrent sessions divided by the number of connections for each dispatcher.

- **SHARED_SERVERS** Specifies the number of shared server processes that will be created when the instance starts up and that will be maintained while the database is up.

- **MAX_SHARED_SERVERS** The maximum number of concurrent shared server processes. The default value of MAX_SHARED_SERVERS is dependent on the value of SHARED_SERVERS. If SHARED_SERVERS is less than or equal to 10, then MAX_SHARED_SERVERS defaults to 20. If SHARED_SERVERS is greater than 10, then MAX_SHARED_SERVERS defaults to two times the value of SHARED_SERVERS.

- **SHARED_SERVER_SESSIONS** The maximum number of sessions that can use the shared server architecture.

Diagnosing and Resolving Performance Issues with Shared Server Processes

In this section, we will discuss monitoring dispatchers, server processes, and memory usage with dynamic performance views. We will also discuss how to address performance issues identified for each shared server component.

Using V$SHARED_SERVER_MONITOR

The V$SHARED_SERVER_MONITOR view is a good starting point for monitoring shared server processes. It indicates general statistics for shared server processes and high watermarks. Here are the columns and their descriptions:

- **Maximum_connections**   The highest number of virtual circuits in use at one time since the instance started. A *virtual circuit* is the term used to describe a user connection to the database through a dispatcher and shared server.

- **Maximum_sessions**   The highest number of shared server sessions in use at one time since the instance started.

- **Servers_started**   The total number of shared servers started since the instance began, but not including those started during instance startup.

- **Servers_terminated**   The total number of shared servers stopped since the instance started.

- **Servers_highwater**   The highest number of shared servers running at one time since the instance started.

Monitoring Dispatchers

You can monitor dispatcher activity by querying V$SHARED_SERVER_MONITOR, V$DISPATCHER, V$QUEUE, and V$DISPATCHER_RATE. V$DISPATCHER is used to gather performance statistics, V$QUEUE indicates queue wait time, and V$DISPATCHER_RATE can be used to analyze detailed dispatcher activity.

Identifying Contention for Dispatchers   The V$DISPATCHER view provides information on the dispatcher processes, including the name, network address, status, and usage statistics.

Query the V$DISPATCHER view with the following SQL:

```
SELECT NETWORK "PROTOCOL",
SUM(BUSY)/(SUM(BUSY)+SUM(IDLE)) "TOTAL BUSY RATE"
FROM V$DISPATCHER
GROUP BY NETWORK
/
PROTOCOL                                                          TOTAL BUSY RATE
------------------------------------------------------------ ----------------
(ADDRESS=(PROTOCOL=tcp)(HOST=packnt02)(PORT=1035))                 .0151321217
```

This query indicates the total busy rate for the dispatcher processes, grouped by protocol. If the rate is greater than .5, indicating the dispatcher processes are busy more than 50 percent of the time, you should consider adding more dispatchers.

The V$QUEUE view contains information about the shared server message queues. You can also check if users are waiting for dispatchers by running the following query:

```
SELECT DECODE(SUM(TOTALQ),0,'No Responses',SUM(WAIT)/SUM(TOTALQ)) "Average Wait Time"
FROM V$QUEUE Q, V$DISPATCHER D
WHERE Q.TYPE = 'DISPATCHER'
AND Q.PADDR = D.PADDR
/
```

The average wait time is in hundredths of seconds; if the wait time increases, consider adding more dispatchers.

The V$DISPATCHER_RATE view contains a sophisticated array of statistics for the dispatcher activities. Columns are grouped into current (CUR_), max (MAX_), and average (AVG_). If CUR_ column values are close to their MAX_ counterparts and dispatcher performance is less than optimal, consider adding more dispatchers for the corresponding protocol.

Dynamically Add or Remove Dispatchers   You can add or remove dispatchers, as in the following command:

```
ALTER SYSTEM SET DISPATCHERS = '(PROTOCOL=TCP)(DISPATCHERS=3)'
/
```

Execute the SHOW PARAMETER DISPATCHER command in SQL*Plus, and you'll see that the VALUE column for dispatchers now indicates the number of dispatchers specified. New user sessions can begin using the additional dispatchers; existing sessions will continue to use the same dispatcher until they log off.

To remove a dispatcher, query the NAME column of the V$DISPATCHER view to determine which dispatcher to shut down. Then use the ALTER SYSTEM command, as in the following example:

```
SELECT NAME FROM V$DISPATCHER
/
D000
D001
...
D004
ALTER SYSTEM SHUTDOWN 'D004'
/
```

Monitoring Shared Servers

PMON adds and removes shared servers as they are needed. If processes are idle, PMON removes them until the value of SHARED_SERVERS is reached. If the shared servers are busy, PMON will start additional processes until the number of MAX_SHARED_SERVERS is reached. Because shared server load is managed dynamically and automatically, less intervention is required. However, if you configure the value of SHARED_SERVERS too high, you'll overuse system resources.

Detecting Shared Server Process Contention   The following query returns the busy rate for the currently running shared servers:

```
SELECT NAME, REQUESTS, BUSY/(BUSY+IDLE) "BUSY RATE", STATUS
FROM V$SHARED_SERVER
WHERE STATUS != 'QUIT'
/
```

Query V$QUEUE to determine if there is contention for the shared servers. The results of this query indicate the average wait time for all requests, in hundredths of seconds:

```
SELECT DECODE(TOTALQ,0,'No Requests',WAIT/TOTALQ) "Average Wait Time Per Request"
FROM V$QUEUE
WHERE TYPE = 'COMMON'
/
```

Steadily increasing wait time in the request queue indicates contention for shared servers.

Dynamically Add or Remove Shared Servers   We dynamically allocate or deallocate server processes with the following command:

```
ALTER SYSTEM SET SHARED_SERVERS=<integer>
/
```

Monitoring Process Usage with V$CIRCUIT

If it appears that a process in the shared server configuration is lagging or stuck, you can query the V$CIRCUIT view to determine where in the virtual circuit the problem lies. The V$CIRCUIT view has columns for DISPATCHER, SERVER, WAITER, STATUS, and QUEUE, as well as statistics. The QUEUE column indicates which queue the circuit is currently on: COMMON (request), DISPATCHER, SERVER, or NONE (idle). Then query V$SHARED_SERVER, V$DISPATCHER, or V$SESSION to investigate why the process is stuck.

The V$CIRCUIT SADDR column can be joined to the V$SESSION SADDR column to determine information about the user who is waiting. Also, the SERVER column of V$SESSION will have the value SHARED for shared server connections.

Shared Servers and Memory Usage

For shared server processes, the User Global Area (UGA) is stored in the shared pool. If you have configured the large pool, then most of the UGA structures are created to the large pool instead. Oracle recommends that you configure the large pool when using shared servers; this reduces the potential for shared pool fragmentation.

Shared servers use the UGA for sorting operations, so it is important that you set the value of SORT_AREA_RETAINED_SIZE smaller than SORT_AREA_SIZE so that the memory used for sorting will be released to the shared pool or large pool when the operation has completed. This assumes you're not using automatic Program Global Area (PGA) memory management.

The overall memory required by shared servers is less than that required by dedicated servers. It is important to remember that you'll need to configure a larger shared pool when using shared servers, but shared server process memory is still less than the sum of the memory requirements for dedicated servers.

Troubleshooting

The shared server environment presents a different set of challenges for the database administrator (DBA) tasked with troubleshooting connectivity issues. Here are a few items that the DBA needs to be aware of when managing a database that utilizes shared servers, as well as some things to investigate when shared server connections fail:

- Shared connections rely on Oracle Net, so the listener must be running in order for connections to reach the database. You should configure the database host to start up the listener when the machine boots up.

- If Oracle Net is not configured properly, then attempts to establish a shared connection will return a TNS_ error message.

- If the INSTANCE_NAME, DB_DOMAIN, or SERVICE_NAMES initialization parameters aren't set properly, then automatic instance registration will fail.

- Shared servers and dispatchers count as processes and are limited by the PROCESSES initialization parameter. Set MAX_SHARED_SERVERS, MAX_DISPATCHERS, and SHARED_SERVER_SESSIONS so that they will all fit within the PROCESSES value.

- Do not kill shared server processes or dispatchers from the OS. If a user needs to be killed, kill the session in the database. Killing the OS process has the potential to affect many other users.

- You must have a dedicated server connection to perform privileged operations such as startup and shutdown.

Configure the Shared Server Environment to Optimize Performance

The shared server environment is ideal for large Online Transaction Processing (OLTP) systems where many users are connected but are inactive the majority of the time they are connected. Shared servers are not designed for batch processing or intense database work; you should use dedicated server processes for those types of activities. For the most part, the shared server environment is self-tuning once you establish the proper number of dispatchers and shared server processes. In this section, we'll discuss configuring the number of dispatchers and shared server processes for optimal performance.

Reducing Contention for Dispatchers

The V$DISPATCHER_RATE view is our primary source for determining the optimal configuration for dispatchers. If the CUR_ column values are near their AVG_ counterparts and below the MAX_ values, and response time is good, then you probably have a good number of dispatchers allocated. If CUR_ and AVG_ are consistently well below MAX_, then consider reducing the number of dispatchers. However, if under system load, you see that CUR_ is close to or equal to MAX_, then consider increasing the number of dispatchers. Adding dispatchers is not always the best solution; you should also consider connection pooling and/or session multiplexing.

Add Dispatchers   The initialization parameters DISPATCHERS and MAX_DISPATCHERS set the number of dispatcher processes started and the maximum dispatcher processes allowed, respectively. When the database is up and running and you detect dispatcher contention, add more dispatchers with ALTER SYSTEM SET DISPATCHERS='dispatch_clause'. You'll need to specify the DISPATCHERS=<integer> attribute in the dispatch_clause.

Enable Connection Pooling   To enable connection pooling for a dispatcher, set the POOL=ON attribute in the dispatch_clause when specifying a dispatcher. By setting the value to ON, TRUE, YES, or BOTH, connection pooling will be enabled for both incoming and outgoing network connections. An integer value indicates pooling on, and the number is the network timeout value in seconds. Setting the value to IN enables incoming pooling only, and OUT enables outgoing pooling only. The default can be NO, OFF, FALSE, or 0, indicating no pooling.

Enable Session Multiplexing   Multiplexing enables a connection manager process to establish and maintain connections from multiple users to individual dispatchers. You can enable multiplexing with the MULTIPLEX=ON attribute in the dispatch_clause. Setting the value to ON, TRUE, 1, YES, or BOTH specifies that multiplexing will be used for incoming and outgoing connections. IN specifies incoming only, and OUT specifies outgoing only. Setting the value to 0, NO, FALSE, or OFF turns off multiplexing.

Reducing Contention for Shared Servers

Oracle automatically manages the number of shared servers based on the activity of requests and the load on the request queue.

Setting and Modifying Shared Server Processes
The initialization parameters SHARED_SERVERS and MAX_SHARED_SERVERS set the initial and maximum number of shared servers, respectively. If SHARED_SERVERS is less than 10, then MAX_SHARED_SERVERS defaults to 20. If SHARED_SERVERS is greater than 10, then MAX_SHARED_SERVERS defaults to 2x SHARED_SERVERS.

When the database starts up, Oracle launches SHARED_SERVERS' number of shared server processes. It will keep at least this many shared server processes running. As the load increases, Oracle will add shared server processes as it determines that they are needed, up to the number of MAX_SHARED_SERVERS. As processing wanes, Oracle will shut down unused servers as it determines they are no longer needed. Again, SHARED_SERVERS is the minimum number of servers that Oracle will keep running. If you see long wait times in the queue, you can manually increase the number of shared servers available for use by issuing the ALTER SYSTEM SET SHARED_SERVERS=<integer>; command. The same command is used to decrease the number of shared servers.

Because shared servers use the shared pool and/or large pool for memory structures, check that the shared pool performance has been optimized. Once you validate that memory is tuned, if you still see shared server contention issues, consider adding more shared servers by increasing MAX_SHARED_SERVERS.

Determining the Optimal Number of Shared Servers and Dispatchers

There is no set formula for determining the optimal number of dispatchers and shared servers for your system. Start by measuring the typical number of users connected to the database and the maximum. Also gather information about the scheduling and frequency of batch and long-running processes.

For DISPATCHERS and MAX_DISPATCHERS, we want to limit the total number of connections per dispatcher. For most systems, a value of 1,000 connections per dispatcher provides good performance. Therefore, set the initialization parameter values at least equal to the maximum number of concurrent sessions divided by the number of connections per dispatcher. If you have a maximum of 10,000 concurrent users, configure at least 10 dispatchers.

For SHARED_SERVERS and MAX_SHARED_SERVERS, start by gradually increasing the values of each while closely monitoring system resources (CPU and swapping). Remember that the SHARED_SERVERS always remain allocated, even if they are idle. It is possible that your system might suffer if you set the initial number of servers too high. Experiment with the number of initial and maximum shared servers, and monitor the response time and performance statistics until you get the targeted performance.

Chapter Summary

The shared server configuration is an alternative to the dedicated server environment and enables the DBA to add a significant number of user connections to the database without changing the existing hardware. With the shared server environment, multiple user processes share a smaller number of server processes, instead of having a dedicated server process for each user process.

The shared server configuration is a better utilization of resources because most user processes are sitting idle the majority of the time, but still consuming memory and CPU resources. shared servers reduce the overall amount of CPU and memory consumed, and enable the DBA to improve system scalability.

In the shared server environment, user processes are assigned to a shared server process. A user process submits a database request to a dispatcher process, which places the request on the request queue in the SGA. The shared server then processes the request and returns the results to the response queue in the SGA. The dispatcher then returns the results to the user process.

An application or database that would benefit from shared servers would have a large number of interactive users, some remote users, a database that is on Unix or NT, performance problems that have been attributed to the dedicated server processes, and a system that is reaching CPU or memory limits. To use shared servers, Oracle Net must be configured.

The shared server configuration can also benefit from multiplexing via the Oracle connection manager and connection pooling. Both features are configured with Oracle Net and when defining the dispatchers.

The CIRCUITS, DISPATCHERS, SHARED_SERVERS, MAX_DISPATCHERS, MAX_SHARED_SERVERS, and SHARED_SERVER_SESSIONS initialization parameters are used to define the startup characteristics and maximum processes allowed for the shared server environment.

The V$SHARED_SERVER_MONITOR view is used to monitor general server, session, and dispatcher statistics. A *virtual circuit* is the term used to describe a user connection to the database through a dispatcher and shared server.

You can monitor the dispatcher busy rate by querying V$DISPATCHER. V$QUEUE is used to monitor the wait queue for each point in the circuit. V$DISPATCHER_RATE contains detailed statistics that can be used to diagnose dispatcher contention. Compare the CUR_ column with its counterpart MAX_ column. Add more dispatchers manually by issuing the ALTER SYSTEM SET

DISPATCHERS='(PROTOCOL=)(DISPATCHERS=)' command, specifying the protocol and number of dispatchers to allocate. You can shut down a dispatcher by issuing the ALTER SYSTEM SHUTDOWN "dispatcher_name" command, where dispatcher_name is derived from the NAME column of V$DISPATCHER.

Shared servers are allocated and deallocated automatically by the Oracle server. PMON adds and removes them as the workload increases and decreases. The SHARED_SERVERS and MAX_SHARED_SERVERS parameters determine the number of shared servers allocated at startup and the maximum that can be allocated at peak usage, respectively. Query V$SHARED_SERVER to determine the shared server busy rate, and query V$QUEUE to determine if there is shared server contention. You can issue the command ALTER SYSTEM SET SHARED_SERVERS=<integer> to dynamically adjust the number of shared servers.

V$CIRCUIT can be used to troubleshoot where a shared server problem may exist. If you see that a server process appears stuck, query V$CIRCUIT to diagnose the location of the holdup.

Configure the large pool if you use shared servers. Oracle will place the majority of the UGA structures, including the sort area, in the large pool if it is configured; otherwise, it will use the shared pool. Set SORT_AREA_RETAINED_SIZE smaller than SORT_AREA_SIZE so that unused memory can be returned to the system.

When troubleshooting, keep in mind that Oracle Net must be running and configured properly for shared server connections to reach the database. Also, the INSTANCE_NAME, DB_DOMAIN, and SERVICE_NAMES initialization parameters must be properly set for automatic listener registration.

The shared server and dispatcher processes count towards the maximum number of PROCESSES allowed, so you'll need to monitor them to make sure you don't run out of processes. Don't kill a shared server or dispatcher process from the OS because you will probably affect other user sessions. If you have to kill an Oracle user session, kill it in the database, not at the OS.

The optimal configuration for dispatchers and shared servers is not deterministic, but should be discovered through trial and error. If response time is poor and statistics are at MAX_ values, increase the number of processes. If response time is good and statistics are not at MAX_ values, then you probably have found an optimal configuration.

If you detect dispatcher contention, consider using session multiplexing or connection pooling before increasing the number of dispatchers. You can set the number of dispatchers for a protocol dynamically and with the DISPATCHERS parameter, and increase the MAX_DISPATCHERS parameter. If you detect shared server contention, increase the MAX_SHARED_SERVERS parameter. Remember, Oracle automatically allocates and deallocates shared servers.

Two-Minute Drill

- The shared server configuration offers the DBA a method for dramatically increasing the number of connections that a database can support using existing hardware.

- With dedicated servers, each user process has an associated server process.

- With shared servers, multiple user processes share a smaller number of server processes.

- In the shared server environment, user processes submit a request to a dispatcher process, which places the request on the request queue in the SGA.

- The request is processed and the results returned to the response queue in the SGA. The dispatcher returns the results from the response queue to the user process.

- Shared servers are useful for large systems with hundreds or thousands of interactive users, Unix servers, or systems that are hardware constrained.

- Shared servers are a better use of limited resources because server processes are more fully utilized.

- To use shared servers, Oracle Net must be configured.

- These initialization parameters define the shared server configuration: CIRCUITS, DISPATCHERS, SHARED_SERVERS, MAX_DISPATCHERS, MAX_SHARED_SERVERS, and SHARED_SERVER_SESSIONS.

- A *virtual circuit* is the term used to describe a user connection to the database through a dispatcher and shared server.

- Query V$SHARED_SERVER_MONITOR to get an overview of shared server processing.

- Query V$QUEUE to determine wait times in the different queues.

- Query V$CIRCUIT to determine where in the virtual circuit bottlenecks may be occurring.

- V$DISPATCHER is used to monitor dispatcher busy rates, and V$DISPATCHER_RATE is used to monitor detailed dispatcher statistics.

- V$SHARED_SERVER is used to monitor the shared server busy rate.

- Configure the large pool if you intend to use shared servers. Sorting occurs in the UGA, which is moved to the large pool in the shared server environment. If you don't configure the large pool, sorting will occur in the shared pool.

■ Set SORT_AREA_RETAINED_SIZE to a value smaller than SORT_AREA_SIZE.

■ When troubleshooting the shared server environment, keep in mind that the Oracle Net listener must be up, the initialization parameters must be set properly to register with the listener, and the PROCESSES parameter is the upper bound for all instance processes.

■ You can increase the number of dispatchers dynamically with the ALTER SYSTEM command. MAX_DISPATCHERS determines the upper bound.

■ Oracle automatically allocates and deallocates shared server processes, but you can manually set the number with the ALTER SYSTEM SET SHARED_SERVERS command. MAX_SHARED_SERVERS determines the upper bound.

Chapter Questions

1. **Which of these factors would *not* contribute to your decision to move to a shared server configuration? (Choose all that apply.)**

   A. The current hardware will not support additional server processes.

   B. The majority of the processing is batch and DSS.

   C. The system is an OLTP system, characterized by long delays between database work.

   D. The database host OS is Unix.

   E. The current dedicated server environment does not suffer from memory swapping.

   F. The current dedicated server environment suffers from memory swapping.

2. **Which of these environments would benefit from moving from dedicated servers to shared servers?**

   A. A Web-based environment, with potentially thousands of concurrent users

   B. A distributed OLTP system

   C. A traditional data warehouse

D. A 25-user Unix database with local connections

E. A batch processing system

F. A DSS or reporting system

3. **You query V$DISPATCHER and note that the dispatcher busy rate is greater than 50 percent. Which of these are plausible courses of action? (Choose three.)**

   A. Decrease the number of dispatcher processes.

   B. Increase the number of dispatcher processes.

   C. Increase the number of shared servers.

   D. Decrease the number of shared servers.

   E. Consider using session multiplexing.

   F. Consider using connection pooling.

4. **It appears that a session has hung up one of the shared servers. You query V$CIRCUIT and V$SESSION, determine the offending session, and take which course of action?**

   A. Get the OS process ID for the session and kill the process at the OS.

   B. Add more shared server processes.

   C. Shut down the shared server process.

   D. Kill the Oracle session with the ALTER SYSTEM KILL SESSION command.

   E. Kill the dispatcher and the server process at the OS.

5. **You notice that the high watermark for shared server processes is continuously at the MAX_SHARED_SERVERS limit. Choose a solution to optimize shared server performance:**

   A. Double the value for SHARED_SERVERS and MAX_SHARED_SERVERS.

   B. Increase MAX_SHARED_SERVERS by a few, and check instance performance.

   C. Increase SHARED_SERVERS by a few, and check instance performance.

6. **Although there is no magic number for dispatchers, which of these is a good guideline to use when determining the optimal number of dispatcher processes?**

   A. Set MAX_DISPATCHERS to the maximum number of concurrent sessions divided by the number of connections per dispatcher.

   B. Set DISPATCHERS to the maximum number of concurrent sessions divided by the number of connections per dispatcher.

   C. Set MAX_DISPATCHERS to the average number of concurrent sessions divided by the number of SHARED_SERVERS.

   D. Set DISPATCHERS to the integer value of concurrent sessions divided by the number of connections per shared server.

Answers to Chapter Questions

1. B, E.   Batch processing and dedicated server memory swapping

Explanation   If the majority of your database processing is batch or long-running Decision Support System (DSS) queries, then shared servers will not help your system scalability. These are characteristics of a dedicated server configuration. If the current dedicated servers show no signs of causing memory swapping, then shared servers may not benefit you. Answers A, C, D, and F are all good reasons to move away from dedicated servers and to shared servers.

2. A, B.   Web-based and OLTP systems

Explanation   The shared server environment is characterized by a large number of nonlocal users whose database usage profile could be described as few and far between. Answers C, D, E, and F each have characteristics that would benefit from dedicated servers. A traditional data warehouse, the batch system, and the DSS system are all characterized by processes that query large amounts of data or insert large amounts of data. These data-intense systems perform better with dedicated servers. Answer D is kinda tricky; Unix systems can benefit from shared servers, but a 25-user system with local connections should probably remain with dedicated servers.

3. B, E, and F.   Increase the number of dispatchers, and/or consider multiplexing and pooling.

Explanation   If the dispatcher processes are busy, consider implementing connection pooling or session multiplexing. If that doesn't solve the problem, add more dispatchers. Answer A, decreasing the number of dispatchers, will not improve the situation. Answers C and D are irrelevant.

4. D. Kill the Oracle session.

Explanation   In the shared server environment, you should never kill the shared server or dispatcher process from the OS. If a session is causing a problem, kill the session within the database, not at the OS. Answers A and E are bad choices; you should never take those steps. Answer B is incorrect, as it is automatically allocated by the Oracle server. Answer C is incorrect because you cannot specify which shared server process to shut down.

5. B. Increase MAX_SHARED_SERVERS by a few.

Explanation   One of the reasons we move to shared servers is to better utilize system resources. If you increase MAX_SHARED_SERVERS by too much, you may cause swapping or CPU starvation. If you increase SHARED_SERVERS by too much, you may cause the same problems; remember, Oracle does not drop shared server processes below the number of SHARED_SERVERS. Increasing SHARED_SERVERS alone will not help if the shared server high watermark is the problem.

6. A. Set MAX_DISPATCHERS to the maximum number of concurrent sessions divided by the number of connections per dispatcher.

Explanation   This is a general guideline, but makes mathematical sense. If one dispatcher can manage up to 1,000 typical users without contention, then divide the maximum number of concurrent sessions by 1,000 to derive the value you should set for MAX_DISPATCHERS. Each of the other answers is incorrect. B and D are incorrect because DISPATCHERS is not a numeric parameter; it is a string that can contain a numeric value for a number of dispatchers. Answer C is incorrect because the number of SHARED_SERVERS is not part of the guideline.

CHAPTER
13

Application Tuning

n this chapter, we will describe the different types of objects that can be used to improve application performance, and we will list the tuning requirements for different types of applications. We will also discuss the role of the database administrator (DBA) in tuning the application. Here are the topics:

- Describe the role of the DBA in application tuning

- Explain different storage structures and why one storage structure may be preferred over another

- Explain and describe clustering options

- Describe the different types of indexes

- Describe index-organized tables (IOTs)

- Describe materialized views and the use of query rewrites

- List requirements for Online Transaction Processing (OLTP), Decision Support Systems (DSS), and hybrid systems

Our primary focus will be on describing the different types of objects that applications may use in the database and the performance implications of each to the DBA. Our emphasis will be on designing the application for performance by using the types of objects that will best suit the application. We will list circumstances that contribute to the choice of one object instead of the other. The emphasis of this chapter is on selecting and maintaining the proper application objects, while the emphasis of Chapter 15 is on tuning the Structured Query Language (SQL) statements that are used to access the application objects. The two chapters should be used by the DBA and developer as a guideline for tuning the application.

Application Tuning

The most important facet of application tuning is getting the design right. In a relational database, the focus is usually on making sure that the tables are designed to some acceptable level of normalization. Once we have the correct logical model for the database, we can begin analyzing the options available for the physical implementation of the logical design. With Oracle9*i* databases, we have several options; we will discuss our options in this chapter.

Describe the Role of the DBA in Tuning Applications

Depending on your business environment or organizational structure, the DBA may be primarily responsible for application design and tuning, or the DBA may have little involvement in the process and the developers are primarily responsible.

In a small or decentralized organization, the DBA may be responsible for all things Oracle, not just the normal DBA tasks. The Oracle DBA may also support other database management systems (DBMSs), operating systems (OSs), or applications.

Typically in larger organizations with a large number of applications that use Oracle databases, DBAs and developers have the opportunity to become highly specialized. In a typical large group of Oracle DBAs, you may have a backup and recovery specialist, an architecture or new features specialist, an infrastructure or OS specialist, a PL/SQL or SQL specialist, production and/or development support specialists, Oracle applications DBAs, tuning specialists, and design specialists. You may also find that DBAs report to different business units, in which case their tasks may more closely resemble those of the DBA in a decentralized or small organization.

In either case, the DBA needs to be familiar with the different schema objects, the performance benefits of using one type of object over another, and which type of object is preferable in certain cases.

We cannot overstate the importance of application tuning, especially at the design phase. If the DBA is not involved in the design, then it is possible that the incorrect or suboptimal object type will be used. Also, the DBA will have to support the suboptimal design once the application is promoted to production, which will impact the DBA's overall effectiveness.

It is important to remember that as the DBA you will be evaluated on the uptime and performance of the systems that you support. Once your customers are satisfied that the database is available when they need it, they will expect it to perform well. If an application is not performing as well as expected, and even if the DBA can prove that the database is perfectly tuned, your customers will expect the DBA to share in the responsibility of tuning the application. Ultimately, your customers are more concerned with application performance than database performance statistics. Most of them have little concern for the buffer cache hit ratio, but are acutely aware of how many seconds a query takes to complete and refresh their application window.

Explain Different Storage Structures

In addition to the regular heap-organized tables, the Oracle9*i* database supports clusters, IOTs, and materialized views for data storage; we also have our choice of several index forms. Which of these structures you should use depends on several factors, including data volume, update frequency, and transaction size. We will use the next several sections to describe each of the available options and explain why one storage structure may be preferred in a given situation.

Explain and Describe Clustering Options

A *cluster* is a physical grouping of one or more tables, all of which have one or more columns in common. The cluster is treated as one structure, so data from the different tables that make up the cluster exist in the same data blocks. The *cluster key* is used to join rows from each of the tables and store them together. Clusters improve performance by prejoining data based on the cluster key, and they reduce storage requirements by only storing the cluster key once for all rows that have the same key value. Clusters are accessed in the same manner as regular tables, so to the application, a cluster is the same as a table.

Types of Clusters

Two types of clusters exist: index and hash. Index clusters use an index to maintain data within the cluster; hash clusters use a hashing algorithm to do the same.

Index Clusters   The index that is used to maintain the index cluster is called, appropriately, the *cluster index*. The cluster index is used to access the block or blocks for the cluster key. The cluster index is similar to a B-Tree unique index; that is, there is one entry in the cluster index for each cluster key value in the cluster. However, the cluster index stores NULL keys. There is only one entry for each cluster key in the index, regardless of how many rows from different tables have the same cluster key.

If all the rows for a given cluster key value cannot fit in one block, the blocks are chained together to speed access to all the values with the given key. The cluster index points to the beginning of the chain of blocks, each of which contains the cluster key value and associated rows.

The CREATE CLUSTER statement has an optional argument, SIZE, which is the estimated number of bytes required by an average cluster key and its associated rows. Oracle uses the SIZE parameter when performing the following tasks:

- Estimating the number of cluster keys (and associated rows) that can fit in a clustered data block.

- Limiting the number of cluster keys placed in a clustered data block. This maximizes the storage efficiency of keys within a cluster.

Hash Clusters   A hash cluster uses a hashing algorithm to find the cluster key within the cluster. The hashing algorithm points directly to the location of the block that holds the cluster key row. This approach means that a query on the cluster key goes directly to the correct block with only one input/output (I/O), which is more efficient than a lookup on an indexed regular table or cluster index and cluster.

Create a Cluster　To create and use a cluster, we first create the cluster and then add tables to it. In the first example, we'll create an index cluster:

```
CREATE CLUSTER ORDER_ENTRIES
  (ORDER_ID    NUMBER(12))
 SIZE 512
 STORAGE (INITIAL 64K NEXT 64K)
/
CREATE INDEX ORDER_ENTRIES_ID_IDX ON CLUSTER ORDER_ENTRIES
/
```

Alternatively, we create a hash cluster, using the default Oracle hashing algorithm:

```
CREATE CLUSTER ORDER_ENTRIES
  (ORDER_ID    NUMBER(12))
 SIZE 512
 HASHKEYS 10
 STORAGE (INITIAL 64K NEXT 64K)
/
```

Finally, we add tables to the cluster. These statements will add the tables to the cluster, regardless of which clustering mechanism we use:

```
CREATE TABLE orders CLUSTER order_entries (order_id)
  AS SELECT * FROM oe.orders
/
CREATE TABLE items CLUSTER order_entries (order_id)
  AS SELECT * FROM oe.order_items
/
```

When to Use and Not Use Clusters　Index clusters are most beneficial when there is uniform key distribution, the keys are rarely updated, and the tables in the cluster are often joined. Hash clusters are a good choice when there is uniform key distribution, evenly distributed key values, and rarely updated keys. Also, if the queries use equijoins and there is a predictable number of key values, consider using a hash cluster. Also, use key columns that have many distinct values, rather than only a few.

If the application uses full table scans, there is no benefit to using clusters. Performance is generally worse because more blocks will be read from the cluster to satisfy the query than if the table were independent. Also, if all rows of a particular cluster key value don't fit within one block, each block that contains rows for the cluster key must be read.

Explain the Different Types of Indexes

Indexes are used to speed the performance of queries' operations. They do so by reducing the overall number of physical reads required to satisfy a request. In general, a small number of block reads on an index results in a direct read to the block and row in the table where the required data resides. This is usually much more efficient than reading an entire table to satisfy the request. In Oracle9*i*, we have several indexing options, so in this section we will discuss B-Tree, bitmap, reverse key, and function-based indexes. The choice of index type should be based on the needs of the application.

B-Tree Indexes

The most common type of index in Oracle is the B-Tree index. The B-Tree index is designed to improve the performance of queries that will be satisfied by reading a small percentage of the rows in a table. There is no absolute threshold that you should use; some guides recommend creating an index when a typical query returns up to 5 percent of the table rows, while others say 10 percent. In reality, you'll have to test and measure query performance with and without indexes. Queries that use indexed columns to join tables can benefit from properly designed B-Tree indexes. Also, query performance can be greatly improved if the index contains all the columns required in the query.

Since indexes are used to improve query performance, it is important to build indexes on the columns that are commonly used to access the table. Also, the order of the columns in a compound index should be based on access paths and the number of distinct values in the column. The more distinct values in a column, the more selective the index will be.

B-Tree Index Growth and Maintenance   The structure of a B-Tree index is similar to an upside-down tree, with the root block at the top of the index and the leaf blocks added at the bottom of the structure. Branch blocks connect the root block to the leaf blocks; large indexes have multiple levels of branch blocks. B-Tree indexes, by design, remain balanced and grow from the leaf blocks up to the root block. New entries are added to the leaf blocks. When a leaf block fills, half its entries are moved to a new block. If adding a new leaf block causes the parent branch block to fill, it will split in a similar manner. This process is repeated throughout the index structure. If the root block requires a split, the same process is followed and then a new root block is created.

Indexes on tables that have a great deal of delete activity will need to be rebuilt regularly. Here's an example of rebuilding an index online, which enables nonparallel Data Manipulation Language (DML) during the operation:

```
ALTER INDEX HR.EMP_DEPARTMENT_IX REBUILD ONLINE
/
```

B-Tree Key Compression   For compound B-Tree indexes, key compression eliminates repeated occurrences of the key column values, potentially saving space and improving performance. Here's an example:

```
CREATE INDEX EMPLOYEE_DEPT_IDX ON EMPLOYEE (DEPT_ID, LAST_NAME, FIRST_NAME)
COMPRESS 2
/
```

The integer following the COMPRESS keyword tells us the number of columns to compress, also known as the *prefix length*. The default and maximum prefix length for nonunique indexes is equal to the number of columns; for unique indexes, the default and maximum is equal to the number of columns minus 1.

Bitmap Indexes

The bitmap index is designed to improve query performance for columns with few distinct values in tables with a large number of rows. It is also effective for resolving Boolean conditions. The bitmap index contains ranges of index rows, and a bitmap that indicates 1 (true) if the key exists in the row or 0 (false) if the key value is not true for the row. Bitmaps are composed of *bitmap segments*, which can be up to one-half a block. The bitmap index is created just as you would create a B-Tree index, except the BITMAP keyword immediately follows the CREATE keyword.

Benefits and Drawbacks of Bitmap Indexes   Bitmap indexes are ideal for columns that have few distinct values (low cardinality), such as the gender column in an employee table, and are ideal for resolving AND or OR operations as well. Because locking is at the bitmap segment level instead of the entry level, Online Transaction Processing (OLTP) or DML-intensive systems can suffer. Bitmap indexes are suited for DSS-type applications with few DML operations. When using bitmap indexes, the memory requirements for the database will most likely need to be increased because the bitmap index requires memory in which to create or merge bitmap segments. Also, bitmap indexes can be partitioned.

Reverse Key Indexes

The reverse key index, as the name implies, reverses the order of the bytes in each column of the index key. For compound indexes, the column order is not reversed. Reverse key indexes are ideal for columns that contain sequential numeric data. In regular B-Tree indexes, sequentially increasing values causes the index height to grow excessively, degrading performance. Reversing the key value causes the indexes to grow in a more normal manner. Reverse key indexes are only useful for exact key match lookups. If you're querying a range of values, then a full table scan is used instead of an index range scan. A reverse key index is created with the same syntax as a regular B-Tree index, except the REVERSE keyword must be included in the statement.

Function-Based Indexes

Another indexing option is the function-based index, which is based on a function or expression that includes one or more columns from the underlying table. The value of the function or expression is precomputed and stored in the index. A function-based index can be implemented as either a B-Tree or a bitmap index. To use a function-based index, the table must be analyzed, you must have the query rewrite system privilege, and query rewrite must be enabled. Here's an example:

```
CREATE INDEX HR.EMPL_LAST_NAME_IDX ON HR.EMPLOYEE (UPPER(LAST_NAME));
```

Applications can use function-based indexes to efficiently evaluate SQL statements that contain functions in WHERE clauses; however, INSERT and UPDATE statements will be slowed because they must first evaluate the function or expression.

Explain IOTs

An IOT is a combination table and primary-key B-Tree index in one structure. Instead of two separate segments, the IOT combines them into one segment. The B-Tree structure is used, and the table columns are stored in the leaf blocks. This reduces storage requirements and improves performance on primary-key lookups. Please note that the primary key is mandatory on an IOT.

Unlike heap-organized tables, IOTs don't have physical ROWIDs. Since access to the physical ROWID in a heap-organized table has proven useful to application developers, an analogous logical ROWID access method has been implemented for IOTs. The method includes a physical guess as to the location of the row, based on the row location when the index was created or rebuilt. When leaf blocks split, the physical guess can be invalidated. So, the second access method used, following a failed or incorrect guess, is via the primary key. Primary key access is fast, but not as fast as a direct physical ROWID or logical ROWID read.

The UROWID data type is provided so that we can create additional performance indexes on IOTs, and also so that developers can use a logical ROWID in the same way they use a physical ROWID. Without the UROWID, nonprimary key lookups would scan the entire IOT structure. Also, an IOT can be partitioned.

Creating an IOT   The syntax for creating an IOT is basically the same as creating a table with a primary key constraint, except the IOT is specified with the ORGANIZATION INDEX clause. Here's an example:

```
CREATE TABLE EMPLOYEES
(EMPLOYEE_ID    NUMBER(10) CONSTRAINT EMPLOYEE_ID_NN NOT NULL,
 LAST_NAME      VARCHAR2(30),
 FIRST_NAME     VARCHAR2(30),
 TITLE VARCHAR2(30),
 CONSTRAINT EMPLOYEE_ID_PK
   PRIMARY KEY (EMPLOYEE_ID))
ORGANIZATION INDEX
PCTTHRESHOLD 20
OVERFLOW TABLESPACE APP_DATA
/
```

Since storing too much information in the leaf blocks can lead to performance problems, the concept of *row overflow* was introduced. By setting the row overflow value, you can move nonprimary key columns to another segment in another tablespace. These keyword settings determine how overflow is handled:

- **PCTTHRESHOLD**   This determines the percentage of space reserved in the IOT leaf block for an IOT row. Valid values are 0 to 50.

- **INCLUDING**   This determines the cutoff point for columns kept in the IOT leaf block, as long as they don't exceed the PCTTHRESHOLD. Any column after the column specified is stored in the OVERFLOW tablespace.

- **OVERFLOW**   This clause specifies the tablespace and storage parameters for the overflow portion of the IOT row. Excessive use of the OVERFLOW table can nullify the performance gains that led you to use IOTs in the first place.

IOT Data Dictionary Views   Since an IOT is a combination table and index, we would expect to see some unique data dictionary entries. An IOT is part-table, so we see an entry in DBA_TABLES for the table name specified in the CREATE TABLE clause. The IOT_TYPE column indicates IOT. If you query the DBA_OBJECTS view using the base IOT table name for OBJECT_NAME, you'll see TABLE for OBJECT_TYPE.

If an overflow segment is defined, it will have its own DBA_TABLES entry; the table name is system generated of the form SYS_IOT_OVER_*nnnn*, where *nnnn* is the OBJECT_ID of the IOT table from DBA_OBJECTS. The DBA_TABLES IOT_TYPE indicates IOT_OVERFLOW, and the IOT_NAME indicates the name of the base IOT table. There is no DBA_SEGMENTS entry for the base IOT table, but there is for SYS_IOT_OVER_*nnnn*.

Additionally, the DBA_INDEXES view will have an entry for the defined primary key; the SEGMENT_TYPE is INDEX.

Using a Mapping Table for Bitmapped Indexes on IOT   In Oracle9*i*, you can create a bitmap index on an IOT table. A *mapping table* is used to resolve the logical ROWIDs needed for the IOT and the physical ROWIDs needed by the bitmap index. The mapping table is built by specifying the MAPPING TABLE clause when creating the IOT. As described previously, the leaf blocks of an IOT can split, causing the performance of the bitmap index via the mapping table to degrade. Analyze the index and query the PCT_DIRECT_ACCESS column of DBA_INDEXES to determine the percentage of rows that have a valid guess on the IOT. To improve performance, rebuild the mapping table with the ALTER TABLE command, including the MAPPING TABLE UPDATE BLOCK REFERENCES clause.

Describe Materialized Views and the Use of Query Rewrites

A *materialized view* is a hybrid between a view and a table, in which the results of the view are stored in the table when the materialized view is created.

The materialized view can be built on an IOT, a partitioned table, or a heap-organized table, and it can be indexed to improve query performance. Queries can be written to go directly against the materialized view, or queries can be redirected by the optimizer to go against the materialized view instead of the base table or tables. Materialized views are useful for meeting aggregate information needs in data warehouses.

Creating Materialized Views   The syntax for creating a materialized view is a combination of view and table create parameters, identical to the syntax used to create a snapshot. You can build a materialized view on a prebuilt table, use an IOT, or create the materialized view with default table storage parameters. A materialized view can be partitioned or use a partitioned base table. You also have the option to enable *query rewrite*, discussed in an upcoming section. Here's a simplified example:

```
CREATE MATERIALIZED VIEW
SALES_AGGREGATE
BUILD IMMEDIATE REFRESH FAST
ENABLE QUERY REWRITE
AS
SELECT REGION_NAME, PERIOD, SUM(SALE_PRICE)
FROM SALES_DETAIL D, SALES_REGION R
WHERE D.REGION_ID = R.REGION_ID
GROUP BY REGION_NAME
/
```

Refreshing a Materialized View

Several techniques can be used to refresh the data in a materialized view; in addition, we can choose to automatically refresh the materialized view or manually refresh with a supplied package. Here are the refresh techniques:

- **Complete**   This truncates the table and executes the view query, reading the base tables to repopulate the materialized view.

- **Fast**   This method only applies changes made to the base tables since the last refresh. Base table materialized view logs or direct loader logs are used to apply the changes.

- **Force**   This indicates to use the fast method, if possible; otherwise, a complete refresh is performed.

- **Never**   The materialized view is not refreshed.

Additionally, two different refresh modes are available:

- **Automatic Refresh mode**   Configured by setting the ON COMMIT clause, this causes committed rows in the base tables to force a fast refresh of the materialized view. The refresh is asynchronous, so the transaction against the base tables is not slowed. Also, you can use the START WITH and NEXT clauses to establish an automatic refresh schedule.

- **Manual Refresh mode**   Use the ON DEMAND clause, then use procedures in the DBMS_MVIEW package to update the view.

Query Rewrites

The query rewrite feature enables the optimizer to rewrite a query to choose the materialized view instead of querying the base tables, improving query performance. This activity is transparent to the end user, except that performance improves. The user doesn't require special privileges on the materialized view for the optimizer to rewrite the query. You must use the cost-based optimizer to enable query rewrites.

Enabling Query Rewrites   A query rewrite is enabled for the instance or at the session by setting the QUERY_REWRITE_ENABLED parameter. The QUERY REWRITE system privilege enables a user to enable or disable a query rewrite for a materialized view for which they own all the base tables. The GLOBAL QUERY REWRITE system privilege enables the privilege for base tables that are in other's schemas. To use a query rewrite, you must have the ENABLE QUERY REWRITE clause in the materialized view, you must be using the cost-based optimizer (CBO), and you must have the QUERY_REWRITE_ENABLED database parameter set to TRUE for either the database or the current session.

The QUERY_REWRITE_INTEGRITY parameter, dynamically set for the instance or session, determines the conditions for a query rewrite. ENFORCED rewrites the query only if the optimizer can guarantee that the data in the materialized view are current and constraints are enabled and validated. STALE_TOLERATED enables query rewrites even if DML has occurred on the base tables since the last refresh. TRUSTED enables a query rewrite if the materialized view has been updated and the constraints have the RELY flag set.

Disabling Query Rewrites   The two methods to explicitly disable query rewrites are to specify a NOREWRITE hint when querying or to use the DISABLE QUERY REWRITE clause when building the materialized view. The hint overrides the setting used when creating the materialized view and the QUERY_REWRITE_ENABLED setting. DISABLE QUERY REWRITE can also be specified with ALTER MATERIALIZED VIEW.

List Requirements for OLTP, DSS, and Hybrid Systems

In this section, we will discuss the different design approaches for OLTP, DSS, and hybrid systems. We will define the requirements of each type of system and then specify which types of objects should be used for each. Later, in Chapter 15, we will also discuss coding techniques, bind variables, hints, analyzing tables and indexes, and the use of histograms in the various types of applications.

OLTP Systems

The typical OLTP system is designed to meet some interactive business process need. Order processing, customer service, inventory tracking, online purchasing, and reservations systems are usually representative of the OLTP application type. These systems are generally used by a large number of users, internal and/or external to the organization. OLTP systems range in size from the very small to the very large.

It is usually expected that these applications will be available 24 hours a day, 365 days a year, with few exceptions. The current quality benchmark is "five 9's," or 99.999 percent availability. That's about 5 minutes, 15 seconds or less per year (not including leap year) that your system can be unavailable. This quality benchmark may not be achievable with a single instance on your current OS and hardware, but your customers will probably expect close to 100 percent uptime. To meet their needs, you may need to consider Oracle's high-availability options, which include Oracle Real Application Clusters (RACs), Advanced Replication, and Oracle Standby database. These alternatives offer improved application uptime and reduce the impact of recovery time following a failure.

Also, it is expected that these systems will perform exceptionally well. Internet application users are notorious for losing interest in applications that don't meet their performance expectations. Although your internal application users may be more tolerant than web customers, they definitely know when response time is poor, especially users of order-entry systems. Users may expect a 1- to 2-second response time for typical queries.

Finally, OLTP systems are generally accessed by a large number of users at the same time; therefore, data concurrency is extremely important.

OLTP Design Considerations   Now that you know about the expectations for an OLTP system, you can design accordingly. Here are some specific design considerations for object types in an OLTP environment.

- **Explicit extent allocation**   Dynamic extent allocation is expensive, so plan the data volume requirements and build the objects with the appropriate size and number of extents. Dynamic extent allocation is not as costly with locally managed tablespaces, but it is still not as desirable as planned extent allocation.

- **Indexing**   Proper indexing is extremely important in an OLTP environment. Too many indexes will slow the performance of insertions, updates, and deletions. If you have indexed properly on columns that are used to look up values or to satisfy join conditions, then you can significantly improve performance. B-Tree indexes are more suited for OLTP systems than bitmap indexes, because a DML operation on a bitmap index entry locks a range of rows, while the same operation on a B-Tree index only requires locking a single row. This can dramatically impact data concurrency. IOTs can be used to speed the performance of information retrieval based on primary key lookups because the index and data are stored together. Also, consider using reverse key indexes for sequences. Finally, rebuild and analyze indexes regularly.

- **Hash clusters**   Hash clusters can be used to improve performance on objects that are used in equijoin queries. However, you should not use hash clusters if the rows are updated frequently with data that causes variable-size columns to grow or if there are frequent row inserts.

DSS/Data Warehouse Systems

DSS systems are typically very large, but support few users compared to the typical OLTP system. The typical application will consist of long-running queries that read a large volume of data and produce summary reports, which are then used by decision makers. full table scans on large tables are common. Data in the DSS is often loaded from other OLTP-type systems, operational control systems, or data collection systems.

The tuning goals for DSS systems include fast query performance and accuracy. These systems may be used for ad hoc querying during normal business hours, and large data loads and scheduled reports after normal business hours.

DSS Design Considerations   Oracle provides us with several design options to improve the performance of long-running queries against large tables. Here are a few design options to consider:

- **Database block size and reads**   If your application reads large volumes of data, it makes sense to read the largest chunks possible in as few physical I/Os as possible. Setting the DB_BLOCK_SIZE and DB_FILE_MULTIBLOCK_READ_COUNT to high values (higher than OLTP) will improve the performance of full table scans on large tables. These settings can also influence the optimizer to choose full table scans instead of index lookups. Also, since rows in DSS systems are rarely updated, you can set the PCTFREE setting very low, increasing data block density.

- **Materialized views**   Materialized views can be used to aggregate data from OLTP sources or from large fact tables. Report runtime can be dramatically reduced.

- **Indexing**   Since many DSS queries scan an entire table or tables, you may not benefit from indexes on large fact tables. Queries against dimension or lookup tables may benefit greatly from proper B-Tree indexing. Also, bitmap indexes can improve query performance on columns with low cardinality. IOTs can be used to speed the performance of queries that use the primary key for exact matches or range searches. Finally, perform regular maintenance on indexes, especially those on tables that are updated frequently.

- **Parallel query**   This can dramatically improve the performance of queries against large tables. Coupled with a correct partitioning implementation, query runtime can be reduced by the factor of parallelism. Parallel query and partitioning are essential for huge DSS systems.

- **Partitioned tables and indexes**   If you purchased the Oracle Partitioning option, you can build partitioned tables and indexes, which provide a substantial performance boost to DSS-type systems. By partitioning the tables and indexes by a partition key, you can optimize parallel query operations and eliminate scans on partitions that are not required to satisfy the query. Partitioning was designed for large DSS systems.

Hybrid Systems

As the name implies, hybrid systems exist on the continuum between absolutely OLTP and absolutely DSS, sharing some design or operational characteristics of each. For instance, your human resources, benefits, and payroll applications may all use the same database, but the human resources application is probably more OLTP-like than the payroll application. The benefits application is probably a good representative hybrid system, with both user interfaces and long-running reports.

With hybrid systems, it is important to focus on tuning the components of the application. For instance, you may want to set the initialization parameter DB_FILE_MULTIBLOCK_READ_COUNT to 8 for the instance, and use the ALTER SESSION command to change the value to 32 for the DSS-like reports. You will probably want to build DSS-like objects in tablespaces that have a larger block size. You also may want to use bind variables for the OLTP-like application components and generate histograms for the DSS-like tables. Use B-Tree indexes for the OLTP-like tables, and use partitioned tables and indexes or bitmap indexes on the DSS-like tables. With hybrid systems, keep in mind that using only one approach to tuning (say, DSS) can cause performance degradation for the components that are more like the other type.

Chapter Summary

In this chapter, we discussed the role of the DBA in tuning the application design, the most important phase of the tuning process. The majority of the chapter was dedicated to describing storage and data access alternatives that can improve application performance. We also discussed the criteria for selecting which type of object to implement.

In many organizations, it is expected that the DBA will take an active role in tuning the application design. Although organizational differences will probably determine the DBA's role in the process, it is extremely important that the DBA understand the options available at database design time.

In addition to heap-organized or regular tables, the Oracle DBA has several other options for storing data. A cluster is used to group one or more tables into a single physical storage structure. The cluster key is the column or columns that each table in the cluster has in common. An index cluster uses a B-Tree index to access rows within the cluster. Alternatively, a hash cluster uses a hashing algorithm to determine row location. You can use the Partitioning option to create partitioned tables, and it can be used to greatly improve the performance of queries against extremely large tables.

The IOT uses a B-Tree primary index structure and places the table row data in the leaf blocks. To reduce performance degradation on an IOT, the DBA can choose to move nonprimary key column data to an overflow segment. IOTs use a logical ROWID method to locate a row. The nonkey columns that fit in the index leaf block are stored as a row headpiece that contains a ROWID field linking it to the next row piece stored in the overflow data segment. Logical ROWIDs are used to support secondary indexes, which locate rows based on the ROWID. The logical ROWID approach uses a guess based on the location of the row when the IOT is created or rebuilt. Secondary indexes can be built on an IOT to improve query performance on nonprimary key lookups. A mapping table is used to make bitmap indexing on an IOT possible. The mapping table relates ROWIDs needed by the IOT and physical ROWIDs needed by the bitmap index.

A materialized view is a summary table and query used to derive data from base tables. The rows of a materialized view are refreshed from data in the base tables using one of three techniques: complete, fast, or force. A materialized view can be configured to refresh data automatically when the underlying tables change or on a schedule. You can also manually refresh the data using procedures from the DBMS_MVIEW package.

Along with materialized views, Oracle provides a query rewrite capability. A query rewrite enables queries to access materialized views instead of the base tables without a modification to the query. A query rewrite is dynamically enabled at the instance or session level and can be enabled or disabled in a query hint or for a specific materialized view.

In addition to the alternative means of storing data, Oracle provides us with several indexing options. The traditional indexing mechanism is the B-Tree index, which is very useful for speeding queries that return a relatively small number of rows from a table. B-Tree indexes are also very useful for speeding join conditions and should be rebuilt regularly if a sizable percentage of rows are deleted, or if the index key values are frequently updated.

Bitmap indexes are useful for columns with few distinct values and millions of rows. They are also effective for resolving Boolean conditions. The bitmap index contains ranges of index rows, and a bitmap that indicates 1 (true) if the key exists in the row or 0 (false) if the key value is not true for the row. In a reverse key index, the bytes of the key are reversed. Reverse key indexes are useful in situations where the key consists of sequentially increasing values. Function-based indexes store the results of a function or expression in the index and speed the performance of queries that match the expression.

In OLTP systems, fast query performance, data concurrency, continuous uptime, and fast recoverability are essential. B-Tree indexes, clusters, and reverse key indexes help speed OLTP queries. DSS systems usually require fast query performance and accuracy. Bitmap indexes, materialized views, and IOTs are tools the DBA should use in the DSS environment. The Partitioning option is also available and is extremely beneficial for a large system with parallel queries.

A hybrid system shares features of both DSS and OLTP. In a hybrid system, the DBA should choose the correct object type for the access method that will be used by the application.

Two-Minute Drill

- In many organizations, the DBA is responsible for choosing and implementing the optimal storage objects for the application.

- OLTP systems generally require high availability and a fast response time.

- DSS systems usually require data accuracy and fast query performance.

- B-Tree indexes are ideal when a large number of distinct values are in a column.

- B-Tree indexes are used to speed query performance when a relatively small number of rows will be returned.

- Bitmap indexes are ideal for low-cardinality data: few distinct values and a large number of rows.

- In a reverse key index, the bytes of the key value are reversed; reverse key indexes are ideal for sequentially increasing values.

- A function-based index implements the results of a function or expression in the index.

- The function-based index speeds the performance of queries that must resolve an expression on the data.

- Clusters store one or more tables together in the same data blocks.

- An IOT places the row data of a table in the leaf blocks of a B-Tree index.

- An IOT can use an overflow segment to store nonkey columns.

- A bitmap index can be added to an IOT by means of a mapping table.

- A materialized view is a snapshot of data from base tables that satisfy the view query.

- A materialized view can be indexed just like a heap-organized table, or it can be implemented as an IOT.

- The data in a materialized view can be refreshed automatically or manually.

- The refresh techniques include complete, force, or fast.

- The query rewrite feature enables an application query to access the materialized view instead of the base tables, potentially showing significant performance improvements.

- A query rewrite is enabled for materialized views by setting the instance or session parameter QUERY_REWRITE_ENABLED.

- Hybrid systems have features of both DSS and OLTP systems.

Chapter Questions

1. In an OLTP environment, three tables share a key column value and are always joined together in queries. Which one of these storage structures is a good design choice?

   A. IOT

   B. Cluster

   C. Materialized view

2. In a DSS application, the sales summary report queries data from seven different tables and groups the data by region and period. Which one of the following storage structures is a good design choice to improve query performance?

   A. IOT

   B. Cluster

   C. Materialized view

3. Which type of index is best suited for low-cardinality data, that is, few distinct column values in a table with many rows?

   A. B-Tree

   B. Bitmap

   C. Compressed key

   D. Reverse key

   E. Function-based

   F. IOT

4. When an IOT is created, the DBA can specify the cutoff point in a row, determining which columns will be stored in the IOT leaf block and which will be stored in the overflow segment by specifying which of the following parameters?

   A. INCLUDING

   B. PCTTHRESHOLD

   C. OVERFLOW

   D. ORGANIZATION INDEX

5. **The DBA can build bitmap indexes on an IOT by creating which of the following?**

   A. An IOT cluster

   B. A bitmap cluster

   C. A mapping table

   D. A bitmap IOT

6. **Which of the following accurately describes the ENFORCED query rewrite integrity parameter?**

   A. A query rewrite is allowed if DML has occurred on the base tables since the last refresh.

   B. A query rewrite is allowed only if the server can guarantee consistency between the base tables and the materialized view.

   C. A query rewrite is enabled in all cases.

7. **This DDL is an example of which type of index?**

   ```
   CREATE INDEX MY_INDEX ON EMPLOYEE (UPPER(LAST_NAME));
   ```

   A. Reverse key

   B. Cluster

   C. Function-based

   D. IOT

   E. Bitmap

   F. B-Tree

8. **Which refresh mode would keep the materialized view in sync with the base tables each time DML occurs on the base table?**

   A. Complete

   B. Automatic using the ON COMMIT clause

   C. Automatic using the START WITH and NEXT clauses

   D. Manual force

   E. Manual complete

Answers to Chapter Questions

1. B.   Cluster

Explanation   The question describes the ideal situation for building a cluster. Since the tables are always joined together with the same key, this key would be an ideal cluster key. We now need to determine if a hash cluster or an index cluster is more appropriate. Answer A is incorrect because an IOT is not the ideal storage structure for the situation described. Answer C might be a good choice in a DSS environment because all the criteria are met except for the environment.

2. C.   Materialized view

Explanation   Materialized views are designed for the type of situation described in the question. A materialized view could be put in place to speed the queries that would have accessed multiple tables to produce summary information. A cluster would probably not be a good structure because the described data is probably volatile and is probably not always queried together. An IOT is not a good way to store data from several tables; however, the materialized view could be stored as an IOT instead of a heap table.

3. B.   Bitmap

Explanation   Bitmap indexes are designed for low-cardinality data, such as gender in an employee table. B-Tree indexes are designed for high-cardinality data, that is, many distinct keys relative to the number of rows. A compressed B-Tree is a compromise between the extremes, but not the correct answer. Reverse key indexes, function-based indexes, and IOTs each have a niche, but none are designed for low-cardinality data.

4. A.   INCLUDING

Explanation   The INCLUDING keyword specifies which columns to keep in the IOT leaf blocks. Those columns after the column specified in the INCLUDING clause will be written to the overflow segment. The PCTTHRESHOLD value indicates how much of the leaf block to reserve for row data; the OVERFLOW clause specifies the storage parameters for the columns that are not kept in the leaf blocks. The ORGANIZATION INDEX clause is used to specify that the table is an IOT.

5. C.   A mapping table

Explanation   The mapping table is used to relate logical ROWIDs required by the IOT to physical ROWIDs required by the bitmap. One mapping table is used for an IOT even if several bitmap indexes are on the structure. Each of the other answers are incorrect because they don't exist.

6. B.   A query rewrite is allowed only if the server can guarantee consistency between the base tables and the materialized view.

Explanation   By setting the QUERY_REWRITE_INTEGRITY parameter to ENFORCED, we specify that the query rewrite should be used only if the data in the materialized view is synchronized with the base table and all integrity constraints are satisfied. Answer A is the condition that describes STALE_TOLERATED. Answer C is incorrect and doesn't accurately describe one particular setting, but is conceptually similar to STALE_TOLERATED.

7. C.   Function-based

Explanation   The DDL clearly shows that the UPPER function is used on the employee's last name column. Answers A, B, D, and E are incorrect because the DDL will not create any one of these types of indexes. Answer F is not the "most correct" answer. The index created is a B-Tree index, but it is a special class of B-Tree indexes called function-based.

8. B.   Automatic using the ON COMMIT clause

Explanation   The ON COMMIT clause specifies that the materialized view will be automatically updated when transactions on the base tables are committed. This guarantees that the materialized view will stay synchronized with the base tables. Answer A doesn't guarantee that the materialized view will stay in sync. Answer C specifies a time to refresh the materialized view, so synchronization is not change-related but time-related. Answers D and E will refresh the materialized view, but will not guarantee synchronization.

CHAPTER
14

Using Oracle
Blocks Efficiently

n this chapter, you will learn how Oracle stores rows in blocks. For the exam, you'll need to know the following:

- Describe the correct usage of extents and Oracle blocks.
- Explain space usage and the high watermark.
- Determine the high watermark.
- Recover space from sparsely populated segments.
- Describe the use of Oracle block parameters.
- Describe, detect, and resolve chaining and migration of Oracle blocks.
- Perform index reorganization.
- Monitor indexes to determine usage.

The performance implications of space management are extremely important. Getting the correct block size and correctly managing how rows are stored in blocks can make a significant difference in database and application performance. We will talk specifically about reorganizing tables and indexes for optimal performance.

Using Oracle Blocks Efficiently

Often neglected for more glamorous items to tune, space management seems to be the most overlooked and misunderstood, but extremely important facet of Oracle database tuning. Reorganizing tables and rebuilding indexes to keep storage at optimal usage and performance are essential database administrator (DBA) functions, but they are often overlooked or given a low priority. In this chapter, I hope to emphasize the importance of using blocks efficiently and explain the operations in such a way that you will not be discouraged from exercising them on your databases.

Describe the Correct Usage of Extents and Oracle Blocks

In this section, we will discuss the hierarchy of data storage in the Oracle database, extent allocation, and locally managed tablespaces. We will also discuss how extent size can affect performance.

Data Storage Hierarchy: Segment, Extent, and Block

In the hierarchy of storage, a segment is comprised of one or more extents, and an extent is comprised of database blocks.

A database block consists of one or more contiguous operating system (OS) blocks. The database block is the smallest unit of storage that can be read from and written to disk; it is the smallest unit of allocation within the database. The default database block size is specified in the init.ora file when the database is created. This default block size is used for the SYSTEM tablespace and is the default for other tablespaces. With Oracle9i, the DBA can specify a nondefault block size for non-SYSTEM tablespaces.

A database extent is a logical group of contiguous database blocks. Extent size is defined at object creation time, with the INITIAL and NEXT storage parameters. If these storage parameters are not specified, then the tablespace storage defaults take effect. You can also dynamically modify the value for NEXT, which does not affect currently allocated extents, but does dictate the size of the next and subsequently allocated extents. The data dictionary view DBA_EXTENTS has a row for each extent in the database.

A segment is a logical storage unit that is made up of one or more extents. With compound objects, such as index-organized tables (IOTs) with overflow, or partitioned tables and indexes, each separate logical storage entity is its own segment. The data dictionary view DBA_SEGMENTS has a row for each segment in the database. Segment types include INDEX PARTITION, TABLE PARTITION, TABLE, CLUSTER, INDEX, ROLLBACK, DEFERRED ROLLBACK, TEMPORARY, CACHE, NESTED TABLE, TABLE SUBPARTITION, INDEX SUBPARTITION, LOB SUBPARTITION, LOBSEGMENT, LOBINDEX, and TYPE2 UNDO.

Extent Allocation

When a process tries to perform an INSERT or UPDATE and cannot find enough free space in the segment, a new extent must be added to the segment. The DBA can manually extend a segment with the ALTER *segment_type segment_name* ALLOCATE EXTENT command, or the Oracle server will do it dynamically. When using dictionary-managed tablespaces, dynamic extent allocation is relatively expensive and can cause performance problems. This is due to the amount of recursive SQL required to update the data dictionary. Dynamic extent allocation is not a performance problem with locally managed tablespaces.

Monitoring for Dynamic Extension

With dictionary-managed tablespaces, we want to avoid dynamic extent allocation as much as possible. To avoid frequent extent allocation, you should focus on determining the correct size that objects will grow to before you build them. Depending on the type of application and volume of data, you may need to build a segment such that it has enough blocks to meet one year's worth of growth. Another approach is to build the object larger than it will ever grow, within reason. After you create and begin populating an object, you should monitor it closely to make sure that it does not frequently extend dynamically. If you determine that an object will extend soon, you should consider manually extending the object to avoid the performance hit that would otherwise occur. Carefully consider the system load at the time, and determine if manually extending the object should be postponed until system load is lower.

Determine Extents That Are Close to Extending   To determine if an object is close to extending, we want to compare the number of used blocks to the number of free blocks. Here's an example that will determine if any tables in the database are above a threshold value:

```
SELECT OWNER, TABLESPACE_NAME, TABLE_NAME, BLOCKS, EMPTY_BLOCKS
FROM DBA_TABLES
WHERE EMPTY_BLOCKS / (BLOCKS+EMPTY_BLOCKS) < .1
AND EMPTY_BLOCKS != 0;
```

You should run this query daily or weekly, depending on the relative growth of the segments in your database. Also, based on the application that uses the database, you may want to use a different threshold value.

Manual Extent Allocation   If you notice from the results of the previous query that an object is close to extending, you may want to take preventative action and force the object to extend before an INSERT or UPDATE statement causes dynamic extension. Here's how:

```
ALTER TABLE HR.EMPLOYEES ALLOCATE EXTENT;
```

Locally Managed Tablespaces
Locally managed tablespaces keep track of the free and used blocks in a datafile by using a bitmap located in the file space header block of each datafile. The bitmap value changes to indicate that a block is free or used. This mechanism avoids the recursive SQL that occurs during dynamic extension of a dictionary-managed tablespace.

Previous to Oracle9*i*, tablespaces were dictionary managed by default. With Oracle9*i*, tablespaces are locally managed by default, except for the SYSTEM tablespace.

You specify extent management when you create the tablespace:

```
CREATE TABLESPACE APP_DATA
DATAFILE 'E:\ORACLE\ORADATA\OR9I\APP_DATA01.DBF'
```

```
SIZE 500 M
EXTENT MANAGEMENT LOCAL
UNIFORM SIZE 5 M;
```

The EXTENT MANAGEMENT LOCAL clause is, as mentioned, the default behavior if the version of Oracle is 9.0.0 or greater and the COMPATIBLE setting in the init.ora file indicates so. There are two versions of the LOCAL option:

- AUTOALLOCATE indicates that the extent size for the tablespace is automatically configured and cannot be changed. This is the default if COMPATIBLE is set to 9.0.0 or higher.

- UNIFORM specifies that the tablespace is managed with uniform extents, each of SIZE bytes, using KB for kilobytes or MB for megabytes. The default SIZE is 1 megabyte.

In my experience, the performance gains with locally managed tablespaces is significant, and you should use them instead of dictionary-managed tablespaces whenever possible.

Also, you should carefully plan the size of your UNIFORM extents and datafiles. Oracle stores only 64KB for the bitmap, but you can lose nearly one extent if it does not fit into your datafile anymore. If, for example, we ask for 5MB extents in a 10MB file, after 64KB is allocated for the bitmap, we are left with one 5MB extent and one less than 5MB extent that is wasted. Locally managed tablespaces should have datafiles that are 64KB larger than a multiple of their extent size when using uniform sizing.

You can migrate a tablespace from dictionary managed to locally managed with the DBMS_SPACE_ADMIN. TABLESPACE_MIGRATE_TO_LOCAL procedure.

The Size of Data Extents: Large versus Small

Whether you choose large or small initial and next extent sizes depends on the data storage requirements of your application. Performance gains from using one large extent versus multiple small extents are negligible for all operations except for those that deallocate extents in a dictionary-managed tablespace. There are some administrative advantages to using large extent sizes:

- Dynamic extent allocation is reduced with large extents.

- The extent map can span multiple blocks if MAXEXTENTS is set to UNLIMITED, reducing performance for operations that must read the extent map. An extent map indicates the location (file ID and block ID) and size (in ORACLE database blocks) of each extent associated with each segment.

- Some extent information is maintained in the data dictionary, so more extents take up more data dictionary entries.

- With dictionary-managed tablespaces, the time required to deallocate extents when we use the DROP or TRUNCATE command is more time consuming when there are more extents to manage. The size of the extents is irrelevant, but the number of extents is relevant.

There are some disadvantages to using large extents instead of small, including

- Large extent sizes can lead to disk space wastage.

- It may be difficult to find contiguous space for large extents.

Explain Space Usage and the High Watermark

Within a segment, there are basically three classifications to which a block belongs:

- **Blocks that are in use** There is currently row data stored in the block. The block may not have filled up, may be full, or may have free space from deleted rows. These rows exist below the high watermark.

- **Empty blocks that have been used** These blocks stored rows at one time, but all the rows have been deleted. These rows exist below the high watermark.

- **Empty blocks that have never been used** No row has been inserted into these blocks. They are part of the segment, but have never had a row written to them. These rows exist above the high watermark.

The high watermark is the cutoff point; all rows above have never been used, and all rows below are currently in use or have been used before. Available blocks below the high watermark are kept on the freelist for insert activity; therefore, blocks below the high watermark are preferred for inserts over blocks above the high watermark. The high watermark is recorded in the segment header block.

The high watermark is reset when the table is completely cleared of row data with the TRUNCATE command. When the TRUNCATE command is executed, the high watermark is set to the beginning of the segment, just as when the segment was created. When new rows are added, the high watermark is raised in five-block increments. The DELETE command does not change the high watermark.

Performance Issues Associated with the High Watermark

Blocks above the high watermark may take up unnecessary space, but they do not affect performance. However, sparsely populated blocks below the high watermark do affect fulltable scan (FTS) performance. Since any FTS must read every block below the high watermark, fewer block reads are required if the same rows are packed into fewer blocks. Index performance can also degrade if the blocks are sparsely populated.

Deallocating Unused Blocks

Blocks above the high watermark can be returned to the tablespace free space pool by issuing a simple command:

```
ALER TABLE HR.EMPLOYEES DEALLOCATE UNUSED;
```

Clusters and the High Watermark

For clusters, the high watermark is different than for tables. Index clusters allocate space for each cluster index entry. For hash clusters, the space for each hash key is allocated below the high watermark. In clusters, space is allocated for all cluster keys, whether they contain data or not.

Determine the High Watermark

The column values used to determine the high watermark are populated when we gather statistics for the table or cluster. You can use the ANALYZE command or the DBMS_STATS package to collect storage information about the object. Use the DBA_TABLES or DBA_CLUSTERS view, whichever is appropriate for the object you're interested in. These columns are of the most importance to us:

- **BLOCKS** Number of blocks below the high watermark
- **EMPTY_BLOCKS** number of blocks above the high watermark; blocks not used since the segment was created or the last TRUNCATE statement was issued
- **NUM_FREELIST_BLOCKS** number of blocks on the freelist

In addition, we can look at the AVG_ROW_LEN, AVG_SPACE, and AVG_SPACE_ FREELIST_BLOCKS to determine the density of data in the blocks below the high watermark.

Recover Space from Sparsely Populated Segments

We've already discussed one way to regain unused space from segments; that is, using the DEALLOCATE UNUSED clause to move table blocks above the high watermark into the tablespace free space pool. In this section, we'll discuss using the DBMS_SPACE package, a tool that we can use to determine space allocation within a segment, and additional methods that we can use to recover unused space from a segment.

Using DBMS_SPACE

The DBMS_SPACE supplied package is useful for determining segment storage statistics and planning segment growth.

DBMS_SPACE.UNUSED_SPACE   This procedure takes as input the segment owner, name, and segment type; it returns the total number of blocks, total bytes, unused blocks, unused bytes, and the last used file, extent, and block, indicating the high watermark.

DBMS_SPACE.FREE_BLOCKS   This procedure takes as input the segment owner, name, segment type, and freelist_group_id (instance); it returns the number of free blocks in the segment. If you're not using real application clusters, then freelist_group_id = 0.

DBMS_SPACE.SPACE_USAGE   This procedure takes as input the segment owner, name, and segment type; it returns the space usage of data blocks under the segment high watermark. The bitmap blocks, segment header, and extent map blocks are not included in the values returned by this procedure.

Methods to Recover Space

As mentioned previously, we can easily recover unused space above the high watermark. If we want to recover unused space below the high watermark, we have a few more options to choose from; however, each one affects data concurrency because rows are moved or removed.

Drop Table   The DROP TABLE command recovers space by dropping the data and definition of a table, and its associated indexes; all extents are freed. The table is removed from the data dictionary, and other objects can now use the space freed up by the drop. Any synonyms or views that reference the table are not dropped, however.

Truncate Table   The TRUNCATE TABLE command recovers space by removing all of the data from a table, but does not alter or drop the table from the database. Index entries are removed, but the index is not dropped. By default, all allocated extents except for the initial extent are returned to tablespace free space. If you specify the REUSE STORAGE clause, then the allocated extents are kept in the segment and not returned to tablespace free space.

Export/Import Table   If you intend to keep the data in a table before you recover the space, you can use the EXPORT command to extract the data from the database. Then use the DROP TABLE or TRUNCATE TABLE command to free the space. Once the space has been freed, run the IMPORT command to return the table data to the database.

There are a few options to consider when importing the table back into the database:

- If you dropped the table after you exported, then you can create the table with new storage parameters that are more suited to the table's storage requirements.

- If you truncated the table, then the object still exists in the database so you'll need to use the IGNORE=Y switch when you import the data.

- If you exported the table with the COMPRESS=Y switch, the import will attempt to create one extent that is large enough to hold all of the table data. You'll need to make sure that there is enough contiguous free space in the tablespace for the initial extent.

- Also, extent management in dictionary-managed tablespaces can be time consuming if many extents are involved.

One last thing to consider, if there are indexes on the table and the table was truncated, the import will be slowed considerably because of index maintenance if you set the import switch INDEXES=Y. It's best to extract the index definitions from the export file by running import using the INDEXFILE switch, drop the indexes, import the data into the table with the INDEXES=N switch, and then build the indexes on the table by executing the index file you created. This may seem like a significant workaround, but it can save you hours on large tables with indexes. Also, you can edit the resulting index creation script to enable parallel index creation.

Move Table   The ALTER TABLE MOVE command is an alternative to the Export/Import option; it enables you to rebuild a table dynamically. You can specify new storage parameters for the table in the STORAGE clause. You will need additional space for the table while it is being moved. Unfortunately, the ROWID for each row in the table will change, so all indexes on the table will have a STATUS of UNUSABLE in the DBA_INDEXES view and must be rebuilt with the ALTER INDEX *index_name* REBUILD; or you can drop and recreate the indexes. The COALESCE option, described in the upcoming section entitled "Coalescing or Rebuilding," cannot be used to make the index usable again.

Describe the Use of Oracle Block Parameters

The block size in an Oracle database has a significant impact on database performance. One of our tuning goals is to reduce the number of blocks read or visited by applications. To reduce the number of blocks visited, we can increase block size, set the PCTFREE lower so that more rows are packed into a block, and also prevent row migrations. Migrations will be covered in the next section "Describe and Detect Chaining and Migration."

The DB_BLOCK_SIZE init.ora parameter determines the default block size for the database. The value is specified when the database is created and cannot be modified afterward. Depending on your platform, the value defaults to 2 or 4KB, and can be 8, 16, 32, or 64KB.

The block size is the minimum input/output (I/O) size for datafile reads. The default database block size should be a multiple of the OS block size for optimal performance.

Creating a Tablespace with a Different Block Size

When creating a tablespace, we can use the BLOCKSIZE clause to use a nonstandard block size for the tablespace. Here's an example:

```
CREATE TABLESPACE test_data
DATAFILE 'E:\ORACLE\ORADATA\OR9I\TEST_DATA01.DBF'
SIZE 10M
BLOCKSIZE 4K
/
```

Before you can create a tablespace with a nonstandard block size, you must have specified the DB_CACHE_SIZE parameter. Also, you must have created a separate buffer cache for the nonstandard block size by setting the DB_*n*K_CACHE_SIZE parameter, where *n* is the same number for the tablespace BLOCKSIZE and the DB_*n*K_CACHE_SIZE. You cannot use a nonstandard block size tablespace for temporary segments.

The Size of Blocks: Large versus Small

Depending on your application needs and the data design, you may need to use a large or small default block size. Remember that you can set up additional tablespaces that have a nonstandard block size.

When to Use Large Blocks
A large block size can significantly improve the performance of large FTSs. Since one block is the smallest unit that is requested in an I/O operation, if a large amount of data can be fetched by the OS and returned to Oracle, then operations become more efficient. In Decision Support System (DSS) environments, you should consider using a larger block size, since FTSs are

expected. One option is to use larger block sizes for tablespaces that contain fact tables that will be read with FTSs, and use the smaller block size tablespaces for dimensions. Index performance is also improved because more index entries can be stored in each block, reducing the overall height of the index. Also, if the row data is very large, a larger block size is more appropriate to reduce row chaining.

When Not to Use Large Blocks   You should not use a large block size in an Online Transaction Processing (OLTP) environment because of possible contention issues. If the majority of reads are random lookups using indexes, then probably too many blocks are read into the buffer cache and then rarely used.

When to Use Small Blocks   Small block sizes are more appropriate for random access lookups like we see in many OLTP systems. They are good for small row sizes and reduce the potential for contention because there are fewer rows per block. Also, random access via index lookups can benefit, and the buffer cache will probably be used more efficiently.

When Not to Use Small Blocks   Small blocks are not a good choice for DSS systems that perform many FTSs. If rows are large and there are relatively few rows per block, then random access may not be very efficient since more blocks may need to be read.

Block Storage Parameters: Setting PCTFREE and PCTUSED

Within each block in an extent in a segment, we can control how much of the space is reserved for row update activity and how much row data must be deleted from a block before it can be returned to the freelist. The PCTFREE block storage parameter specifies how much space to reserve for row updates to rows that already exist in the block. The PCTUSED parameter specifies a threshold that when enough rows are deleted from a block, the block is placed back on the freelist. Each of these parameters is set with the CREATE TABLE/CLUSTER command, and you can change the values of PCTFREE or PCTUSED with the ALTER TABLE/CLUSTER command. When you change these values with the ALTER command, the existing blocks are not immediately affected; however, any subsequent Data Manipulation Language (DML) will adhere to the new settings.

Setting PCTFREE   Rows are inserted into blocks that are on the freelist. Once the volume of block overhead and row data reaches 100-PCTFREE, the block is taken off the freelist and no new rows are inserted into the block. The value you choose for PCTFREE should consider the volume and frequency of row updates that cause rows to grow, the type of table access used by the application, and the type of application. If rows are updated frequently such that column values grow (for example, varchar2 columns), then you should consider keeping a higher PCTFREE, reserving space for the rows to grow. If tables are accessed with FTSs, then a lower PCTFREE leads to more densely populated blocks, which are more efficient than sparsely populated blocks. The default value is 10; consider the ratio of the average update size to the average row length when estimating a value. DSS applications that only insert rows and never update them are good candidates for low (or zero) PCTFREE. For OLTP systems, you may need to keep the PCTFREE higher than the default if row chaining or migration becomes an issue.

Setting PCTUSED   When a block is not on the freelist and we begin deleting rows, the row will remain off the freelist until the percentage of block overhead and row data drops below PCTUSED. Once below PCTUSED, the block becomes a candidate for new row inserts.

The PCTUSED parameter is only significant if you have row deletes. If the table in question has heavy delete and insert activity, then you should closely consider the value for PCTUSED. If the value is too low, then there may be contention for blocks on the freelist because blocks are not returned to the freelist quickly. If the setting is too high, then blocks may be added to and removed from the freelist too quickly. Careful consideration should be followed up with monitoring. The default value for PCTUSED is 40.

The PCTUSED parameter is used for tables and clusters, but not indexes. Consider the average row length, the number of rows to delete before returning the block to the freelist, and the block size when estimating a value. Here's a formula that you can use for estimating what PCTUSED should be set to:

$$PCTUSED = 100\text{-}PCTFREE - (100 \times rows \times average\ row\ length)/block\ size$$

Coalescing Block Free Space   When there is delete activity, or update activity that causes rows to become smaller, blocks can become fragmented. There is no command that enables the DBA to coalesce free space from deleted rows inside a block. Free space is not automatically coalesced by Oracle when rows are deleted or updated. However, Oracle does coalesce block free space under these circumstances:

- An INSERT or UPDATE finds enough free space in a data block.

- There is not enough contiguous free space to update the row piece.

The noncontiguous free space is coalesced, and the row piece is put into the block.

Describe and Detect Chaining and Migration of Oracle Blocks

Migration and chaining are two distinctly different types of problems that can exist when a row is too large to fit into a single data block. In this section, we will define each, the circumstances that can cause each, how to detect them, and how to fix them.

Row Chaining

Row chaining occurs when a row is too large to fit into a single empty data block. When this occurs, Oracle will spread the row across as many blocks as are needed, chaining the row from one block to the next. For example, you have an 8K block size, but each row is 10K or 18K long. In the former case, a minimum of two blocks would be required; in the latter, a minimum of three blocks would be required. Chaining occurs when a row is inserted or updated.

Chaining is prevalent when large objects (LOB) are used. Generally, the only way to fix row chaining is to increase the block size. With Oracle9i, we can create tablespaces with a block size other than the database default; therefore, we can move tables that exhibit significant row chaining to a tablespace with a larger block size.

Row Migration

Row migration occurs when a row is updated and it will not fit back into the original block. When this happens, the Oracle server attempts to find another block that the entire row can be moved to. If it does find a block, the entire row is moved to the new block. The row piece (head ROWID) remains in the original block, with the original ROWID, and points to the migrated row in the new block. This means that indexes are not invalidated and do not need to be rebuilt when a row migrates. Row migration occurs when the PCTFREE value is set too low, and Oracle is unable to update a row using available free space in the same block.

Performance Implications of Row Chaining and Migration

Both row chaining and migration cause performance problems. Querying on chained or migrated rows requires greater consumption of memory, CPU, and I/O. The buffer cache is cycled more quickly because more blocks must be read into the cache. CPU consumption is greater because the Oracle server has to read a block and process the information required to find the remaining pieces of the row. More I/O is required, unless all the needed blocks are read with one I/O because of the DB_FILE_MULTIBLOCK_READ_COUNT setting, or the blocks already exist in the buffer cache; both are unlikely. With a migrated row, a ROWID lookup will require an additional read to the secondary block.

For both chained and migrated rows, queries that use an index to return row data will be less efficient, since more than one block must be read, than if all the data were returned from one block.

Detecting Row Chaining and Migration

The CHAIN_CNT column of DBA_TABLES is updated with the number of chained and migrated rows for the table specified when we run the ANALYZE TABLE *table_name* COMPUTE STATISTICS command or run DBMS_STATS.gather_table_stats. We can then calculate a ratio of chained rows to total rows (NUM_ROWS) to determine if there is a problem. There is no set ratio that we use as a threshold value; you'll have to compare the absolute number of rows, chained and migrated rows, and the ratio to determine if action is required.

You can also measure the impact that the chained and migrated rows have on the instance by viewing the Statspack Instance Activity Stats *table fetch continued row* statistic or by querying the V$SYSSTAT view.

How to Fix Migrated Rows

Setting PCTFREE higher will generally reduce the number of row migrations, but that does not fix previous problems. For rows that are currently migrated, there are several steps we can take to move the rows in their entirety to a new block.

Detecting the Migrated Rows   We use the ANALYZE TABLE . . . LIST CHAINED ROWS command to determine which rows have migrated and write information about them to a table. The CHAINED_ROWS table is defined in $ORACLE_HOME/rdbms/admin/utlchain.sql; you should run this script before you run the ANALYZE command as specified previously. You can run the ANALYZE command for many tables since the CHAINED_ROW table stores the OWNER and TABLE_NAME. Here's the definition for the CHAINED_ROWS table:

```
create table CHAINED_ROWS (
  owner_name          varchar2(30),
  table_name          varchar2(30),
  cluster_name        varchar2(30),
  partition_name      varchar2(30),
  subpartition_name   varchar2(30),
  head_rowid          rowid,
  analyze_timestamp   date
);
```

You can either use the CHAINED_ROWS table or create a similar table of your own design, as long as it has the same column names, datatypes, and sizes as the CHAINED_ROWS table.

Fixing Migrated Rows   The options for fixing migrated rows are similar to the options for recovering space from sparsely populated blocks: move the table, or export, then truncate or drop and then import. Additionally, we can use this method:

1. Create a temporary table as an empty copy of the first

2. Copy rows from the old table into the temporary table where the old table ROWID equals the value in the HEAD_ROW column of the CHAINED_ROWS table.

3. Delete the rows from the old table where the ROWID equals the HEAD_ROW values.

4. Copy the rows from the temporary table into the old table.

5. Drop the temporary table, and clean up the CHAINED_ROWS table. You might also run the ANALYZE command on the old table just to get current statistics and to validate that there are no more chained rows.

   In this scenario, we won't invalidate any indexes, so they don't need to be rebuilt; however, you will need to disable any foreign key constraints that would be violated during the drop.

Perform Index Reorganization

Maintenance is essential for indexes on tables that have a large percentage of change. By default, B-Tree indexes are always balanced; however, significant delete activity can cause index blocks to become sparsely populated. Sparsely populated blocks must still be maintained in the index, and the indexes can become a performance problem instead of a performance asset.

   When rows are deleted from a data block, the data block will be put on the freelist once the row data volume drops below the PCTUSED threshold. Any new row can be added to basically any block on the freelist, so rows in a block are likely nonsequential. This is not true for index blocks, where there is no PCTUSED parameter and entries must be written to the correct block based on the key value. For applications that delete old key values and insert new key values, index blocks can become sparsely populated on one side of the index and fully populated on the other—at least transiently. The index maintains a block even if it has only one entry in it. Once all entries from an index block are deleted, the block can then be put on the freelist. If an index has a significant amount of sparsely populated blocks, you should consider rebuilding the index.

Monitoring Index Storage Statistics

The ANALYZE INDEX *index_name* VALIDATE STRUCTURE command or the DBMS_STATS.gather_index_stats procedure can be used to gather statistics about the storage characteristics of an index. Once an index is analyzed, we'll look at three data dictionary views that hold the statistics.

DBA_INDEXES　The DBA_INDEXES view tells us just about everything we want to know about an index. When we gather statistics, we update the following columns: LAST_ANALYZED, BLEVEL, LEAF_BLOCKS, DISTINCT_KEYS, AVG_LEAF_BLOCKS_PER_KEY, AVG_DATA_BLOCKS_PER_KEY, and CLUSTERING_FACTOR. For each of these except CLUSTERING_FACTOR, you should be able to derive what the column stores based on the column name. The CLUSTERING_FACTOR is an indicator of how well ordered the index structure is. A CLUSTERING_FACTOR close to the number of blocks in the associated table indicates a well-ordered block; a CLUSTERING_FACTOR close to the number of rows in the table indicates a randomly ordered table. For example,

```
SELECT I.INDEX_NAME, T.NUM_ROWS, T.BLOCKS, I.CLUSTERING_FACTOR
FROM USER_INDEXES I, USER_TABLES T
WHERE I.TABLE_NAME = T.TABLE_NAME;
```

INDEX_NAME	NUM_ROWS	BLOCKS	CLUSTERING_FACTOR
ORDER_PK1	5	1	1
ORDER_ITEMS_PK	665	4	252
ORDER_ITEMS_UK	665	4	196
PROD_NAME_IX	8640	360	6806
PROD_SUPPLIER_IX	288	12	121

INDEX_STATS　The INDEX_STATS view is populated when we use the VALIDATE STRUCTURE clause; the view is session specific, like a temporary table. The view contains only one row, just for the last ANALYZE INDEX . . . VALIDATE STRUCTURE command. It is not truncated when we use the DELETE STATISTICS clause. The single row is replaced each time the VALIDATE STRUCTURE clause is used. If you drop the index for which you have stats in the INDEX_STATS view, the INDEX_STATS table is cleared.

For the INDEX_STATS view, we're mostly interested in the following columns:

- **LF_ROWS** Number of values (leaf rows) in the index
- **LF_ROWS_LEN** Sum of the lengths of all the values in bytes
- **DEL_LF_ROWS** Number of values deleted from the index
- **DEL_LF_ROWS_LEN** Sum of the lengths of all the deleted values

The following query can be used to determine how sparsely populated the blocks are, which is also known as *wastage*:

```
SELECT NAME, (DEL_LF_ROWS_LEN/LF_ROWS_LEN) * 100 "Wastage"
FROM INDEX_STATS
/
NAME                                  Wastage
------------------------------  ----------
MY_EMPLOYEES_IDX                    46.7248908
```

If wastage is greater than 20 percent, you should consider rebuilding or coalescing the index. In the previous case, I should do something to the index soon.

INDEX_HISTOGRAM   The INDEX_HISTOGRAM view is also updated when you use the ANALYZE INDEX . . . VALIDATE STRUCTURE command. There are two columns: REPEAT_COUNT indicates how many times a key value is repeated; KEYS_WITH_REPEAT_COUNT indicates the number of index keys that are repeated for the value of REPEAT_COUNT. For a primary key index, you'll see that the KEYS_WITH_REPEAT_COUNT is always 0.

Unlike the row in INDEX_STATS, the rows in INDEX_HISTOGRAM are not deleted if you drop the last-analyzed index; however, the table data is still session specific.

Coalescing or Rebuilding

Now that I've determined that my index is in bad shape, I should decide whether to rebuild or coalesce the index. The basic syntax for both is ALTER INDEX *index_name* COALESCE|REBUILD. Coalescing works on leaf blocks within the same branch tree, does not require additional disk space during the operation, and operates faster. Rebuilding requires additional disk space because the index is actually moved to different blocks; however, you can specify new storage parameters, including a different tablespace. Coalescing does not guarantee that wastage will drop to zero, but rebuilding does. Both are alternatives to dropping the index and recreating it. You can also rebuild or coalesce an index while other sessions are using the index. The ALTER INDEX *index_name* REBUILD ONLINE command enables you to rebuild an index while it is in use.

Additional Parameters When Rebuilding an Index   In addition to the full list of storage parameters available with the REBUILD option, you can specify NOLOGGING or LOGGING, and RECOVERABLE or UNRECOVERABLE. You can also use the COMPUTE STATISTICS clause to gather statistics for the index during the rebuild operation.

NOLOGGING or LOGGING are permanent attributes of an index. If you rebuild an index with the NOLOGGING clause, no redo log entries are written for index changes until the LOGGING option is specified. There is no restriction as to whether the database must be in archievelog mode or not.

UNRECOVERABLE and RECOVERABLE are specific to the index rebuild or create operation; they are not permanent attributes of the index. If you rebuild an index with the UNRECOVERABLE clause, no redo log entries are written during the rebuild operation. The RECOVERABLE option is only allowed if the database is in archivelog mode. RECOVERABLE and UNRECOVERABLE are deprecated; they are maintained for backward compatibility.

Monitor Indexes to Determine Usage

It is possible to over-index a table—that is, create indexes that are never used but require system resources to maintain, and use valuable disk space. With Oracle9i, we can monitor an index for usage; if it's not being used, then we should drop it.

We begin monitoring an index for usage by issuing the ALTER INDEX *index_name* MONITORING USAGE command. When the command is executed, a row is written to the V$OBJECT_USAGE view, indicating the INDEX_NAME, TABLE_NAME, that MONITORING is YES, and the START_MONITORING time when the monitoring started. If the index gets used once monitoring is turned on, the USED column will indicate YES. We can monitor multiple indexes for usage at the same time.

We stop monitoring index usage by issuing the ALTER INDEX ... NOMONITORING USAGE command. When the command is executed, the STOP_MONITORING column is populated to show the time when the monitoring was stopped, and the MONITORING column will also change to NO. If we issue the MONITORING USAGE clause again, the STOP_MONITORING column is cleared and the START_MONITORING clause is populated with the new start time.

Again, if you monitor an index for an extensive amount of time and discover that it was not used, you should drop it. Consult with the application developer before you drop the index, of course.

Chapter Summary

The most fundamental storage unit for Oracle databases is the block. A database block is made up of one or more contiguous OS blocks. An extent is made up of one or more database blocks, and a segment is made up of one or more extents.

Extents are allocated as segments grow due to INSERT or UPDATE activity. You can manually allocate an extent by issuing the ALTER ... ALLOCATE EXTENT command. With dictionary-managed tablespaces, dynamic extension of segments is a performance problem, so you should monitor for extents that are close to extending. With locally managed tablespaces, recursive SQL is eliminated and dynamic extent allocation is not a performance problem.

Large extents may waste storage space, but they reduce the likelihood of dynamic extent allocation, reduce the need to read multiple blocks if the MAXEXTENTS UNLIMITED option is used for the segment, and reduce data dictionary storage since fewer extents are used. Small extents utilize space more efficiently; large extents may have trouble finding contiguous space within the tablespace. As the number of extents in a segment increases, deallocating extents from the segment can become a performance problem.

Within a segment, there are blocks that are in use, empty blocks that have been used, and blocks that have never been used. Blocks that are in use and blocks that have been used exist below the high watermark. Blocks that have never been used exist above the high watermark. Rows are inserted into available blocks below the high watermark first. The high watermark is reset when the table is completely cleared of row data with the TRUNCATE command. The DELETE command does not reset the high watermark. Empty blocks below the high watermark can cause performance issues with full table scans (FTSs).

Unused blocks above the high watermark are returned to the tablespace free space by issuing the ALTER TABLE . . . DEALLOCATE UNUSED command.

We must analyze a table to determine the high watermark. The BLOCKS column in DBA_TABLES indicates the number of blocks below the high watermark; the EMPTY_BLOCKS column is the number of blocks above the high watermark.

We recover space below the high watermark from sparsely populated tables by exporting the table, dropping or truncating the table, and then importing the table. Another option is to use the ALTER TABLE . . . MOVE command. If a table is moved, indexes on the table are invalidated and must be rebuilt before they can be used.

The Oracle block size can have a significant impact on application performance. We set the default block size for the database at create time with the DB_BLOCK_SIZE initialization parameter. With Oracle9*i*, we can also use a nondefault block size for tablespaces other than SYSTEM or TEMPORARY tablespaces.

The default block size should be a multiple of the OS block size. Valid default database block sizes are 2 or 4KB (OS dependent), and can be 8, 16, 32, or 64KB, again, OS dependent.

To use a nondefault block size, you must specify the DB_CACHE_SIZE init.ora parameter and the DB_*n*K_CACHE_SIZE parameter, where *n* is one of the valid block sizes mentioned in the previous paragraph. You can then specify the BLOCKSIZE *n* parameter when you build a tablespace.

Large blocks are beneficial for DSS applications that mostly perform FTSs or index range scans, and request large I/Os. Large blocks should not be used for OLTP systems, due to potential contention issues and index efficiency. Small blocks are ideal for OLTP systems with random lookups.

The PCTFREE and PCTUSED block storage parameters are used to specify thresholds within a data block. The PCTFREE threshold specifies the amount of free space in the block reserved for row updates. The PCTUSED threshold specifies the point delete activity must reach before a block is returned to the freelist and made available for new inserts.

If a segment has significant update activity, you should size the PCTFREE parameter to allow for updates. If there is no delete activity, then PCTUSED is irrelevant. PCTUSED is not used for indexes. Within data blocks, free space caused by deletes or updates to a smaller row size will not be coalesced automatically. Free space is coalesced automatically when there is enough space for a row to be inserted into or updated in the block, but the space is not contiguous.

Row chaining occurs when a row is too big to fit into one block, so parts of it must exist in two or more blocks. Migration occurs when a block is updated and it won't fit back into the original block. Oracle moves the entire row to another block, but keeps a row piece in the original block. This prevents the invalidation of indexes that would occur if the ROWID was moved.

Both row chaining and migration are bad performance problems because they at least double the amount of I/O required to fetch each chained or migrated row.

We can see if there are any fetch activities that encounter chained rows by select the *table fetch continued row* statistic in the V$SYSSTAT view. We detect chaining and migration by using the ANALYZE TABLE command to update the CHAIN_CNT column in DBA_TABLES.

We fix migrated rows by using the ANALYZE . . . LIST CHAINED ROWS command, which populates the CHAINED_ROWS table, unless we specify another table. The CHAINED_ROWS table is created by the $ORACLE_HOME/rdbms/admin/utlchain.sql script. We can eliminate row migration by moving the migrated rows from the original table into a temp table and then back again. Setting PCTFREE higher will generally reduce the number of row migrations. We can also move the table to a tablespace with a larger block size if row chaining has been identified as a problem.

We may need to perform index reorganization when delete activity is significant. Index blocks become sparsely populated if the index key distribution changes due to high turnover of deletes and inserts. The ANALYZE INDEX . . . VALIDATE STRUCTURE command populates the DBA_INDEXES, INDEX_STATS, and INDEX_HISTOGRAM views. The INDEX_STATS view contains the number of rows deleted from the index and the number of leaf rows in the index. If the ratio of deleted to leaf rows exceeds 20 percent, consider rebuilding the index.

Coalescing an index does not require the additional space needed to rebuild an index. Also, it does not guarantee that all empty or sparsely populated blocks will be eliminated. Rebuilding also gives us the opportunity to change the storage parameters for the index, which coalescing does not.

To determine if an index is being used, issue the ALTER INDEX .. MONTORING USAGE command. When we want to stop monitoring for usage, we issue the ALTER INDEX . . . NOMONITORING USAGE command. The V$OBJECT_USAGE view is populated with information about the index; specifically, the USED column will indicate NO if the index has not been used while monitoring was turned on.

Two-Minute Drill

- In the hierarchy of storage, a segment is comprised of one or more extents, and an extent is comprised of database blocks.

- A database block consists of one or more contiguous OS blocks.

- The database block is the smallest unit of storage that can be read from and written to disk.

- The default database block size is specified in the init.ora file when the database is created.

- This default block size is used for the SYSTEM tablespace and is the default for other tablespaces.

- With Oracle9*i*, the DBA can specify a nondefault block size for nonSYSTEM tablespaces, except TEMPORARY tablespaces.

- A database extent is a logical group of contiguous database blocks.

- Extent size is defined at object creation time, with the INITIAL and NEXT storage parameters.

- When all the blocks in extents in a segment become full due to INSERT or UPDATE activity, a new extent must be added to the segment.

- The DBA can manually extend a segment with the ALTER *segment_type segment_name* ALLOCATE EXTENT command.

- With dictionary-managed tablespaces, we want to avoid dynamic extent allocation as much as possible.

- Dictionary-managed tablespaces keep extent map information for the tablespace in the data dictionary.

- Segment extent maps are stored in the segment header blocks. The data dictionary keeps track of what extents in the tablespace are free (FET$) or used (UET$).

- To avoid frequent extent allocation, you should focus on determining the correct size that objects will grow to before you build them.

- Locally managed tablespaces keep track of the free and used blocks in a tablespace by using a bitmap located in the header block of each datafile.

- Dynamic extent allocation is reduced with large extents.

- The segment extent map can span multiple blocks if MAXEXTENTS is set to UNLIMITED, reducing performance for operations that must read the extent map.

- Large extent sizes can lead to disk space wastage.

- With dictionary-managed tablespaces, the time required to deallocate extents when we use the DROP or TRUNCATE command is more time consuming when there are more extents to manage.

- The high watermark is the cutoff point; all rows above have never been used, all rows below are currently in use or have been used before.

- The high watermark is recorded in the segment header block.

- The high watermark is reset when the table is completely cleared of row data with the TRUNCATE command.

- The DELETE command does not change the high watermark.

- Blocks above the high watermark may take up unnecessary space, but they do not affect performance.

- However, sparsely populated blocks below the high watermark do affect FTS performance.

- Blocks above the high watermark can be returned to the tablespace free space by issuing the ALTER TABLE . . . DEALLOCATE UNUSED command.

- Analyze a table to populate the BLOCKS and EMPTY_BLOCKS columns of the DBA_TABLES view.

- BLOCKS indicates the number of blocks below the high watermark.

- EMPTY_BLOCKS indicates the number of blocks above the high watermark.

- We can recover space used by a table by using the TRUNCATE or DROP commands.

- The DROP TABLE command removes all references to the table except for synonyms and views.

- You can use the export/import utility programs to recover space from a sparsely populated table.

- You can also use the ALTER TABLE . . . MOVE command, specifying new storage parameters.

- The DB_BLOCK_SIZE init.ora parameter determines the default block size for the database.

- The value of DB_BLOCK_SIZE is specified when the database is created and cannot be modified afterward.

- Depending on your platform, the value of DB_BLOCK_SIZE defaults to 2 or 4 KB, and can be 8, 16, 32, or 64KB.

- When creating a tablespace, we can use the BLOCKSIZE clause to use a nonstandard block size for the tablespace.

- To use a nondefault block size, you must have specified the DB_CACHE_SIZE parameter.

- You must create a separate buffer cache for the nonstandard block size by setting the DB_nK_CACHE_SIZE parameter, where n is the same number for the tablespace BLOCKSIZE and the DB_nK_CACHE_SIZE.

- A large block size can significantly improve the performance of large FTSs.

- Also, if each row is very large, a larger block size is more appropriate.

- You should not use a large block size in an OLTP environment because of possible contention issues.

- Small block sizes are more appropriate for random access lookups like we see in many OLTP systems. They are good for small row sizes and reduce the potential for contention because there are fewer rows per block.

- The PCTFREE block storage parameter specifies how much space to reserve for row updates to rows that already exist in the block.

- The PCTUSED parameter specifies a threshold that when enough rows are deleted from a block, the block is placed back on the freelist.

- The default value for PCTFREE is 10.

- The default value for PCTUSED is 40.

- The PCTUSED parameter is used for tables and clusters, but not indexes or IOTs.

- Row chaining occurs when a row is too large to fit into a single empty data block. Oracle writes different row pieces to additional blocks.

- Row migration occurs when a row is updated and it will not fit back into the original block. Oracle keeps the original row piece in the original block, but moves the row data to another block; the ROWID is not invalidated.

■ Run the ANALYZE TABLE . . . COMPUTE STATISTICS command to update the CHAIN_CNT column of DBA_TABLES. Compare this to NUM_ROWS to determine the scope of chaining problems in a table.

■ Setting PCTFREE higher will generally reduce the number of future row migrations.

■ Use the ANALYZE . . . LIST CHAINED ROWS command to determine which rows have migrated and write information about them to the CHAINED_ROWS table.

■ The CHAINED_ROWS table is defined in $ORACLE_HOME/rdbms/admin/utlchain.sql (OS dependent).

■ To fix migrated rows, copy them from the source table to a new table using the list of ROWIDs inserted into the CHAINED_ROWS table. Delete the original rows from the source table and then copy the rows from the new table back to the source table.

■ Indexes can become a performance liability if too many deletes occur.

■ Oracle maintains an index block even if it only has one entry in it.

■ Execute the ANALYZE INDEX *index_name* VALIDATE STRUCTURE command, and then query the INDEX_STATS view within the same session to determine index wastage.

■ If index wastage is greater than 20 percent, rebuild the index.

■ Rebuilding the index enables us to specify new storage parameters.

■ Coalescing is an alternative to rebuilding, but does not guarantee that all sparse blocks will be removed.

■ Use the ALTER INDEX . . . MONITORING USAGE command to begin monitoring for index usage.

■ Use the ALTER INDEX . . . NOMONITORING USAGE command to stop monitoring for use.

■ Query the V$OBJECT_USAGE view to determine if the index was used during the monitoring period.

Chapter Questions

1. **Which of these rules should you follow to gain optimal database block performance? (Choose two.)**

   A. Size the Oracle database block to one half the size of the OS block size for OLTP systems.

   B. Size the Oracle database block size to a multiple of the OS block size.

   C. Use large blocks for DSS databases.

   D. Use large blocks for OLTP databases.

   E. Block size is dynamically configurable, so you can size blocks as needed.

2. **Which of the following is true about allocating extents?**

   A. Always let Oracle allocate extents dynamically.

   B. You should avoid dynamic extent allocation.

   C. You can monitor segments that are close to extending by querying DBA_EXTENTS.

   D. You should extend a table manually with the ALTER TABLE . . . ALLOCATE NEXT command.

   E. You should extend a table manually with the ALTER TABLE . . . AUTOEXTEND command.

3. **Which of these statements accurately describes blocks below the high watermark?**

   A. EMPTY_BLOCKS are blocks below the high watermark that have never been used.

   B. SPARSE_BLOCKS are blocks below the high watermark that have been used.

   C. EMPTY_BLOCKS are blocks above the high watermark that have been used, but have been cleared with the DELETE command.

   D. BLOCKS is the total number of blocks in the segment.

   E. BLOCKS is the total number of blocks below the high watermark.

   F. None of the above.

4. **The high watermark is effectively moved to the start of the segment by which of these commands?**

   A. DELETE ALL

   B. RESET HIGHWATER

   C. TRUNCATE

   D. COALESCE

   E. DEALLOCATE UNUSED

   F. DROP TABLE

5. **You can recover space from a sparsely populated table, but you should be prepared for which of the following scenarios? (Choose two.)**

   A. You may have to rebuild some of the indexes on a table if you use the ALTER TABLE . . . MOVE command because some of the indexes can become invalidated.

   B. You will have to rebuild all of the indexes on a table if you use the ALTER TABLE . . . MOVE command because all of the indexes will become invalidated.

   C. When importing into a new table, you should always build the indexes before importing the table rows.

   D. If you set INDEXES=Y when importing into a new table, performance will suffer due to index maintenance.

   E. When a table is moved, all indexes are marked INVALID.

   F. After a table is moved, you can save time and space by coalescing all associated indexes instead of rebuilding.

6. **Which of these options to recover space will cause the least impact on your application users?**

   A. Export, drop, and import table.

   B. Move the table.

   C. Rebuild an index.

   D. Truncate a table.

   E. Delete a table.

   F. Fix migrated rows.

7. You're building a large fact table for a data warehouse where there will be no updates or deletes. Which of the following settings for PCTFREE and PCTUSED makes the best performance combination?

A. 0, 20

B. 90, 10

C. 10, 95

D. 0, 40

E. 20, 60

F. 100, 0

8. We've discovered that too many blocks in an index are sparsely populated due to delete activity and will choose which course of action to correct it?

A. Increase the PCTFREE block storage parameter to cause denser index blocks.

B. Increase the PCTFREE block storage parameter, but monitor for index row migration.

C. Decrease the PCTFREE parameter, which will allow room for index updates.

D. Decrease the PCTUSED parameter, so that blocks get back onto the freelist more quickly.

E. Increase the PCTUSED parameter so that blocks get back onto the freelist more quickly.

F. None of the above.

9. Which one of the following is a plausible solution for a row chaining problem?

A. Export, truncate, and import the chained rows.

B. Move the tables with the chaining problem to a tablespace that has a larger block size.

C. Increase the DB_FILE_MULTIBLOCK_READ_COUNT.

D. Use the CHAINED_ROWS table, which is memory resident, to store chained rows separate from the base table.

   E. Use the ANALYZE TABLE . . . REBUILD CHAINED ROWS command to eliminate chaining.

   F. Move the tables with the chaining problem to a tablespace that has a smaller block size.

10. **When copying migrated rows to a new table, you should use the _____ column of the CHAINED_ROWS table as a reference to make sure you move the correct rows?**

   A. ROWID

   B. LOGICAL ID

   C. UROWID

   D. HEAD_ROWID

   E. HEAD_ROW

   F. ROW_COUNT

11. **You can use either the ALTER INDEX . . . COALESCE or REBUILD to accomplish which goal?**

   A. Eliminate duplicate key values.

   B. Eliminate all sparsely populated blocks.

   C. Eliminate all blocks above the high watermark.

   D. Quickly eliminate some or all of the sparsely populated blocks.

   E. Make an unusable index usable again.

12. **Deleted entries in an index are handled differently than deleted rows in a table for what reason?**

   A. Index key values are never written over previous key values.

   B. Entries in an index block are inserted based on a range of key values, whereas table data is inserted based on freelist status.

   C. Deleted entries in an index are never reused; that's why we don't have the PCTUSED option for indexes.

   D. Oracle automatically coalesces deleted entries in B-Tree indexes.

   E. Table data blocks are automatically coalesced when associated index entries are deleted.

13. **If you suspect that an index is rarely used, you can query the V$OBJECT_USAGE view; but what is the possible problem you can encounter?**

   A. The view only contains a YES/NO to indicate if an index has been used since it was created.

   B. The view only contains a YES/NO to indicate if an index has been used since monitoring was turned on.

   C. There's only one row at a time in V$OBJECT_USAGE, so you cannot monitor all indexes in your schema at the same time.

   D. You can only monitor a particular index for 24 hours, and then you must restart monitoring with a DBMS_JOB procedure.

14. **To begin monitoring an index for usage, issue which ALTER INDEX clause?**

   A. START_MONITORING

   B. MONITORING_USAGE

   C. BEGIN_MONITORING

   D. NOMONITORING USAGE

   E. MONITORING USAGE

   F. NOMONITORING_USAGE

Answers to Chapter Questions

1. B and C.   Size the Oracle database block size to a multiple of the OS block size, and use large blocks for DSS databases.

Explanation   Making the Oracle database size a multiple of the OS block size is a good general guideline to follow; this includes the situation where the OS and database block size are the same. If the database block size were less than the OS block size, you would read more data from disk than necessary. This is actually okay with some systems that perform many FTSs and need to fetch many OS blocks. A large block size makes sense for DSS databases because we want to read more data with one physical I/O. We do not want to use large block sizes for OLTP systems because of possible contention. And finally, database block size is a static init.ora parameter tablespace block size cannot be changed.

2. B.   You should avoid dynamic extent allocation.

Explanation   Dynamic extent allocation can cause performance problems for application SQL statements that are inserting or updating. Answer A is incorrect because we don't want Oracle to dynamically extend segments. Answer C, DBA_EXTENTS, does not give us information about segments close to extending. Answers D and E are not valid ALTER TABLE clauses.

3. E.   BLOCKS is the total number of blocks below the high watermark.

Explanation   From DBA_TABLES, the number of BLOCKS is the total number of blocks below the high watermark. EMPTY_BLOCKS are blocks above the high watermark; they have never been used. SPARSE_BLOCKS is not a valid statistic.

4. C.   TRUNCATE

Explanation   The TRUNCATE command removes all rows from a table and sets the high watermark to the start of the segment. Answers A and B are not valid statements. The COALESCE clause is used when rebuilding indexes or coalescing the free space in a tablespace. The DEALLOCATE UNUSED command will recover all blocks above the high watermark that are not in the first extent of the segment. DROP TABLE doesn't move the high watermark; it removes it.

5. B and D.   You will have to rebuild all of the indexes on a table if you use the ALTER TABLE . . . MOVE command because all of the indexes will become invalidated, and if you set INDEXES=Y on your import, performance will suffer due to index maintenance.

Explanation   When a table is moved, all indexes on that table are marked UNUSABLE, and they must be rebuilt or dropped and created new before they can be used. Also, if you import with the indexes in place or build the indexes before loading the data, index maintenance will cause performance degradation. Answer A is semantically incorrect. Answer C is a direct contradiction to answer D. Answer F is incorrect because you cannot coalesce an unusable index; you must rebuild or drop and recreate it.

6. C. Rebuild an index.

Explanation You can rebuild an index online with no impact to the users. Each of the other answers causes some impact. Answers A, D, and E are the most traumatic to application users because the data will be unavailable. Answer B will cause the indexes to be unusable, so there is a possibility for performance degradation. Answer F causes rows to be moved out of the original table, which could affect table users.

7. A. 0, 20

Explanation A large fact table in a data warehouse is usually a table that is not updated. It is usually loaded, and then queried with FTSs. Setting PCTFREE as low as possible makes best sense, because there will be no updates into the table, and the table will be read with FTSs. Answers C and F are not possible. Answer B is the opposite of what we would expect, and dangerous because we would keep moving the block on and off the freelist with each inserted or deleted row. Answer D is a acceptable answer, but there's really no need to set PCTUSED to anything since we won't drop below that threshold. Answer E is a compromise—but not optimal.

8. F. None of the above.

Explanation Answers A and B are incorrect; increasing PCTFREE would cause less dense index blocks and reduce row migration, if that were a potential problem with indexes. Answer C is incorrect because decreasing PCTFREE would allow less room for index updates. Answers D and E are not valid because the PCTUSED parameter is not used with indexes.

9. B. Move the tables with the chaining problem to a tablespaces that has a larger block size.

Explanation Moving the table with chained rows to a tablespace that was built with a larger block size is the only possible solution, other than breaking the table into multiple tables, each with fewer columns. Answer A does not fix chained rows, but will fix migrated rows. Answer C might seem like a way to get around the fact that the row now exists in multiple blocks, but DB_FILE_MULTIBLOCK_READ_COUNT doesn't specify to get the blocks with the row chains in them. The CHAINED_ROWS table is not a memory-resident table used to store chained rows. It is used to store the ROWID of each row that has migrated to another block. Answer E, REBUILD CHAINED ROWS, is not a valid ANALYZE TABLE clause. Answer F is the opposite of the correct answer B.

10. E. HEAD_ROW

Explanation The HEAD_ROW column contains the ROWID for each row that has migrated to another block. We will match it with the actual ROWID to copy, delete, and copy back migrated rows. Answers B, C, D, and F are fictitious column names.

11. D. Quickly eliminate some or all of the sparsely populated blocks.

Explanation Rebuilding and coalescing are two options that we can use to quickly fix an index that has performance problems. The COALESCE clause only coalesces within tree branch, but the REBUILD clause does a complete rebuild of the index. Answers B and E are true for the REBUILD clause, but not for coalescing. Answers A and C are not accomplished by using the REBUILD or COALESCE feature.

12. B. Entries in an index block are inserted based on a range of key values, whereas table data is inserted based on freelist status.

Explanation When rows are deleted from a data block, new rows can come in and overwrite the free space, as long as the block is on the freelist after the delete. With indexes, entries in a block are based on the range of key values. If you delete an entry, that space will remain unused until another index key with the same value is inserted into the index. Answer A is incorrect because identical entries could overwrite each other. Answer C is incorrect because deleted entries can be reused; PCTUSED is irrelevant, however. Answers D and E are both incorrect; Oracle does not coalesce in either case.

13. B. The view only contains a YES/NO to indicate if an index has been used since monitoring was turned on.

Explanation The view is designed to track a simple YES or NO if the index was used during the monitoring period. This is not a good indicator of how heavily used the index is, but it does let us know if no one is using the index. Answer C is incorrect; information about multiple objects can exist in V$OBJECT_USAGE. The MONITORING USAGE command does not require 24-hour increments.

14. E. MONITORING_USAGE

Explanation The only possible correct answer is E because all the other clauses are invalid. MONITORING USAGE indicates that if anyone accesses the index, it should update the USED column to indicate YES.

CHAPTER
15

SQL Statement Tuning

n this chapter, you will learn about tuning Structured Query Language (SQL) statement performance. In Chapter 13, we describe different objects that can be used to improve performance and under what circumstances we would implement a particular type of object. In this chapter, we will discuss tools and operations that can improve and stabilize application SQL performance. From reading this chapter, you will be able to perform the following tasks:

- Describe how the optimizer is used
- Explain the concept of plan stability
- Use stored outlines
- Describe how hints are used
- Collect statistics on indexes and tables
- Describe the use of histograms
- Copy statistics between databases
- Online Transaction Processing (OLTP) and Decision Support Systems (DSS) considerations
- Use SQL Trace and TKPROF

Central to SQL performance is understanding how the optimizer works and what we can do to make sure the optimizer is using the best-performing execution plan for a query. We will discuss the different optimizer modes and the tuning features available if we use the cost-based optimizer (CBO). The focus here is not on specific SQL tuning techniques, but on the tools and methods available to the database administrator (DBA) and developer for SQL statement tuning.

SQL Statement Tuning

As you are well aware of by now, application performance is absolutely dependent on properly tuned SQL statements. To optimize SQL statement performance, the DBA needs to understand and implement certain Oracle features. Without a sound understanding and proper implementation of these features, application performance will be random at best.

When an SQL statement is submitted by an application, the SQL statement is processed by the SQL compiler. The main components of the SQL compiler are the parser, the optimizer, and the row source generator. The parser checks the SQL syntax and validates database references. The optimizer determines the most efficient way to execute the SQL statement. The row source generator takes the optimizer plan and generates the execution plan. The SQL execution engine then processes the plan for the SQL statement.

In this chapter, we will discuss how we can influence the choices made by the optimizer.

Describe How the Optimizer Is Used

The optimizer is responsible for determining the most efficient way to execute and produce the results of an SQL statement. Depending on table size, the number of rows, the density of data blocks, and the columns indexed, there may be many different ways to get the table data required by an SQL statement. If the SQL statement requires the joining of tables, then the number of different execution plans available becomes even greater. For each SQL statement, the optimizer performs the following tasks:

- Evaluates expressions and conditions

- Transforms statements, if needed

- Chooses the optimizer approach: rule-based optimizer (RBO) or cost-based optimizer (RBO)

- Chooses an access path for each table

- Chooses the join order, if more than two tables are joined

- Chooses the method to join the tables

The highest level of influence that we can have on the optimizer is the choice of optimizer mode. The static OPTIMIZER_MODE initialization parameter determines which optimizer, RBO or CBO, to use for the entire instance.

Rule-Based Optimizer

The RBO examines the SQL statement and applies a set of rules and rankings to determine the access paths. The RBO looks at the syntax of the SQL statements, uses data dictionary information about the structure of the referenced objects, and then applies its set of heuristics to determine which plan will work best. The RBO will use 15 different access paths and associated rankings to determine the execution plan. In general, an access path with a lower ranking is faster than an access path with a higher ranking, so the RBO will use the access path with the lower ranking if multiple access paths are available. Table 15-1 shows the 15 different RBO access paths and their associated rankings.

The RBO does not use ANALYZE or DBMS_STATS-gathered statistics to choose the optimal execution plan. For some applications, the developer understands the data access paths extremely well and can code the SQL statements for optimal

Path 1	Single row by ROWID
Path 2	Single row by cluster join
Path 3	Single row by hash cluster key with unique or primary key
Path 4	Single row by unique or primary key
Path 5	Clustered join
Path 6	Hash cluster key
Path 7	Indexed cluster key
Path 8	Composite index
Path 9	Single-column indexes
Path 10	Bounded range search on indexed columns
Path 11	Unbounded range search on indexed columns
Path 12	Sort-merge join
Path 13	MAX or MIN of indexed column
Path 14	ORDER BY on indexed column
Path 15	Full table scan

TABLE 15-1.   *Rule-Based Optimizer Access Path Ranking*

performance using the RBO. In cases like this, it may be best to continue using the RBO on a case-by-case basis. Otherwise, the RBO is maintained for backward compatibility, and new development should use the CBO. Oracle continues to improve the CBO, and several Oracle9*i* features require the use of the CBO:

■ Partitioned tables and indexes

■ Partition pruning

■ Index-organized tables (IOTs)

■ Reverse key indexes

■ Function-based indexes

■ Start schema queries

- Parallel query and parallel Data Manipulation Language (DML)
- Query rewrites with materialized views

Cost-Based Optimizer (CBO)

The CBO is a statistics-driven optimizer that evaluates multiple access paths and chooses an optimal plan based on the relative resource cost of the operation. When we gather statistics about an object, either with the ANALYZE command or the DBMS_STATS package, the CBO gains necessary information about data distribution and storage characteristics, which are then used to optimize the execution plan of the SQL statements. The relative cost of an SQL statement is based on the estimated computing resources required to complete the task: input/output (I/O), central processing unit (CPU), and memory. The CBO can also be influenced by hints supplied in the SQL statement. The CBO performs the following steps:

1. Generates potential plans that consider available access paths and hints.

2. Estimates the cost of each plan, based on gathered statistics.

3. Compares the cost of each plan and chooses the one with the lowest cost.

In general, we should use the CBO instead of the RBO.

Setting the Optimizer Mode

The optimizer mode or approach can be set for the entire instance, for a session, or for a single SQL statement. The order of precedence is that the SQL statement overrides the session mode, and the session mode overrides the instance mode.

Instance Level   The DBA can set the optimizer mode for the entire instance by setting the OPTIMIZER_MODE initialization parameter. The setting cannot be changed dynamically for the entire instance. These are the valid settings for the parameter, each of which exhibits a different default behavior:

- **RULE**   Use a rule-based approach for all SQL statements, even if statistics are available.

- **ALL_ROWS**   Optimize with the goal of best throughput (minimize response time), even if no statistics are available.

- **FIRST_ROWS_*n***   Optimize with a goal of best response time for *n* number of rows, where *n* = 1, 10, 100, or 1,000.

- **FIRST_ROWS**   The optimizer uses costs and heuristics to find the optimal plan for returning the first few rows. FIRST_ROWS is used for plan stability and backward compatibility.

- **CHOOSE** This is the default value. If statistics are available for at least one of the tables in an SQL statement, or the degree of parallelism for any of the tables is greater than 1, use a cost-based approach and optimize for best throughput (ALL_ROWS); otherwise, the rule-based approach will be used.

Query the V$SYSTEM_PARAMETER view to determine the current optimizer setting:

```
SELECT NAME, VALUE, ISDEFAULT, ISMODIFIED, DESCRIPTION
FROM V$SYSTEM_PARAMETER
WHERE NAME LIKE '%optimizer_mode%'
/
NAME                                VALUE       ISDEFAULT ISMODIFI DESCRIPTION
----------------------------------- ----------- --------- -------- --------------
optimizer_mode                      CHOOSE      TRUE      FALSE    optimizer mode
```

Also, there is a column of some interest, ISADJUSTED, which indicates that the Relational Database Management System (RDBMS) adjusted the input value to a more suitable value. For example, the parameter value should be prime, but the user input a nonprime number, so the RDBMS adjusted the value to the next prime number. You can also use the V$SYSTEM_PARAMETER2 view, which makes the distinction between the list parameter values clear.

Session Level For an individual session, we can set the optimizer mode to any one of the previously mentioned optimizer settings, and the session mode will override the instance mode for the current session. Use the ALTER SESSION SET OPTIMIZER_MODE=*mode* command to set the session optimizer mode.

You can query the V$PARMETER view to determine the current session setting:

```
SELECT NAME, VALUE, ISDEFAULT, ISMODIFIED, DESCRIPTION
FROM V$PARAMETER
WHERE NAME LIKE '%optimizer_mode%'
/
NAME                                VALUE       ISDEFAULT ISMODIFIED DESCRIPTION
----------------------------------- ----------- --------- ---------- --------------
optimizer_mode                      RULE        TRUE      MODIFIED   optimizer mode
```

Statement Level At the SQL statement level, the application developer can code a hint into the SQL statement to influence the optimizer mode. As mentioned previously, the optimizer mode coded into the hint overrides the session setting and the instance setting, just for this SQL statement. The same list of optimizer modes applies. Here's an example:

```
SELECT /*+ ALL_ROWS */
EMPLOYEE_ID, LAST_NAME
FROM MY_EMPLOYEES E, MY_DEPT D
WHERE E.DEPARTMENT_ID = D.DEPARTMENT_ID
AND D.DEPARTMENT_ID=100
/
```

In this section, we only discussed how we can use SQL hints to change the optimizer mode for a single SQL statement. Later in this chapter in the "Describe How Hints are Used" section, we will discuss how SQL hints can be used to further influence the access path and execution plan.

Explain the Concept of Plan Stability

If you're the DBA for large, dynamic Oracle databases, then you've seen that when using the CBO, SQL execution plans can change without any changes to the actual SQL statements. SQL execution plans change due to modifications to the optimizer mode setting, initialization parameters affecting the size of memory structures, DB_FILE_MULTIBLOCK_READ_COUNT, data block storage parameters, table reorganizations, schema changes (including adding indexes), and the accuracy and timeliness of optimizer statistics. Upgrading or migrating the database to a newer Oracle version can also dramatically affect the execution plan and SQL performance. The initialization parameter OPTIMIZER_MODE_ENABLE=*release* will keep the CBO features at the specified prior or current release, which can be useful for maintaining known CBO behavior during or after an upgrade.

Plan stability prevents execution plans, and therefore application performance, from changing due to environmental and configuration changes. Plan stability is made possible by keeping execution plans in *stored outlines*. When you enable stored outlines, the optimizer generates equivalent execution plans from the outlines, thereby stabilizing the access paths for the SQL statement. The plans in the stored outlines do not change, even if the database configuration or the Oracle release changes.

You can create public or private stored outlines for one or all SQL statements. Plan stability also helps stabilize application performance when you migrate from the RBO to the CBO, and also when you upgrade to a new Oracle release.

Plan Equivalence and Stability   For a stored outline to work, the SQL statements executed must match the stored SQL statements exactly. The stored outlines rely on hints in the SQL statements to set the execution plan and will remain stable even if the database environment changes.

Use of Stored Outlines

Plan stability is implemented with stored outlines. A stored outline is the execution plan for a specific SQL statement; it can be generated automatically for all SQL statements, or you can create a stored outline for an individual SQL statement. Stored outlines are grouped into categories. The default category for a database is DEFAULT; you can create as many categories as you wish. You can dynamically set a stored outline for the instance or specify a stored outline to use for a session. The same SQL statement can have a stored outline in more than one category.

Oracle keeps stored outlines in the OUTLN schema, which is created automatically when the database is created. Be sure that you change the default password, which is OUTLN. These are the tables used by the stored outline processes:

- **OL$**   Stores the actual SQL statement text.

- **OL$HINTS**   Stores the hints used for the execution plan of a stored outline.

- **OL$NODES**   Describes the tree structure of the query.

You should use the views DBA_OUTLINES and DBA_OUTLINE_HINTS to query the OUTLN tables. Direct manipulation of the OL$, OL$HINTS, and OL$NODES tables is prohibited.

Creating and Maintaining Stored Outlines

The DBA can configure the instance to create stored outlines for all executed SQL statements by issuing the ALTER SYSTEM SET CREATE_STORED_OUTLINES=*category_name* command. If *category_name* is DEFAULT or TRUE, then stored outlines will be written to the DEFAULT category. You can specify some other *category_name* to create or add to a user-defined category. You can specify FALSE to stop creating stored outlines.

When creating stored outlines using the instance-wide method, the outline name for each outline created (OL_NAME column in the OUTLN tables) is system generated.

Creating Statement-Level Stored Outlines   You can create a stored outline for a specific SQL statement by issuing the CREATE OR REPLACE OUTLINE command. With this command, you can specify which category to use and create a user-defined outline name. Here's an example:

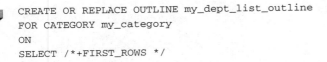

```
CREATE OR REPLACE OUTLINE my_dept_list_outline
FOR CATEGORY my_category
ON
SELECT /*+FIRST_ROWS */
```

```
EMPLOYEE_ID, LAST_NAME
FROM MY_EMPLOYEES E, MY_DEPT D
WHERE E.DEPARTMENT_ID = D.DEPARTMENT_ID
/
Outline created.
```

Maintaining a Stored Outline   The OUTLN_PKG (public synonym DBMS_OUTLN) package is used to drop, rename, and perform other maintenance procedures on stored outlines. Here are some of the procedures in the package, with a brief description of each:

- **DROP_BY_CAT**   Drops outlines that belong to a specified category.

- **DROP_EXTRAS**   Cleans up after an import by dropping extra hint rows not accounted for by HINTCOUNT.

- **DROP_UNREFD_HINTS**   Drops hint rows that have no corresponding outline in the OL$ table.

- **DROP_UNUSED**   Drops outlines that have never been applied in the compilation of an SQL statement.

- **UPDATE_BY_CAT**   Changes the category of outlines in one category to a new category.

You can use the ALTER OUTLINE command to rename a stored outline, change its category, or rebuild the outline data and execution plan by compiling the outline's SQL statement. You can also drop a stored outline with the DROP OUTLINE commands. Here's an example of rebuilding an outline to regenerate the execution plan under current conditions; we've supplied the outline name from the OL_NAME column of OUTLN.OL$:

```
ALTER OUTLINE SYS_OUTLINE_020119192534968 REBUILD
/
```

Private Outlines

A private outline can be used to test changes to a publicly used stored outline without affecting the public users. You simply create the outline tables in your schema, copy a public stored outline to your private outline tables, and alter your session to use the private outline. You can edit the private outline and publish it back to the public stored outlines.

Editing a Private Stored Outline   We use the DBMS_OUTLN_EDIT package to edit stored outlines. These are the steps to editing stored outlines:

1. Create the OL$ editing tables in the current schema:

   ```
   EXEC DBMS_OUTLN_EDIT.CREATE_EDIT_TABLES;
   ```

2. Copy the selected outline to the editing tables, creating a private outline, with the CREATE PRIVATE OUTLINE command. Here's an example:

   ```
   CREATE PRIVATE OUTLINE MY_TEST FROM SYS_OUTLINE_020119192534968;
   ```

3. Edit the private outline using the DBMS_OUTLN_EDIT.CHANGE_JOIN_POS procedure. Then update the private outline:

   ```
   EXEC DBMS_OUTLN_EDIT.REFRESH_PRIVATE_OUTLINE('MY_TEST');
   ```

4. Use the private outline. Issue the following statement, and then run the query:

   ```
   ALTER SESSION SET USE_PRIVATE_OUTLINES=TRUE;
   ```

5. Publish the private outline by overwriting the stored outline:

   ```
   CREATE OR REPLACE OUTLINE SYS_OUTLINE_020119192534968 FROM PRIVATE MY_TEST;
   ```

6. Disable private outline usage, and clean up the private outline tables:

   ```
   ALTER SESSION SET USE_PRIVATE_OUTLINES=FALSE;
   EXEC DBMS_OUTLN_EDIT.DROP_EDIT_TABLES;
   ```

Using Stored Outlines

For the current session to begin using the stored outlines that have been created, simply enter the ALTER SESSION SET USE_STORED_OUTLINES=*category_name*. If you specify TRUE or DEFAULT for *category_name*, you'll begin using the DEFAULT category. To specify a stored outline category for the instance, use the ALTER SYSTEM command instead of ALTER SESSION. Here's an example of how we would begin using the DEFAULT category for the instance, but the *my_category* category for the current session:

```
ALTER SYSTEM SET USE_STORED_OUTLINES=TRUE              ---- or DEFAULT
/
ALTER SESSION SET USE_STORED_OUTLINES=MY_CATEGORY
/
```

If there is no match for an SQL statement in MY_CATEGORY, but there is a match in the DEFAULT group, then the execution plan for the outline in the

DEFAULT group will be used. If there is no match in the DEFAULT category, then the statement is executed as it normally would be if there were no stored outlines in use. If an object that is referenced in a stored outline hint cannot be used, then the hint will not be used by the statement.

When the USE_PRIVATE_OUTLINES parameter is enabled and an outlined SQL statement is issued, the optimizer retrieves the outline from the session private area rather than the public area used when USE_STORED_OUTLINES is enabled. If no outline exists in the session private area, then the optimizer will not use an outline to compile the statement.

Describe How Hints Are Used

In this brief section, we will discuss how hints are used. We will not provide the list of valid SQL hints, but instead will introduce the concept and demonstrate the use of a hint.

Sometimes the CBO will choose an execution plan that is suboptimal. The developer may understand the distribution of the data better than the CBO and its bevy of statistics. In such a case, the developer can code a hint to the optimizer directly into the SQL statement. The hint tells the CBO which access path to use, so use it instead of the CBO's choice. This is a very good way to begin to impose plan stability on your applications.

Using Hints in SQL Statements

The syntax used to insert a hint is straightforward, and you've already seen examples several times in this chapter. We'll use the same SQL with a slight modification. In this example, the hint is on the second line, and it tells the optimizer to use the EMP_DEPT_IDX index on the MY_EMPLOYEES table:

```
SELECT
/*+ INDEX (E EMP_DEPT_IDX) */
EMPLOYEE_ID, LAST_NAME
FROM MY_EMPLOYEES E, MY_DEPT D
WHERE E.DEPARTMENT_ID = D.DEPARTMENT_ID
AND D.DEPARTMENT_ID=100
/
```

You can code SQL hints in subqueries and use multiple hints for multitable joins. If the hint has a syntax error, there is no error, and the hint will not be used. The /* */ characters indicate a comment, so if you leave off the + following the first asterisk, then the hint actually becomes a regular comment.

Collect Statistics on Indexes and Tables

In Chapter 3, we discussed using the ANALYZE command and the DBMS_STATS package to collect table, index, and column information and store it in the data dictionary. In this section, we'll expand on the use of the tools and discuss how the optimizer uses the statistics to improve SQL statement performance.

ANALYZE Command

The ANALYZE command is used to gather statistics for tables, clusters, and indexes. The CBO uses the statistics to determine optimal access paths for SQL statements. When you use ANALYZE on an object, you overwrite existing statistics held in the data dictionary for the object. If your data changes frequently, you should consider analyzing the objects frequently. If you see sudden drastic performance degradation on specific queries against specific tables, consider analyzing the tables and associated indexes before spending too much time investigating the performance problem.

With the ANALYZE command, we can specify COMPUTE or ESTIMATE statistics. COMPUTE statistics is the more thorough, locking the object and performing a full scan. COMPUTE can interfere with data concurrency. ESTIMATE statistics enables us to specify a percentage of rows or a number of rows to sample. If you specify over 50 percent, COMPUTE is used. DELETE statistics will remove statistics from the data dictionary.

Here's an example of the ANALYZE command, used to gather statistics for a table:

```
ANALYZE TABLE JENNYP.STATS_TAB ESTIMATE STATISTICS;
Table analyzed.
```

The DBMS_UTILITY package has two procedures that enable you to collect statistics on collections of objects, rather than use multiple individual ANALYZE commands. The two procedures are ANALYZE_SCHEMA and ANALYZE_DATABASE. The ANALYZE_DATABASE procedure also collects statistics on the data dictionary tables, which is not recommended. The ANALYZE command is kept for backward compatibility. The DBMS_STATS package, introduced in Oracle8i, is capable of gathering more sophisticated and useful statistics than the ANALYZE command.

DBMS_STATS Package

The DBMS_STATS package gathers more sophisticated statistics for tables, indexes, and clusters. One of the added benefits of the DBMS_STATS package is that you can gather statistics in parallel on an object.

Here's an example of a DBMS_STATS procedure that gathers table statistics, similar to the ANALYZE command demonstrated in the previous section, except here we're able to specify that we want to parallelize the gathering and use block sampling instead of row sampling:

```
EXEC DBMS_STATS.GATHER_TABLE_STATS (OWNNAME=> 'JENNYP', -
TABNAME=> 'STATS_TAB', -
ESTIMATE_PERCENT=> 20, -
BLOCK_SAMPLE=> TRUE, -
CASCADE=> TRUE, -
DEGREE=> 6)
```

Here's a brief description of the DBMS_STATS procedures that we use to gather statistics:

- **GATHER_TABLE_STATS** Gathers statistics for a specific schema table
- **GATHER_INDEX_STATS** Gathers statistics for a specific schema index
- **GATHER_SCHEMA_STATS** Gathers statistics for all the objects in a specific schema
- **GATHER_DATABASE_STATS** Gathers statistics for all objects in the database

Data Dictionary Statistics

Whether you use the ANALYZE command or the DBMS_STATS package to gather statistics, the data dictionary will be updated to reflect the new statistics values. Depending on the type of object analyzed, you'll see that different statistics are gathered.

Table Statistics   The following statistics are gathered for tables and kept in the DBA_TABLES data dictionary view: NUM_ROWS, BLOCKS, EMPTY_BLOCKS, AVG_SPACE, CHAIN_CNT, AVG_ROW_LEN, AVG_SPACE_FREELIST_BLOCKS, NUM_FREELIST_BLOCKS, SAMPLE_SIZE, GLOBAL_STATS, USER_STATS, and LAST_ANALYZED.

Index Statistics   For indexes, the following statistics are gathered and kept in DBA_INDEXES: BLEVEL, LEAF_BLOCKS, DISTINCT_KEYS, AVG_LEAF_BLOCKS_PER_KEY, AVG_DATA_BLOCKS_PER_KEY, NUM_ROWS, CLUSTERING_FACTOR, SAMPLE_SIZE, PCT_DIRECT_ACCESS, GLOBAL_STATS, USER_STATS, and LAST_ANALYZED.

Column Statistics   For columns, the following statistics are stored in DBA_TAB_COL_STATISTICS: NUM_DISTINCT, LOW_VALUE, HIGH_VALUE, DENSITY, NUM_NULLS, NUM_BUCKETS, LAST_ANALYZED, SAMPLE_SIZE,

GLOBAL_STATS, USER_STATS, and AVG_COL_LEN. The NUM_BUCKETS column
indicates the number of histogram buckets that are used for the column.

Describe the Use of Histograms

A *histogram* puts the values of the column into a series of buckets, so that all
column values within the same range are in the same bucket. The CBO can use
histograms to store more detailed estimates of the distribution of column data and
improve selectivity and execution plans when the column data is skewed. By
default, 75 distinct buckets are used; you may need to change this number based on
the distribution of your column data.

Height-Based and Value-Based Histograms   The CBO uses height-based and
value-based histograms. Height-based histograms place approximately the same
number of values into each bucket so that the endpoints of each bucket are
determined by the number of values in each. You can have multiple buckets with the
same endpoint if the data is highly skewed.

Value-based histograms, also known as frequency histograms, are used when
the number of distinct column values is less than or equal to the number of
histogram buckets specified (or the default if none is specified).

Creating Histograms

The DBMS_STATS package can be used to create histograms for a table. The
following example creates a 15-bucket histogram on the MY_EMPLOYEES table in
the JENNYP schema:

```
EXECUTE DBMS_STATS.GATHER_TABLE_STATS
('JENNYP','MY_EMPLOYEES', METHOD_OPT => 'FOR COLUMNS SIZE 15 salary');
```

You can also create histograms by using the SIZE *nn* keyword in the ANALYZE
command, where *nn* is the number of buckets created for the histogram. Here's an
example:

```
ANALYZE TABLE JENNYP.MY_EMPLOYEES COMPUTE STATISTICS
FOR COLUMNS SIZE 15 salary
/
```

When to Use Histograms

Histograms can adversely affect performance if misused. You should consider
creating histograms only on columns that have highly skewed data and that are
often used in WHERE clauses. If you use histograms, keep in mind that the
histograms are static and can become outdated, so you should update them on a

regular basis. If the columns have any of the following characteristics, don't use histograms:

- Bind variables are used exclusively to compare against the columns.
- The column data is uniformly distributed.
- The column is not used in WHERE clauses of queries.
- The column is unique and is used only with equality predicates.

Histogram Data Dictionary Views   Information about histograms can be queried from the DBA_TAB_HISTOGRAMS, DBA_PART_HISTOGRAMS, DBA_SUBPART_HISTOGRAMS, DBA_SUBPART_COL_STATISTICS, DBA_TAB_COL_STATISTICS views.

Copy Statistics Between Databases

SQL statements often exhibit unique behavior depending on the database they're run in. For example, you may see excellent statement performance in a test environment, but then see extremely poor performance in a production environment. One feature that Oracle has provided is the capability to copy optimizer statistics from the data dictionary to a schema table and back again. You can use this feature to copy data dictionary statistics from one database to another, or to make a backup copy of the statistics that can then be put back into the data dictionary at a later time. You can copy statistics from a production database to a test database to verify that the SQL performance is comparable. Also, you can also copy execution plans from one database to another if you use OUTLINES.

Steps for Copying Statistics

The DBMS_STATS package and the export/import utilities are used to copy statistics from one database to another. Here are the basic steps:

1. Execute DBMS_STATS.CREATE_STAT_TABLE to create a statistics table in your schema. Here's an example:

   ```
   EXEC DBMS_STATS.CREATE_STAT_TABLE(OWNNAME=> 'JENNYP', -
   STATTAB=> 'STATS_TAB', -
   TBLSPACE=> 'TOOLS')
   ```

2. Export the data dictionary statistics for a specific schema to the user-defined table:

   ```
   EXEC DBMS_STATS.EXPORT_SCHEMA_STATS(OWNNAME=> 'JENNYP', -
   STATTAB=>'STATS_TAB')
   ```

3. Use the Oracle export utility to export the statistics table from the current database, and use the import utility to import the table into the target database.

4. Import the schema statistics into the data dictionary on the target database:

```
EXEC DBMS_STATS.IMPORT_SCHEMA_STATS(OWNNAME=> 'JENNYP', -
STATTAB=> 'STATS_TAB')
```

You can use this same process for database, system, table, index, and column statistics; they each have their own set of DBMS_STATS procedures.

OLTP and DSS Considerations

As mentioned in Chapter 13, OLTP and DSS applications differ in the types of objects they most benefit from. Also, specific SQL statement tuning considerations exist for OLTP and DSS systems.

OLTP Application Coding Techniques   For OLTP systems, quick execution, data concurrency, and continuous uptime are extremely important. To improve on these requirements, consider the following SQL statement coding techniques:

- Shared code and bind variables should be used because quick parsing is required.

- Carefully consider the performance differences when using the RBO versus the CBO. If you use the CBO, analyze tables and indexes regularly using DBMS_STATS or ANALYZE. This should be table and index specific.

- Cursor sharing should be SIMILAR. Since parse time is a more significant portion of the overall SQL execution time, reductions in parse time will improve SQL statement performance.

DSS Coding Techniques   For DSS systems, fast response time, data accuracy, and availability are important. You should consider the following techniques to improve application performance:

- Use literals, not bind variables, in your application code.

- Use hints and test on valid data volumes. Parsing is a relatively small percentage of the total query time.

- Generate histograms for columns that contain data that is distributed nonuniformly if the application uses literals in queries instead of bind variables.

- Use parallelized queries and parallel DML.

- Execute Explain Plan and/or autotrace if performance degrades.

- Use HINTS in your SQL statements if you know a better access plan.

- Cursor sharing should be EXACT. This forces an exact match based on the numeric value of the SQL statement.

- Use the CBO rather than the RBO.

Use SQL Trace and TKPROF

A DBA can use several tools to determine which SQL statements are causing performance problems. In Chapter 3, you were introduced to Statspack and learned that it produces a report of SQL statements in the shared pool; this is one simple tool that indicates what may have been causing problems before or at the time the report was generated. For more real-time analysis and investigation, we can use SQL trace and TKPROF. We can also use the Explain Plan command or SQL*Plus Autotrace to determine how a query will behave without running it. Finally, we can query the V$SQL_PLAN dynamic performance view to determine the actual execution plan of an SQL statement in the shared pool.

Capturing Current Session Events with SQL Trace and TKPROF

If you notice that a session is behaving abnormally and performance has degraded, you can trace the session, generate a trace file, and format the output so that it can be further analyzed. SQL trace is used to create a session trace file; TKPROF is used to format the trace file so that it can be more easily interpreted.

SQL Trace   This utility is used to gather detailed information about the execution of SQL statements within a session and generate a trace file in the USER_DUMP_DEST directory. If you want to trace the current session, either execute the ALTER SESSION SET SQL_TRACE=true command or execute the stored procedure DBMS_SESSION.SET_SQL_TRACE(TRUE). The SQL trace utility can be turned on for the entire instance by setting the SQL_TRACE=TRUE initialization parameter; however, you should be warned that this will cause a trace file to be created for each session in the database, including background processes. The only way to turn off SQL tracing for the entire instance is to change the setting to FALSE in the init.ora file and restart the database.

   To turn SQL trace on for another session, use the DBMS_SYSTEM.SET_SQL_TRACE_IN_SESSION procedure. Here's an example:

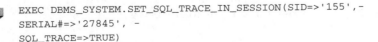

```
EXEC DBMS_SYSTEM.SET_SQL_TRACE_IN_SESSION(SID=>'155',-
SERIAL#=>'27845', -
SQL_TRACE=>TRUE)
```

The catproc.sql script does not create a public synonym for the DBMS_SYSTEM package, nor does it grant privileges on the package; therefore, you'll need to log in as SYS to execute the SET_SQL_TRACE_IN_SESSION procedure or grant the appropriate privileges. You turn off SQL Trace in a session by using FALSE in place of TRUE in the previously mentioned commands. If you want to gather timing data for the SQL statements executing in the session, be sure to set TIMED_STATISTICS=TRUE either for the session to be traced or for the instance. Also, the MAX_DUMP_FILE_SIZE parameter specifies the maximum number of operating system (OS) blocks that the trace file can grow to; specify K or M to change this to Kilobytes or Megabytes.

TKPROF   TKPROF is a formatting utility specifically designed to read the trace files generated by SQL Trace and convert them into something that the DBA can read, analyze, and act on. There are several command-line options for TKPROF; we'll discuss a few of them here:

- **Tracefile**   The name of the file created by SQL Trace.
- **Outputfile**   The name of the formatted report file generated by TKPROF.
- **Sort**   The sort order of the SQL statements listed in the report. Several sort options are available; I prefer to sort the report by SQL statement CPU time, which is an indicator of relative query performance.
- **Explain**   If specified with a username and password, the explain process will log on to the database and run the Explain Plan command for the SQL statements and then return the plan report to the output file.
- **SYS**   When set to NO, ignore recursive SQL statements.

The TKPROF report consists of SQL statements executed by the session, statistics that indicate system impact, and, if specified, the Explain Plan report for each SQL statement. Some of the important statistics include execution calls, CPU seconds, total elapsed time, physical reads, logical reads, and rows processed. You can use these statistics to determine which SQL statements in a session require tuning.

Explain Plan and SQL*Plus Autotrace
If you want to test a query to see the execution plan that the optimizer will use without actually running the query, you can use the Explain Plan command. You can also automate the Explain Plan process by using SQL*Plus Autotrace.

Explain Plan   Before you can use the Explain Plan command successfully, you must have built the PLAN_TABLE in the current schema by using the utlxplan.sql-supplied script. Once the table has been built, you can use Explain Plan on a common query, as in this example:

```
EXPLAIN PLAN
SET STATEMENT_ID = '2002-12-31.01'
FOR
SELECT * FROM HR.EMPLOYEES
WHERE EMPLOYEE_ID=100
/
```

Once Explain Plan has run, we can query the PLAN_TABLE to check the execution plan by using the utlxpls.sql script or the utlxplp.sql script for parallel queries.

Be sure to truncate or drop the PLAN_TABLE when you're no longer using it.

Using Autotrace   If you would like to see the execution plan for each SQL statement run in a session, but you don't want to issue multiple Explain Plan commands and maintain the PLAN_TABLE table, then consider using SQL*Plus autotrace. Autotrace is an improvement over the Explain Plan command and enables us to collect information about the SQL statements as they run.

Enable SQL*Plus autotrace by running the $ORACLE_HOME/sqlplus/admin/plustrce.sql command; this script grants SELECT privileges on certain V$ views. Once enabled, begin tracing by issuing the following command:

```
SET AUTOTRACE TRACEONLY EXPLAIN;
```

This statement specifies to set AUTOTRACE, TRACEONLY, and EXPLAIN. This will trace each SQL statement without returning data rows (TRACEONLY) and generate an execution plan (EXPLAIN) for the SQL statement. By setting TRACEONLY STATISTICS, we only see the statistics in the output. So now, if you type in the query

```
SELECT * FROM HR.EMPLOYEES
WHERE EMPLOYEE_ID = 206
/
```

instead of seeing the query results, the Explain Plan for the query is displayed instead:

```
Execution Plan
----------------------------------------------------------
   0         SELECT STATEMENT Optimizer=CHOOSE
```

```
                          (Cost=1 Card=1 Bytes=62)
  1     0    TABLE ACCESS (BY INDEX ROWID) OF 'EMPLOYEES'
                          (Cost=1 Card=1 Bytes=62)
  2     1        INDEX (UNIQUE SCAN) OF 'EMP_EMP_ID_PK' (UNIQUE)
```

To turn tracing off, enter SET AUTOTRACE OFF at the SQL*Plus prompt.

V$SQL_PLAN View

In addition to the previously mentioned tools and utilities, Oracle has provided us with the V$SQL_PLAN view, which can be used to query the actual execution plan for an SQL statement. The V$SQL_PLAN view can be used along with the previously mentioned tools to tune the SQL statement. This view is best queried with a script that formats the display and selects only columns of interest to the DBA.

Chapter Summary

In this chapter, we discussed how SQL statement performance is influenced by the optimizer. We discussed how to influence optimizer decisions by gathering statistics on objects, using stored outlines for plan stability, and including hints in queries. We also discussed how to copy statistics from one database to another so that we can accurately test application performance. In addition, we discussed the tools used to investigate SQL statement performance.

Oracle uses two different SQL optimizers: the rule-based optimizer (RBO) and the cost-based optimizer (CBO). The RBO depends on syntax and ranking rules to determine an execution plan for the SQL statement. The CBO relies on statistics to determine an optimal execution plan. The RBO is maintained for backward compatibility. Oracle recommends that you use the CBO for all new development. The CBO is mandatory if you use partitioned tables, partitioned indexes, IOTs, reverse key indexes, function-based indexes, parallel query and parallel DML, and query rewrites with materialized views.

The dynamically configurable OPTIMIZER_MODE initialization parameter determines the optimizer approach that will be used by the instance. Valid choices are RULE, CHOOSE, ALL_ROWS, FIRST_ROWS_*n*, and FIRST_ROWS.

You can set the OPTIMIZER_MODE at the session level using the same set of choices. You can set the OPTIMIZER_MODE for a single SQL statement by including a hint in the SQL statement. The session setting takes precedence over the instance setting, and the hint takes precedence over the session setting.

Environmental changes, such as modifying initialization parameters, upgrading to a newer Oracle release, and modifiying object storage parameters, can influence the execution plan generated by the CBO, even if the actual SQL statement has not changed. The concept of plan stability was introduced to keep SQL execution plans constant even when the database environment changes. Plan stability is implemented with stored outlines. For plan stability to work, a submitted SQL statement must match exactly a stored outline SQL statement.

Stored outlines are kept in the OUTLN schema, in the OL$, OL$HINTS, and OL$NODES tables. To create stored outlines for all SQL statements executed in the database, use the ALTER SYSTEM SET CREATE_STORED_OUTLINES command, specifying the *category_name* for the stored outlines. You can generate a stored outline for an individual SQL statement by using the CREATE OR REPLACE OUTLINE command, immediately followed by the SQL statement. Stored outlines are maintained with the DBMS_OUTLN (OUTLN_PKG) package and with the ALTER and DROP OUTLINE SQL commands.

Private stored outlines are used to edit and test changes to stored outlines without influencing current stored outlines. The DBMS_OUTLN_EDIT package is used to create locally private OL$* tables, edit a copy of a stored outline, and publish the modified outline back to the public stored outlines. To use a stored outline, use the ALTER SYSTEM SET USE_STORED_OUTLINES=*category_name*; for an individual session, use the ALTER SESSION version of the command.

Hints are used to influence how the optimizer chooses an execution plan. The developer who understands the data distribution can sometimes provide better information and a better access method to the data than the optimizer can determine on its own. A hint is coded inline with the SQL statement; multiple hints can be used, and hints can be used in subqueries.

The ANALYZE command, the DBMS_UTLITY.ANALYZE_* procedures, and the DBMS_STATS package are used to collect statistics on tables, indexes, and clusters for the CBO. Valid and up-to-date statistics can make a significant difference in SQL statement performance. With the ANALYZE command, you can use the COMPUTE option, which scans the entire object to get exact statistics, or use the ESTIMATE option to sample a number or percent of rows. The DBMS_STATS package can be used to gather more sophisticated statistics and gather them in parallel. Whichever method you choose, the statistics are written to the DBA_TABLES, DBA_INDEXES, DBA_CLUSTERS, and DBA_TAB_COL_STATISTICS data dictionary tables for the objects analyzed.

The CBO can use histograms, gathered on table column data, to do a better job choosing an access path under certain conditions: when the data is skewed or distribution is nonuniform and when bind variables are not used. Histograms use a number of buckets to distribute data by value. Height-based histograms place approximately the same number of column values in each bucket based on the range of values; value-based histograms place column values in a bucket based on the unique value of the column. Histograms are created by using the ANALYZE command or the DBMS_STATS package.

The DBMS_STATS package can also be used to copy statistics from the data dictionary to a schema table. From there, the table can be exported and imported into another database. The DBMS_STATS package is also used to populate statistics in the data dictionary tables from the exported objects. This is useful for comparing test and production execution plans, and stabilizing statistics between databases.

Several tools are available for real-time analyses on SQL statements. The SQL Trace utility is used to trace the SQL statements in a session and write a trace file to the USER_DUMP_DEST directory. The TKPROF utility is then used to format the trace file into a readable report. Within an SQL*Plus session, you can automatically trace all SQL statements by issuing the SET AUTOTRACE command. If you want to manually create an execution plan for an SQL statement, use the Explain Plan command. Both Autotrace and Explain Plan populate the plan_table. The V$SQL_PLAN table shows execution plans for SQL statements that are currently in the shared pool.

Two-Minute Drill

- The rule-based optimizer (RBO) is enabled by setting OPTIMIZER_MODE=RULE.

- The RBO uses syntax rules and access path ranking to determine the execution plan.

- The cost-based optimizer (CBO) is enabled by setting OPTIMIZER_MODE=ALL_ROWS, CHOOSE, FIRST_ROWS, or FIRST_ROWS_*n*.

- ALL_ROWS optimizes for total throughput.

- FIRST_ROWS and FIRST_ROWS_*n* optimizes response time for the first *n* number of rows.

- CHOOSE specifies that the CBO should be used if statistics are available; otherwise, use the RBO.

- The OPTIMIZER_MODE can be set for the instance in the init.ora file or with the ALTER SYSTEM command for the session with the ALTER SESSION command or for a single SQL statement by coding an SQL hint.

- The OPTIMIZER_MODE precedence is the session setting overrides the instance setting, and the SQL hint setting overrides the session setting.

- The CBO is highly dependent on statistics gathered with the ANALYZE command, the DBMS_UTILITY package, or the DBMS_STATS package.

- Execution plans can change due to environmental changes.

- Plan stability, implemented with stored outlines, stabilizes the execution plans even when the environment changes.

- Stored outlines are implemented in the OUTLN schema in the OL$* tables.

- For a stored outline to be used, the SQL statement submitted must exactly match an SQL statement in the active stored outline.

- To create stored outlines for all SQL generated in the instance, issue the ALTER SYSTEM CREATE_STORED_OUTLINES=*category_name* command.

- If *category_name* = TRUE, then the DEFAULT outline is created.

- Stop creating stored outlines by setting the *category_name* to FALSE.

- You can create a stored outline for an individual SQL statement by issuing the CREATE OR REPLACE OUTLINE command immediately preceding your SQL statement.

- Stored outlines are maintained by using the DBMS_OUTLN (OUTLN_PKG) package.

- A private outline can be used to edit a stored outline without affecting other users.

- The DBMS_OUTLN_EDIT package is used to create editing tables, edit the SQL hints and execution plans, and drop the private outline tables when no longer needed.

- Use the CREATE OR REPLACE OUTLINE command to copy the modified outline to the public stored outlines schema.

- Begin using a stored outline for the session by issuing the ALTER SESSION SET USE_STORED_OUTLINES=*category_name* command.

- For the instance, use ALTER SYSTEM SET USE_STORED_OUTLINES=*category_name*.

- USE_STORED_OUTLINES and CREATE_STORED_OUTLINES are not valid initialization parameters.

- To influence the optimizer's choice of execution plan access paths, code a hint directly in the SQL statement.

- The syntax for a hint is /*+ <hint> */.

- You can code SQL hints in subqueries and use multiple hints for multitable joins.

- Use the ANALYZE command or the DBMS_STATS package to gather statistics for schema objects.

- ANALYZE . . . COMPUTE reads the entire object and computes statistical information.

- The ESTIMATE option samples a number or percentage of rows and calculates the statistics.

- The DBMS_STATS package replaces the ANALYZE command and is able to sample blocks or rows and gather statistics in parallel.

- Statistics are kept in the DBA_TABLES, DBA_INDEXES, DBA_CLUSTERS, and DBA_TAB_COL_STATISTICS data dictionary views.

- Histograms are used to assist the CBO by distributing column data into range or value buckets.

- Histograms can be useful if data is skewed and not accessed with bind variables.

- The DBA_TAB_HISTOGRAMS, DBA_PART_HISTOGRAMS, DBA_SUBPART_HISTOGRAMS, and DBA_TAB_COL_STATISTICS views keep information about histograms.

- Since histograms are gathered as statistics on data, they can become stale when the data changes.

- The DBMS_STATS package can be used to copy data dictionary statistics from one database to another.

- The DBMS_STATS.CREATE_STAT_TABLE and EXPORT_SCHEMA_STATS procedures are used to get the statistics.

- Use the Oracle export utility to export the schema statistics table and the Oracle import utility to import the schema table into the target database.

- Use the DBMS_STATS.IMPORT_SCHEMA_STATS procedure to populate the data dictionary in the target database with the imported statistics.

- SQL statements can be traced in a session or for the instance by setting SQL_TRACE=TRUE.

- DBMS_SESSION.SET_SQL_TRACE can be used to turn tracing on or off in the current session.

- Use DBMS_SYSTEM.SET_SQL_TRACE_IN_SESSION to turn tracing on or off in another session.

- The session trace file is written to the USER_DUMP_DEST directory.

- Use TKPROF to format the session trace file.

- Use the Explain Plan command to create an execution plan report for a SQL statement.

- Set AUTOTRACE in SQL*Plus to automatically trace all SQL statements in the session.

- Both Autotrace and Explain Plan require the PLAN_TABLE, which is created with the utlxplan.sql script.

- The V$SQL_PLAN dynamic performance view displays the execution plan for all the SQL statements in the shared pool.

Chapter Questions

1. **Which of the following statements accurately describes how the RBO determines optimal execution plans? (Choose two.)**

   A. It creates execution plans based on the syntax and structure of the SQL statement.

   B. It uses access path rankings to determine an optimal execution plan.

   C. Performance is driven by the validity of statistics gathered by the ANALYZE command.

   D. It can use histograms to determine optimal execution against skewed data.

2. **Which of the following statements accurately describes how the CBO determines optimal execution plans? (Choose three.)**

   A. It creates execution plans based on the syntax and structure of the SQL statement.

   B. It uses access path rankings to determine an optimal execution plan.

   C. Performance is driven by the validity of statistics gathered by the ANALYZE command.

   D. It can use histograms to determine optimal execution against skewed data.

   E. It uses rules for SQL statement structure and dictionary information.

3. **To create stored outlines for all SQL statements executed in the database, you should issue which command?**

   A. ALTER SYSTEM SET CREATE_STORED_OUTLINES=TRUE

   B. ALTER SESSION SET CREATE_STORED_OUTLINES=TRUE

   C. Set the init.ora parameter CREATE_STORED_OUTLINES=TRUE.

   D. Use the DBMS_OUTLN.CREATE_STORED_OUTLINES procedure.

   E. Enter the CREATE OR REPLACE OUTLINE command.

4. **To begin using the default stored outlines for the current session only, which of the following commands should you use?**

   A. DBMS_SESSION.USE_STORED_OUTLINES(TRUE)

   B. DBMS_OUTLIN.USE_STORED_OUTLINES(TRUE)

   C. ALTER SESSION SET USE_STORED_OUTLINES=TRUE

   D. ALTER SYSTEM SET USE_STORED_OUTLINES=TRUE

   E. Set the init.ora parameter USE_STORED_OUTLINES=TRUE.

5. **Which of these pairs of tools would be useful for generating an SQL statement trace file for an active session and formatting the output?**

   A. Autotrace and TRACEONLY EXPLAIN

   B. DBMS_SYSTEM.SET_SQL_TRACE_IN_SESSION and TKPROF

   C. PLAN_TABLE and TKPROF

   D. Statspack report and TKPROF

   E. V$SQL_PLAN and Explain Plan

   F. Explain Plan and PLAN_TABLE

6. **Which of the following TKPROF command lines will explain the SQL statements traced?**

   A. Tkprof tracefile=ora_0123.trc explain=true sys=yes

   B. Tkprof tracefile=ora_0123.trc explain=system/password sys=no

   C. Tkprof tracefile=ora_0123.trc outputfile=ora_0123.out explain=true sys=no

   D. Tkprof tracefile=ora_0123.trc explain=system sys=yes

   E. Tkprof tracefile=ora_0123.trc outputfile=ora_0123.out sys=no

7. **Which of the following are reasons to gather statistics with the DBMS_STATS package instead of the ANALYZE command? (Choose two.)**

   A. The ANALYZE command doesn't support HISTOGRAMS.

   B. DBMS_STATS enables gathering statistics in parallel.

   C. The ANALYZE command does not compute statistics on indexes.

   D. DBMS_STATS enables block-level sampling.

   E. ANALYZE does not enable row-level sampling.

8. **What is the purpose of gathering schema object statistics with ANALYZE or DBMS_STATS? (Choose all that apply.)**

   A. To assist the CBO in determining optimal execution plans

   B. To assist the RBO in determining optimal execution plans

   C. To reorganize data in an object so that the optimizer will find the optimal execution plan

   D. To allow the function of bitmap indexes on heap-organized tables

   E. To allow the use of function-based indexes

9. **When creating a local statistics table with the DBMS_STATS.CREATE_STAT_TABLE procedure, which of the following fields are required? (Choose all that apply.)**

   A. ownname

   B. stattab

   C. tblspace

   D. statown

10. **From the following list, choose the only valid step in the process of moving statistics from one database to another.**

    A. Export the data dictionary using the Oracle export utility.

    B. Import the data dictionary using the Oracle import utility.

    C. Use the DBMS_STATS.COPY_STATS procedure to copy data dictionary stats from one database to another through a DB_LINK.

    D. Use the DBMS_STATS.EXPORT_SCHEMA_STATS to extract the data dictionary statistics into a schema table.

    E. Use the DBMS_STATS.EXTRACT_SCHEMA_STATS to extract the data dictionary statistics into a schema table.

    F. Use the DBMS_STATS.EXPORT_SCHEMA_STATS to export the data dictionary statistics into a dump file in the USER_DUMP_DEST directory.

Answers to Chapter Questions

1. A, B.   It creates execution plans based on the syntax and structure of the SQL statement, and it uses access path rankings to determine an optimal execution plan.

Explanation   The RBO uses access path rankings and the structure of the SQL statements to determine the execution plan. The RBO does not use histograms, and it does not use statistics gathered by the ANALYZE command.

2. A, C, D.   It creates execution plans based on the syntax and structure of the SQL statement, performance is driven by the validity of statistics gathered by the ANALYZE command, and it can use histograms to determine optimal execution against skewed data.

Explanation   The CBO uses statistics gathered by ANALYZE (or DBMS_STATS) and stored in the data dictionary to determine optimal execution plans. The CBO also uses histograms, if available, to determine optimal paths if the column data is skewed. The syntax and the structure of the SQL statement has a big impact on which indexes the optimizer would choose and also the join order of tables. Answers B and E are descriptive of the RBO.

3. A.   ALTER SYSTEM SET CREATE_STORED_OUTLINES=TRUE

Explanation   To enable stored outline creation, use the ALTER SYSTEM command. You cannot set the CREATE_STORED_OUTLINES command in the init.ora file. Answer B is incorrect because it only affects the current session. Answer D refers to an nonexistent procedure. Answer E will create a stored outline for the SQL statement that follows.

4. C.   ALTER SESSION SET USE_STORED_OUTLINES=TRUE

Explanation   This command will cause the current session to begin using the default stored outline. Answers A and B are incorrect because they do not exist. Answer D will enable the use of the default stored outline for the entire instance. Answer F is incorrect because there is no USE_STORED_OUTLINES initialization parameter.

5. B.   DBMS_SYSTEM.SET_SQL_TRACE_IN_SESSION and TKPROF

Explanation   To generate a trace file in the USER_DUMP_DEST directory for an active session, use the SET_SQL_TRACE_IN_SESSION procedure. Then use the TKPROF command to format the output. Answer A is incorrect because no trace file is created. Answers C, D, and E are incorrect because the two tools paired are not used together. The PLAN_TABLE is used by Explain Plan and autotrace. TKPROF doesn't format the output from the PLAN_TABLE or the Statspack report. The Explain Plan command is not used with the V$SQL_PLAN view. Answer F is incorrect because neither generates a trace file.

6. B.   Tkprof tracefile=ora_0123.trc explain=system/password sys=no

Explanation   The explain=system/password parameter tells TKPROF to connect to the database and run Explain Plan for each of the SQL statements in the trace file. The execution plan created is not necessarily the same plan that was used by the actual SQL statement being traced because they are explained in separate sessions. Each of the other answers is incorrect because they don't specify the explain=username/password parameter.

7. B, D.   DBMS_STATS enables gathering statistics in parallel and also block-level sampling.

Explanation   These are two advantages that DBMS_STATS has over the ANALYZE command. Answers A, C, and E are incorrect because each is not true about the ANALYZE command; the ANALYZE command does create histograms, it does compute statistics on indexes, when specified, and it does enable row-level sampling. Although each of these are true, they are also available with DBMS_STATS.

8. A, E.   To assist the CBO in determining optimal execution plans, and to allow the use of function-based indexes.

Explanation   Statistics are vital to the proper function of the CBO. Whether statistics are gathered with the ANALYZE command or with the DBMS_STATS package, they will assist the CBO. Also, function-based indexes are enabled by gathering statistics and using the CBO. Answer B is incorrect because statistics don't help the RBO. Answer C is incorrect because gathering statistics doesn't modify or reorganize object data. Answer D is incorrect because statistics are not required for bitmap indexes on heap-organized tables to work; however, statistics can change the execution plan and help the query performance.

9. A, B.   Ownname and stattab

Explanation   The ownname and stattab fields are required. Ownname specifies in which schema to create the table specified with the stattab variable. Answer C, tblspace, is optional if you want to create the table in some tablespace other than the default for the user specified in ownname. Answer D, statown, is not a CREATE_STAT_TABLE parameter.

10. D.   Use the DBMS_STATS.EXPORT_SCHEMA_STATS to extract the data dictionary statistics into a schema table.

Explanation   We use the EXPORT_SCHEMA_STATS procedure to extract data dictionary statistics for a schema into a schema table. We do this step after we create the stats table in the schema and before we export the stats table. Next, we would import the stats table into a target database and use the IMPORT_SCHEMA_STATS procedure to populate the target data dictionary. Answers A and B are incorrect because these utilities are not used to directly touch the data dictionary, at least when we're moving statistics from one database to another. Answers C and E refer to nonexistent procedures. Answer F is incorrect because the procedure is not used to create a dump file.

CHAPTER
16

OS Considerations and Oracle Resource Manager

n this chapter, you will learn about operating system (OS) issues that must be considered when tuning the Oracle database environment. Specifically, you will learn to do the following:

- Describe different system architectures
- Describe the primary steps of OS tuning
- Identify similarities between OS and database (DB) tuning
- Understand virtual memory and paging
- Explain the difference between a process and a thread
- Configuring resource management with Oracle Resource Manager
- Administer Resource Manager

This chapter focuses on OS and system environment issues that you must be aware of when tuning the Oracle database. We will also discuss the Oracle Resource Manager in this chapter, because it can be used to restrict OS resource consumption by database users.

OS Considerations

Depending on your organization and environment, the database administrator (DBA) may also be the OS system administrator (SA). If not, you'll find that the DBA and SA share similar responsibilities and tuning goals. This chapter can be used by both the DBA and the SA as a set of topics for discussion, and as a guide for OS tuning on systems that host Oracle databases.

Just like the DBA, the SA considers memory usage, input/output (I/O) levels, central processing unit (CPU) usage, and network traffic. We're not going to discuss networking in this chapter, as that is an entirely different OCP exam. Just like the DBA, the SA should tune memory, I/O, and CPU in that order. In order to reach common ground on these tuning issues, we will introduce various types of hardware that the Oracle database may exist on, and then briefly discuss our primary concerns about memory, I/O, and CPU.

Describe Different System Architectures

In this section, we will discuss the different fundamental architectures that support the Oracle database software.

Uniprocessor   This type of system has only one CPU and one memory area.

Symmetric Multiprocessor (SMP) Systems   Symmetric Multiprocessor (SMP) systems have multiple CPUs, generally ranging from 2 to 64. All the CPUs in the SMP configuration share the same memory, system bus, and I/O system. A single copy of the OS runs all the CPUs.

Massively Parallel Processor (MPP)Systems   A Massively Parallel Processor (MPP) system consists of several nodes (up to several thousand) connected together. Each node has its own CPU, memory, system bus, and I/O; each runs its own copy of the OS.

Nonuniform Memory Access (NUMA) Systems   A Nonuniform Memory Access (NUMA) system is composed of several SMP systems. The memory from each system is combined to form one large memory space. A single copy of the OS runs across all nodes.

Clustered Systems   In a clustered system, the nodes are connected via a local area network (LAN). Each loosely coupled node runs its own copy of the OS, but also runs clustering software that enables workload balancing and high availability. Nodes in a clustered system can be combinations of SMP and uniprocessor systems.

Understand Virtual Memory and Paging

As we've discussed previously, Oracle background processes and server processes use memory. Some of this memory is in the System Global Area (SGA), and some is in the Program Global Area (PGA). For the most part, the SGA is fixed in size, and the total PGA memory consumed is based on the number of server processes and their activity. When the memory required for these processes (and other OS processes) exceeds real memory, the OS relies on *virtual memory*. Virtual memory is disk space used to accommodate memory blocks (pages) that have been *paged* out of real memory because other processes need the real memory for current processing.

The map for virtual memory pages is kept in real memory. On multiprocessor systems, each processor has its own virtual memory map, so some wastage occurs. On some platforms such as Solaris, virtual memory mapping is in a shared memory area called intimate shared memory (ISM), which is locked into physical memory. This reduces real memory wastage and keeps the SGA in real memory.

Paging happens when a process needs a block of virtual memory. Because the block must be read from disk into real memory, I/O occurs. Also, we may need to write to virtual memory the block of real memory that was replaced.

Swapping is when the entire memory space of a process is moved from real memory to virtual memory. Any amount of swapping is bad. Paging and swapping are reduced or eliminated by adding more real memory, or by reducing the amount of memory consumed by processes. If you are unable to add more real memory, consider reducing the size of the SGA gradually until swapping and paging diminish.

Describe the Primary Steps of OS Tuning

As with tuning the database, there is a method to tuning the OS that supports the Oracle database. The process is straightforward: tune memory, I/O, and the CPU, in that order. This process should be followed regardless of the OS, but individual differences in the type of system or OS will lead you to focus more on one area or another.

Tuning Memory

When tuning the database and instance, we usually start with tuning the SGA. A well-tuned SGA is the foundation of a well-tuned database system. One of the most important guidelines is to not size the SGA larger than available real memory. In addition, we should consider these steps:

1. *Lock SGA into real memory.* On some OSs, setting the initialization parameter LOCK_SGA to TRUE will lock the SGA in real memory, and it will not be paged out to disk. Only use this if you have plenty of available memory.

2. *Use intimate shared memory, if it is available.* On some systems, such as Solaris, the use of intimate shared memory (ISM) can dramatically improve performance. ISM enables page table entries for SGA pages to be shared between processes.

3. *Monitor real and virtual memory.* Whether or not your system supports ISM or LOCK_SGA, you should monitor real and virtual memory usage, paging, and swapping.

Tuning I/O

Once you have tuned memory, turn your efforts to the I/O subsystem. In general, you should focus on balancing I/O across multiple controllers and storage devices. Choose many smaller physical devices instead of a few larger devices. This reduces the likelihood that one disk will cause performance problems for the overall system. Also consider using more I/O channels instead of fewer. Here are some additional guidelines:

- **Use raw devices**   With raw devices, there is a tradeoff between performance and ease of administration. Also, some systems may not benefit from the use of raw devices.

- **Synchronous versus asynchronous I/O**   When synchronous I/O calls are used, Oracle has to wait on an I/O request until it completes. With asynchronous I/O calls, Oracle doesn't have to wait on a request to complete; it can issue other I/O requests and continue processing. Depending on your OS, however, you may be better off using synchronous I/O and multiple DBW processes or I/O slaves, rather than asynchronous I/O.

At the OS, monitor the number of reads and writes, the reads and writes per second, and I/O request queue lengths.

Tuning CPU

Finally, we want to tune our CPU resources. Generally, more CPUs are better than fewer, and faster CPUs are better than slower. If you note high CPU utilization, investigate why. A good place to start is with the long-running application queries, which generally are your worst CPU consumers. Properly tuned application queries can dramatically reduce CPU consumption. We should monitor the following resources:

- **CPU busy rate**   If the overall CPU busy rate is greater than 90 percent, you probably are in need of more CPU resources.

- **OS to user-processing ratio**   Our tuning goal is to have the CPU resources working predominantly on user applications, not system tasks. If system-related tasks are using more than 40 percent of the CPU, investigate.

- **CPU load balance**   On all systems except uniprocessors, verify that processes are balanced across the available CPUs.

Identify Similarities Between OS and DB Tuning

A well-tuned database, a well-tuned OS, and a properly tuned application all contribute to a high-performance system. Each affects the other. For example, a poorly tuned query with multiple full table scans can cause I/O contention, high CPU usage, and rapid buffer cache block turnover. Tune the query or add indexes, and I/O contention will be reduced, the buffer cache will be used more efficiently, and CPU usage will drop. In this way, the OS, database, and application performance will improve.

Tune the OS Using Oracle Statistics   Oracle dynamic performance views can be used to diagnose OS-related issues. One such view is the V$FILESTAT view, which indicates read and write times for each data file in the database. Use V$FILESTAT to determine file system performance problems, and assist with load balancing. V$FILESTAT can also be used to help diagnose where full table scans occur, which can be used for application tuning.

Explain the Difference Between a Process and a Thread

On most OSs, each Oracle process is a separate OS process. On some OSs, such as those based on Microsoft Windows NT, Oracle is a single OS process with multiple threads. Each Oracle background and server process is a thread within the same OS process. A *thread* is a sequence of instructions that can execute independently of other threads within the same process.

On Unix, if you use the *ps* command, you'll notice a separate OS process running for SMON, Process Monitor (PMON), and each of the other background processes for the instance. On NT, if you use the Process Manager utility, you'll notice only one OS process named *oracle.exe* running for the instance; however, V$PROCESS indicates several processes running in the database.

Database Resource Manager

The Oracle Resource Manager feature enables the DBA to place limits on resource usage by groups of users, known as consumer groups. With the Resource Manager, the DBA can guarantee a minimum amount of processing to a group of users, allocate percentages of CPU resources, limit the degree of parallelism for a group of users, and dynamically configure an instance to use a specific resource allocation plan.

Resource Manager Concepts

The Resource Manager consists of three basic components: resource consumer groups, resource plan directives, and resource plans.

Resource consumer groups are groups of users with similar resource requirements. A user can belong to many consumer groups, but only one group at a time can be active for a session.

Resource plan directives are used to assign consumer groups or subplans to a resource plan, and to allocate resources among consumer groups in a resource plan. A resource plan serves as a collection of resource plan directives. Only one resource plan can be active in an instance. The active resource plan is specified with the RESOURCE_MANAGER_PLAN initialization parameter and is dynamically configurable.

Resource Allocation Methods   The Resource Manager uses the *absolute* resource allocation method to limit the degree of parallelism for operations, and the method may be specified only in a plan directive that refers to a resource consumer group. The absolute method specifies the maximum number of processes that may be assigned to an operation.

The Resource Manager uses the *emphasis* resource allocation method to allocate CPU to a specific resource consumer group in a resource plan. CPU usage is prioritized from levels 1 through 8; level 1 is the highest priority. The percentage (emphasis) on the CPU is specified for each consumer group at each level. These are the basic rules for CPU resource allocation:

- At any given level, the sum of assigned percentages to consumer groups must be less than or equal to 100.

- If a level has no plan directive, then all consumer groups get 0 percent at that level.

- If any CPU is available after all resource consumer groups at a given level have had the opportunity to use the resource, the available CPU will be made available to the next level.

- If CPU is still available, then the consumer groups get another opportunity to use the CPU, starting at level 1 and according to the previous rules.

These rules become important when the system is fully utilized. If the CPU resources are not fully utilized, then Oracle will attempt to maximize throughput instead of prioritizing among consumer groups. CPU allocation is distributed between sessions in a group in a round-robin manner.

The System Plan and Consumer Groups   When you create the database, the SYSTEM_PLAN is created, as well as these default consumer groups:

- **SYS_GROUP**   This includes users SYSTEM and SYS, and has high priority.

- **LOW_GROUP**   This group has the lowest priority of the consumer groups.

- **DEFAULT_CONSUMER_GROUP**   This is automatically assigned to each database user.

- **OTHER_GROUPS**   This is used to allocate resources to groups that are not assigned to the active resource plan. The active plan must contain a plan directive for this group.

Subplans   A plan contains consumer groups and plan directives, but can also include subplans. A subplan is simply a plan that is assigned to a parent plan. A subplan can belong to more than one plan, but loops are not allowed. The highest-level plan in a hierarchy is referred to as the top-level plan.

Configuring Resource Management

Oracle has supplied us with two Procedural Language/Structured Query Language (PL/SQL) packages that we use to configure resource management. The DBMS_RESOURCE_MANAGER package is used to create and manage pending areas, resource plans, consumer groups, and resource plan directives. It is also used to validate and submit resource plans, and then assign the plans to consumer groups. The DBMS_RESOURCE_MANAGER_PRIVS package is used to assign users and roles to consumer groups. You must have the ADMINISTER RESOURCE MANAGER system privilege to use these packages; it is automatically granted to the DBA and is granted to others with the DBMS_RESOURCE_MANAGER_PRIVS.grant_system_privilege procedure. The privilege is revoked with the revoke_system_privilege procedure.

The correct sequence of events when configuring resource management is as follows:

1. Create a resource plan, which first requires a pending area.

2. Create a resource consumer group(s).

3. Create resource plan directives.

4. Validate and submit the resource plan and directives.

5. Assign users or roles to consumer groups.

6. Once these steps have been completed, you can specify one plan that will be used by the instance.

Creating a Pending Area   Before you can create a resource plan, you must create a pending area by simply issuing the DBMS_RESOURCE_MANAGER.create_pending_area procedure. The pending area is used as a staging area for creating plans, directives, and consumer groups before they are submitted to the database.

Creating Resource Plans   As mentioned previously, the SYSTEM_PLAN is created when the database is created. To create a plan, execute the DBMS_RESOURCE_MANAGER.create_plan procedure, supplying a plan name string and a plan description string. Here's an example:

```
EXEC DBMS_RESOURCE_MANAGER.CREATE_PLAN('OLTP','OLTP Application Plan')
```

There is also the DBMS_RESOURCE_MANAGER.CREATE_SIMPLE_PLAN procedure, which creates a simple resource plan containing up to eight consumer groups, all in one step.

Creating Consumer Groups   As mentioned previously, four consumer groups are created for you when the database is created. You can create additional consumer groups with the DBMS_RESOURCE_MANAGER.create_consumer_group procedure, again supplying a consumer group name string, a consumer group description string, and a CPU resource allocation method. At this time, the only CPU resource allocation method available is ROUND-ROBIN. Here's an example:

```
EXEC DBMS_RESOURCE_MANAGER.CREATE_CONSUMER_GROUP('OLTP_USERS','OLTP
Application Users')
```

Create Resource Plan Directives   Here's where the fun begins. This is the step where we configure a resource directive for a consumer group and assign it to a plan. We use the DBMS_RESOURCE_MANAGER.create_plan_directive procedure, supplying the following information:

- **Plan**   The name of the plan this directive is assigned to.
- **Group_or_subplan**   The consumer group or subplan name.
- **Comment**   A comment.
- **Cpu_pn**   The percentage of CPU, where n is the priority level, 1 through 8.
- **Parallel_degree_limit_p1**   The degree of parallelism.
- **Active_sess_pool_p1**   The maximum number of sessions allowed for a consumer group.
- **Queueing_p1**   The length of time in seconds for which a queued session should wait before timing out.
- **Switch_group**   The consumer resource group to switch to once switch_time is reached.
- **Switch_time**   The number of seconds that a session must be active before switching resource groups.
- **Switch_estimate**   If TRUE, Oracle will use the execution time estimate to switch the sessions to the SWITCH_GROUP consumer group before the operation starts. The default is FALSE.
- **Max_est_exec_time**   The maximum estimated time an operation can take.
- **Undo_pool**   The quota of undo space per resource consumer group in KB.

Here's an example:

```
exec DBMS_RESOURCE_MANAGER.create_plan_directive(plan => 'OLTP', -
group_or_subplan => 'OLTP_USERS', -
comment => 'regular OLTP users', -
cpu_p1 => 10, -
parallel_degree_limit_p1 => 16)
```

Confirm Group and Plan Configuration   Now that you've created a plan, a consumer group, and a directive, it's time to validate the plan and submit it. Before you validate the plan, however, make sure that you've created a plan directive for OTHER_GROUPS. Validate the plan using the DBMS_RESOURCE_MANAGER.validate_pending_area procedure, which verifies that the plan follows these rules:

- No subplan loops.
- Referenced subplans and/or consumer groups must exist.
- The sum of percentages for resources that use the emphasis method cannot exceed 100 at any given priority level.
- Plans and resource consumer groups cannot have the same name.
- The plan must have a directive for OTHER_GROUPS.
- A plan has a maximum of 32 consumer groups and 32 subplans.
- The parallel_degree_limit_p1 directive parameter can only be used with consumer group directives, not subplan directives.
- Each directive at the lowest level in a plan must refer to consumer groups, not subplans, and each directive that references the top-level plan must be a consumer group directive.

Once the pending area has been validated, submit the pending area with the DBMS_RESOURCE_MANAGER.submit_pending_area procedure. The submit_pending_area procedure also performs validation, so you are not forced to call the validate_pending_area procedure. However, debugging is often easier if you incrementally validate your changes, especially if you are manipulating complex plans.

Administer Resource Manager

Now that you have configured a Resource Manager plan and directives, we need to complete a few more steps before the system will use the plan. We need to assign users to consumer groups and assign the plan that the instance will use. We also need to know how to switch a user to a different consumer group and, of course, monitor the resource manager with data dictionary views and performance views.

Assigning Users to Consumer Groups

Users must be assigned to resource consumer groups before the Resource Manager can be used. We use the DBMS_RESOURCE_MANAGER_PRIVS.grant_switch_consumer_group procedure to grant a consumer group and the privilege to switch to a consumer group to a user.

Here's an example:

```
exec DBMS_RESOURCE_MANAGER_PRIVS.grant_switch_consumer_group( -
grantee_name=>'JENNYP', -
consumer_group=>'OLTP_USERS', -
grant_option=>FALSE)
```

To set the user's default consumer group, that is, the consumer group to which a user belongs at session signon, use the set_initial_consumer_group procedure. The user or PUBLIC must have been granted the privilege to switch to the consumer group before it can be the user's initial consumer group. This switch privilege must be granted to the user, not to a role that is then granted to the user. Here's an example:

```
exec DBMS_RESOURCE_MANAGER.set_initial_consumer_group( -
user=>'JENNYP', -
consumer_group=>'OLTP_USERS')
/
```

If you don't set the initial consumer group for a user, they will by default be assigned to the DEFAULT_CONSUMER_GROUP.

Set the Resource Plan for the Instance

To use the Resource Manager, we must set the top-level resource plan for the instance. To assign the plan at startup, set the initialization parameter RESOURCE_MANAGER_PLAN=*resource_plan_name*. If the plan specified in the initialization parameter does not exist in the database, the instance will not open, and the ORA-07452 error message is written to the alert log. We must correct the problem and restart the instance. To activate, deactivate, or change the current the top-level plan dynamically, issue the ALTER SYSTEM SET RESOURCE_MANAGER_PLAN command.

Changing Consumer Groups

A user session may need to switch from one consumer group to another during processing, or the DBA may need to switch a user or a particular session to another consumer group.

Changing Consumer Groups Within a Session   To switch from one consumer group to another during a session, simply invoke the DBMS_SESSION.switch_current_consumer_group procedure. The user must have been granted the privilege to switch to the new consumer group. If the procedure is called from another procedure, the user can switch to a consumer group for which the owner of that procedure has a switch privilege.

Here's an anonymous PL/SQL block that will switch the current session to another consumer group, and display the old consumer group:

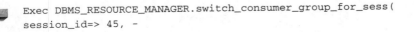

```
SET serveroutput on
DECLARE
  v_old_group VARCHAR2(30);
BEGIN
   DBMS_SESSION.SWITCH_current_CONSUMER_GROUP(
       new_consumer_group => 'OLTP_USERS',
       old_consumer_group => v_old_group,
       initial_group_on_error => TRUE);
   DBMS_OUTPUT.PUT_LINE(' OLD GROUP = ' || v_old_group);
END;
/
OLD GROUP = DEFAULT_CONSUMER_GROUP
```

In this example, the session is switching to the OLTP_USERS consumer group. The old_consumer_group is returned to a variable that we can later use to switch the session back to the original consumer group. The BOOLEAN initial_group_on_error, when set to TRUE, sets the current consumer group of the session to the initial consumer group if the procedure cannot switch the session to the new consumer group.

Changing Consumer Groups for a Session or Sessions   The DBA, or anyone with the ADMINISTER_RESOURCE_MANAGER privilege, can switch a session, or all sessions for a user, to a different consumer group that the user has the privilege to switch to. With the given procedures, the switch to the new consumer group is immediate. This is a convenient way for the DBA to lower or raise the priority of a running session or sessions. Here's an example of switching the consumer group for a session:

```
Exec DBMS_RESOURCE_MANAGER.switch_consumer_group_for_sess(
session_id=> 45, -
```

```
session_serial=> 4106, -
consumer_group=> 'OLTP_USERS')
```

Here's an example of switching all sessions for a particular user:

```
Exec DBMS_RESOURCE_MANAGER.switch_consumer_group_for_user( -
user=> 'JENNYP', -
consumer_group=> 'OLTP_USERS')
```

Again, the switch is immediate. With both procedures, the parallel query slave sessions associated with the session or sessions that are switched will also switch to the new consumer group.

Monitoring Resource Manager

In this section, we will introduce the data dictionary views that we can query to obtain information about the resource plans, consumer groups, and plan directives. We will also introduce the dynamic performance views that we can use to monitor resource utilization.

Data Dictionary Views   In this section, we introduce the data dictionary views that you can use to check resource manager objects. These views are used to get information about the plans, plan directives, and consumer groups that have been defined in the database:

- **DBA_RSRC_PLANS**   Lists information about each resource plan, including the plan name, status (PENDING or ACTIVE), and number of directives.

- **DBA_RSRC_PLAN_DIRECTIVES**   Lists information about all resource plan directives in the database, including the plan, group or subplan, CPU percentage for each level, and status (PENDING or ACTIVE).

- **DBA_RSRC_CONSUMER_GROUPS**   Lists information about consumer groups, such as the name, status, and comments.

- **DBA_RSRC_CONSUMER_GROUP_PRIVS**   Lists information about which users and roles are assigned to which consumer groups, and whether or not the consumer group is the initial consumer group for the user or role.

- **DBA_RSRC_MANAGER_SYSTEM_PRIVS**   Lists all the users that have the ADMINISTER_RESOURCE_MANAGER privilege.

- **DBA_USERS**   The INITIAL_RSRC_CONSUMER_GROUP column indicates the default consumer group for the user.

Dynamic Performance Views   The V$SYSSTAT row for *CPU used by this session* indicates CPU utilization for all sessions. The V$SESSTAT view shows the CPU utilization for each session. In addition, these views can be used to check the Resource Manager information:

- **V$RSRC_PLAN**   Shows the active plan for the instance.

- **V$RSRC_CONSUMER_GROUP**   Shows CPU utilization for the currently active consumer groups.

- **V$RSRC_PLAN_CPU_MTH and V$RSRC_CONSUMER_GROUP_CPU_MTH**   Shows the resource allocation methods defined for the CPU and the consumer groups.

Chapter Summary

The emphasis of this chapter was on OS considerations as part of the tuning process. We discussed the different system architectures that you may encounter as an Oracle DBA. We discussed the primary steps of OS tuning and the similarities between OS and database tuning. We explained at a very high level virtual memory, paging, and swapping, and also the difference between a process and a thread.

This chapter also introduced the Database Resource Manager. The Resource Manager is used to place limits on resource usage by groups of users. The Resource Manager enables the DBA to allocate percentages of CPU resources to priority levels and to limit the degree of parallelism for a group of users.

The three basic components of the Resource Manager implementation are resource consumer groups, resource plans, and resource plan directives. A resource consumer group consists of users with similar resource consumption requirements. A resource plan is a collection of resource plan directives. A resource plan directive is used to assign a consumer group or subplan to a resource plan, and to allocate resources among consumer groups in a plan.

CPU utilization between user sessions within a group is allocated in a round-robin manner, while CPU utilization between consumer groups is based on the *emphasis* method. This means that groups assigned to level 1 receive a greater emphasis than groups assigned to level 8. The Resource Manager uses the *absolute* method to limit the degree of parallelism; that is, the DBA specifies the maximum number of parallel processes allowed for an operation. Additionally, the DBA can establish resource plan directives for the maximum number of sessions allowed in a consumer group, parameters for switching between consumer groups, and an UNDO space quota.

When the database is created, the SYSTEM_PLAN is created, along with four consumer groups: SYS_GROUP, LOW_GROUP, DEFAULT_CONSUMER_GROUP, and OTHER_GROUPS.

The DBA uses the DBMS_RESOURCE_MANAGER package to create a pending area, resource plans, consumer groups, and resource plan directives. The DBA can also use the package to assign the initial consumer group for users. The DBA can grant other users the privilege to execute procedures in the package by using the DBMS_RESOURCE_MANAGER_PRIVS.grant_system_privilege procedure.

The DBMS_RESOURCE_MANAGER_PRIVS package is used to assign users to resource consumer groups, to grant users the privilege to switch from one consumer group to another, and to revoke privileges.

The RESOURCE_MANAGER_PLAN initialization parameter is used to specify the resource plan that the instance will use on startup. If the parameter value is not a valid resource plan in the database, then the instance will not open. The DBA can change the current plan, activate, or deactivate it with the ALTER SYSTEM command.

A user session can switch from one consumer group to another valid group by using the DBMS_SESSION.switch_current_consumer_group procedure. The DBA can switch a session from one consumer group to another with the DBMS_RESOURCE_MANAGER.switch_consumer_group_for_sess procedure, and switch all the sessions for a user from one consumer group to another with the DBMS_RESOURCE_MANAGER.switch_consumer_group_for_user procedure.

The DBA can query information about Resource Manager objects by using several data dictionary views and dynamic performance views. The DBA_RSRC_PLANS, DBA_RSRC_PLAN_DIRECTIVES, DBA_RSRC_CONSUMER_GROUPS, DBA_RSRC_CONSUMER_GROUP_PRIVS, and DB_RSRC_MANAGER_SYSTEM_PRIVS data dictionary views list information about the Resource Manager objects. The V$RSRC_PLAN view provides information about the currently active top-level resource plan, and the V$RSRC_CONSUMER_GROUP view shows CPU utilization for currently active consumer groups.

Two-Minute Drill

- The systems administrator (SA) and the DBA share similar tuning goals.

- The SA tunes the OS memory, I/O, and CPU, in that order.

- A uniprocessor system has one CPU.

- A Symmetric Multiprocessing (SMP) system has multiple CPUs that share the same memory, system bus, and I/O system.

- A Massively Parallel Processor (MPP) system consists of several nodes, each running its own copy of the OS on its own CPU, memory, system bus, and I/O.

- A Nonuniform Memory Access (NUMA) system consists of several SMP systems that run a single copy of the OS in one large combined memory space.

- In loosely clustered systems, the nodes are connected via a LAN, and each node runs its own OS and clustering software.

- When tuning memory, the SA and DBA should consider locking the Shared Global Area (SGA) into real memory, use intimate shared memory where applicable, and monitor real and virtual memory consumption.

- When tuning I/O, choose a large number of small devices over a small number of large devices. Consider raw devices, more I/O channels instead of fewer, and asynchronous I/O.

- Monitor the number of reads and writes, reads and writes per second, and I/O request queue lengths.

- When tuning CPU resources, monitor the busy rate, the OS-to-user-processing ratio, and the CPU load balance on multiprocessor systems.

- Oracle dynamic performance views, such as V$FILESTAT, can be used to help tune the OS resources.

- Virtual memory is disk space that is used to accommodate memory blocks that have been paged out of real memory because other processes need the real memory for current operations.

- Paging occurs when a block of memory is moved from disk to memory or memory to disk.

- Swapping occurs when the entire memory space is moved from real memory to virtual memory.

- Paging and swapping are reduced by adding more real memory, or by reducing the amount of memory used by processes.

- On most systems, each Oracle process is a separate OS process.

- On MS Windows NT, Oracle is a single OS process with each Oracle process implemented as a thread within the OS process.

- The Database Resource Manager enables the DBA to place limits on resource utilization.

- The Resource Manager uses resource plans, plan directives, and consumer groups.

- A resource consumer group is a collection of users with similar resource requirements.

- A resource plan directive is a mapping of resource requirements to users, and a way to assign consumer groups or subplans to a resource plan.

- A resource plan is a collection of resource plan directives.

- Only one resource plan can be used at a time in an instance.

- The RESOURCE_MANAGER_PLAN initialization parameter sets the initial resource plan for the instance. The setting is dynamically configurable.

- The Resource Manager uses the *absolute* resource allocation method to limit the degree of parallelism for operations.

- The Resource Manager uses the *emphasis* resource allocation method to allocate CPU to a specific resource consumer group in a resource plan.

- CPU allocation is distributed between sessions in a consumer group in a round-robin manner.

- The SYSTEM_PLAN is created when the database is created.

- Four consumer groups are created when the database is created: SYS_GROUP, LOW_GROUP, DEFAULT_CONSUMER_GROUP, and OTHER_GROUPS.

- A subplan is a resource plan that is assigned to a parent plan.

- The DBMS_RESOURCE_MANAGER package is used to create and manage pending areas, resource plans, consumer groups, and resource plan directives.

- It is also used to validate and submit resource plans, and then assign the plans to consumer groups.

- The DBMS_RESOURCE_MANAGER_PRIVS package is used to assign users and roles to consumer groups.

- You must have the ADMINISTER RESOURCE MANAGER system privilege to use the DBMS_RESOURCE_MANAGER and DBMS_RESOURCE_MANAGER_PRIVS packages; it can only be granted with the DBMS_RESOURCE_MANAGER_PRIVS.grant_system_privilege procedure.

- The privilege is revoked with the DBMS_RESOURCE_MANAGER_PRIVS.revoke_system_privilege procedure.

■ The correct sequence of events when configuring resource management is as follows:

1. Create a pending area (DBMS_RESOURCE_MANAGER.create_ pending_area procedure).

2. Create a resource plan (create_plan).

3. Create a resource consumer group or groups (create_consumer_group).

4. Create resource plan directives (create_plan_directive).

5. Validate and submit the resource plan and directives (validate_pending_area).

6. Assign users or roles to consumer groups (DBMS_RESOURCE_ MANAGER_PRIVS.grant_switch_consumer_group and DBMS_RESOURCE_MANAGER.set_initial_consumer_group).

7. Specify one plan that will be used by the instance at startup by setting the RESOURCE_MANAGER_PLAN initialization parameter, or set it dynamically with the ALTER SYSTEM command.

■ A session can switch consumer groups with the DBMS_SESSION.switch_current_consumer_group procedure.

■ The DBA, or anyone with the ADMINISTER_RESOURCE_MANAGER privilege, can switch the consumer group for a session with the DBMS_RESOURCE_MANAGER.switch_consumer_group_for_sess procedure. All sessions for a user can be switched with the DBMS_RESOURCE_MANAGER.switch_consumer_group_for_user procedure.

■ The DBA_RSRC_PLANS, DBA_RSRC_PLAN_DIRECTIVES, DBA_RSRC_CONSUMER_GROUPS, DBA_RSRC_CONSUMER_GROUP_PRIVS, and DBA_RSRC_MANAGER_SYSTEM_PRIVS data dictionary views are used to query the current resource manager objects in the database.

■ The V$RSRC_PLAN view shows information about the current active plan for the instance.

■ The V$RSRC_CONSUMER_GROUP view shows CPU utilization for the currently active consumer groups.

Chapter Questions

1. The DBA notices that a user has opened several sessions that are consuming too much of the CPU resource and decides to move the users to a lower-priority resource group in the current plan. Which procedure should the DBA use to accomplish this task?

   A. DBMS_RESOURCE_MANAGER.switch_consumer_group_for_user

   B. DBMS_RESOURCE_MANAGER.switch_consumer_group_for_sess

   C. DBMS_RESOURCE_MANAGER_PRIV.switch_consumer_group_for_user

   D. DBMS_SESSION.switch_current_consumer_group

2. In order to switch another user's session from one consumer group to another, you'll need which one of these roles?

   A. The ADMINISTER RESOURCE MANAGER privilege, granted by the GRANT command.

   B. The ADMINISTER RESOURCE MANAGER privilege, granted with the DBMS_RESOURCE_MANAGER_PRIVS.grant_system_privilege procedure.

   C. The RESOURCE MANAGER ADMIN privilege, granted with the DBMS_RESOURCE_MANAGER_PRIVS.grant_system_privilege procedure.

   D. The ADMINISTER RESOURCE MANAGER privilege, granted with the DBMS_RESOURCE_MANAGER.grant_system_privilege procedure.

3. From the following, choose the correct sequence of events to configure Resource Manager:

   A. Create a pending area, create a plan, create plan directives, and create consumer groups.

   B. Create a pending area, create consumer groups, create plan directives, and create a plan.

   C. Create a pending area, create a plan, create consumer groups, and create plan directives.

4. **Before a resource plan can become the active top-level plan, which of the following rules must be validated? (Choose all that apply.)**

   A. All referenced subplans and consumer groups must exist.

   B. The sum of percentages for resources that use the emphasis method cannot exceed 100 at any given priority level.

   C. The plan must have a directive for OTHER_GROUPS.

   D. All plans must contain at least one subplan.

   E. A plan has a maximum of 32 consumer groups and 32 subplans.

Answers to Chapter Questions

1. A.   DBMS_RESOURCE_MANAGER.switch_consumer_group_for_user

Explanation   The switch_consumer_group_for_user procedure is used by the DBA to switch all sessions for a user to another consumer group. The switch is immediate. The DBA would use the procedure specified in answer B to switch a single session from one consumer group to another. Answer C is incorrect; it does not exist. The procedure specified in answer D would be used by a session to switch from one group to another.

2. B.   The ADMINISTER RESOURCE MANAGER privilege, granted with the DBMS_RESOURCE_MANAGER_PRIVS.grant_system_privilege procedure.

Explanation   The DBA is automatically granted the ADMINISTER_RESOURCE_ MANAGER role; however, all other users who require the role must have it granted through the DBMS_RESOURCE_MANAGER_PRIVS.grant_system_privilege procedure. The GRANT command will not work for this role. Also, to revoke the privilege, issue the revoke_system_privilege procedure from the same package. Answer C specifies an incorrect role, and answer D specifies an incorrect package name.

3. C.   Create a pending area, create a plan, create consumer groups, and create plan directives.

Explanation   This specifies the correct sequence of events. We did not include the validate and submit steps, nor did we assign users or roles to consumer groups. However, the steps specified in answer C are in the correct order. Answers A and B are both incorrect because the sequence of events is incorrect.

4. A, B, C, and E are correct.

Explanation Each of the rules specified must be met for a plan to be validated. All referenced subplans and consumer groups must exist. CPU percentages for resources in the emphasis method cannot exceed 100 percent at any level, and there must be a directive for OTHER_GROUPS in the plan. There is a maximum of 32 consumer groups allowed in a plan, and a maximum of 32 subplans in a plan. Answer D is incorrect; no plan is required to have a subplan.

PART
II

Practice Exams

CHAPTER
17

Practice Exam 1 and 2

his is the first of two practice exams, each approximately the same length as the actual OCP exam. For your convenience, the exam questions are sorted according to the exam content checklist. The actual OCP exam is not sorted for your convenience. Answers to the questions begin after the last question. Give yourself 90 minutes to complete this practice exam.

Practice Exam 1 Questions

1. **To minimize production application issues, the database administrator (DBA) should begin tuning during which design stage?**

   A. Conceptual design

   B. Database configuration

   C. End-user acceptance testing

   D. Postproduction implementation

2. **Which of these do not represent valid tuning goals?**

   A. Reduce or eliminate waits

   B. Improve overall system throughput

   C. Improve the performance of specific SQL statements

   D. Reduce the number of data blocks cached in memory

   E. Improve cache hit ratios

3. **Which of these is a common problem addressed by performance tuning?**

   A. Long-running full table scans

   B. SQL cursors reused

   C. Sorts in memory instead of to disk

   D. Persistent database connections

4. **The system alert log is written to which directory specified in the init.ora file?**

   A. USER_DUMP_DEST

   B. BACKGROUND_DUMP_DEST

   C. CORE_DUMP_DEST

   D. ALERT_DUMP_DEST

5. **The V$FILESTAT dynamic performance view could best be categorized as which type of view?**

    A. Accumulator view

    B. Informational view

    C. Current state view

    D. Materialized view

6. **You need to generate a STATSPACK report and have decided to name it daytime_OLTP.rpt. What other two pieces of information will you need to successfully create a report? (Choose two.)**

    A. Ending snapshot ID

    B. Start time

    C. Beginning snapshot ID

    D. End time

7. **By default, STATSPACK objects are written to which schema and tablespace?**

    A. PERFSTAT, SYSTEM

    B. PERFSTAT, user-defined or SYSTEM

    C. SYS, SYSTEM

    D. SYSTEM, SYS

    E. PERFSTAT, user-defined nonsystem

    F. SYSTEM, user-defined

8. **The STATSPACK report is similar in nature to which of the following?**

    A. OEM Oracle Expert

    B. OEM Tuning Template

    C. SQL Trace and TKPROF

    D. UTLESTAT report.txt

9. **Name the two primary tuning goals when tuning the library cache. (Choose two.)**

    A. Minimize reparsing

    B. Reuse data blocks

    C. Eliminate disk reads

    D. Cache database blocks in the library cache

    E. Avoid memory fragmentation

10. **The Dictionary cache hit ratio measures the ratio of which two statistics from V$ROWCACHE? (Choose two.)**

    A. PINS

    B. RELOADS

    C. GETS

    D. GETMISSES

    E. KEEPS

11. **You notice that a large and seldom used package is pinned in the shared pool. Which of these would remove the package from the shared pool?**

    A. Exec SYS.DBMS_SHARED_POOL.KEEP('AP.ANNUAL_RPT')

    B. Exec SYS.DBMS_SHARED_POOL.UNPIN('AP.ANNUAL_RPT')

    C. Exec SYS.DBMS_SHARED_POOL.UNKEEP('AP.ANNUAL_RPT')

    D. None of the above

12. **Your application frequently compiles large PL/SQL objects, and this leads to shared pool fragmentation. You note that SHARED_POOL_RESERVED_SIZE is set at the default, and you determine that increasing it is a good step. What percent of the SHARED_POOL_SIZE should you set SHARED_POOL_RESERVED_SIZE to?**

    A. 10

    B. 50

    C. 75

    D. 5

13. **In the shared server environment, the UGA components *user session data* and *cursor state information* are stored in which memory structures?**

    A. PGA

    B. VBA

    C. Shared pool

    D. Buffer cache

    E. Log buffer

14. **RMAN will use which pools to cache buffers for input/output (I/O) slaves during backup and restore operations? (Choose two.)**

    A. The large pool when it is configured

    B. The shared pool exclusively, in all cases

    C. The Program Global Area (PGA)

    D. The shared pool if the large pool is not configured

    E. The large pool if the shared pool is not configured

15. **Which of the following best describes a *buffer cache miss*?**

    A. When buffers are moved to the dirty list before they are written to disk.

    B. Changed data that has not been written to disk.

    C. An Oracle user process is searching for a free buffer and reaches the threshold limit.

    D. Data is not in the cache and the block of data must be read into the cache from a datafile on disk.

16. **Which of these steps are taken by the server process as it searches for a free buffer in the buffer cache? (Choose two.)**

    A. The buffer is moved up to the most recently used (MRU) end of the least recently used (LRU) list and a logical read occurs.

    B. The server process moves dirty buffers to the dirty list as it searches the LRU list for a free buffer.

    C. The server process signals DBWn to read dirty buffers from the data files.

    D. The server process signals DBWn to flush the dirty buffers from the buffer cache.

17. **The *free buffer waits* system wait event is an indicator of which type of problem?**

    A. There are too many DBWn processes.

    B. The DBWn processes are not keeping up with the number of dirty buffers that must be written to disk.

    C. There is a wait for the current copy of a data block in memory due to unselective indexes.

    D. System page faulting is taking place.

18. **Dynamic SGA allocation enables the DBA to increase the size of the SGA components up to?**

    A. MAX_SGA_SIZE

    B. SGA_MAX_SIZE

    C. SHARED_POOL_SIZE+BUFFER_CACHE_SIZE

    D. DB_BLOCK_SIZE

19. **You're concerned that the buffer cache hit ratio is too low, and you believe that increasing the size of DB_CACHE_SIZE will improve performance. Which initialization parameter and dynamic performance view can you use to help determine the optimal DB_CACHE_SIZE? (Choose two.)**

    A. DB_CACHE_SIZE

    B. DB_CACHE_ADVICE parameter

    C. V$DB_CACHE

    D. DB_BUFFER_CACHE

    E. V$DB_CACHE_ADVICE

    F. V$CACHE_ADVICE

20. **Which one of these statements is true about the buffer cache in Oracle9*i*?**

    A. The size of the KEEP and RECYCLE buffer pools are subtracted from the DEFAULT buffer pool.

    B. You assign objects to the KEEP or RECYCLE buffer pools using the DBMS_BUFFER_POOL package.

    C. You assign objects to the KEEP or RECYCLE buffer pool at startup time using the DB_CACHE_KEEP and DB_CACHE_RECYCLE initialization parameters.

    D. The KEEP and RECYCLE buffer pools are separately defined memory areas from the DEFAULT buffer pool.

21. **Freelist contention can be eliminated by using automatic segment-space management, which is designated when?**

    A. At the table create time

    B. At the tablespace create time

C. At the database create time

D. At the query run time

22. **When a user makes changes to the database with INSERT, UPDATE, DELETE, CREATE, ALTER, or DROP commands, the information required to reconstruct or redo the changes is written from the user's memory space into redo log buffer entries by which Oracle process?**

   A. The server process

   B. SMON

   C. PMON

   D. DBWn

   E. LGWn

   F. LGWR

23. **Which of these environmental influences would lead you to increase the size of the java pool? (Choose two.)**

   A. Large client-side applications are written in Java.

   B. The application uses large Java stored procedures.

   C. Shared servers are used for the Java components.

   D. Dedicated servers are used.

   E. Application users are spread across multiple continents.

24. **Multiple DBW processes are preferred over DBWR I/O slaves because?**

   A. The DBW0 process is freed to gather dirty buffers when I/O slaves are used.

   B. DBWn processes gather, batch, and write dirty buffers independently.

   C. I/O slaves gather, batch, and write dirty buffers.

   D. I/O slaves are more efficient because they focus only on reads.

25. **Which of the following are good techniques to reduce I/O contention?**

   A. Place REDO logs and ROLLBACK segment tablespaces on the same device.

   B. Place all REDO logs on the same RAID-5 device.

   C. Place all heavily used tables in the same tablespace.

   D. Separate data and indexes into different tablespaces on different physical devices.

26. **Which of these statements is true about assigning a default temporary tablespace to a user?**

    A. If you do not specify a SYSTEM TEMPORARY TABLESPACE when you create the database, the SYSTEM tablespace will be defined as the temporary tablespace for each new user.

    B. If you do not specify a DEFAULT TEMPORARY TABLESPACE when you create the database, the TEMP tablespace will be defined as the temporary tablespace for each new user.

    C. If you do not specify a TEMPORARY TABLESPACE when you create the database, the TEMPORARY tablespace will be defined as the temporary tablespace for each new user.

    D. If you do not specify a DEFAULT TEMPORARY TABLESPACE when you create the database, the SYSTEM tablespace will be defined as the temporary tablespace for each new user.

27. **The purpose of a checkpoint is to? (Choose two.)**

    A. Write the current redo log to the archived redo log.

    B. Synchronize the modified data blocks in memory with the datafiles on disk.

    C. Ensure database consistency.

    D. Ensure that data blocks are read into memory as quickly as possible.

    E. Keep track of redo entries.

28. **Which of these factors would lead you to increase the value of LOG_CHECKPOINT_TIMEOUT? (Choose two.)**

    A. Checkpoints occur too frequently, causing performance problems.

    B. Checkpoints occur too frequently, lengthening the time to recover the database.

    C. Checkpoints occur infrequently, lengthening the time to recover the database.

    D. Checkpointing is not a performance problem, but you need to recover the database more quickly.

    E. Checkpointing is a performance problem, and database recovery time is not an issue.

29. **Which of these tuning approaches can be used to improve the performance of redo logging? (Choose two.)**

    A. Place redo logs on RAID-5 disks.

    B. Place redo logs on separate RAID-0 disks.

    C. Smaller redo logs improve performance by reducing checkpoint frequency.

    D. Larger redo logs improve performance by reducing checkpoint frequency.

30. **To reduce unnecessary sorting, you can employ which of the following SQL techniques? (Choose two.)**

    A. Use the UNION operator instead of UNION ALL.

    B. Use DISTINCT when selecting the primary key.

    C. Don't use DISTINCT when selecting the primary key.

    D. Use the UNION ALL operator instead of UNION.

    E. Use the NOSORT option when building indexes on unsorted table data.

31. **To monitor current session sort operations, you should join which two dynamic performance views?**

    A. V$SORT and V$PROCESS

    B. V$SORT_USAGE and V$PROCESS

    C. V$SORT_SEGMENT and DBA_SEGMENTS

    D. V$SORT_USAGE and V$SQL

    E. V$SORT_USAGE and V$SESSION

    F. V$SORT_SEGMENT and V$SESSION

32. **Which of the following does not require a sort?**

    A. Analyzing a table

    B. Truncating a table

    C. Building an index

    D. Select using the DISTINCT keyword

    E. Sort-merge join

33. Oracle uses latches for what purpose?

   A. To queue access to database objects such as tables

   B. To protect access to memory structures

   C. To keep memory doors closed

   D. To speed access to database tables

   E. To allow two or more processes to access and modify the same structure at the same time

34. The Statspack report contains several sections that can be used to identify latch performance issues. In which section should you look first to determine if latch wait problems are significant?

   A. Top 10 Wait Events

   B. Top 5 Wait Events

   C. Wait Events

   D. Latch Activity

   E. Latch Sleep Breakdown

35. Which of the following tuning steps can be taken to minimize redo allocation latch contention in Oracle9*i*? (Choose two.)

   A. Use the NOLOGGING option to reduce the amount of redo log entries for certain operations.

   B. Increase the LOG_BUFFER parameter.

   C. Increase the size of the redo logs.

   D. Increase the number of redo allocation latches.

   E. Increase the number of redo copy latches.

36. Which of the following system events indicates that PMON is rolling back a dead transaction?

   A. The undo segment recovery wait event

   B. The redo segment recovery wait event

   C. The transaction wait event

   D. The undo segment tx slot wait event

   E. The undo PMON transaction recovery wait event

37. **Which answer best describes rollback segment header contention in an Online Transaction Processing (OLTP) system?**

   A. Some transactions are required to update the rollback segment transaction table, and contention can occur if a transaction tries to update the header block.

   B. No transactions are required to update the rollback segment transaction table, so contention does not occur because multiple transactions do not try to update the header block.

   C. Every transaction must be able to update the rollback segment transaction table, but contention does not occur when multiple transactions try to update the header block.

   D. Every transaction must be able to update the rollback segment transaction table, and contention can occur if multiple transactions try to update the header block.

38. **When configuring manual rollback segments for optimal performance in an OLTP system, you should follow which general guidelines? (Choose two.)**

   A. Use relatively small rollback segments.

   B. Allocate a rollback segment for every four concurrent transactions.

   C. Use relatively larger rollback segments.

   D. Allocate one rollback segment per concurrent transaction.

   E. Keep larger rollback segments online at all times.

39. **Which of the following performance advantages would be gained by using automatic undo management instead of manual undo management?**

   A. The SYSTEM rollback segment is used for undo.

   B. You can assign multiple active undo tablespaces for an instance.

   C. Undo segments are statically defined by the Oracle server, so the DBA doesn't have to tune them.

   D. Undo segments are dynamically allocated by the Oracle server, so the DBA doesn't need to add or remove undo segments based on usage.

40. **The DBA must configure which of these parameters in the init.ora file to begin using automatic undo management?**

   A. UNDO_TABLESPACE

   B. UNDO_RETENTION

C. UNDO_MANAGEMENT

D. UNDO_SUPPRESS_ERRORS

41. **Which two locks are acquired automatically for a DELETE statement? (Choose two.)**

   A. A shared (subexclusive) TM lock

   B. A shared (subexclusive) TX lock

   C. An exclusive TX lock

   D. A shared TX lock

   E. An exclusive DDL lock

42. **Which of these are possible causes of lock contention? (Choose two.)**

   A. Manual undo management is used.

   B. Long-running operations that do not commit regularly.

   C. Long-running batch jobs that commit frequently.

   D. Long-running queries.

   E. Explicitly coded table locks.

43. **Choose from the following list one reason why utllockt.sql would not be run when there are known lock contention problems?**

   A. Utllockt.sql scans each table that is locked to determine why.

   B. Utllockt.sql can contribute to the contention because it also must acquire locks.

   C. Utllockt.sql must acquire locks to read the DBA_LOCKS view.

   D. Utllockt.sql releases all DML locks, which can lead to data corruption.

44. **One possible solution to resolving a lock contention issue is to use the ALTER SYSTEM KILL SESSION command to kill a session that has acquired locks that others need. How does killing the session resolve lock contention?**

   A. The transaction is forced to commit, which releases all locks.

   B. The transaction is forced to commit, which converts all locks to SHARE.

   C. The transaction is forced to roll back changes to the most recent savepoint, which will release all DML locks.

    D. The transaction is aborted and PMON commits the changes that were pending, thus releasing the DML locks.

    E. The transaction is aborted and PMON rolls back the uncommitted changes, thus releasing DML locks.

45. **A DML lock is held until which of the following occurs? (Choose three.)**

    A. COMMIT

    B. ROLLBACK

    C. ROLLBACK to a SAVEPOINT defined prior to the DML lock request

    D. COMMIT up to a SAVEPOINT

    E. Another DML lock is acquired

    F. ROLLBACK to a SAVEPOINT is defined after the DML lock request

46. **Which of these performance issues would lead you to switch to the Oracle shared server environment? (Choose two.)**

    A. The database server is memory constrained.

    B. Dedicated servers have not been identified as a performance problem.

    C. The database server is on NT or UNIX, and supports hundreds of concurrent sessions.

    D. Sessions predominantly use local connections to the server.

    E. There are a few batch users and no interactive users.

47. **If the TOTAL BUSY RATE is greater than 50 percent for a particular protocol in V$DISPATCHER, what course of action should you take?**

    A. Increase the size of the dispatcher process memory space.

    B. Add more protocols for each busy dispatcher.

    C. Add more space to the DBA_DISPATCHERS process table.

    D. Increase the size of the shared pool.

    E. Increase the number of dispatchers for the protocol.

48. **Through monitoring, you notice that the average number of shared server processes is consistently below the value set for MAX_SHARED_SERVERS and there are no waits in the queue. What should you do to optimize shared server performance?**

    A. Consider reducing MAX_SHARED_SERVERS.

    B. Consider reducing SHARED_SERVERS.

    C. Consider increasing SHARED_SERVERS.

    D. Consider increasing MAX_SHARED_SERVERS.

49. **Which of the following application characteristics would contribute to the decision to use an index cluster?**

    A. The application generally performs full table scans.

    B. The tables in the cluster grow rapidly.

    C. The index keys are frequently updated.

    D. The index keys are rarely updated.

50. **Which of the following application and column data characteristics would lead the database designer to choose a B-Tree index instead of a bitmap index to improve query performance on a table?**

    A. The data is high-cardinality, meaning many distinct values for a relatively small number of rows.

    B. The data is low-cardinality, meaning few distinct values for a relatively large number of rows.

    C. The data in the table is rarely updated.

    D. Data concurrency is not an issue, because the application is Decision Support Systems (DSS).

51. **Performance of an index-organized table (IOT) can degrade because of what reason?**

    A. Leaf blocks split, causing the physical ROWID to become invalidated.

    B. Leaf blocks split, causing the physical guess to become invalidated.

    C. Leaf blocks merge, causing the physical ROWID to become invalidated.

    D. Leaf blocks merge, causing the primary key to become invalidated.

    E. Leaf blocks split, causing the primary key to become invalidated.

52. **How can we improve the performance of a DSS aggregate query without modifying the query?**

    A. Implement a materialized view and disable a query rewrite for the session.

    B. Implement a materialized view, and set the QUERY_REWRITE_ENABLED parameter to TRUE.

C. Add a reverse key index to the aggregate table.

D. Use a stored outline with the /*+ RULE */ hint.

53. **Which of these is not a performance advantage of large table extents?**

A. Dynamic extent allocation is reduced with large extents instead of small extents.

B. The object has space preallocated for future growth.

C. It is possible to read the entire extent map with one I/O.

D. Some of the space may be wasted until the object grows into the large extents.

54. **Which of these will cause performance degradation on full table scans?**

A. Empty blocks above the high watermark

B. Performance indexes on nonpimary key columns

C. Empty blocks in the region of a segment that have never been used

D. Empty or underused blocks below the high watermark

55. **For a data warehouse fact table, which of the following block storage table parameter settings can improve full table scan performance on large tables?**

A. Set PCTUSED high.

B. Set PCTUSED low.

C. Set PCTUSED to 50 percent of PCTFREE.

D. Set PCTFREE to 50 percent of PCTUSED.

E. Minimize PCTFREE.

F. Maximize PCTUSED.

56. **To recover unused space from a table that has never been used but keeps the data intact, which of these options will cause the least impact on application users?**

A. Export the table, drop the table, and import the table.

B. Export the table, truncate the table, and import the table.

C. Truncate the table.

D. Drop the table.

    E. Deallocate unused blocks.

    F. Truncate unused blocks.

    G. Move the table.

57. Which of these guidelines will reduce potential row migration?

    A. Use the ANALYZE command on the table regularly.

    B. Use the DBMS_STATS.unchain procedure.

    C. Increase PCTUSED.

    D. Increase PCTFREE.

    E. Decrease PCTFREE.

58. Why is it necessary to reorganize an index because of delete activity?

    A. Empty blocks are read during index lookups.

    B. Empty blocks are skipped during an index lookup.

    C. Index blocks that contain only a single entry still must be maintained.

    D. Empty branch nodes are still visited during an index scan.

59. If you have enabled MONITORING for an index, determine if the index can be dropped by querying which dynamic performance view?

    A. V$QUERY_USAGE

    B. V$INDEX_USAGE

    C. V$TABLE_USAGE

    D. V$OBJECT_USAGE

    E. V$SORT_USAGE

60. Which of these functions are performed by the optimizer? (Choose four.)

    A. Evaluates expressions and conditions

    B. Transforms statements, if needed

    C. Checks the SQL syntax

    D. Validates database references

    E. Chooses the optimizer approach (rule- or cost-based)

    F. Chooses an access path for each table

    G. Processes the execution plan

61. **To create a stored outline that has a nonsystem generated outline name, you'll need to perform which of the following?**

    A. Use the CREATE or REPLACE OUTLINE command.

    B. Use the DBMS_OUTLIN.CREATE_OUTLINE procedure.

    C. Set the CREATE_STORED_OUTLINES initialization parameter.

    D. Use the ALTER SYSTEM SET CREATE_STORED_OUTLINES command.

62. **When using TKPROF to format a SQL trace file from a user session, which of the following parameters should you specify to remove recursive SQL statements from the output?**

    A. Recursive=no

    B. Sys_sql=no

    C. Explain=no

    D. Sys=no

    E. Recursive_sql=no

63. **The DBA should gather statistics regularly for which reason?**

    A. If the CBO is used, performance can be adversely affected if statistics are stale.

    B. If the CBO is specified and there are no statistics on any of the tables referenced in a query, then the RBO is automatically used.

    C. If the RBO is used, performance can be adversely affected if statistics are stale.

    D. If the RBO is specified and there are no statistics on any of the tables referenced in a query, then the CBO is automatically used.

64. **For what purpose would you copy statistics between databases?**

    A. To configure an accurate model of a production environment on a test system

    B. So that the data in the schema tables will be the same

    C. So that stored outline execution plans can be modified in the source database

    D. So that the data dictionaries between the two databases can be synchronized

65. Before you can create a resource plan directive, which of the following steps must you complete? (Choose two.)

    A. Validate the resource plan.

    B. Submit the resource plan.

    C. Specify which plan will be used by the instance.

    D. Create a pending area.

    E. Create a resource plan.

66. A user session can change from one consumer group to another within a session by using which of the following methods?

    A. DBMS_SESSION.switch_current_consumer_group

    B. DBMS_SESSION.join_new_consumer_group

    C. DBMS_SESSION.old_consumer_group

    D. DBMS_SESSION.jump_current_consumer_group

Answers to Practice Exam I Questions

1. B.   Database configuration

Explanation   The DBA may play a role during the conceptual design stage; however, the DBA must become fully involved in the application development process during the database design and configuration stage. The likelihood of performance problems increases dramatically if the DBA doesn't get involved until user acceptance testing or, even worse, after the database is moved to production.

2. D.   Reduce the number of data blocks cached in memory

Explanation   We would prefer to cache as many data blocks in memory as possible, based on physical constraints because memory access is significantly faster than disk access. Reducing waits, improving the performance of individual SQL statements, improving overall system throughput, and improving cache hit ratios are all valid tuning goals.

3. A.   Long-running full table scans

Explanation   Long-running full table scans are a common tuning problem. The SQL executing the full table scan is not the only session affected, as full table scans cause greater disk I/O, cause greater turnover in the DB buffer cache, and consume too much central processing unit (CPU) memory for the desired results. Each of these side effects can interfere with other sessions. We would rather reuse our SQL cursors, sort in memory instead of to disk, and maintain persistent database connections when they should be used; each of these reduces system load.

4. B.   BACKGROUND_DUMP_DEST

Explanation   Specified in the init.ora file, and also dynamically configurable, the BACKGROUND_DUMP_DEST specifies the location for dump files from server background processes, and also the alert log. The USER_DUMP_DEST is used for user process trace output, and the CORE_DUMP_DEST directory is used for core dumps. The ALERT_DUMP_DEST is not a valid initialization parameter.

5. A.   Accumulator view

Explanation   There are three basic types of dynamic performance views: accumulator, informational, and current state. Accumulator views record occurrences of events, such as a disk read or write. Informational views, such as V$SYSTEM_PARAMETER, show current values for system settings. Current state views, such as V$SYSTEM_EVENT, record system state changes as they occur.

6. A, C.   Ending snapshot ID and beginning snapshot ID

Explanation   The Statspack report must have a beginning and ending snapshot ID; that is used as the key to select the rows that will be used to calculate the differences in values between the times snapshot data was gathered. The start time and end time are derived from the snapshot IDs.

7. E. PERFSTAT, user-defined nonsystem

Explanation The PERFSTAT schema owns the STATSPACK objects. When you install STATSPACK, it will prompt you for a default tablespace name for the PERFSTAT user; SYSTEM is strictly not allowed. You must input a default tablespace for the PERFSTAT user.

8. D. UTLESTAT report.txt

Explanation The Statspack report is meant to replace UTLBSTAT/UTLESTAT and the resulting report.txt. Statspack enables the retention of multiple snapshots of performance statistics in the database, so you can generate a Statspack report to calculate the difference between parameters taken at two different snapshots.

9. A, E. Minimize reparsing and avoid memory fragmentation

Explanation We can minimize reparsing by reusing similar code, usually enforced with bind variables instead of literals. We avoid memory fragmentation by pinning large chunks of PL/SQL code instead of reloading and unloading. Answers B and C are more appropriate for the DB buffer cache, and answer D is incorrect because we don't cache database blocks in the library cache.

10. C, D. GETS and GETMISSES

Explanation The actual formula is (sum(gets) -sum(getmisses))/sum(gets). You should try to keep this ratio in the high 80's or better. The dictionary cache hit ratio is an indicator of how often the correct data dictionary information is found in memory when needed. GETS indicates the number of data dictionary requests; GETMISSES indicates the number of requests that were not met by reading the cache and required an I/O.

11. D. None of the above

Explanation You can use SYS.DBMS_SHARED_POOL.UNKEEP('AP.ANNUAL_RPT') to tell Oracle not to pin the package, but this does not automatically flush the package from the cache. You can remove the package from the cache by flushing the shared pool with the ALTER SYSTEM FLUSH SHARED_POOL command or passively allowing the LRU process to age the package out.

12. A. 10

Explanation The reserved space in the shared pool is made available for large cursors that need to use the shared pool and have the potential to cause fragmentation. We reduce fragmentation by keeping them away from the regular shared pool. The default value is 5, so the next increment should be 10. Fifty percent and 75 percent are both invalid answers, since SHARED_POOL_RESERVED_SIZE cannot be 50 percent or greater of the SHARED_POOL_SIZE.

13. C.   Shared pool

Explanation   In the shared server environment, some of the UGA components are moved into the shared pool. These components reside in the PGA when dedicated servers are used. The session stack space remains in the PGA regardless of server configuration.

14. A, D.   The large pool when it is configured; otherwise, it is the shared pool

Explanation   RMAN will attempt to use the large pool, if it is present, to buffer slave process I/O. If the large pool is not present, RMAN will attempt to use the shared pool to buffer the I/O. If neither can be used, RMAN will use local process memory.

15. D.   Data is not in the cache and the block of data must be read into the cache from a datafile on disk.

Explanation   A buffer cache miss indicates that the data block required for an operation was not found in the buffer cache. The server process then has to perform an I/O to retrieve the block from a data file.

16. B, D.   The server process moves dirty buffers to the dirty list as it searches the LRU list for a free buffer, and the server process signals DBWn to flush the dirty buffers from the buffer cache.

Explanation   These two steps are part of the search operation when a server process is looking for a free buffer in the buffer cache. Dirty blocks are moved onto the dirty buffer list and then written to disk. Answer A indicates that the required block was found in the cache. Answer C is incorrect. DBWn doesn't read dirty buffers from disk; it writes them to disk.

17. B.   The DBWn processes are not keeping up with the number of dirty buffers that must be written to disk.

Explanation   If there's a row in V$SYSTEM_EVENT where the EVENT column equals free buffer wait, this indicates that the DBWn processes aren't writing dirty blocks fast enough to make room for new blocks. It's possible that the I/O system isn't keeping up. Also, a high number may indicate that the buffer cache is too small.

18. B.   SGA_MAX_SIZE

Explanation   The SGA_MAX_SIZE parameter indicates the maximum size that you can dynamically increase the SGA components up to. The buffer cache, redo buffers, the Java pool, large pool, shared pool, and reserved shared pool all must fit inside the SGA_MAX_SIZE limit.

19. B, E.   DB_CACHE_ADVICE parameter and V$DB_CACHE_ADVICE view

Explanation   By setting the DB_CACHE_ADVICE parameter to READY, the system allocates memory structures in the shared pool. Set it to ON, and the system begins collecting statistics that can be used to size the DB buffer cache. The parameter is dynamically configurable. The V$DB_CACHE_ADVICE view will show you estimated physical read reductions if the DB_CACHE_SIZE parameter is increased, or read increases if the value is reduced.

20. D.   The KEEP and RECYCLE buffer pools are separately defined memory areas from the DEFAULT buffer pool.

Explanation   In the previous version of Oracle, the KEEP and RECYCLE were subtracted from the total DB buffer cache size. In Oracle9*i*, the KEEP, RECYCLE, and DEFAULT are all sized separately with the initialization parameters DB_KEEP_CACHE_SIZE, DB_RECYCLE_CACHE_ SIZE, and DB_CACHE_SIZE respectively.

21. B.   At the tablespace create time

Explanation   Automatic segment-space management is designated at the time the tablespace is created by issuing the EXTENT MANAGEMENT LOCAL clause in the CREATE TABLESPACE command.

22. A.   The server process

Explanation   The server process is responsible for writing changes to the redo log buffer. LGWR reads the redo log buffer and writes to the redo log files. DBWn is responsible for writing dirty blocks from the DB buffer cache to the data files.

23. B, C.   The application uses large Java stored procedures, and shared servers are used for the Java components.

Explanation   If the application uses large Java stored procedures, then a large java_pool setting will contribute to system performance. Also, if Java components are used in the database and the database uses shared servers, some of the Java process memory structures are kept in the Java pool. Answers A, D, and E do not directly affect the Java pool requirements.

24. B.   DBWn processes gather, batch, and write dirty buffers independently.

Explanation   As opposed to I/O slaves, which only write the dirty buffers to data files, multiple DBWn processes perform their tasks in parallel with each other. If one DBW0 process is used with multiple I/O slaves, then the DBW0 process still must gather, batch, and then hand off the batch to an available I/O slave for writing.

25. D.   Separate data and indexes into different tablespaces on different physical devices.

Explanation   This is a good practice because generally a table and its associated indexes are usually read in the same time frame by the same server process or processes. Also, if large amounts of DML are on a table, I/O contention can be a major performance problem if the data files and index files are stored on the same physical device.

26. D.   If you do not specify a DEFAULT TEMPORARY TABLESPACE when you create the database, the SYSTEM tablespace will be defined as the temporary tablespace for each new user.

Explanation   The good news is that if you do specify a DEFAULT TEMPORARY TABLESPACE when you create the database, you don't have to worry about applications building temporary segments in your SYSTEM tablespace, or assigning a TEMPORARY tablespace to each user that you create.

27. B, C.   Synchronize the modified data blocks in memory with the datafiles on disk, and ensure database consistency.

Explanation   Checkpoints are used to make sure that we have a consistent point to which we can recover in case of a system crash. To get there, we need to write the dirty blocks from the DB buffer cache to disk, and make sure that redo is available in the redo logs.

28. A, E.   Checkpoints occur too frequently, causing a performance problem, or checkpointing is a performance problem, and database recovery is not an issue.

Explanation   Frequent checkpointing reduces the recovery window in case of a failure, but can also impact performance because of the I/O. If the frequency is too often, and fast recovery time is not as important as good performance while the system is functioning normally, then consider increasing the time between checkpoints.

29. B, D.   Place redo logs on separate RAID-0 disks, and/or larger redo logs improve performance by reducing checkpoint frequency.

Explanation   Since LGWR writes continuously and sequentially to the redo logs, and they're only read in case of recovery (or by LogMiner), it makes sense to put them on the fastest write devices available. RAID-0 provides the fastest write performance of the RAID options. Also, if checkpoint processes are a performance problem, consider reducing the frequency by increasing the size of the redo logs. There is a tradeoff, as longer times between checkpoints can increase the time required to recover.

30. C, D.   Don't use DISTINCT when selecting the primary key, and use the UNION ALL operator instead of UNION.

Explanation   There's no need to use the DISTINCT keyword if you know you're selecting on a primary key; the DISTINCT causes an unnecessary sort. Also, the UNION operator sorts the return set and removes duplicates; if you know there are no duplicates between the queries, then use UNION ALL instead.

31. E.   V$SORT_USAGE and V$SESSION

Explanation   The V$SORT_USAGE view describes user sorting activities, the extents allocated, and the type of segment created. Join the SESSION_ADDR column with the ADDR column of V$SESSION to gather session information.

32. B.   Truncating a table

Explanation   Truncating a table does not require a sort. Each of the others, analyzing a table, building an index, using the DISTINCT keyword, and performing a sort-merge join, requires at least one sort operation.

33. B.   To protect access to memory structures

Explanation   Latches are one of the methods used to protect Oracle structures; locks are the other. Latches have no queueing feature; they do not speed performance, nor do they allow simultaneous or shared access. Latches are exclusive and held briefly.

34. B.   Top 5 Wait Events

Explanation   The Top 5 Wait Events section of the STATSPACK report should be the first place you look to determine the impact of different types of performance problems on your database. If latches are not in the Top 5 Wait Events section, that means that you have some other performance problems to address first.

35. A, B.   Use the NOLOGGING option to reduce the amount of redo log entries for certain operations, and increase the LOG_BUFFER parameter.

Explanation   These two steps reduce contention by reducing the overall workload, and by reducing the frequency of redo log buffer flushing to the redo log files. You cannot increase the number of redo allocation latches, as there is only one. Increasing the size of the redo logs has no effect on the redo log buffer. You cannot increase the number of redo copy latches.

36. A.   The undo segment recovery wait event

Explanation   As the name implies, the event indicates that recovery is taking place following an abend, and PMON is using the undo segment to recover the transaction.

37. D.   Every transaction must be able to update the rollback segment transaction table, and contention can occur if multiple transactions try to update the header block.

Explanation   In an OLTP system, data concurrency among multiple users is expected. The solution to roll back segment header contention increases the number of rollback segments.

38. A, B.   Use relatively small rollback segments, and allocate a rollback segment for every four concurrent transactions.

Explanation   These are general guidelines, not absolute rules. However, OLTP systems generally have lots of small transactions, which would be better matched to lots of small rollback segments. The general rule of four per concurrent transaction is based on an average number of transactions; you may find that a very large number of rollback segments is unmanageable, so increasing the ratio may be necessary.

39. D.   Undo segments are dynamically allocated by the Oracle server, so the DBA doesn't need to add or remove undo segments based on usage.

Explanation   The purpose of automatic undo management is to eliminate the manual configuration of rollback segments, which seems to be a universal problem. Undo segments are brought online or taken offline as load demands change. This reduces the likelihood of application failures and also reduces the workload on the DBA.

40. C.   UNDO_MANAGEMENT

Explanation   Setting UNDO_MANAGEMENT to AUTO in the init.ora file is a requirement to begin using automatic undo management. You can create an UNDO tablespace while the database is running in manual mode, specify the UNDO_MANAGEMENT=AUTO parameter, and also specify the UNDO_TABLESPACE parameter. If you don't specify UNDO_TABLESPACE, Oracle will use the first UNDO tablespace it finds; otherwise, the SYSTEM rollback segment will be used (which is bad).

41. A, C.   A shared (subexclusive) TM lock, and an exclusive TX lock

Explanation   When you delete rows from a table, a shared or subexclusive table lock (TM) is placed on the table. The exclusive TX lock is used to enforce the row locks on the rows that are marked for delete.

42. B, E.   Long-running operations that do not commit regularly and explicitly coded table locks

Explanation   Both contribute to lock contention; an explicitly coded table lock will more than likely prevent other requestors from updating what they need, and long-running operations that do not commit regularly will probably also prevent others from acquiring requested locks.

43. B.   Utllockt.sql can contribute to the contention because it also must acquire locks.

Explanation   Utllockt.sql creates two tables for temporary use while it queries the DBA_LOCKS view and prepares the lock hierarchy report. If the database is suffering badly because of locking problems, don't exacerbate the problem by requesting more locks. Chances are the shared DDL locks requested and acquired when utllockt.sql creates the LOCK_HOLDERS and DBA_LOCKS_TEMP tables will not cause major locking issues.

44. E.   The transaction is aborted and PMON rolls back the uncommitted changes, thus releasing DML locks.

Explanation   Killing the session will cause the transaction to abend. PMON will reconstruct the data files to the before state from the rollback segment entries. All locks held by the transaction will be released.

45. A, B, C.   COMMIT, ROLLBACK, and ROLLBACK to a SAVEPOINT defined prior to the DML lock request

Explanation   An implicit or explicit COMMIT, a ROLLBACK due to transaction abend, or a normal ROLLBACK command will cause a transaction to end and all DML locks to be released. A ROLLBACK to a SAVEPOINT will cause all DML locks requested since the SAVEPOINT to be released.

46. A, C.   The database server is memory constrained, or the database server is on NT or UNIX and supports hundreds of concurrent sessions.

Explanation   Oracle shared server requires less overall memory than the dedicated server environment. Dedicated servers each have their own private process memory, which when summed can be huge on Unix, Linux, or NT. The UGA memory structures could be more efficiently allocated and managed in the SGA if the shared servers were used instead.

47. E.   Increase the number of dispatchers for the protocol.

Explanation   A busy rate greater than 50 percent indicates contention for dispatcher processes. By issuing the command, basically of the form, ALTER SYSTEM SET DISPATCHERS = '(PROTOCOL=TCP)(DISPATCHERS=n)', where n is greater than the current value, you can increase the number of dispatchers available for a protocol, thus reducing potential dispatcher contention issues.

48. B.   Consider reducing SHARED_SERVERS

Explanation   We usually don't think about reducing the number of processes to improve performance, but if there are too many shared servers allocated, then keeping them allocated wastes resources. MAX_SHARED_SERVERS is not an issue in this case because this ceiling value is probably not reached. The SHARED_SERVERS parameter indicates how many shared servers are brought online at system startup and maintained while the system is up. Reducing this number will simply lower the baseline resource consumption.

49. D.   The index keys are rarely updated.

Explanation   With index clusters, updating the index key too frequently will cause increased cluster maintenance. If the keys are rarely updated, then cluster efficiency and performance will be less impacted. Each of the other answers would lead you to not use a cluster.

50. A.   The data is high-cardinality, meaning many distinct values for a relatively small number of rows.

Explanation   Another way to answer this is that B-Tree indexes should be highly selective. If there are few or only one row for each distinct key value, then a B-Tree index provides the best performance. Low-cardinality implies that a bitmap index could be used to improve query performance.

51. B.   Leaf blocks split, causing the physical guess to become invalidated.

Explanation   In an IOT, data rows are stored in the leaf blocks of the index. When rows are added and leaf blocks split, then half the rows go to the new block. For those rows, the physical guess has become invalid, so the primary key index must be used for lookup.

52. B.   Implement a materialized view, and set the QUERY_REWRITE_ENABLED parameter to TRUE.

Explanation   By using a materialized view and enabling a query rewrite, the CBO will automatically rewrite a query to use the materialized view instead of the base tables. No change to the SQL is required. Materialized views are most useful as aggregates in a DSS environment.

53. D.   Some of the space may be wasted until the object grows into the large extents.

Explanation   If you size segments so that they don't extend frequently, then you will have unused space in the extents until the objects become fully populated. This wasted space is not a performance advantage and probably is not a disadvantage either.

54. D.   Empty or underused blocks below the high watermark

Explanation   Empty or underused blocks below the high watermark will be visited by every full table scan, thus degrading performance. If full table scans are used frequently, then consider reorganizing the table to eliminate the empty and underused blocks.

55. E.   Minimize PCTFREE

Explanation   Because we're looking to perform full table scans against traditionally large tables, we want to make sure that we read as many rows as we can for each I/O. By minimizing PCTFREE, we will probably fit more rows into a block (higher block density) and improve the performance of full table scans. PCTUSED is irrelevant because we should not have delete activity in a data warehouse fact table.

56. E.   Deallocate unused blocks.

Explanation   Execute the command ALTER TABLE table_name DEALLOCATE UNUSED. This will deallocate space from the table that is above the high watermark and return it to the free space in the tablespace. There is no impact to the user because the data blocks that have rows in them will not be affected. Each of the other methods mentioned will affect users that need the data.

57. D.   Increase PCTFREE.

Explanation   Row migration occurs because there is not enough free space in the data block where the row was initially placed. Increasing the PCTFREE setting will reduce the likelihood of row migration, but the modification does not change existing data blocks. The new settings apply to all data blocks used by the table, including blocks already allocated and subsequently allocated for the table. However, the blocks already allocated for the table are not immediately reorganized when space usage parameters are altered, but are necessary after the change. Once the PCTFREE is changed, DML will utilize the new setting.

58. C.   Index blocks that contain only a single entry still must be maintained.

Explanation   Sparsely populated index blocks degrade performance. If you have deleted a significant number of rows from the table that the index is on, you should reorganize the index. The general guideline is 20 percent of the rows deleted should trigger the DBA to reorganize the index. D is not correct because you would not have an empty branch node in a B-Tree index (must be balanced). A and B are not correct because index lookups only apply to populated leaf blocks. However, empty blocks are read during index scans, which is another reason why you should rebuild your index after a large number of rows have been deleted.

59. D. V$OBJECT_USAGE

Explanation The V$OBJECT_USAGE view indicates if an index has been used during the monitoring period. You can enable monitoring for an index by using the ALTER INDEX . . . MONITORING USAGE clause. This is not a valid clause when creating the index.

60. A, B, E, F. Evaluates expressions and conditions; transforms statements, if needed; chooses the optimizer approach (rule- or cost-based); and chooses an access path for each table

Explanation These are the functions of the optimizer. The parser is responsible for validating SQL syntax and database references. The SQL execution engine then executes the query.

61. A. Use the CREATE or REPLACE OUTLINE command.

Explanation You can create a named stored outline for one query at a time with the CREATE or REPLACE OUTLINE command. Answers B and C are invalid answers; answer D will create stored outlines with system-generated names for all executed SQL statements.

62. D. Sys=no

Explanation Recursive SQL statements are not written to the formatted output file if you indicate the sys=no parameter and value pair. Each of the other answers are invalid parameter/value pairs.

63. A. If the CBO is used, performance can be adversely affected if statistics are stale.

Explanation The CBO relies heavily on the accuracy of the gathered statistics. If the data is modified or turned over rapidly, then the statistics will become stale rapidly. The solution to stale statistics is to gather new statistics.

64. A. To configure an accurate model of a production environment on a test system

Explanation Many times the statistics gathered in a test environment are not equivalent to those gathered in the production environment because data distribution and volume are not the same. By copying statistics from one environment to the next, you can get a more accurate performance analysis on SQL statements.

65. D, E. Create a pending area and a resource plan.

Explanation If you want to create a resource plan directive, you must first create a resource plan and resource consumer groups. Before you can create a resource plan, you must create a pending area. Validate and submit a resource plan after you create the resource plan directives. Once the plan has been submitted, you can specify that the plan will be used by the instance.

66. A.   DBMS_SESSION.switch_current_consumer_group

Explanation   If the user has been granted the right to switch consumer groups with the DBMS_RESOURCE_MANAGER_PRIVS.grant_switch_consumer_group, then the user can switch the consumer group for the current session by using the DBMS_SESSION package, and the switch_current_consumer_group procedure. The remaining procedures mentioned do not exist.

Practice Exam Two

This is the second of two practice exams, each approximately the same length as the actual OCP exam. The questions are sorted by subject according to the exam content checklist. Answers to the questions begin after the last question. Give yourself 90 minutes to complete this practice exam.

Practice Exam 2 Questions

1. **Which of the following is not considered an important goal of the database configuration phase?**

    A. Tuning disk I/O

    B. Tuning memory

    C. Tuning application code

    D. Tuning CPU utilization

2. **Which of these tuning goals are appropriate for a data warehouse system?**

    A. Subsecond response time

    B. 24x7 availability

    C. High data concurrency

    D. Improve the performance of specific SQL statements

3. **You notice that all SQL statements that have a join condition on one particular table appear to be running very slowly. Which of these steps should you take first to help identify the performance problem?**

    A. Check to see if the database is running the CBO or RBO.

    B. Check file I/O statistics for the data file and tablespace that the table is in.

    C. Verify that there are no missing indexes from the table.

    D. Verify that the table blocks are stored in the buffer cache.

4. **One way to determine the frequency of checkpoints is to set which of the following parameters and then check the alert.log file for messages?**

    A. LOG_SIMULTANEOUS_COPIES

    B. LOG_CHECKPOINT_TIMEOUT

    C. LOG_CHECKPOINTS_TO_ALERT

    D. ALERT_LOG_CHECKPOINTING

5. **Which dynamic performance view is the primary place to look for system performance and resource usage information?**

    A. V$SYSTEM_EVENT

    B. V$PERFORMANCE

    C. V$RESOURCE

    D. V$SYSSTAT

    E. V$SYSTEM_STATS

6. **A Statspack snapshot is a(n) _____ collection of data?**

    A. Ongoing

    B. Dynamic

    C. Point-in-time

    D. Continuously refreshed

7. **Which of these initialization parameters is required for Statspack to collect statistics automatically with spauto.sql?**

    A. DB_JOB_QUEUE_PROCESSES

    B. JOB_QUEUE_INTERVAL

    C. JOB_QUEUE_PROCESSES

    D. STATSPACK_JOB_AUTO

8. **Which of these is an accurate statement about the performance tuning tool?**

    A. OEM Statspack is an optional product, but can help provide expert advice on configuration parameters.

    B. OEM Oracle Expert is an optional product, but can help provide expert advice on configuration parameters.

    C. OEM Oracle Performance Manager is an optional product, but can help provide expert advice on configuration parameters.

    D. OEM Oracle Expert is an optional product, but provides real-time monitoring of database performance.

    E. OEM Utlestat is an optional product, but can help provide expert advice on configuration parameters.

9. **Which of the following columns will you use to calculate the library cache hit ratio? (Choose two.)**

   A. PINS

   B. RELOADS

   C. GETS

   D. GETMISSES

   E. KEEPS

10. **Which of these are true statements about tuning the dictionary cache? (Choose two.)**

    A. The algorithm that manages data in the shared pool prefers to keep library cache data over dictionary cache data.

    B. The algorithm that manages data in the shared pool prefers to keep dictionary cache data over library cache data.

    C. When using sequences, the CACHE option improves dictionary cache performance.

    D. The DBA should perform DDL during peak activity hours.

11. **When is the best time to pin large, frequently used objects in the shared pool?**

    A. Immediately after shutdown

    B. On startup, by specifying the PIN_LARGE_OBJECTS parameter

    C. On startup, by specifying the FAST_LOAD_OBJECTS parameter

    D. Immediately after startup

    E. Immediately prior to their use

12. **You query the V$SHARED_POOL_RESERVED dynamic performance view and notice that REQUEST_FAILURES is greater than zero and increasing. What should you do?**

    A. Reserved pool is too small; increase the SHARED_POOL_RESERVED_SPACE init.ora parameter.

    B. No action is required as long as REQUEST_MISSES is not increasing.

    C. Reserved pool is too small; increase the SHARED_POOL_RESERVED_SIZE init.ora parameter.

    D. REQUEST_FAILURES will always be zero if the shared pool reserved space is configured.

13. **Which of these accurately describes how the UGA is configured?**

   A. In both shared server and dedicated server environments, the session stack space is kept in the SGA.

   B. The sort areas and private SQL areas are included in the SGA in the dedicated server environment.

   C. In both shared server and dedicated server environments, the session stack space is kept in the PGA.

   D. The sort areas and private SQL areas are included in the PGA, regardless of the server configuration.

14. **Which of the following is true when CURSOR_SPACE_FOR_TIME=TRUE ?**

   A. The cursor will be deallocated from memory as soon as all application cursors are closed.

   B. The cursor cannot be deallocated from memory while an application cursor that is associated with it is open.

   C. The cursor management algorithm will attempt to deallocate used cursors from memory while an application cursor that is associated with it is open, if the library cache hit ratio is less than the specified threshold.

   D. The cursor must be deallocated from memory as soon as an application cursor that is associated with it is open.

15. **Which of these statements about processes and the buffer cache is accurate?**

   A. The server processes are responsible for writing dirty data blocks back to disk.

   B. The server processes are responsible for reading dirty data blocks from disk.

   C. The LGWR process writes dirty data blocks to the redo log.

   D. The ARCH process reads dirty data blocks from the buffer cache and writes them to the archive log destination.

   E. The server processes are responsible for reading blocks of data in or into the buffer cache.

16. **When LGWR signals a checkpoint, what happens in the buffer cache?**

   A. DBWn copies dirty data blocks from the LRU list to the write list and writes the data blocks to datafiles.

   B. The reading, batching, and writing of dirty data blocks are parallelized.

C. The server process copies dirty data blocks from the LRU list to the write list, and DBWn writes the data blocks to datafiles.

D. LGWR copies dirty data blocks from the LRU list to the write list, and the server process writes the data blocks to datafiles.

17. **Buffer cache performance is measured by selecting and comparing what information from which dynamic performance views?**

A. Logical and consistent reads from V$SYSSTAT

B. Physical and logical reads from V$SYSSTAT

C. Consistent gets and logical reads from V$BUFFER_POOL

D. Physical and logical reads from V$BUFFER_POOL

18. **The default buffer cache can be expanded dynamically if needed, but only in granule-size increments of? (Choose two.)**

A. 2Mb if the SGA is less than 128Mb

B. 4Mb if the SGA is less than 128Mb

C. 8Mb if the SGA is less than 128Mb

D. 8Mb if the SGA is larger than 128Mb

E. 16Mb if the SGA is larger than 128Mb

19. **You want to allocate the memory structures in the shared pool so that you can begin collecting cache advice information at a later time. What is the correct setting for the DB_CACHE_ADVICE parameter?**

A. FALSE

B. OFF

C. READY

D. ON

E. ALLOCATE

20. **To support tablespaces that use a block size other than the default, the DBA can configure separate buffer caches. Which of the following accurately describes configuring these separate buffer caches?**

A. The init.ora parameter DB_CACHE_BLOCK_SIZE can be set to any one of the values 2, 4, 8, 16, or 32.

B. Set the init.ora parameters DB_nK_CACHE_SIZE to the required cache size where n is some block size in the range of 1 to 32, including the default block size.

   C. Set the init.ora parameters DB_*n*K_CACHE_SIZE to the required cache size where *n* is some block size in the range of 2 to 32, excluding the default block size.

   D. Set the init.ora DB_*n*K_CACHE_SIZE parameters to the required cache size where *n* is some block size in the series 2, 4, 8, 16, and 32, excluding the default block size.

   E. Set the init.ora DB_*n*K_CACHE_SIZE parameters to the required cache size where *n* is some block size in the series 2, 4, 8, 16, and 32, including the default block size.

21. **Contention can occur on the cache buffer LRU chain latch on very busy systems because?**

   A. A latch must be obtained when moving, adding, or removing a buffer from one of the LRU lists.

   B. A latch must be obtained only when removing a buffer from one of the LRU lists.

   C. A latch must be obtained only when adding a buffer to one of the LRU lists.

   D. A latch must be obtained only when moving or removing a buffer from one of the LRU lists.

22. **Which events trigger the log writer process, LGWR, to begin writing from the redo log buffer to the online redo log file or to members of the active redo log group? (Choose three.)**

   A. The redo log file becomes one-third full.

   B. The log buffer becomes one-third full.

   C. A DBWn process tells LGWR to write.

   D. A server process performs a COMMIT or ROLLBACK.

   E. The server process tells ARCH to write.

23. **What does the result of this query indicate?**

```
SELECT * FROM V$SGASTAT
WHERE POOL LIKE '%java%'
```

   A. The number of Java session memory structures allocated

   B. The amount of Java pool free memory and memory in use

   C. The size of each Java session memory structure

24. **Which of the following is true about multiple DBWn processes? (Choose three.)**

    A. Configured by setting the DB_WRITER_PROCESSES initialization parameter to a value greater than 1 and less than or equal to 10.

    B. The processes are named DBW0 through DBW9.

    C. The processes are named DBW1 through DBW10.

    D. They can improve dirty buffer write performance on multiprocessor systems.

    E. The number of processes is dynamically configurable by the DBA.

    F. Oracle automatically allocates DBWn processes as they are needed.

25. **Which of these is an accurate implementation of manual striping?**

    A.
    ```
    CREATE TABLESPACE APP_DATA
    DATAFILE 'D:\ORACLE\ORADATA\OR9I\APP_DATA01.DBF' SIZE 10 M,
             'E:\ORACLE\ORADATA\OR9I\APP_DATA02.DBF' SIZE 10 M,
             'F:\ORACLE\ORADATA\OR9I\APP_DATA03.DBF' SIZE 10 M,
             'G:\ORACLE\ORADATA\OR9I\APP_DATA04.DBF' SIZE 10 M
    /
    ```

    B.
    ```
    CREATE TABLESPACE APP_DATA
    DATAFILE 'E:\ORACLE\ORADATA\OR9I\APP_DATA01.DBF' SIZE 10 M,
             'E:\ORACLE\ORADATA\OR9I\APP_DATA02.DBF' SIZE 10 M,
             'E:\ORACLE\ORADATA\OR9I\APP_DATA03.DBF' SIZE 10 M,
             'E:\ORACLE\ORADATA\OR9I\APP_DATA04.DBF' SIZE 10 M
    /
    ```

    C.
    ```
    CREATE TABLESPACE APP_DATA
    DATAFILE 'D:\ORACLE\ORADATA\OR9I\APP_DATA01.DBF' SIZE 10 M,
             'E:\ORACLE\ORADATA\OR9I\APP_DATA02.DBF' SIZE 10 M,
             'D:\ORACLE\ORADATA\OR9I\APP_DATA03.DBF' SIZE 10 M,
             'E:\ORACLE\ORADATA\OR9I\APP_DATA04.DBF' SIZE 10 M
    USING MANUAL STRIPING
    /
    ```

26. **Which of these views would be used to diagnose tablespace performance problems?**

    A. V$TABLESPACE

    B. V$FILESTAT

C. V$FILE_IO

D. V$TABLESPACE_USAGE

E. DBA_TABLESPACES

27. **Which of these events does not trigger a checkpoint?**

   A. A redo log file switch

   B. Issuing the ALTER SYSTEM CHECKPOINT command

   C. Issuing the ALTER SYSTEM SWITCH LOGFILE command

   D. When LOG_CHECKPOINT_TIMEOUT is reached

   E. When (LOG_CHECKPOINT_INTERVAL* size of LOG_BUFFER) bytes of data is written to the current redo log file

   F. When (LOG_CHECKPOINT_INTERVAL* size of IO OS blocks) bytes of data is written to the current redo log file

28. **Checkpoints occur too frequently, causing performance problems. Which of these are valid solutions? (Choose two.)**

   A. Increase the size of the redo logs.

   B. Decrease the size of the redo logs.

   C. Decrease LOG_CHECKPOINT_TIMEOUT.

   D. Increase LOG_CHECKPOINT_TIMEOUT.

29. **Which of the following would indicate a performance problem with the redo logs?**

   A. The EVENT *log file parallel write* in the V$SYSTEM_EVENT view

   B. The EVENT *redo log file parallel write* in the V$SYSSTAT view

   C. The EVENT *redo log file parallel write* in the V$SYSTEM view

   D. The EVENT *log file parallel write* in the V$SYSSTAT view

30. **Which of the following SQL operations require sort operations? (Choose two.)**

   A. Index creation on ordered data using the NOSORT option

   B. Creating a B-Tree index on ordered data

   C. Creating a function-based index

   D. ANALYZE with the DELETE STATISTICS option

31. **When a process needs to use the defined temporary tablespace for sorting operations, which of the following does it do?**

A. It looks in the PGA sort extent pool (SEP) to determine if there are free extents in the system tablespace.

B. It looks in the SGA sort extent pool (SEP) to determine if there are free extents in the sort segment.

C. It looks in the PGA sort extent pool (SEP) to determine if there are free extents in the sort segment.

32. **Which of the following will reduce the number of disk sorts?**

A. Increasing SORT_AREA_SIZE

B. Decreasing SORT_AREA_RETAINED_SIZE

C. Increasing the SORT_MEMORY_ALLOCATED parameter

D. Altering SORT_AREA_SIZE dynamically, based on available memory within SGA_MAX_SIZE

33. **Which of these statements is true about latches?**

A. One process can scan a memory structure while another process holds a latch on the structure.

B. While one process holds a latch on a memory structure, no other process can access or scan the memory structure.

C. All latches are in one of two modes: scan or lock.

D. Scan latches are used on the LRU lists in the buffer cache.

34. **Which of the following steps should you take to diagnose contention for latches? (Choose two.)**

A. Query V$SYSTEM_EVENT to see if the *latch free* event has a high value for the TIME_WAITED column.

B. Query V$SYSSTAT to see if the *latch free* event has a high value for the TIME_WAITED column.

C. Query V$LATCH and V$LATCH_CHILDREN based on the results of V$SYSTAT.

D. Query V$LATCH and V$LATCH_CHILDREN based on the results of V$SYSTEM_EVENT.

35. **In most cases, the DBA can tune latches and minimize latch contention by configuring which latch parameters?**

    A. DB_LATCH_COUNT

    B. Setting DB_LATCH_MONITORING=AUTO

    C. Setting DB_LATCH_CONTENTION=SAFE

    D. The DBA doesn't tune latches; instead, the DBA tunes the processes that contribute to latch contention.

    E. By setting the values for individual problem latches in the init.ora file

36. **V$ROLLSTAT can be used to determine?**

    A. The performance characteristics of all undo segments defined in the database.

    B. The performance characteristics of all manually managed redo segments defined in the database only.

    C. The performance characteristics of all undo segments currently online in the database.

    D. The performance characteristics of all manually configured rollback segments defined in the database only.

    E. Only the STATUS of an undo segment is ONLINE or OFFLINE.

37. **Which of the following are not tuning goals for undo segment management?**

    A. Transactions should never wait for access to undo segments.

    B. Undo segments should never extend during normal operation.

    C. No transaction should ever run out of undo segment space.

    D. Undo segments should never wrap during normal operation.

    E. Readers should always see the read-consistent images they need.

38. **On large DSS systems where the transactions are relatively few and large, which approach should you use to define the number and size of rollback segments?**

    A. Fewer and smaller rollback segments

    B. Larger and more rollback segments

    C. Smaller and more rollback segments

    D. Larger and fewer rollback segments

39. **The DBA reduces the likelihood of application failure due to ORA-01555 errors by setting which parameters?**

   A. UNDO_RETENTION and REDO_RETENTION

   B. UNDO_RETENTION and UNDO_SUPPRESS_MESSAGES

   C. UNDO_RETENTION and UNDO_SUPPRESS_ERRORS

   D. UNDO_RETENTION and UNDO_SPACE_MANAGEMENT

   E. REDO_RETENTION

40. **What happens when the DBA issues the ALTER SYSTEM SET UNDO_TABLESPACE=<another_undo_tablespace> command? (Choose two.)**

   A. All new transactions will begin using the newly activated undo tablespace.

   B. Existing transactions will be forced to roll back; however, they will automatically restart in the newly activated tablespace, transparent to the end user.

   C. Existing transactions will continue to use the previous tablespace for read consistency, but use the new tablespace for undo segment updates.

   D. Existing transactions will continue to use the previous tablespace until they are complete.

41. **The DBA can modify the default locking mechanism by setting which init.ora parameter?**

   A. ROW_LOCKING=ROW

   B. ROW_LOCKING=TABLE

   C. ROW_LOCKING=DEFAULT

   D. ROW_LOCKING=INTENT

42. **When users inform the DBA that a resource is unavailable or that queries are not responding, which views should the DBA use to determine the locking and waiting sessions? (Choose two.)**

   A. DBA_LOCKS_HELD

   B. DBA_BLOCKERS

   C. V$SESSIONS_WAITING

   D. V$BLOCK_AND_WAIT

   E. DBA_WAITERS

43. **What are the results of this query? (Choose all that apply.)**

```
SELECT * FROM v$lock
MINUS
SELECT * FROM v$enqueue_lock
/
```

   A. All the DDL locks on the system

   B. All user locks on the system

   C. All DML locks on the system

   D. Always 0 rows, since the views are synonymous

44. **Querying the DBA_WAITERS view will give us which vital piece of information that we can use to resolve lock contention in an emergency?**

   A. BLOCKING_SESSION

   B. WAITING_SESSION

   C. SESSION_SID

   D. HOLDING_SESSION

45. **Which of these is not a condition that would lead to a deadlock in the current session?**

   A. Another session is holding a lock on a resource in an incompatible mode.

   B. The resource is required by the current session.

   C. The other session is waiting for a resource that is also requested by a third session.

   D. The other session is waiting for a resource that is locked in an incompatible mode by the current session.

46. **Which of the following describes features that enable scalability for users in an Oracle shared server environment? (Choose two.)**

   A. Remote Dispatcher Management enables web-based users to dynamically allocate additional dispatcher resources based on load balancing algorithms.

   B. Oracle Remote Sensing enables DBAs to switch users from a dedicated server to a shared server and back based on Resource Manager connection groups.

   C. Oracle Connection Manager enables multiple client network sessions to be multiplexed through a single network connection to a database.

D. Connection pooling enables you to reduce the number of physical network connections to a dispatcher.

E. Dedicated servers enable systems to scale even when memory is constrained.

47. **Which of these views can you use to monitor usage of Oracle shared server processes?**

A. V$SHARED_SERVER_MONITOR

B. V$SHARED_SERVERS

C. V$SHARED_PROCESSES

D. V$SS_PROCESSES

48. **When determining the optimal configuration for dispatchers by querying the V$DISPATCHER_RATE view, which of the following is not true?**

A. If the CUR_ column values are near their AVG_ counterparts and below the MAX_ values, and response time is good, then you probably have a good number of dispatchers allocated.

B. If, under system load, you see that CUR_ is close to or equal to MAX_, then consider increasing the number of dispatchers.

C. If CUR_ and AVG_ are consistently well below MAX_, then consider reducing the number of dispatchers.

D. If, under system load, you see that CUR_ is close to or equal to MAX_, then consider decreasing the number of dispatchers.

49. **An index-organized table (IOT) might be the best storage structure to implement, given which of the following conditions? (Choose two.)**

A. All queries will use full table scans on the IOT.

B. Rows are frequently deleted and updated to expand character columns.

C. All queries will use the primary key for lookup.

D. Rows are frequently added, but not updated or deleted.

E. There is no primary key, but a unique index is used to enforce unique entries.

50. **To use a function-based index on a table, which of the following must occur? (Choose three.)**

A. The table must be analyzed.

B. The RBO must be used.

    C. You must have a query rewrite system privilege.

    D. A query rewrite must be enabled for the session or instance.

    E. The function-based index must be on a materialized view.

51. **Which of the following is true about the physical guess on an IOT?**

    A. The physical guess is the same thing as the physical ROWID on heap-organized tables.

    B. Following a failed or incorrect guess, access is via the UROWID.

    C. Following a failed or incorrect guess, access is via the primary key.

    D. Following a failed or incorrect guess, access is via the secondary key.

    E. The physical guess is updated when a block splits.

52. **In a materialized view, which of these refresh modes may be chosen as a performance-improving alternative?**

    A. COMPLETE

    B. MANUAL

    C. AUTOMATIC

    D. FAST

    E. DIFFERENTIAL

53. **Which of these are performance advantages of using a small block size? (Choose two.)**

    A. Reduced block contention.

    B. Random access is relatively more efficient.

    C. A small number of rows per block.

    D. Fewer fetches are required to perform full table scans.

    E. Good for sequential access.

54. **Which of these are not true about the high watermark of a data segment? (Choose two.)**

    A. Recorded in the header block of the segment

    B. Reset by a DELETE statement

    C. Reset by a TRUNCATE statement

    D. Recorded in the data dictionary

55. **Which two conditions are necessary for free space in a block to be coalesced automatically? (Choose two.)**

   A. Free space is not coalesced automatically; it must be done manually.

   B. Free space is coalesced automatically on instance startup.

   C. An INSERT or UPDATE statement attempts to update a block that has enough free space.

   D. A DELETE statement is issued, and there are noncontiguous rows below the PCTFREE mark.

   E. The free space in the block is fragmented such that no new rows can fit into contiguous free space.

56. **You can recover space from a sparsely populated table by using the ALTER TABLE MOVE command, but what are the negative side effects? (Choose two.)**

   A. All indexes are dropped because the physical ROWID no longer exists.

   B. All indexes become invalidated because the physical ROWID of each row in the table changes.

   C. The rows are sorted and coalesced, but no new storage parameters are allowed.

   D. The indexes must be rebuilt before they can be used.

   E. The indexes must be dropped before the move statement will succeed.

57. **Which of the following statements accurately describes the chaining and migration of Oracle blocks? (Choose two.)**

   A. Chaining occurs when a row is too large to fit into a single data block.

   B. Chaining occurs when a row is updated and will not fit back into the block where its physical ROWID points to.

   C. Migration occurs when a row is too large to fit into a single data block.

   D. Migration occurs when a row is updated and will no longer fit back into the block where its physical ROWID points to, but will fit into another data block.

   E. The physical ROWID changes to the new block in both chaining and migration.

   F. Chaining invalidates indexes on the rows that move to another data block.

58. **Index reorganization is essential for volatile indexes because? (Choose three.)**

   A. Deleted row entries are reused based on index key value.

   B. Deleted row entries are reused based on the PCTUSED block parameter.

   C. Delete activity will degrade the index performance.

   D. Modified index keys are moved to less sparse blocks.

   E. Leaf blocks with only one entry are still maintained.

59. **To start and stop monitoring an index to determine usage, use which ALTER INDEX command clause?**

   A. START MONITORING USAGE/STOP MONITORING USAGE

   B. MONITORING USAGE/NOMONITORING USAGE

   C. START MONITORING/STOP MONITORING

   D. START USAGE/STOP USAGE

60. **The rule-based optimizer (RBO) relies on which of the following? (Choose three.)**

   A. The syntax of the SQL statements

   B. Data dictionary information about the structure of the referenced objects

   C. Its set of heuristics to determine which plan will work best

   D. Statistics gathered by the DBMS_STATS package

61. **To begin using a stored outline for the instance, what should you do?**

   A. Set init.ora parameter USE_STORED_OUTLINES=*category_name*.

   B. Execute the ALTER DATABASE USE_STORED_OUTLINES=*category_name* command.

   C. Execute the ALTER SYSTEM USE_STORED_OUTLINES=*category_name* command.

   D. Execute the procedure DBMS_OUTLN.USE_SYSTEM_STORED_OUTLINES('*category_name*').

62. **The EXPLAIN PLAN command, the Autotrace feature in SQL*Plus, and the TKPROF utility each have the following in common?**

    A. A plan table is required for each, and for TKPROF when explain=username/password.

    B. They each run within a SQL*Plus session.

    C. The PLAN_TABLE must exist for each in all conditions.

    D. Each requires the DBA or Unix administrator to execute.

    E. Each requires the explain_table in the schema of the SQL originator.

63. **In which of these cases should statistics be run on database schema objects? (Choose two.)**

    A. The RBO is used exclusively by setting OPTIMIZER_MODE=TRUE.

    B. OPTIMIZER_MODE=CHOOSE

    C. OPTIMIZER_MODE=COST

    D. OPTIMIZER_MODE=ALL_ROWS

    E. OPTIMIZER_MODE=RULE

64. **Which of these tools are used to copy statistics between databases? (Choose three.)**

    A. SQL*Plus copy

    B. DBMS_JOB

    C. spauto.sql

    D. DBMS_STATS

    E. export

    F. import

    G. DBMS_COPY

    H. A database link

65. **Which of the following Resource Manager rules must be validated with the DBMS_RESOURCE_MANAGER.validate_pending_area procedure? (Choose three.)**

    A. No subplan loops.

    B. Each subplan must reference the top-level plan's consumer group.

   C. The plan must have a directive for SYSTEM_GROUP.

   D. The plan must have a directive for SYS_GROUP.

   E. The plan must have a directive for OTHER_GROUPS.

   F. Referenced subplans and/or consumer groups must exist.

66. **Which of the following are true about Resource Manager consumer groups? (Choose two.)**

   A. A user can only belong to one consumer group.

   B. Resource consumer groups are groups of users with similar resource requirements.

   C. A user can belong to many consumer groups, but only one group at a time can be active for a session.

   D. A user can only switch between OTHER_GROUPS and LOW_GROUP, if the privilege is granted with the GRANT RESOURCE MANAGER PRIV command.

Answers to Practice Exam 2 Questions

1. C.   Tuning application code

Explanation   At the database configuration phase of the application design process, we are mostly concerned with tuning memory, I/O, and CPU. The application code should have already been tuned in the development and test environments. There are usually user acceptance testing and post-implementation opportunities to tune the application SQL code.

2. D.   Improve the performance of specific SQL statements

Explanation   In a data warehouse system, specific SQL statement performance, accuracy, and availability are key tuning issues. Subsecond response times, 24x7 availability, and high data concurrency are usually requirements for an OLTP system.

3. C.   Verify that there are no missing indexes from the table.

Explanation   The problem statement clearly identifies at least one possible problem; that is the missing index on the columns in the join condition. If all queries were experiencing performance problems, then we might first verify that there are recent statistics on tables if the CBO is used. If objects in a specific tablespace were seen as performance constrained, we would check the file I/O statistics for the files in the tablespace.

4. C.   LOG_CHECKPOINTS_TO_ALERT

Explanation   Setting LOG_CHECKPOINTS_TO_ALERT causes the checkpoint process to write a message to the alert log for the instance. You can then compare the timestamp of each message to determine checkpoint frequency. Answer D is not a valid parameter. LOG_SIMULTANEOUS_COPIES was used to configure redo copy latches prior to Oracle8*i* and is no longer supported. LOG_CHECKPOINT_ TIMEOUT specifies the maximum amount of time in seconds a dirty buffer can remain in the database buffer cache before DBWn must write it to disk.

5. D.   V$SYSSTAT

Explanation   System performance and resource usage stats are kept in the V$SYSSTAT view. Hit ratios, cumulative logons, total CPU usage, parse counts, total physical reads and writes, and in-memory and to-disk sorts are just a few of the vital statistics that are available in this view. Wait events are recorded in the V$SYSTEM_EVENT view; V$PERFORMANCE, V$RESOURCE, and V$SYSTEM_ STATS are fictitious.

6. C.   Point-in-time

Explanation   Each snapshot, executed with the stored procedure STATSPACK.snap, is a point-in-time gathering of cumulative and current statistics in the database. The snapshot is not continuously refreshed, ongoing, or a dynamic collection of data. Each snapshot reads the instance views and populates the PERFSTAT tables with current point-in-time data.

7. C.   JOB_QUEUE_PROCESSES

Explanation   The spauto.sql script performs automatic statistics gathering for STATSPACK. To run, it must use the DBMS_JOB package; for jobs to run, the JOB_QUEUE_PROCESSES value must be 1 or greater. Each of the other answers are invalid parameters.

8. B.   OEM Oracle Expert is an optional product, but can help provide expert advice on configuration parameters.

Explanation   OEM Oracle Expert, which is an optional product (not part of the base OEM installation or pricing model), provides expert advice for configuring the database. Statspack is not an optional product, UTLESTAT is not optional and is not part of OEM (but can be launched from OEM), OEM Performance Manager does not provide expert configuration advice (Oracle Expert does), and Oracle Expert is not used for real-time monitoring (Performance Manager is).

9. A, B.   PINS and RELOADS

Explanation   Here's the formula for the library cache hit ratio, selected from V$LIBRARYCACHE: ((PINS-RELOADS)/PINS)*100. The library cache hit ratio should be greater than 90 percent.

10. B, C.   The algorithm that manages data in the shared pool prefers to keep dictionary cache data over library cache data, and when using sequences, the CACHE option improves dictionary cache performance.

Explanation   It is important to remember that dictionary cache misses are more expensive than library cache misses, so the algorithm that manages the shared pool prefers to keep objects in the dictionary cache. If the library cache statistics look good, that means the library cache is sized appropriately and infers that the dictionary cache is sized appropriately. If you do not use the CACHE option on a sequence, each call to NEXTVAL creates a get in the dc_sequences dictionary cache item. Also, the DBA should perform DDL during off-peak hours.

11. D.   Immediately after startup

Explanation   We can eliminate answers A, B, and C; we cannot pin objects when the database is down, and the two parameters mentioned are not valid init.ora parameters. So that leaves D or E; if we choose to pin large objects immediately prior to their use, then the first process that accesses the object will take a performance hit. To avoid this hit, and possible fragmentation, load the large frequently used objects immediately after startup.

> **12.** C. Reserved pool is too small; increase the SHARED_POOL_RESERVED_SIZE init.ora parameter.

Explanation The REQUEST_FAILURES column indicates the number of times the reserved list did not have a free piece of memory to satisfy the request and started flushing objects from the LRU list. To remedy this, increase the size of the shared pool reserved space by increasing the SHARED_POOL_RESERVED_SIZE parameter.

> **13.** C. In both shared server and dedicated server environments, the session stack space is kept in the PGA.

Explanation By definition, the session stack space is kept in the PGA, whether the process memory is assigned to a shared server or a dedicated server. The sort areas and private SQL areas are stored in the PGA for dedicated servers, and in the SGA for shared servers.

> **14.** B. The cursor cannot be deallocated from memory while an application cursor that is associated with it is open.

Explanation Setting CURSOR_SPACE_FOR_TIME=TRUE indicates that the cursor will not be deallocated from memory as long as the application cursor is open. Only set this to TRUE if you have no library cache misses; the library cache hit ratio is almost 100 percent. Each of the other statements is an incorrect assessment of how the setting influences cursor retention.

> **15.** E. The server processes are responsible for reading blocks of data in or into the buffer cache.

Explanation Server processes look for a data block in the buffer cache. If it is found, we have a hit. If not, the server process will scan for dirty blocks that can be moved out of the cache and be replaced by the block that needs to be read from disk. Once the free block is made available, the server process reads the required block from disk and places it in the free block in the buffer cache. DBWn writes blocks to disk; LGWR writes log buffer entries into the redo log files, and the ARCH process reads the redo log files and writes them to the archived redo log file destinations.

> **16.** A. DBWn copies dirty blocks from the LRU list to the write list and writes the data blocks to datafiles.

Explanation One of the primary functions of the checkpoint is to synchronize dirty blocks in memory with blocks on disk. LGWR signals the checkpoint, and DBWn copies the dirty blocks from the LRU list to the write list and then writes them to disk. The reading, batching, and writing of dirty blocks is parallelized when we use multiple DBW processes. In answers C and D, we have obfuscated the responsibilities.

17. B.   Physical and logical reads from V$SYSSTAT

Explanation   The formula is $1 - ((physical\ reads - physical\ reads\ direct - physical\ reads\ direct\ (lob))/session\ logical\ reads)$. Each of these values is obtained from the VALUE column of V$SYSSTAT. We are measuring the hit ratio as the ratio of logical to physical reads. Logical reads are on a buffer cache block. Physical reads, of course, result in an I/O operation against a disk device. The V$BUFFER_POOL view is legitimate, but consistent gets, logical reads, and physical reads are not accumulated in this view.

18. B, E.   4Mb if the SGA is less than 128Mb, and 16Mb if the SGA is larger than 128Mb

Explanation   The granule is defined as a unit of allocation in the dynamic SGA. When an SGA component (DB buffer cache, shared pool) is expanded or shrunk, it must be in granule increments. The minimum number of granules allocated is 1 for each of the SGA structures (buffer cache, shared pool, and fixed SGA). The maximum number of granules is determined by MAX_SGA_SIZE, which is measured in bytes.

19. C.   READY

Explanation   Setting DB_CACHE_ADVICE to READY allocates the memory structures in the shared pool to collect the statistics needed to populate the V$DB_CACHE_ADVICE view. The memory structures, and the view, are not populated with data until the DB_CACHE_ADVICE is set to ON, which signals the collection of buffer cache advice statistics. Setting the parameter to OFF stops collecting data and deallocates the shared pool memory structures.

20. D.   Set the init.ora DB_*n*K_CACHE_SIZE parameters to the required cache size where *n* is some block size in the series 2, 4, 8, 16, and 32, excluding the default block size.

Explanation   The DBA can create separate buffer caches based on the nondefault block sizes. Acceptable block size values are 2, 4, 8, 16, and 32, excluding the value for DB_BLOCK_SIZE, which is the default database block size and the block size for the system tablespace.

21. A.   A latch must be obtained when moving, adding, or removing a buffer from one of the LRU lists.

Explanation   Any activity that affects the status of a block of data in the DB buffer cache requires obtaining a LRU latch. The cache buffer LRU chain latch is responsible for protecting the LRU list.

22. B, C, and D.   If the log buffer becomes one-third full, DBWn tells LGWR to write, or a server process performs a COMMIT or ROLLBACK

Explanation   By definition, these are the events that trigger LGWR to write all the log buffer entries to the redo log file or files. The server processes do not tell ARCH to write to the redo logs; ARCH is responsible for writing to the archived redo logs.

23. B.   The amount of Java pool free memory and memory in use

Explanation   V$SGASTAT has two entries for the Java pool: free memory and memory in use. The sum of these two values is equal to the java_pool_size.

24. A, B, D.   Configured by setting the DB_WRITER_PROCESSES initialization parameter to a value greater than 1 and less than or equal to 10, the processes are named DBW0 through DBW9, and they can improve dirty buffer write performance on multiprocessor systems.

Explanation   The DB_WRITER_PROCESSES, default value 1, and values 1 through 10 set the number of DBW processes. If 1, then only the DBW0 process will be used. The valid processes are DBW0 through DBW9. Multiple DBW processes can reduce write contention due to the DBW0 process being overworked. The number of processes is set in the init.ora parameter and is not dynamically configurable or automatically adjusted.

25. A.

Explanation   The CREATE TABLESPACE command specifically creates datafiles of equal size on four separate disk devices. This is a good example of manual striping. Answer B is incorrect because all four data files are created on the same device. Answer C is incorrect because the MANUAL STRIPING clause is invalid.

26. B.   V$FILESTAT.

Explanation   The V$FILESTAT view contains accumulated data about the number of physical reads and writes, blocks read and written, and the total read and write time. These statistics can be used to determine hot spots or disks that are much more active than others, and to evaluate the average read and write time for the files in a tablespace. The information can then be used to determine if files need to be moved to different disk drives.

27. E.   When (LOG_CHECKPOINT_INTERVAL* size of LOG_BUFFER) bytes of data is written to the current redo log file

Explanation   A checkpoint is triggered when there is a redo log file switch, when the ALTER SYSTEM CHECKPOINT or ALTER SYSTEM SWITCH LOGFILE command is entered, or when LOG_CHECKPOINT_TIMEOUT is reached. The remaining checkpoint trigger is when the bytes of data written to the current redo log file are equal to the product of LOG_CHECKPOINT_INTERVAL and the OS block size.

28. A, D.   Increase the size of the redo logs or increase LOG_CHECKPOINT_TIMEOUT.

Explanation   Increasing the size of the redo logs will reduce the frequency of checkpoints caused by a log switch, called *complete* checkpoints. Increasing the LOG_CHECKPOINT_TIMEOUT will also reduce the number of *incremental* checkpoints.

29. A.   The EVENT *log file parallel write* in the V$SYSTEM_EVENT view

Explanation   The wait event *log file parallel write* indicates that there may be an I/O performance issue. Each of the other answers uses an incorrect wait event or an incorrectly specified dynamic performance view.

30. B, C.   Creating a B-Tree index on ordered data or creating a function-based index

Explanation   Creating a B-Tree index on sorted data will still cause a sorting operation because the NOSORT parameter was not specified. The sort is required to get the key values into the correct order in the B-Tree. Function-based indexes also require a sort because correct order must be built into the B-Tree.

31. B.   It looks in the SGA sort extent pool (SEP) to determine if there are free extents in the sort segment.

Explanation   A sort segment is created when the first sort operation uses the tablespace and is dropped when the database is closed. The sort segment grows as needed and is made up of extents that can be used by different sort operations. When a process needs sort space, it looks in the SGA sort extent pool (SEP) to determine if there are free extents in the sort segment.

32. A.   Increasing SORT_AREA_SIZE

Explanation   The value of SORT_AREA_SIZE determines the amount of memory that can be used for sorting operations; a lower value increases the likelihood that sorting will overflow the area and require disk extents. Increasing the size of the sort area will reduce free memory available to the remaining processes on the database server, but will also reduce the likelihood that sort operations will require disk space allocated from the temporary tablespace. SORT_AREA_SIZE, if too large, can contribute to paging and swapping.

33. B.   While one process holds a latch on a memory structure, no other process can access or scan the memory structure.

Explanation   Latches, with only a few exceptions, are exclusive. The structure of a latch is simple; it does not support queueing or sharing. The idea is that a latch will only be held briefly. Scanning a memory structure requires a latch because otherwise the memory structure could be changed by another process, invalidating the first scan.

34. A, D.   Query V$SYSTEM_EVENT to see if the *latch free* event has a high value for the TIME_WAITED column, and query V$LATCH and V$LATCH_CHILDREN based on the results of V$SYSTEM_EVENT.

Explanation   The first place to start is in the V$SYSTEM_EVENT view, looking for *latch free* waits. If the TIME_WAITED column has a high value, then query the V$LATCH and V$LATCH_CHILDREN, if needed, to investigate the specific latch or child latch that is contributing the most to the time waited. Answers B and C specify an incorrect dynamic performance view for wait events.

35. D.   The DBA doesn't tune latches; instead, the DBA tunes the processes that contribute to latch contention.

Explanation   In Oracle9*i*, no parameters directly tune latches. Latch contention is evidence that some other application code or database parameter needs to be tuned. Hidden parameters (_*) can be used to configure some latches, but they are usually unsupported unless you have been specifically instructed to use them by Oracle Support.

36. C.   The performance characteristics of all undo segments currently online in the database

Explanation   The V$ROLLSTAT view is used for either manually or automatically configured undo segments, but not both at the same time because the database will only support one or the other. V$ROLLSTAT is limited to one row for each undo segment that is currently online.

37. D.   Undo segments should never wrap during normal operation.

Explanation   Wrapping is expected and a normal operation. Each of the other answers are valid undo tuning goals. Transactions should never wait for access to undo segments and they should never run out of undo space; undo segments should not dynamically extend, and readers should always see the read-consistent view that they require for their application. Unnecessary waits can be remedied with more undo segments. Space issues can usually be resolved by adding more space to the undo tablespace. Dynamic extension, in a manually configured undo environment, is controlled by properly setting the extent size and optimal number of extents. Read-consistency issues can usually be resolved by adding more space to rollback segments, adding more rollback segments, or by increasing the UNDO_RETENTION parameter.

38. D. Larger and fewer rollback segments

Explanation Since there are few concurrent transactions, there are fewer demands on rollback segment header blocks, which should result in us choosing to create fewer rollback segments. However, transactions will probably be much larger and run longer, so we should increase the size of the rollback segments appropriate. Smaller and more rollback segments apply to OLTP standard operations. Of course, there will be a mix for hybrid systems.

39. C. UNDO_RETENTION and UNDO_SUPRESS_ERRORS

Explanation When using automatic undo management, the initialization parameter UNDO_RETENTION specifies how long to keep a read-consistent block in the undo segment after the transaction completes. REDO_RETENTION, UNDO_SPACE_MANAGEMENT, and UNDO_SUPPRESS_MESSAGES are not valid parameters; therefore, you can eliminate answers A, B, D, and E. That leaves answer C as the only valid answer.

40. A, D. All new transactions will begin using the newly activated undo tablespace, and existing transactions will continue to use the previous tablespace until they are complete.

Explanation The DBA can change the current undo tablespace to a new one, but existing transactions will continue to use the tablespace that they were using when the transaction started. So although only one tablespace can be the active tablespace, it is possible to have active undo segments in multiple tablespaces. This is true while the old UNDO tablespace has a setting of OFFLINE PENDING. Once it goes OFFLINE, access to the old UNDO tablespace is not permitted.

41. D. ROW_LOCKING=INTENT

Explanation The DBA can modify the default locking mechanism by setting the ROW_LOCKING initialization parameter. The default value is ALWAYS; this causes default locking at the row level during DML statements. This is the least restrictive. You can also specify DEFAULT, which is synonymous with ALWAYS. Setting the value to INTENT causes default locking at the table level, except for SELECT. . .FOR UPDATE statements, which cause row-level locking.

42. B, E. DBA_BLOCKERS and DBA_WAITERS

Explanation The DBA_BLOCKERS and DBA_WAITERS views are used to determine who is causing lock contention, and who is waiting on lock requests. DBA_LOCKS can be used, but the DBA_BLOCKERS and DBA_WAITERS views are predefined to display the basic information needed for problem resolution. V$SESSIONS_WAITING and V$BLOCK_AND_WAIT are not valid views.

43. B, C.   All user locks and DML locks on the system

Explanation   The V$LOCK view shows all locks on the system. The V$ENQUEUE_LOCK view has the same columns as V$LOCK, except it displays all locks owned by enqueue state objects only. The difference is user and DML locks.

44. D.   HOLDING_SESSION

Explanation   The DBA_WAITERS view also indicates the lock mode held and the mode requested by the WAITING_SESSION. We can use the HOLDING_SESSION along with information from V$SESSION to issue the ALTER SYSTEM KILL SESSION command.

45. C.   The other session is waiting for a resource that is also requested by a third session.

Explanation   The conditions A, B, and D are the prerequisite conditions that make a deadlock happen. Multiple users can wait for the same resource without causing a deadlock. However, multiple users could also be involved in a deadlock if the correct (but unlikely) conditions occur.

46. C, D.   Oracle Connection Manager enables multiple client network sessions to be multiplexed through a single network connection to a database, and connection pooling enables you to reduce the number of physical network connections to a dispatcher.

Explanation   Answers A and B are not Oracle products, but I think they should consider developing them. Answer E is a direct contradiction to what we know about dedicated servers and shared servers. Both Connection Manager and connection pooling are specified when a dispatcher is defined.

47. A.   V$SHARED_SERVER_MONITOR

Explanation   The V$SHARED_SERVER_MONITOR view is a good starting point for monitoring shared server processes. It indicates general statistics for shared server processes and high watermarks. Columns include MAXIMUM_CONNECTIONS, MAXIMUM_SERVERS, MAXIMUM_SESSIONS, SERVERS_STARTED, SERVERS_TERMINATED, and SERVERS_HIGHWATER.

48. D.   If, under system load, you see that CUR_ is close to or equal to MAX_, then consider decreasing the number of dispatchers.

Explanation   Each of the other answers is an approach you could use to tune the number of dispatchers. The basic concept that if your dispatcher load is close to MAX_, then you should consider adding more dispatchers.

49. C, D. All queries will use the primary key for lookup, and rows are frequently added but not updated or deleted.

Explanation   IOTs are best suited for physical guess lookups, based on the primary key value. An IOT is also a good choice when there is minimal maintenance required on the index structure. Too many deletes can cause performance problems due to sparsely populated blocks. An IOT must have a primary key.

50. A, C, D. The table must be analyzed, you must have a query rewrite privilege, and a query rewrite must be enabled for the session or instance.

Explanation   A function-based index relies on statistics gathered for the CBO. Also, the query will be rewritten by the optimizer to use the function or expression, but only if the query rewrite parameters have been set.

51. C. Following a failed or incorrect guess, access is via the primary key.

Explanation   The physical guess is a ROWID guess of the actual location of a row in the IOT. If, for whatever reason, a row moves in an IOT, the physical guess becomes invalid. The primary key is then used for IOT lookup; the primary key is slower.

52. D. FAST

Explanation   The FAST refresh mode only sends individual changes to the target materialized view; this is usually significantly faster than a COMPLETE refresh, which resends all rows in the master table. Manual and automatic describe modes used to schedule the refresh jobs. DIFFERENTIAL is something I just made up.

53. A, B. Reduce block contention and random access becomes more efficient.

Explanation   A small block size means that you'll get fewer rows into a block. However, random access improves because they don't have to read as much erroneous information.

54. B, D. Reset by a DELETE statement, or recorded in the data dictionary

Explanation   The high watermark indicates the block in the table for which all blocks below it have been used, and all blocks above it have not been used; it is recorded in the segment header block. The TRUNCATE command resets the high watermark to the minimum. The DELETE command does not reset the high watermark.

55. C, E. An INSERT or UPDATE statement attempts to update a block that has enough free space, and the free space in the block is fragmented such that no new rows can fit into contiguous free space.

Explanation   Free space within a data block is not coalesced manually; it is not coalesced automatically when rows are deleted, or when the instance starts up. Free space within a block is coalesced when there is enough free space (when the block is on the free list), an INSERT or UPDATE occurs, and the free space within the block is fragmented such that the INSERT or UPDATE cannot occur in the block unless coalescing occurs.

> **56.** B, D.   All indexes become invalidated because the physical ROWID of each row in the table changes, and the indexes must be rebuilt before they can be used.

Explanation   When the table is moved, indexes are invalidated because the ROWID for each index entry is not automatically converted to the new physical ROWID. Therefore, we must rebuild an index before it can be used. Check the STATUS column in DBA_INDEXES to verify.

> **57.** A, D.   Chaining occurs when a row is too large to fit into a single data block, and migration occurs when a row is updated and will no longer fit back into the block where its physical ROWID points to, but will into another data block.

Explanation   Chaining and migration are two distinctly different events that can occur to rows of data in a data block. An INSERT or UPDATE can cause chaining usually if the row is very large. Migration occurs when a row is updated, and the row will not fit back into the block. If Oracle finds enough free space and has to move the row to another block, a small piece of the row remains in the original block, so the ROWID doesn't change. Neither row chaining nor migration requires index rebuilds.

> **58.** A, C, E.   Deleted row entries are reused based on index key value, delete activity will degrade index performance, and leaf blocks with only one entry are still maintained.

Explanation   Compared to an index with no empty row slots, an index with deleted rows will have an overall reduction in effectiveness because more block reads will be required to process the same number of rows. When a row is deleted, a new entry into the index will only replace it if the index key value is identical; therefore, there is the potential that deleted row entries will not be reused. Each block in the index is maintained, even if there is only one row in it.

> **59.** B.   MONITORING USAGE/MONITORING USAGE

Explanation   The MONITORING USAGE clause is used to both start and stop monitoring index usage. The V$OBJECT_USAGE view will indicate if the index was used during the monitoring period.

60. A, B, C.   The syntax of the SQL statements, data dictionary information about the structure of the referenced objects, and its set of heuristics to determine which plan will work best

Explanation   The RBO does not use statistics to determine execution plans; it uses the syntax of the SQL statement, uses dictionary information about the structure of each object referenced in the statement, and applies a set of rules to determine optimal execution plans.

61. C.   Execute the ALTER SYSTEM USE_STORED_OUTLINES=*category_name* command.

Explanation   If *category_name* is DEFAULT or TRUE, then the DEFAULT outline is used. Otherwise, specify a named stored outline. USE_STORED_OUTLINES is not an initialization parameter.

62. A.   The plan table is required for each and for TKPROF when explain=username/password.

Explanation   Both the EXPLAIN PLAN command and the Autotrace option require a plan table. The TKPROF command requires the plan table only if the *explain* parameter is included.

63. B, D.   OPTIMIZER_MODE=CHOOSE and OPTIMIZER_MODE=ALL_ROWS

Explanation   TRUE and COST are not valid OPTIMIZER_MODE settings. When RULE is specified, statistics are not used. ALL_ROWS and CHOOSE are both CBO settings; that is, ALL_ROWS indicates to the CBO that it should optimize for throughput, and CHOOSE indicates to use the CBO if statistics are available on any table in the SQL statement. If any table in the SQL statement has statistics on it, then performance is better under the CHOOSE option; however, performance will be best if all the tables have statistics on them.

64. D, E, F.   DBMS_STATS, export, and import

Explanation   DBMS_STATS is used to create and populate the statistics table in a schema. The export and import utilities are used to extract the object from the source database and bring it into the target database. DBMS_STATS is then used on the target database to move the statistics into the data dictionary.

65. A, E, F.   No subplan loops, the plan must have a directive for OTHER_GROUPS, and referenced subplans and/or consumer groups must exist.

Explanation   The validate_pending_area procedure checks the entries in the resource plan against the Resource Manager rules. The plan must specify a directive for OTHER_GROUPS. No subplan loops are allowed; that is, no subplan can have a directive that includes a higher-level plan as a subplan. All referenced subplans and consumer groups are verified.

66. B, C.   Resource consumer groups are groups of users with similar resource requirements, and a user can belong to many consumer groups, but only one group at a time can be active for a session.

Explanation   Resource Manager consumer groups are user-defined (or DBA-defined) groups of schema users that have similar resource requirements. The DBA can assign a user to as many consumer groups as is required. A session logs on with the default consumer group for the user, and the user session can then switch to other allowed consumer groups as needed.

GLOSSARY

Glossary

■ **Archived redo log**   Optionally, filled online redo files can be archived before being reused, creating an archived redo log. Archived (offline) redo log files constitute the archived redo log.

■ **Asynchronous I/O**   Asynchronous I/O is an input/output mechanism that enables processes to proceed with the next operation without having to wait after issuing a write. Asynchronous I/O improves the system performance by minimizing the wasted idle time.

■ **Automatic Undo Management**   Configuration that utilizes undo segments managed automatically by the Oracle server, and eliminates the need for manually configured rollback segments. This enables DBAs to allocate their undo space in a single undo tablespace with the database taking care of issues such as undo block contention, consistent read retention, and space utilization.

■ **Autotrace**   A SQL*Plus option that generates a report on the execution path used by the SQL optimizer and the statement execution statistics. The report is useful to monitor and tune the performance of DML statements.

■ **Background processes**   Background processes consolidate functions that would otherwise be handled by multiple Oracle programs running for each user process. The background processes asynchronously perform I/O and monitor other Oracle processes to provide increased parallelism for better performance and reliability. Oracle creates a set of background processes for each instance. The essential background processes are LGWR, SMON, PMON, CKPT, and DBW0.

■ **Bind variable**   A variable in a SQL statement that must be replaced with a valid value, or the address of a value, in order for the statement to successfully execute. Bind variables are most useful for OLTP-type queries, where SQL statement parsing should be kept to a minimum.

■ **Bitmap index**   Bitmap indexes store the rowids associated with a key value as a bitmap. Each bit in the bitmap corresponds to a possible rowid, and if the bit is set, it means that the row with the corresponding rowid contains the key value. The internal representation of bitmaps is best suited for applications with low levels of concurrent transactions, such as data warehousing.

■ **Bottleneck**   The delay in transmission of data, typically when a system's bandwidth cannot support the amount of information being relayed at the speed it is being processed. There are, however, many factors that can create a bottleneck in a system. When performance tuning, one of the goals is to eliminate bottlenecks.

■ **Checkpoint**   An event that causes all modified database buffers in the buffer cache to be written to the datafiles by DBWn. The checkpoint process is responsible for signaling DBWn at checkpoints and updating all the datafiles and control files of the database to indicate the most recent checkpoint.

■ **Cluster**   Optional structure for storing table data. Clusters are groups of one or more tables physically stored together because they share common columns (cluster key) and are often used together. Because related rows are physically stored together, disk access time improves.

■ **Commit**   Make permanent changes to data (inserts, updates, and deletes) in the database. Before changes are committed, both the old and new data exist so that changes can be stored or the data can be restored to its prior state.

■ **Concurrency**   Simultaneous access of the same data by many users. A multiuser database management system must provide adequate concurrency controls so that data cannot be updated or changed improperly, compromising data integrity.

■ **Contention**   When some process has to wait for a resource that is being used by another process. Reducing contention is a tuning goal.

■ **Cost-based optimizer (CBO)**   Uses data distribution statistics for database segments, generates a set of potential execution plans for SQL statements, estimates the cost of each plan, calls the plan generator to generate the plan, compares the costs, and chooses the plan with the lowest cost. The CBO is made up of the query transformer, the estimator, and the plan generator.

■ **Cursor**   A cursor is a name or pointer for the memory associated with a specific SQL statement.

■ **Database buffer cache**   The database buffer cache is the memory structure in the SGA that holds copies of data blocks read from datafiles. All user processes concurrently connected to the instance share access to the database buffer cache.

■ **Database resource manager**   A set of tools within the Oracle database that gives database administrators more control over resource management decisions, through the use of resource plans, consumer groups, and plan directives.

- **Database writer process (DBWn)**   An Oracle background process that writes the contents of buffers in the buffer cache to datafiles.

- **Data block**   The minimum unit of I/O and smallest logical unit of data storage in an Oracle database. Also called logical blocks, Oracle blocks, or pages. Every database has a default block size, although data blocks in different tablespaces can have different sizes. One data block corresponds to a specific number of bytes of physical database space on disk. A segment is composed of one or more extents, and an extent is formed from contiguous blocks.

- **Data consistency**   In a multiuser environment, where many users can access data at the same time (concurrency), data consistency means that each user sees a consistent view of the data, including visible changes made by the user's own transactions and transactions of other users.

- **Data Definition Language (DDL)**   Data Definition Language. The category of SQL statements that define or delete database objects such as tables or views. Examples are the CREATE, ALTER, and DROP statements.

- **Data dictionary**   The set of tables and views that are used as a read-only reference for a particular database. A data dictionary stores such information as the logical and physical structure of the database, users of the database, information about integrity constraints, how much space is allocated for a schema object, and how much of it is in use. The data dictionary is created when a database is created and is automatically updated when the structure of the database is updated.

- **Data Manipulation Language (DML)**   The category of SQL statements that query and update the database data. Common DML statements are SELECT, INSERT, UPDATE, and DELETE.

- **Data segment**   A segment that contains table data. Each cluster has a data segment, and the data of every table in the cluster is stored within the cluster data segment. Each nonclustered segment has its own data segment. For partitioned tables, each partition has its own data segment.

- **Data warehouse**   A database that is used for business analysis rather than transaction processing (OLTP). Usually very large volumes of data that are frequently added to but rarely modified.

- **Decision Support System (DSS)**   Type of database and application that usually has a small number of concurrent users who use the database for reporting or decision-making processes. These are usually large batch inserts, with few or no updates and deletes. Examples are data warehouses and reporting systems.

- **Dedicated server** A database server configuration in which there is a one-to-one relationship between a server process and a user process.

- **Dictionary cache** A set of memory structures in the shared pool of the SGA, which holds a collection of definitions of data dictionary objects. Also known as the row cache because it holds data as rows instead of buffers.

- **Dictionary-managed tablespace** Extent allocation, and information about free and used extents in a tablespace is stored in the data dictionary.

- **Dispatcher processes (D*nnn*)** Optional background processes, present only when a shared server configuration is used. At least one dispatcher process is created for every communication protocol configured. (D000, . . . , Dnnn). Each dispatcher process is responsible for routing requests from connected user processes to available shared server processes and returning the responses back to the appropriate user processes.

- **Dynamic performance views** The set of V$ views the DBA uses to monitor an Oracle instance. Dynamic performance views are called *fixed views* because they cannot be altered or removed by the DBA.

- **Enqueue** Enqueues are shared memory structures that serialize access to database resources and are associated with a session or transaction. To *enqueue* means to place on a waiting list, as in lock requests waiting for a lock to be released.

- **Equijoin** A join condition containing an equality operator.

- **Explain Plan** A SQL statement that enables you to examine the execution plan chosen by the optimizer for DML statements. Explain Plan causes the optimizer to choose an execution plan and then to put data describing the plan into a database table. Also, an Explain Plan is an access path determined by the query optimizer.

- **Export** Oracle utility program that enables the extraction of schema objects from an Oracle database into a binary dump file. The binary file can then be used by the Oracle import utility program.

- **Extent** An extent is a specific number of contiguous data blocks obtained in a single allocation and is used for storing a specific type of information.

- **Histogram** Used by the CBO; partitions the values in a column into bands so that all column values in a band fall within the same range. Histograms provide improved selectivity estimates in the presence of data skew, resulting in optimal execution plans with nonuniform data distributions.

- **Import**   Oracle utility program used to load binary dump files created by the export utility into an Oracle database. It can be used to import database schema objects and data, enable tablespace transport between databases, or copy statistics or execution plans between databases.

- **Index**   An optional structure associated with tables and clusters. You can create an index on one or more columns of a table, or a function or expression, to speed SQL statement execution on that table.

- **Index-organized table (IOT)**   A schema object whose storage organization is a variant of a primary B-Tree. Unlike an ordinary (heap-organized) table whose data is stored as an unordered collection (heap), data for an index-organized table is stored in a B-Tree index structure in a primary key sorted manner. Each index entry in the B-Tree also stores the nonkey column values.

- **Index segment**   Each index has an index segment that stores all of its data. For a partitioned index, each partition has its own index segment.

- **Instance**   A System Global Area (SGA) and the Oracle background processes constitute an Oracle instance. Every time an instance is started, an SGA is allocated and Oracle background processes are started. The SGA is deallocated when the instance shuts down.

- **Instance recovery**   Recovery of an instance in the event of software or hardware failure, so that the database is available to users again. If the instance terminates abnormally, then the instance recovery automatically occurs at the next instance startup.

- **Join**   A query that selects data from more than one table. A join is characterized by multiple tables in the FROM clause. Oracle pairs the rows from these tables using the condition specified in the WHERE clause and returns the resulting rows. This condition is called the *join condition* and usually compares columns of all the joined tables.

- **Key**   Column or set of columns included in the definition of certain types of integrity constraints or indexes. Keys are a logical concept, and they describe the relationships between the different tables and columns of a relational database.

- **Large pool**   Optional area in the SGA that provides large memory allocations for Oracle RMAN backup and restore operations, I/O server processes, and session memory for the shared server.

- **Latch**   A simple, low-level serialization mechanism to protect shared data structures in the SGA.

- **Library cache** A memory structure containing shared SQL and PL/SQL areas. The library cache is one of the components of the shared pool.

- **Literal** A constant value, written at compile time and read only at run time. Literals can be accessed quickly and are used when modification is not necessary. Literals are preferred over bind variables for DSS-type systems and when histograms are in use.

- **Locally managed tablespace** A tablespace that manages its own extents maintains a bitmap in each datafile to keep track of the free or used status of blocks in that datafile.

- **Log writer process (LGWR)** The log writer process (LGWR) is responsible for redo log buffer management and writing the redo log buffer to a redo log file on disk. LGWR writes all redo entries that have been copied into the buffer since the last time it wrote.

- **Materialized view** A materialized view provides indirect access to table data by storing the results of a query in a separate schema object.

- **Mirroring** Maintaining identical copies of data on one or more disks. Typically, mirroring is performed on duplicate hard disks at the operating system level, so that if one of the disks becomes unavailable, the other disk can continue to service requests without interruptions.

- **Online Transaction Processing (OLTP)** A type of database and application system that typically has a large number of concurrent users and high volume of small data transactions: inserts, updates, and deletes; usually response time is extremely important. Examples include order processing, reservations, and point-of-sale systems.

- **Optimizer** Determines the most efficient way to execute SQL statements by evaluating expressions and translating them into equivalent, quicker expressions. The optimizer formulates a set of execution plans and picks the best one for a SQL statement.

- **Optimizer hint** A directive to the optimizer that is included in the SQL statement. A hint is used to override the plan that the optimizer would normally generate.

- **Oracle Trace** Used by the Oracle database to collect performance and resource utilization data, such as SQL parse, execute, fetch statistics, and wait statistics. Oracle Trace provides several SQL scripts that can be used to access server event tables, collects server event data and stores it in memory, and enables data to be formatted while a collection is occurring.

- **Paging**   A technique for increasing the memory space available by moving infrequently used parts of a program's working memory from main memory to a secondary storage medium, usually a disk. The unit of transfer is called a *page.*

- **Parallel execution**   Multiple processes work together simultaneously to execute a single SQL statement to improve throughput and overall SQL execution time.

- **Parse**   A *hard parse* occurs when a SQL statement is executed, and the SQL statement is either not in the shared pool or it is in the shared pool but it cannot be shared. A SQL statement is not shared if the metadata for the two SQL statements is different. This can happen if a SQL statement is textually identical as a preexisting SQL statement but the tables referred to in the two statements resolve to physically different tables, or if the optimizer environment is different. A *soft parse* occurs when a session attempts to execute a SQL statement, the statement is already in the shared pool, and it can be used (that is, shared). For a statement to be shared, all data (including metadata, such as the optimizer execution plan) pertaining to the existing SQL statement must be equally applicable to the current statement being issued.

- **Parse call**   A call to Oracle to prepare a SQL statement for execution. This includes syntactically checking the SQL statement, optimizing it, and building (or locating) an executable form of that statement.

- **Parser**   Performs syntax analysis and semantic analysis of SQL statements, and expands views (referenced in a query) into separate query blocks.

- **Physical I/O**   A block read that could not be satisfied from the buffer cache, either because the block was not present or because the I/O is a direct I/O (and bypasses the buffer cache).

- **Plan generator**   Tries out different possible plans for a given query so that the CBO can choose the plan with the lowest cost. It explores different plans for a query block by trying out different access paths, join methods, and join orders.

- **Plan stability**   The concept of preventing certain database environment changes from affecting the performance characteristics of applications. Such changes include changes in optimizer statistics, changes to the optimizer mode settings, and changes to parameters affecting the sizes of memory structures. Plan stability is enforced with stored outlines.

- **PL/SQL**   Oracle's procedural language extension to SQL. PL/SQL enables you to mix SQL statements with procedural constructs. With PL/SQL, you can define and execute PL/SQL program units such as procedures, functions, and packages.

■ **Process** Each process in an Oracle instance performs a specific job. By dividing the work of Oracle and database applications into several processes, multiple users and applications can connect to a single database instance simultaneously.

■ **Program Global Area (PGA)** A nonshared memory region that contains data and control information for a server process, and is created when the server or background process is started. Also referred to as the Process Global Area.

■ **Query transformer** Decides whether to rewrite a user query to generate a better query plan, merges views, and performs subquery unnesting.

■ **RAID** Redundant arrays of inexpensive disks. RAID configurations provide improved data reliability with the option of striping (manually distributing data). Different RAID configurations (levels) are chosen based on performance and cost, and are suited to different types of applications, depending on their I/O characteristics.

■ **Read consistency** In a multiuser environment, Oracle's read consistency ensures the following: The set of data seen by a statement remains constant throughout statement execution (statement-level read consistency). Readers and writers of database data do not wait for other writers or other readers of the same data. Writers of database data wait only for other writers who are updating identical rows in concurrent transactions.

■ **Redo log** The redo log is a set of two or more redo log files that record all changes made to the database, including both uncommitted and committed changes, and is used to protect altered database data in memory that has not been written to the datafiles. Redo entries are temporarily stored in redo log buffers of the SGA, and the background process LGWR writes the redo entries sequentially to an *online* redo log file. If the database is in archivelog mode, then the ARCn process is responsible for writing the online redo log file to one or more archived log file destinations.

■ **Redo log buffer** Memory structure in the SGA that stores redo entries—a log of changes made to the database.

■ **Roll back** Undo any changes to data that have been performed by SQL statements within an uncommitted transaction. After a transaction has been committed, it cannot be rolled back. Oracle uses rollback or undo segments to store old values. The redo log contains a record of changes made to the rollback or undo segments.

- **Rollback segment** Logical database structure created by the DBA to temporarily store undo information. Rollback segments store old data changed by SQL statements in a transaction until it is committed.

- **ROWID** A globally unique identifier for a row in a database. It is created at the time the row is inserted into a table and destroyed when it is removed from a table.

- **Row source generator** Receives the optimal plan from the optimizer and outputs the execution plan for the SQL statement. A row source is an iterative control structure that processes a set of rows in an iterated manner and produces a row set.

- **Rule-based optimizer (RBO)** Chooses an execution plan for SQL statements based on the access paths available and the ranks of these access paths (if there is more than one way, then the RBO uses the operation with the lowest rank). The RBO is used if no statistics are available and also depending on the value of OPTIMIZER_MODE.

- **Schema** A collection of database objects, including logical structures such as tables, views, sequences, stored procedures, synonyms, indexes, clusters, and database links. A schema has the name of the user who controls it, referenced throughout data dictionary views as the "OWNER."

- **Segment** A set of extents allocated for a specific type of database object such as a table, index, or cluster.

- **Server processes** Server processes handle requests from connected user processes. A server process is in charge of communicating with the user process and interacting with the Oracle database to carry out requests of the associated user process.

- **Session** A specific connection of a user to an Oracle instance through a user process. A session lasts from the time the user connects until the time the user disconnects, is terminated, or exits the database application.

- **Shared pool** Portion of the SGA that contains shared memory constructs such as shared SQL areas. A shared SQL area is required to process every unique SQL statement submitted to a database. A single shared SQL area is used by multiple applications that issue the same statement, leaving more shared memory for other uses.

- **Shared Server** A database server configuration that enables many user processes to share a small number of server processes, minimizing the number of server processes and maximizing the use of available system resources.

- **SQL** Structured Query Language. A nonprocedural industry-standard language for creating, updating, and querying relational database management systems. The internationally accepted standard for relational systems, covering not only query, but also data definition, manipulation, security, and some aspects of referential integrity.

- **SQL compiler** Compiles SQL statements into a shared cursor. The SQL compiler is made up of the parser, the optimizer, and the row source generator.

- **SQL*Loader** Reads and interprets input files. It is the most efficient way to load large amounts of data.

- **SQL*Plus** Oracle tool used to execute SQL statements against an Oracle database. Oracle SQL includes many extensions to the ANSI/ISO standard SQL language.

- **SQL statements (identical)** Textually identical SQL statements do not differ in any way.

- **SQL statements (similar)** Similar SQL statements differ only due to changing literal values. If the literal values were replaced with bind variables, then the SQL statements would be textually identical.

- **SQL Trace** A basic performance diagnostic tool to help monitor and tune applications running against the Oracle database. SQL Trace lets you assess the efficiency of the SQL statements an application runs and generates statistics for each statement. The trace files produced by this tool are used as input for TKPROF.

- **Statspack** A set of SQL, PL/SQL, and SQL*Plus scripts that allow the collection, automation, storage, and viewing of performance data. Statspack supersedes the traditional UTLBSTAT/UTLESTAT tuning scripts.

- **Stored outline** An abstraction of an execution plan generated by the optimizer at the time the outline was created; represented primarily as a set of hints. When the outline is used, these hints are applied at various stages of SQL statement compilation.

- **Striping** The interleaving of a related block of data across disks. Proper striping reduces I/O and improves performance.

- **System Global Area (SGA)** A group of shared memory structures that contain data and control information for one Oracle database instance. If multiple users are concurrently connected to the same instance, then the data in the instance's SGA is shared among the users. Consequently, the SGA is sometimes referred to as the Shared Global Area.

■ **Temporary segment**   Temporary segments are created by Oracle when a SQL statement needs a temporary work area to complete execution. When the statement finishes execution, the temporary segment's extents are returned to the system for future use.

■ **TKPROF**   A diagnostic tool to help monitor and tune applications running against the Oracle database. TKPROF primarily processes SQL trace output files and translates them into readable output files, providing a summary of user-level statements and recursive SQL calls for the trace files. It can also assess the efficiency of SQL statements, generate execution plans, and create SQL scripts to store statistics in the database.

■ **Trace file**   Information about a process is dumped into a trace file. Trace files are generated for a process when an internal error is detected or if SQL tracing is turned on for the session.

■ **Transaction**   A logical unit of work that contains one or more SQL statements. All statements in a transaction are committed or rolled back together.

■ **Transaction recovery**   Transaction recovery involves rolling back all uncommitted transactions of a failed instance. These are in-progress transactions that did not commit and that Oracle needs to roll back. It is possible for uncommitted transactions to get saved to disk. In this case, Oracle uses undo data to reverse the effects of any changes that were written to the datafiles but not yet committed.

■ **User Global Area (UGA)**   The UGA is memory that is associated with a user session. The UGA normally comes from the SGA to allow the migration of sessions across processes (shared server configuration). If session migration is disabled (dedicated server configuration), UGA memory will be allocated from the PGA.

■ **Wait events**   Statistics that are incremented by a server process/thread to indicate that it had to wait for an event to complete before being able to continue processing. Wait events are one of the first places for investigation when performing reactive performance tuning.

Index

Q–R

W–X

INTERNATIONAL CONTACT INFORMATION

AUSTRALIA
McGraw-Hill Book Company Australia Pty. Ltd.
TEL +61-2-9900-1800
FAX +61-2-9878-8881
http://www.mcgraw-hill.com.au
books-it_sydney@mcgraw-hill.com

CANADA
McGraw-Hill Ryerson Ltd.
TEL +905-430-5000
FAX +905-430-5020
http://www.mcgraw-hill.ca

GREECE, MIDDLE EAST, & AFRICA
(Excluding South Africa)
McGraw-Hill Hellas
TEL +30-1-656-0990-3-4
FAX +30-1-654-5525

MEXICO (Also serving Latin America)
McGraw-Hill Interamericana Editores S.A. de C.V.
TEL +525-117-1583
FAX +525-117-1589
http://www.mcgraw-hill.com.mx
fernando_castellanos@mcgraw-hill.com

SINGAPORE (Serving Asia)
McGraw-Hill Book Company
TEL +65-863-1580
FAX +65-862-3354
http://www.mcgraw-hill.com.sg
mghasia@mcgraw-hill.com

SOUTH AFRICA
McGraw-Hill South Africa
TEL +27-11-622-7512
FAX +27-11-622-9045
robyn_swanepoel@mcgraw-hill.com

SPAIN
McGraw-Hill/Interamericana de España, S.A.U.
TEL +34-91-180-3000
FAX +34-91-372-8513
http://www.mcgraw-hill.es
professional@mcgraw-hill.es

UNITED KINGDOM, NORTHERN,
EASTERN, & CENTRAL EUROPE
McGraw-Hill Education Europe
TEL +44-1-628-502500
FAX +44-1-628-770224
http://www.mcgraw-hill.co.uk
computing_neurope@mcgraw-hill.com

ALL OTHER INQUIRIES Contact:
Osborne/McGraw-Hill
TEL +1-510-549-6600
FAX +1-510-883-7600
http://www.osborne.com
omg_international@mcgraw-hill.com

GET YOUR **FREE SUBSCRIPTION**
TO ORACLE MAGAZINE

Oracle Magazine is essential gear for today's information technology professionals. Stay informed and increase your productivity with every issue of **Oracle Magazine**. Inside each free bimonthly issue you'll get:

- Up-to-date information on Oracle Database, E-Business Suite applications, Web development, and database technology and business trends
- Third-party news and announcements
- Technical articles on Oracle Products and operating environments
- Development and administration tips
- Real-world customer stories

IF THERE ARE OTHER ORACLE USERS AT YOUR LOCATION WHO WOULD LIKE TO RECEIVE THEIR OWN SUBSCRIPTION TO ORACLE MAGAZINE, PLEASE PHOTOCOPY THIS FORM AND PASS IT ALONG.

Three easy ways to subscribe:

① Web
Visit our Web site at www.oracle.com/oraclemagazine.
You'll find a subscription form there, plus much more!

② Fax
Complete the questionnaire on the back of this card and fax the questionnaire side only to +1.847.647.9735.

③ Mail
Complete the questionnaire on the back of this card and mail it to P.O. Box 1263, Skokie, IL 60076-8263

Oracle Publishing

ORACLE®

FREE SUBSCRIPTION

○ Yes, please send me a FREE subscription to *Oracle Magazine*. ○ **NO**

To receive a free subscription to Oracle Magazine, you must fill out the entire card, sign it, and date it (incomplete cards cannot be processed or acknowledged). You can also fax your application to +1.847.647.9735.
Or subscribe at our Web site at www.oracle.com/oraclemagazine/

○ From time to time, Oracle Publishing allows our partners exclusive access to our e-mail addresses for special promotions and announcements. To be included in this program, please check this box.

○ Oracle Publishing allows sharing of our mailing list with selected third parties. If you prefer your mailing address not to be included in this program, please check here. If at any time you would like to be removed from this mailing list, please contact Customer Service at +1.847.647.9630 or send an e-mail to oracle@halldata.com.

signature (required)   date

X

name   title

company   e-mail address

street/p.o. box

city/state/zip or postal code   telephone

country   fax

YOU MUST ANSWER ALL NINE QUESTIONS BELOW.

① WHAT IS THE PRIMARY BUSINESS ACTIVITY OF YOUR FIRM AT THIS LOCATION?
(check one only)

- ☐ 01 Application Service Provider
- ☐ 02 Communications
- ☐ 03 Consulting, Training
- ☐ 04 Data Processing
- ☐ 05 Education
- ☐ 06 Engineering
- ☐ 07 Financial Services
- ☐ 08 Government (federal, local, state, other)
- ☐ 09 Government (military)
- ☐ 10 Health Care
- ☐ 11 Manufacturing (aerospace, defense)
- ☐ 12 Manufacturing (computer hardware)
- ☐ 13 Manufacturing (noncomputer)
- ☐ 14 Research & Development
- ☐ 15 Retailing, Wholesaling, Distribution
- ☐ 16 Software Development
- ☐ 17 Systems Integration, VAR, VAD, OEM
- ☐ 18 Transportation
- ☐ 19 Utilities (electric, gas, sanitation)
- ☐ 98 Other Business and Services

② WHICH OF THE FOLLOWING BEST DESCRIBES YOUR PRIMARY JOB FUNCTION?
(check one only)

Corporate Management/Staff
- ☐ 01 Executive Management (President, Chair, CEO, CFO, Owner, Partner, Principal)
- ☐ 02 Finance/Administrative Management (VP/Director/ Manager/Controller, Purchasing, Administration)
- ☐ 03 Sales/Marketing Management (VP/Director/Manager)
- ☐ 04 Computer Systems/Operations Management (CIO/VP/Director/ Manager MIS, Operations)

IS/IT Staff
- ☐ 05 Systems Development/ Programming Management
- ☐ 06 Systems Development/ Programming Staff
- ☐ 07 Consulting
- ☐ 08 DBA/Systems Administrator
- ☐ 09 Education/Training
- ☐ 10 Technical Support Director/Manager
- ☐ 11 Other Technical Management/Staff
- ☐ 98 Other

③ WHAT IS YOUR CURRENT PRIMARY OPERATING PLATFORM? (select all that apply)

- ☐ 01 Digital Equipment UNIX
- ☐ 02 Digital Equipment VAX VMS
- ☐ 03 HP UNIX
- ☐ 04 IBM AIX
- ☐ 05 IBM UNIX
- ☐ 06 Java
- ☐ 07 Linux
- ☐ 08 Macintosh
- ☐ 09 MS-DOS
- ☐ 10 MVS
- ☐ 11 NetWare
- ☐ 12 Network Computing
- ☐ 13 OpenVMS
- ☐ 14 SCO UNIX
- ☐ 15 Sequent DYNIX/ptx
- ☐ 16 Sun Solaris/SunOS
- ☐ 17 SVR4
- ☐ 18 UnixWare
- ☐ 19 Windows
- ☐ 20 Windows NT
- ☐ 21 Other UNIX
- ☐ 98 Other
- 99 ☐ None of the above

④ DO YOU EVALUATE, SPECIFY, RECOMMEND, OR AUTHORIZE THE PURCHASE OF ANY OF THE FOLLOWING? (check all that apply)

- ☐ 01 Hardware
- ☐ 02 Software
- ☐ 03 Application Development Tools
- ☐ 04 Database Products
- ☐ 05 Internet or Intranet Products
- 99 ☐ None of the above

⑤ IN YOUR JOB, DO YOU USE OR PLAN TO PURCHASE ANY OF THE FOLLOWING PRODUCTS? (check all that apply)

Software
- ☐ 01 Business Graphics
- ☐ 02 CAD/CAE/CAM
- ☐ 03 CASE
- ☐ 04 Communications
- ☐ 05 Database Management
- ☐ 06 File Management
- ☐ 07 Finance
- ☐ 08 Java
- ☐ 09 Materials Resource Planning
- ☐ 10 Multimedia Authoring
- ☐ 11 Networking
- ☐ 12 Office Automation
- ☐ 13 Order Entry/Inventory Control
- ☐ 14 Programming
- ☐ 15 Project Management
- ☐ 16 Scientific and Engineering
- ☐ 17 Spreadsheets
- ☐ 18 Systems Management
- ☐ 19 Workflow

Hardware
- ☐ 20 Macintosh
- ☐ 21 Mainframe
- ☐ 22 Massively Parallel Processing
- ☐ 23 Minicomputer
- ☐ 24 PC
- ☐ 25 Network Computer
- ☐ 26 Symmetric Multiprocessing
- ☐ 27 Workstation

Peripherals
- ☐ 28 Bridges/Routers/Hubs/Gateways
- ☐ 29 CD-ROM Drives
- ☐ 30 Disk Drives/Subsystems
- ☐ 31 Modems
- ☐ 32 Tape Drives/Subsystems
- ☐ 33 Video Boards/Multimedia

Services
- ☐ 34 Application Service Provider
- ☐ 35 Consulting
- ☐ 36 Education/Training
- ☐ 37 Maintenance
- ☐ 38 Online Database Services
- ☐ 39 Support
- ☐ 40 Technology-Based Training
- ☐ 98 Other
- 99 ☐ None of the above

⑥ WHAT ORACLE PRODUCTS ARE IN USE AT YOUR SITE? (check all that apply)

Software
- ☐ 01 Oracle9i
- ☐ 02 Oracle9i Lite
- ☐ 03 Oracle8
- ☐ 04 Oracle8i
- ☐ 05 Oracle8i Lite
- ☐ 06 Oracle7
- ☐ 07 Oracle9i Application Server
- ☐ 08 Oracle9i Application Server Wireless
- ☐ 09 Oracle Data Mart Suites
- ☐ 10 Oracle Internet Commerce Server
- ☐ 11 Oracle interMedia
- ☐ 12 Oracle Lite
- ☐ 13 Oracle Payment Server
- ☐ 14 Oracle Video Server
- ☐ 15 Oracle Rdb

Tools
- ☐ 16 Oracle Darwin
- ☐ 17 Oracle Designer
- ☐ 18 Oracle Developer
- ☐ 19 Oracle Discoverer
- ☐ 20 Oracle Express
- ☐ 21 Oracle JDeveloper
- ☐ 22 Oracle Reports
- ☐ 23 Oracle Portal
- ☐ 24 Oracle Warehouse Builder
- ☐ 25 Oracle Workflow

Oracle E-Business Suite
- ☐ 26 Oracle Advanced Planning/Scheduling
- ☐ 27 Oracle Business Intelligence
- ☐ 28 Oracle E-Commerce
- ☐ 29 Oracle Exchange
- ☐ 30 Oracle Financials
- ☐ 31 Oracle Human Resources
- ☐ 32 Oracle Interaction Center
- ☐ 33 Oracle Internet Procurement
- ☐ 34 Oracle Manufacturing
- ☐ 35 Oracle Marketing
- ☐ 36 Oracle Order Management
- ☐ 37 Oracle Professional Services Automation
- ☐ 38 Oracle Projects
- ☐ 39 Oracle Sales
- ☐ 40 Oracle Service
- ☐ 41 Oracle Small Business Suite
- ☐ 42 Oracle Supply Chain Management
- ☐ 43 Oracle Travel Management
- ☐ 44 Oracle Treasury

Oracle Services
- ☐ 45 Oracle.com Online Services
- ☐ 46 Oracle Consulting
- ☐ 47 Oracle Education
- ☐ 48 Oracle Support
- ☐ 98 ther
- 99 ☐ None of the above

⑦ WHAT OTHER DATABASE PRODUCTS ARE IN USE AT YOUR SITE? (check all that apply)

- ☐ 01 Access
- ☐ 02 Baan
- ☐ 03 dbase
- ☐ 04 Gupta
- ☐ 05 IBM DB2
- ☐ 06 Informix
- ☐ 07 Ingres
- ☐ 08 Microsoft Access
- ☐ 09 Microsoft SQL Server
- ☐ 10 PeopleSoft
- ☐ 11 Progress
- ☐ 12 SAP
- ☐ 13 Sybase
- ☐ 14 VSAM
- ☐ 98 Other
- 99 ☐ None of the above

⑧ DURING THE NEXT 12 MONTHS, HOW MUCH DO YOU ANTICIPATE YOUR ORGANIZATION WILL SPEND ON COMPUTER HARDWARE, SOFTWARE, PERIPHERALS, AND SERVICES FOR YOUR LOCATION? (check only one)

- ☐ 01 Less than $10,000
- ☐ 02 $10,000 to $49,999
- ☐ 03 $50,000 to $99,999
- ☐ 04 $100,000 to $499,999
- ☐ 05 $500,000 to $999,999
- ☐ 06 $1,000,000 and over

⑨ WHAT IS YOUR COMPANY'S YEARLY SALES REVENUE? (please choose one)

- ☐ 01 $500,000,000 and above
- ☐ 02 $100,000,000 to $500,000,000
- ☐ 03 $50,000,000 to $100,000,000
- ☐ 04 $5,000,000 to $50,000,000
- ☐ 05 $1,000,000 to $5,000,000

123101

About the BeachFrontQuizzer™ CD-ROM

BeachFrontQuizzer provides interactive certification exams to help you prepare for certification. With the enclosed CD, you can test your knowledge of the topics covered in this book with more than 175 multiple choice questions.

Installation

To install BeachFrontQuizzer:

1. **Insert the CD-ROM in your CD-ROM drive.**

2. **Follow the Setup steps in the displayed Installation Wizard. (When the Setup is finished, you may immediately begin using BeachFrontQuizzer.)**

3. **To begin using BeachFrontQuizzer, enter the 12-digit license key number of the exam you want to take:**

   1Z0-033 Oracle9*i* Performance Tuning   307967757177

Study Sessions

BeachFrontQuizzer tests your knowledge as you learn about new subjects through interactive quiz sessions. Study Session Questions are selected from a single database for each session, dependent on the subcategory selected and the number of times each question has been previously answered correctly. In this way, questions you have answered correctly are not repeated until you have answered all the new questions. Questions that you have missed previously will reappear in later sessions and keep coming back to haunt you until you get the question correct. In addition, you can track your progress by displaying the number of questions you have answered with the Historical Analysis option. You can reset the progress tracking by clicking on the Clear History button. Each time a question is presented the answers are randomized so that you will not memorize a pattern or letter that goes with the question. You will start to memorize the correct answer that goes with the question instead.

Practice Exams

For advanced users, BeachFrontQuizzer also provides Simulated and Adaptive certification exams. Questions are chosen at random from the database. The Simulated Exam presents a specific number of questions directly related to the real exam. After you finish the exam, BeachFrontQuizzer displays your score and the passing score required for the test. You may display the exam results of this specific exam from this menu. You may review each question and display the correct answer.

NOTE
For further details of the feature functionality of this BeachFrontQuizzer software, consult the online instructions by choosing Contents from the BeachFrontQuizzer Help menu.

Technical Support

If you experience technical difficulties, please call (888) 992-3131. Outside the United States call (281) 992-3131. Or, you may e-mail **bfquiz@swbell.net**.

WARNING: BEFORE OPENING THE DISC PACKAGE, CAREFULLY READ THE TERMS AND CONDITIONS OF THE FOLLOWING COPYRIGHT STATEMENT AND LIMITED CD-ROM WARRANTY.

Copyright Statement

This software is protected by both United States copyright law and international copyright treaty provision. Except as noted in the contents of the CD-ROM, you must treat this software just like a book. However, you may copy it into a computer to be used and you may make archival copies of the software for the sole purpose of backing up the software and protecting your investment from loss. By saying, "just like a book," The McGraw-Hill Companies, Inc. (ìOsborne/McGraw-Hillî) means, for example, that this software may be used by any number of people and may be freely moved from one computer location to another, so long as there is no possibility of its being used at one location or on one computer while it is being used at another. Just as a book cannot be read by two different people in two different places at the same time, neither can the software be used by two different people in two different places at the same time.

Limited Warranty

Osborne/McGraw-Hill warrants the physical compact disc enclosed herein to be free of defects in materials and workmanship for a period of sixty days from the purchase date. If the CD included in your book has defects in materials or workmanship, please call McGraw-Hill at 1-800-217-0059, 9am to 5pm, Monday through Friday, Eastern Standard Time, and McGraw-Hill will replace the defective disc.

The entire and exclusive liability and remedy for breach of this Limited Warranty shall be limited to replacement of the defective disc, and shall not include or extend to any claim for or right to cover any other damages, including but not limited to, loss of profit, data, or use of the software, or special incidental, or consequential damages or other similar claims, even if Osborne/McGraw-Hill has been specifically advised of the possibility of such damages. In no event will Osborne/McGraw-Hill's liability for any damages to you or any other person ever exceed the lower of the suggested list price or actual price paid for the license to use the software, regardless of any form of the claim.

OSBORNE/McGRAW-HILL SPECIFICALLY DISCLAIMS ALL OTHER WARRANTIES, EXPRESS OR IMPLIED, INCLUDING BUT NOT LIMITED TO, ANY IMPLIED WARRANTY OF MERCHANTABILITY OR FITNESS FOR A PARTICULAR PURPOSE. Specifically, Osborne/McGraw-Hill makes no representation or warranty that the software is fit for any particular purpose, and any implied warranty of merchantability is limited to the sixty-day duration of the Limited Warranty covering the physical disc only (and not the software), and is otherwise expressly and specifically disclaimed.

This limited warranty gives you specific legal rights; you may have others which may vary from state to state. Some states do not allow the exclusion of incidental or consequential damages, or the limitation on how long an implied warranty lasts, so some of the above may not apply to you. This agreement constitutes the entire agreement between the parties relating to use of the Product. The terms of any purchase order shall have no effect on the terms of this Agreement. Failure of Osborne/McGraw-Hill to insist at any time on strict compliance with this Agreement shall not constitute a waiver of any rights under this Agreement. This Agreement shall be construed and governed in accordance with the laws of New York. If any provision of this Agreement is held to be contrary to law, that provision will be enforced to the maximum extent permissible, and the remaining provisions will remain in force and effect.

NO TECHNICAL SUPPORT IS PROVIDED WITH THIS CD-ROM.